NEW HORIZONS IN CONSTRUCTION LAW

Edited by

John Uff QC

&

Martin Odams de Zylva

Construction Law Press
London
1998

Construction Law Press® is the imprint of the Centre of Construction Law and Management, King's College London.

Published in Great Britain by
Centre of Construction Law and Management
King's College London
The Old Watch House
Strand
London WC2R 2LS
Tel: 44 (0) 171 873 26 85
Fax: 44 (0) 171 872 02 10
Email: cclm@kcl.ac.uk

ISBN 0-9514866-8-3

A copy of the CIP entry for this book is available from the British Library.

Printed in Great Britain by Redwood Books Limited
Trowbridge, Wilts.

Acknowledgments

The editors express thanks to all who made contributions to the two conferences on which this work is based. They also express gratitude for their continuing co-operation in the preparation of these papers for publication. Thanks are also due to the contributors of the additional papers without which proper coverage of the subject matter in such depth or breadth would not have been achieved.

The editors express their thanks to Pauline Gale, Manager of the Centre of Construction Law and Management for the 9th annual conference and to Linda Jones who succeeded her before the 10th annual conference.

Professor John Uff QC   Martin Odams de Zylva

London
May 1998

Contents

Introduction

Part I
The Place of Construction in
Commercial Law

Part II
Procurement and Project Strategy

Part III
Construction and the Regulated Industries

Part IV
Damage, Proof and Recovery

Part V
Disputes and their Resolution

Contributors

Professor James Barlow BA, PhD Reader, Faculty of the Built Environment, University of Westminster.

Lord Bingham of Cornhill, Lord Chief Justice

Michael Black, QC, LLB, FCIArb, Visiting Research Fellow, Building Engineering Department, University of Manchester Institute of Science and Technology.

Penny Brooker BA, LLB, PhD, Dip Ed., Senior Lecturer, School of Social Sciences and Law, Oxford Brookes University.

Professor Phillip Capper, MA.(OXON), BA(Dunelm), Solicitor, Partner, Masons; Masons Professor of Construction Law, King's College London.

Bruce Claxton MA(Cantab), LLB(LOND), MSc.(LOND), CEng FICE ACIArb MAPM, Rendell Palmer Tritton.

John Dorter, Solicitor, Partner, Allen Allen & Hemsley, Sydney.

Colin Gallani, CEng, BSc, MICE, MIHT, MInstCES, Consulting Engineer

Geoff Haley MBA, Solicitor, Partner, S J Berwin & Co.

Eur Ing. **Geoffrey Beresford Hartwell**, FIMechE, Companion IEE, FCIArb, Cromwell House Associates

Chris Head, BSc.(Hons)(LOND), FICE, FIWEM, FCIArb, Director Knight Piesold

Jonathan Hosie, LLB.(Hons), MSc.(LOND), ACIArb, Solicitor, Partner, Edge & Ellison.

Adrian Hughes, MA.(OXON), Barrister.

Simon Hughes, MA.(OXON), Barrister.

Professor Anthony Lavers, LLB, MPhil, PhD, Barrister, Professor of Law, Oxford Brookes University.

Christopher Lemar MA(ECON)(Cantab), FCA, MAE, Partner, Coopers & Lybrand.

Sir Nicholas Lyell, QC, MP.

Kristine Morais, BA, LLB, MSc.(LOND), Solicitor, Masons.

Professor Mike O'Reilly, BEng, PhD, LLB, CEng, MICE, ACIArb, Barrister. Professor of Civil Engineering, Kingston University.

Martin Odams de Zylva, BSc.(Hons), MSc.(LOND), FRICS, ACIArb.

Sir Philip Otton, Lord Justice of Appeal.

John L Powell, QC, MA, LLB(Cantab).

John Redmond, BA, FCIArb, Partner Laytons

Nigel Robson, BA, FCIArb, Partner Eversheds Solicitors

Edmund C Ryan, MSc.(LOND), CEng, MICE, FCIArb, Senior Lecturer, Kingston University.

Alan W Shilston, BSc, CEng, FICE, FCIWEM, FIHT, FCIArb.

John Tackaberry QC, MA(Cantab), LLM(Cantab), FCIArb, FFB.

His Honour Judge Anthony Thornton, QC, Official Referee.

Professor John Uff, QC, Ph.D, FEng., FICE, FCIArb, Nash Professor of Engineering Law, Director, Centre of Construction Law, Kings College London.

Peter Vass, MSc.(ECON), CPA, School of Management, University of Bath.

Jeremy Winter, LLB, Solicitor, Partner, Baker & Mackenzie.

Caselist

Australia

Pakistan

European Union

New Zealand

Scotland

Legislation

Australia

England

New Zealand

Subordinate Legislation

England

European Union

Treaty of Rome 1957

Directives

Introduction

1. Keynote Address to the 1996 Conference – New Challenges in Construction Law

Lord Bingham of Cornhill, Lord Chief Justice

I feel very greatly honoured and flattered to be the keynote speaker at this conference sponsored by Eversheds and conscious of my complete lack of qualification to fill that role. Unlike most of those present I am not an engineer, I am not a contractor, I am not a designer, I am not a surveyor, I am not a construction arbitrator and I cannot even claim to have been a construction specialist when in practice at the Bar or to have been such on the Bench. Doing my best to see what qualifications I could claim, I have dredged up three tenuous qualifications. The first is some exposure to construction litigation at the Bar and on the Bench, and I suppose some wider experience of contractual litigation. Secondly, I can claim some experience (including current experience) as that rather dignified figure, the building owner, namely the paying customer. And thirdly I can claim experience, admittedly forty years old, as a member of a concreting gang employed by Sir Alfred McAlpine to lay the runway at Gatwick. Some of you will recall that when the Pope visited this country the first thing he did on arrival at Gatwick was to kneel and kiss the concrete, and I have nurtured the hope that it was my concrete which received that papal blessing.

Working on a concrete gang was an extremely formative experience in some ways. We were very generously rewarded at the rate of four and a penny ha'penny an hour, which was extremely good money in those days, and it was reinforced by the fact that one received time and a half after six o'clock every evening and on Saturday, and double time on Sunday. This however did make the conditions of service extremely arduous, because it meant that for the second half of every weekday you could not really do any work at all, in order to make sure that there was plenty left at six o'clock that you had to wait to do, and these conditions became even more excruciating towards the end of the week since one had to make sure on Thursday and Friday that one did almost nothing at all in order to guarantee that it was necessary to come in at the weekend. Whether these are more general problems in the construction industry, I do not know.

What is obvious to any lawyer or indeed any citizen viewing the construction industry is, and this goes without saying, that it is a hugely important industry in the national economy. It represents a substantial portion of our gross domestic product. It is also I think true (and this is a constant theme of the papers which I have seen relating to this conference) that its an industry in which our dispute resolution procedures do not show up at their best. By dispute resolution procedures I embrace both litigation and arbitration and alternative dispute resolution. That is a point which could be put a great deal more strongly than that. It would, I think, be true to say that all the problems of excessive cost, excessive delay, excessive prolixity, excessive paper and so on are seen at their worst in this particular field. That prompts the question why this should be so. Many explanations can be proffered, and indeed a large number are canvassed in the various papers. But it seems to me, having looked at these papers, that there are eight main reasons why this is so.

The first of those is what I call, not very happily perhaps, the fluidity of the product. Compared with most contracts it seems to me that building and engineering and construction contracts generally unquestionably permit an unusual degree of variation of the product to be supplied under the contract. In other contracts some degree of fluidity is not unknown but surely not to the same extent, and the more novel and the more complex the structure to be built then the more this is so. It is, I think, a constant, familiar feature of this kind of contract that the works are subject to constant change from the beginning of the construction period to virtually the end so that it is certainly not unknown, I am sure, to all of you to find the contract document actually being executed at the very end of the works because then for the first time the parties really know what it is that is to be built. So that seems to me to be the first feature which of necessity makes any kind of litigation in this field very difficult, because the changing nature of the product gives ample opportunity for dispute.

The second and linked feature is what, again perhaps not very happily, I have described as the fluidity of the price. Again, some degree of fluidity is not unknown in other contracts but, again as I would suggest, not to the same extent as in building contracts. Of course there is a very good reason for the price to be subject to change as new conditions are encountered, variations have to be priced and so on, but it does, as it seems to me almost inevitably, give enormous opportunity for dispute.

The third contributory factor is the period of time over which contractual performance takes place in this kind of contract. Compare it, for example, with a purchase of a cargo of oil on a vessel, perhaps on the spot market for delivery at a named port. The consideration payable under such a contract may be very large but the period for performance of the contract is likely to be a matter of days or at most weeks as compared with a major construction contract, which as we all know, may go on for years. The longer the contract period, of course, the greater the opportunity for contingencies to occur, whether it be the weather, or currency fluctuation or changes in market conditions, or changes in the international climate or whatever.

The fourth contributing factor I have called factual complexity. It is, I think, clear that even with a relatively simple building considerable foresight and very careful attention to detail are needed to foresee in advance what needs to be done to avoid having to undo work you have already done in order to make good deficiencies later, and I am thinking of ducts and pipes and services and wiring etc. etc. etc. That is so even with a relatively simple building. With a complex or innovative building clearly that is a difficulty which needs to be magnified ten thousandfold or perhaps more. So one is, I think inevitably, dealing with a field of quite unusual factual complexity.

The fifth factor is the number of active participants in performance. One has of course a designer, a supervisor, an engineer, a contractor, a multitude of sub-contractors. One of the papers which I have seen, and which no doubt you will be discussing, interestingly discusses a change in the structure of the contracting industry suggesting that whereas once upon a time you would have had a general contractor with a big contract who would do the bulk of the building work and contract out the specialist trades to sub-contractors, now this is somewhat altered. You may have a general contractor who is little more than a distributor of sub-contracts and perhaps a supervisor of the works, with virtually everything being sub-contracted out to specialist sub-contractors. That must I think, in comparison with almost any other class of contract that one can think of, increase the possibility of misunderstandings, confusion and, of course, at worst, buck passing.

Sixthly, one is dealing with contracts in which very often huge sums are at stake, large enough to make long and expensive litigation appear worth while. I think it is perhaps worth emphasising the word "appear" because an Official Referee is said to have remarked recently that in every large case he tried his real choice was as to which of the two contesting parties in the case would go bust. So that I think one is dealing with contests in which the stakes are in every sense very high indeed and that of course increases the difficulty and weight of the whole exercise.

Seventhly, the contracts use contract documentation, often in a standard form not necessarily well designed for the particular project in hand and not necessarily easy to understand and construe. Certainly I think a number of lawyers find these contract forms difficult and I have for my part often wondered how the manager on the site, who one hopes is not a lawyer, copes with trying to give practical effect to documents which are very difficult and obscure. One imagines a practical-minded contractor sitting down in his hut and trying to make sense of this material and one's heart goes out to him, or her.

Eighthly, I think one should include what has been described in some of the papers as the claims culture, which exists I think to an unusual extent in this industry. It is of course understandable that, in time of recession particularly, competition is very fierce, contractors are desperate to acquire work, they tender at cost or little above cost and then seek to make a reasonable profit by presenting claims ex post facto in order to try and make the contract worth while from their point of view. No doubt the recession has made things worse and others will have much more experience of this issue than I have, but I think this is not an entirely new phenomenon. I can recall acting for a concern, which shall certainly be nameless, some years ago. I suppose occasionally they built something somewhere but their real business was making claims. From the moment that the contract began they began to compile a dossier, to start giving notices, to get the correspondence bundle into good shape and to set about preparing the way for massive claims against the building owner.

Surely this situation is exacerbated by the inequality in the commercial muscle of many of those engaged in the performance of these contracts, particularly as between the larger contractors and the smaller sub-contractors which, as I understand, is a longstanding and recognised source of abuse. I had understood that section 108 of the Housing Grants, Construction and Regeneration Act was really intended to address this problem by enabling a sub-contractor to obtain an adjudication in his favour and obtain payment *pro tem*, with the expectation or the possibility that the whole matter would be re-opened subsequently but with the hope that he would at least have something in his pocket to keep him going, rather than being faced with the prospect of bankruptcy if he did not accept something less than he thought he was really entitled to recover. But clearly this section is a controversial topic. I understand that there are those who feel that it is a step in entirely the wrong direction.

Now of course it must be true that those engaged in the construction industry, like everybody else, are motivated by self interest and commercial incentives and human nature and so on. But I do wonder whether this is quite a sufficient explanation of the claims culture which does exist and which I think, but I shall be corrected by others who know more about this, is less marked elsewhere than it is here. And I think, but again it is very difficult to speak positively, that this culture is less evident in other fields where one might expect it to exist, such as for example shipbuilding. Now it is very difficult to be dogmatic, and I myself have experience of shipowners who order ships at the top of the market and then there are currency fluctuations against them and they find that they have ordered a ship much bigger than they think the market really needs, and so they then make complaints about the building of the vessel as an excuse for not taking it or paying much less. So plainly this kind of activity is not unknown elsewhere. But I have an impression, which may be unreliable that in other fields such as that one does not get the same incidence of dispute as one does in the mainstream construction/engineering field.

Now I am very conscious indeed that what I have said so far is a typical lawyer's contribution, long on diagnosis and very short on prescription. One can only hope that an accurate diagnosis is not a necessary precondition of effective prescription. And I am very conscious indeed that you will be discussing in the rest of this conference various prescriptions which will no doubt include structural change, cultural change, contractual change and legal change more generally. I was interested by one of the papers which discussed the possibly, I emphasise possibly, emerging doctrine of good faith in the negotiation and operation of a contract and it may be that there is room for some approximation to the European view of these matters. So I end, as is I think probably appropriate, on a completely inconclusive note, expressing the hope that the conference may enable you to move towards effective prescriptions for this malady, if it has been accurately diagnosed.

2. General Introduction

The Editors

This volume brings together the edited proceedings of the 9th and 10th Annual Conferences of the Centre of Construction Law at King's College, held in September 1996 and 1997. The themes and papers of the two conferences were complementary and now form one volume of collated material covering the major construction law themes current at the end of first decade of the Centre of Construction Law.

Lord Bingham's keynote speech for the 9th Annual Conference is reproduced as paper 1 in this volume. For the 10th Annual Conference, Sir Nicholas Lyell, Attorney General under the Major Government until May 1997 was the keynote speaker. He recalled the speech which he delivered at the First Annual Conference in 1988, then as Solicitor General under Mrs Thatcher. In 1988 the UK construction industry accounted for some 10 per cent. of GDP amounting to some £34 billion per annum. The industry then employed 1.5 million people. Within 12 months of that conference there occurred a major property slump which led to five or more truly difficult years for the economy. Contracts for public works, however, particularly road building provided exceptional value which the government of the day took full advantage of in its construction programme. Over the ten-year span since 1988 the construction industry has truly undergone a sea-change. In money terms, its output in 1997 was about the same figure (£34 billion) as in 1988, but effectively reduced by inflation. And now the figure represents not 10 per cent. but 5 per cent. only of GDP, partly because of the change in the value of money, but also reflecting a very great growth in productivity.

Over the ten-year period since 1988 the number of employees in the industry has shrunk from 1.5 million to about 800,000. But there were other more encouraging statistics: new work started in 1988 accounted for £19 billion whereas the figure for 1997 was nearly £28 billion. The value of contract works undertaken abroad has also shown steady growth. In 1988 the figure was £1.9 billion while the latest figure for 1997 amounted to £3.4 billion. Overseas earnings by Architects, Consulting Engineers and Surveyors have also doubled over the same period to a current figure of £1.2 billion. Currently the private housing market is rising by 10-15 per cent. per annum, although road construction has suffered a sharp downturn.

The real sea-change over the ten-year period has been in attitudes. It was this change which provided the real challenge and the real hope for the construction industry in future years. The challenge for construction lawyers was to ensure that legal structures and practices kept pace with the real changes in, and the new aspirations of the industry. These included the rise of Design and Build, the PFI and Partnering. Impending implementation of the Housing Grants, Construction and Regeneration Act 1996, represented a major step forward. Although there were sceptical voices, it should not be overlooked that these changes had come from a profound sense of dissatisfaction with what we were and to some extent still are doing in the construction industry. Clients are tired of conflict, disputes and cost escalation which have become the hallmarks of the UK construction industry for many decades. They are tired of the old system of low tenders followed by a running battle to ratchet up the costs. Typical of this, was one national contractor who often encountered out-turn prices which exceeded the bid value by 50 per cent. – well above the National Audit Office figure of 28 per cent.

One solution lay in the new system of partnering, now firmly supported by major employers such as BAA, Railtrack, the water companies, local authorities and now the MoD and the Highways Agency. Major private employers such as Marks and Spencers, Tesco and Boots were also using their power to offer continuity of work on a similar basis. It was this desire for change which led to setting up the Latham Committee and which underpinned its report, which lay at the heart of the HGCR Act.

Partnering was also identified by Nigel Robson, Head of Construction at Eversheds, sponsors of the 9th Annual Conference, as one of the areas which significantly influenced risk management. Current risk management philosophies in the UK cover a broad spectrum. But the prevailing practice is still for risks to be allocated to, or one might say "dumped" upon, the contractor. This includes both foreseeable and unforeseeable risks. The Promoter is seeking price certainly for which he is willing to pay a premium. Whilst this approach has some theoretical appeal, it breaks down in practice. Given that the award will be to the lowest tenderer, the foundation is laid for the acrimony which has bedevilled our construction industry. At best the project will be dispute prone, at worst, the owner employer faces a defaulting contractor.

Nigel Robson's introductory paper identified five areas of current significance. First, partnering represents an increasingly popular approach to construction projects. There are many definitions of partnering, but the necessary ingredients should be regarded as embracing the following elements: trust; collaborative not adversarial approach; close and open communication; and common objectives and incentives. These ingredients are not properly reflected in the majority of contract documentation. Some cannot escape the notion that contracting is a war of attrition. In the United States, partnering has been shown to be remarkably successful in reducing claims, and therefore total contract price and time on public works contracts. A major component of partnering is a brain-storming session amongst project participants at which issues of concern are raised, including risk identification. The product of this exercise eventually forms part of the partnering charter to be signed by all participants in the project. Analysis of any typical partnering charter reveals that the achievement of the individual goals of the parties is based upon the effective management of risks during the performance of the contract.

Second, the allocation of risk arising from sub-surface conditions often leads to major disputes where unforeseen conditions are found to exist. Each of the standard form contracts attempts to allocate the risk by allowing the contractor to recover additional cost in particular circumstances. There is a temptation, however, to make the contractor fully responsible for site conditions, or to alter the wording so as to load more of the risk on the contractor. The effect on pricing and on claims can be dramatic.

Third, pre-project planning is invariably repaid by greater efficiency and cost saving. The American Construction Industry Institute has identified the management of risk as an essential and integral part of pre-project planning which should also cover analysis of the financial, business, regulatory, project and operational risks and contingencies. Their search showed that pre-project planning can reduce project costs by as much as 20 per cent., and the total design and construction period by up to 39 per cent.

Fourth, some aspects of insurance will repay close attention. In regard to third party liability, and interesting approach has been adopted by one major oil company whereby, the contractor accepts liability for third party claims up to a certain limit (dependent on the magnitude of the contract). Thus, even if it is clear that the employer or his personnel were to blame for the incident which gave rise to the third party claim, the contractor remains liable. In practice, it will not always be clear what caused or contributed to an accident. This is an example of allocating the risk to the party who is most in control of that risk. It is also a way of managing and avoiding the risk of litigation. Conversely, the owner accepts liability for third party damage above the cap, even if the contractor is at fault. This is partly a response to contractors being unwilling to accept unlimited liability, but again it avoids the risk of litigation between owner and contractor. The arrangement also accords with common practice since in most cases injured parties will sue the site owner not least because they are seen to have the deeper pocket.

Fifth, Alternative Dispute Resolution (ADR) in its many forms is growing in popularity and status. There is a danger, however, of over-proceduralising the process. It should not become too legal. A balance needs to be struck between procedure, informality and flexibility. Most experienced employers regard ADR as a sensible tool which can save time and money, and which can be especially helpful in long term contracts where there is need to maintain good relationships. It also instils in both employer and contractor organisations a better "claims management" discipline. It is helpful to keep in mind that disputes are mostly factual and technical rather than legal, and so involve construction professionals. Consequently, professionals have a valuable role to play both in resolving and in preventing the occurrence of disputes. Striking the right balance was particularly important in large projects where Dispute Review Boards had an important role.

The themes of risk, partnering and ADR are addressed further in the papers which follow. Likewise, the themes of procurement, including PFI, and the regulated industries, identified by Sir Nicholas Lyell, are addressed in specific papers. The collated papers from both conferences have been arranged under four broad headings dealing, first, with the place which construction law holds in commercial law generally. In his introductory paper, Sir Philip Otton makes the apposite observation that construction cases contribute significantly to the development of commercial law. As is examined in the last paper of the introductory section dissemination of the developments in, and standardisation in the teaching of, the law pertinent to the construction sector represent the aims of the Society of Construction Law and the Centre of Construction Law & Management at King's College London.

The second section dealing with procurement and project strategy examines important new developments which are likely to bring about fundamental changes in the contracting arrangements within the industry. The first paper examines current views on the issues of efficiency and reform in construction contracts and procurement, and the wider influences on forms of contract and procurement methods and concludes that there is an in-built resistance in the industry to change. This paper does however serve to reinforce the importance of the relationship between economics, construction and law, and despite those resistant to change seeking to blur the focus, it highlights that fact that those who adapt to changed requirements will remain important contributors to the long-term efficiency of the industry. One of these changes is the advent of the Private Finance Initiative, the prevailing and emerging principles of which undergo analysis in Geoff Haley's paper. Similarly an interesting contribution to the debate is provided by the following paper which examines the difficulties in securing private finance for infrastructure projects, which, prior to widescale privatisation, were in the public domain. Whether the long term durability of PFI can be guaranteed by the present Government remains to be seen, but it is obvious from the emerging caselaw and financing techniques that PFI has and will continue to have a profound effect on the procurement of public contracts.

The current buzzword in construction procurement is 'Partnering', the success and inherent difficulties of which are the subject of analysis in the final papers in this section. John Barlow explores the relationship between institutional economics in the construction sector and the emergence of partnering. John Dorter examines the fundamental conceptual differences between partnering and contracting. In conclusion he illustrates what can go wrong if these differences are overlooked or glossed over by the draftsman.

In section three, papers are presented on aspects of the regulated industries – a wholly new field of study generated by the privatisation programme of the 1980s, which has replaced the former nationalised industries with new privately owned industries operating under a variety of systems of regulation. Of particular note is the paper by Kristine Morais, in which she comprehensively reviews the structure of power generation plant and considers the principal risks involved in the procurement and the implementation of such plant generally. She goes on to examine the ways in which sponsors, otherwise known as financiers, may safeguard against such risks when analysing the major project documentation and suggests how the return on the capital invested may be protected.

Fourthly, a series of papers continuing the theme of damage, its proof and recovery, themes which are also covered in papers from earlier published conference proceedings. John Powell's paper deals with loss containment and proposes the emergence of the principle of proportionality, Johnathan Hosie examines how the liquidated damage provision has developed and how it now can best be developed to enhance certainty in the case of default. The following two papers are related by a common them: cost. Colin Gallani examines how the costs of construction can be kept to an acceptable level by analysing and managing the factors which lead to cost overruns. Christopher Lemar then examines *ex post facto* how and if recovery from the client can be achieved.

The final part of the collection contains a series of papers on current aspects of disputes and their resolution, which also complement papers in earlier published proceedings. The first paper by Phillip Capper examines the relevance and continued application of arbitration as the primary means of settling disputes arising in construction. Secondly, Penny Brooker and Anthony Lavers report on a major academic survey into attitudes within the contracting and sub-contracting sectors to dispute resolution. Michael O'Reilly then examines how statutory reform streamlines the arbitration process and promotes cost efficiency in the dispute resolution process. The final paper by Michael Black QC examines how the institution of ADR is perceived and managed by the courts.

The editors, the publishers and the Centre of Construction Law and Management wish to record the great and valued assistance of the conference sponsors and supporters. Eversheds Solicitors were sponsors for the 9th Annual Conference and the Society of Construction Law for the 10th. Keynote speakers were Lord Bingham, Lord Chief Justice of England (whose speech is reproduced above) and Sir Nicholas Lyell whose speech forms part of this General Introduction. Finally thanks are due to the two conference Chairmen, Nigel Robson of Eversheds and Sir Phillip Otton, Lord Justice of Appeal and President of the Society of Construction Law, both of whom contributed greatly to the proceedings.

3. A Contemporary Review of Construction Law and Its Institutions

Introduction

Construction law might once have been seen as minor branch of common law with some particular features deriving from special contract forms. Since the rise and dramatic re-shaping of the law of negligence in the 1980s, it would be difficult to see construction law as either minor, or as a branch of anything else. A more contemporary picture would see construction law as probably the major generator of new commercial law in the 1980s and 1990s. Of equal importance, construction law has given rise to what is here referred to as a number of major "institutions" which facilitate the development and dissemination of construction law. It is these institutions which form the compendious subject of this paper, whose contents originally formed separate contributions at the 10th Annual Conference, respectively by John Redmond, Chairman of the Society of Construction Law, Alan Shilston, Civil Engineer, Adrian Hughes, Barrister, John Tackaberry QC, and John Uff QC, Director of the Centre of Construction Law and Management.

This composite paper first outlines the origin and activities of the Society of Construction Law, currently (1998) celebrating its 15th anniversary. It then reviews international developments in construction law generally and considers specific activity in a range of countries with which the Society of Construction Law maintains active links. The paper then considers the contemporary position of the Official Referees, the primary generators of construction law. Finally, some observations are offered on the academic future of construction law through the perspective of the Centre of Construction Law at King's College, London.

The Society of Construction Law

The Society of Construction Law, founded in 1983 by a small band of practitioners in the field of construction law, has grown in 15 years beyond expectation to a membership of over 700. While not the first Society of Construction Law in Europe SCL is now the largest and the most active society in Europe or elsewhere.

The Society entered a new phase in 1996 when Lord Justice Otton agreed to become President and the senior elected member became Chairman of its Council. The Society's objective is *"to promote for the public benefit, education, study and research (and publication of the useful results of such research) in the field of construction law and related subjects both in the United Kingdom and overseas"*.

The principal activities of the Society are the monthly meetings held in London. The subjects covered at meetings are extraordinarily varies and have been led by a wide range of eminent and well-known speakers from the UK or elsewhere. Other meetings, are held in Manchester, Bristol, Cardiff, Birmingham, Edinburgh and Newcastle, and in fact anywhere where an enthusiastic core of members wish to organise a meeting. Many of the papers delivered at the evening meetings are subsequently published and distributed to members. Members of the Society overseas who never attend meetings feel that this supply of published material amply justifies their subscription.

The Society of Construction Law has grown and flourished despite the fact that construction, for much of the period, has been in decline. This growth has not been the result of a major marketing campaign – the Society has done little to attract members. The reason is that construction law has become an area of immense significance, not merely to the construction industry but to the development of commercial law generally, particularly the law of contract and tort. Construction has indeed given rise to a host of widely significant cases for the Common Law.

Much of the Society's success is attributable to the mix of professions and interests represented by the first members who met in October 1983. That mix has been maintained, without conscious effort. The majority of members are Solicitors, but they include a wide range of specialisms and represent only a bare majority (56%). Other significant groups comprise Quantity Surveyors (15%), Engineers (12%), Barristers (8%) and Architects (4%). The range is not just horizontal, spanning virtually every profession involved in the construction industry. It is also vertical, as members include the most senior members of each of the professions, as well as some of the most junior, often within the first years of qualification. The society's meetings therefore offer a unique opportunity for lawyer to meet engineer, and junior to meet senior.

The increasing acceptance of new contractual approaches in construction, the changes in arbitration law and practice and the extraordinarily radical measures being introduced by the Housing Grants, Construction and Regeneration Act, 1996 are each dramatically affecting the development of construction law. All those who participate in the industry are aware that great changes are afoot. Some welcome them and others are cynical about their potential. But all are interested in the fate of the industry. There are more construction lawyers writing for the construction press than quantity surveyors, architects or engineers. Law is central to the industry and the need for the Society to provide a forum for practitioners from the different professional groups is greater than ever. The Society of Construction Law will continue to promote way in which members may communicate and debate these vital matters.

There has been a massive growth in the academic study of the subject over the ten years since the founding of the Centre of Construction Law at King's College. The industry has derived great benefit from the availability of formal academic qualifications in the filed of construction law, initially from King's College and latterly from many other colleges and universities. The Society provides a bridge between the colleges and universities and the construction professions, which is already providing very real benefits in each direction. The Society was founded with the object of promoting the study of construction law, and is particularly proud to have been associated with the development of the Centre of Construction Law which has in turn provided support and enthusiasm from which the Society has benefited hugely.

Construction law in international developments

The scale and complexity of international construction projects nowadays render inevitable joint venture contracting arrangements to enable risks and skills to be shared. Thus, a joint venture might have a Japanese lead contractor with consortium members selected from a wide range of jurisdictions from the developed countries with advanced construction industries, such as Germany, France Sweden, Italy, Holland UK and US. Promoters will often be identified with the developing countries. To deal with their lack of knowledge and experience, coupled with a desire to transfer maximum risk to contractors, lump sum fixed price turnkey contracting is the most usual form of procurement favoured by promoters.

Promoters, constructors, and non-lawyer service providers concerned with international construction, interface with construction lawyers at various stages in the construction process. They need to know what is the nature of the lawyers' duties owed to their clients. Are these controlled by statutory regulation, custom or the edicts of national professional bodies? Or are they just personal to the practitioners? Without such understanding there will be tensions between non-lawyers and lawyers, who are not as forthcoming as they might be about the nature of the skills they deploy. Non-lawyers, at least from an English perspective, are more appreciative of the creative as distinct from negative exercise of legal skills.

In the international construction law field, particularly in the ever-expanding world of lump sum fixed price turnkey contracting, the valuation of changed or disorganised work can only realistically be achieved by reference to evidence of actual cost. At an international level, there is increasing convergence across the cultures as to standardised accountancy practices and conventions. The major accountancy firms operate on a truly international scale. They necessarily adopt global standard practices where staff are moved between offices throughout the world to deal with short-term peak workloads.

During the assessment competitive bid proposals, promoters would be well advised to explore what accountancy arrangements a short-listed contracting organisation had in contemplation: who are its global auditors and which branch of the auditing firm will be responsible for monitoring and auditing the contract in contemplation. The matter of how the exchange of cost information between promoter and contractor external auditors would be achieved, also needs to be established as part of the contract negotiations.

While the practice of international law is not primarily concerned with the resolution of disputes, the development of international law in the abstract is very much specialist lawyer territory into which non-lawyers, however self-confident, should hesitate to intrude. However, in the field of dispute resolution and in particular international arbitration which, spanning national boundaries, will be the usual way of deciding international construction disputes, non-lawyers must take account of relevant national law in establishing and quantifying liability.

In the effective conduct of international arbitration, the common ingredient, whether the arbitrators are non-lawyers or lawyers or a mixture of both, is that arbitrators necessarily must be pro-active, effective communicators, tactful, patient, culturally neutral and possess the imagination to be procedurally creative. Party representatives need to possess the capability of shedding home-grown habits and prejudices, with a healthy curiosity as to how colleagues from other jurisdictions operate. Even if an adversarial procedure is still appropriate English courts, that does not justify such an approach in international arbitration. Arbitration, wherever it is to be conducted, posits the need for continuation in business relationships and accordingly the absence of confrontation in its procedures. Procedural co-operation should be the name of the game.

All commercial people are familiar with and regularly handle business reports. They conform to a readily identifiable general style. Arbitration is an aspect of business management. Arbitration awards should be written with this in mind. They should be well reasoned and written in a user-friendly communicating style with which commercial people across the cultures can easily relate, in the same way as business reports.

Foreign construction law institutions

Equivalent bodies to the Society of Construction Law exist in most of the other European countries. These societies provide a channel of communication for the exchange of ideas between different jurisdictions and a point of contact for the development of comparative research. Harmonisation of principles of construction law between European countries, and indeed on a wider international basis, may still be at an early stage, but efforts are being made. The existence of national societies provides a structure which can assist such exercises and promote international co-operation and understanding to further these ends.

Apart from the UK Society of Construction Law, thriving associations exist in Italy, France, Germany, Belgium, Netherlands, Norway, Sweden, Denmark, Greece, Austria, Switzerland and the Czech Republic. Each of these organisations belongs to the European Society of Construction Law. The national presidents meet once a year after a conference organised by one of the members states. For 1997, the host nation was Greece. The Hellenic Society for Technology and Construction Law ran a conference on the subject of "Disturbances in the Construction Process" in Athens, including contributions from different countries on the subject of causation, delay and loss of productivity, risk allocation and dispute resolution in construction projects. In addition, member societies hold their own domestic conferences. The Association Française pour le Droit de la Construction held a conference in Paris in 1997 on the allocation of risk in construction projects. The French Society's annual conference proceedings are published in the Revue de Droit Immobilier.

In the Netherlands, there are two main societies for construction law. The programme of the Dutch Society of Construction Law during the past year has included sessions on project management, planning, architect's copyright and the legal aspects of a large redevelopment project in Rotterdam. The Dutch Institute for Construction Law has held seminars during the past year on developments in the law of tenders and competition and a review of developments over the previous 25 years in honour of a distinguished past president. The Dutch Institute has recently formed a separate society of construction advocates, the equivalent of ORBA/ORSA.

The Danish Society of Construction Law has been engaged in discussing the progress of the DKK 22 Billion coast to coast link between Sweden and Denmark, the construction of which commenced in 1996, in particular the efficacy of the ADR provisions in the contract. The Society is also to consider the general subject of contractors' claims for disruption.

The GAIPEC fact finding exercise

An interesting and important exercise was conducted at the Danish Society's 10th Anniversary conference in Copenhagen in September 1994. Speakers from the difference European member states and the United States were asked to consider issues of liability of contractors and supervisors in their particular jurisdiction through a consideration of the factual circumstances of four specimen cases. The exercise was considered sufficiently important in establishing the comparative position on liability under construction contracts, for the European Commission in 1995/6 to conduct (through GAIPEC) an exercise along similar lines through questionnaires addressed to each of the EU member states. Nine specimen cases and a comprehensive set of questions were included in a questionnaire for legal experts.

The questionnaires[1] sought to establish the legal and factual position on liability for damage in construction contracts in each of the member states. The European Commission was concerned to establish that there were no material barriers to freedom of establishment and service or inequalities in consumer protection warranting its intervention. The results of the exercise will be of considerable interest. A similar approach could be followed through the channel of the national construction law associations in other areas of comparative importance.

Developments in other jurisdictions

A brief review of the recent developments reported by the national presidents or published in the Correspondents' Reports in the International Constructions Law Review, indicates some of the international developments in construction law considered by foreign lawyers to be of particular importance.

New Zealand The common law in New Zealand has importantly diverged from that in the United Kingdom in relation both to limitation and the existence of a duty of care in a local authority. The Privy

---

[1]   Specimen forms are found at page 120 of 1996 International Construction Law Review.

Council upheld the New Zealand Court of Appeal in *Invercargill City Council v. Hamlin*[2] to the effect that neither *Pirelli* nor *Murphy* represented the law in Zealand. In the Court of Appeal, Sir Robin Cooke had stated:

> "...*Whilst disharmony may be regrettable, it is inevitable now that the Commonwealth jurisdictions have gone on their own paths without taking English decisions as the invariable starting point. The ideal of a uniform common law has proved as unattainable as any ideal of a uniform civil law. It could not survive the independence of the United States; constitutional evolution in the Commonwealth has done the rest. What of course is both desirable and feasible, within the limits of judicial and professional time, is to take into account and learn from decisions in other jurisdictions...*"

The Privy Council endorsed this approach by stating:

> "...*in the present case the Judges in the New Zealand Court of Appeal were consciously departing from English case law on the ground that conditions in New Zealand are different. Were they entitled to do so? The Answer must surely be Yes. The ability of the common law to adapt itself to the differing circumstances of the countries in which it has taken root is not a weakness but one of its greatest strengths. Were it not so, the common law would not have flourished as it has with all the common law countries learning from each other.*"

Canada and Australia In March 1995, both Canada through *Winnipeg v. Bird*[3] and Australia through *Bryan v. Maloney*[4] had rejected *Murphy*. These instances involve areas of substantive law which have proved inappropriate for harmonisation even between jurisdictions with a common tradition. Whilst comparative study is beneficial for the development of the substantive law in a given jurisdiction, differing conditions and attitudes will support the maintenance of different legal principles between different jurisdictions in substantial areas of construction law.

---

[2]   [1996] AC 624

[3]   (1995) 121 DLR (4th) 93

[4]   (1995) 128 ALR 163

France The most important current development in construction law in France is considered to be the creation of a new public procurement code which will come into effect next year. This will be based upon a March 1996 report on the public procurement regulations with the aim of strengthening and clarifying the existing code. In 1996, a court of first instance in Strasbourg had for the first time invalidated a public works contract which had been awarded in breach of the current competition rules which as amounted to a criminal office.

Hungary A new Public Procurement Act was brought into force in Hungary from November 1995. The Act was passed as part of the harmonisation process with a view to compliance with EU law. The Act has provisional effect only, however, in that it retains a preference in favour of Hungarian companies which it is recognised would have to be removed in the event of Hungary being admitted to the EU.

Netherlands In February 1995, the Court of First Instance of the European Union upheld the view of the European Commission that certain pre-tender practices of Dutch contractors intended to ensure collaboration in the exchange of price and other information were in breach of Article 85 of the Treaty in restricting fair competition. The contractors have appealed.

Denmark As noted above, the vast Sweden to Denmark coast to coast link project is at the forefront of the Danish construction industry. The contract involved the establishment of an ADR board. After the first year of construction there has been no need for resort to ADR and there have been no request for arbitration. A previous very large civil engineering project, the 18 kilometre Great Belt link led to an important European Court judgment in June 1993 in relation to the Public Procurement Directive. The state-owned Danish company responsible for the project had issued a restricted invitation to tender for part of the works. The case is important as part of the EU's attempt to enforce its public procurement rules throughout the Union. Denmark does not have direct legislation governing contracts for building and civil engineering. A revised version of the Danish General Conditions for Works and Supplies for Building and Civil Engineering Works (AB92) was issued in December 1992.

Sweden Sweden has similarly recently issued a revised standard contract, referred to also as "AB92", for use both domestically and by foreign parties.

Finland Finland has recently allowed, for the first time, a privately funded government Design, Build, Finance and Operate construction project. Tenders were invited internationally for the construction of a 69 kilometre highway as a test project for similar private sector large scale construction projects. Work started in May 1997.

Greece Two major construction projects in Greece have provided the opportunity for the creation of two different dispute resolution procedures in the contracts. The Athens International Airport contract contains a multi-step procedure which provides first for a mandatory primary attempt at an amicable and friendly resolution with the assistance of a two member resolution panel; certain time deadlines are imposed. If not capable of such resolution, the next step is a voluntary referral to a three member mediation panel The procedure is flexible and non-binding unless formalised. There is a final provision for reference to arbitration to the London Court of Arbitration to be conducted in English in London, the award to be final and binding.

The Rio Antirio Bridge contract contains a difference series of procedures. There is a non-mandatory exhortation to amicable settlement. If unsuccessful, there is then provision for mandatory reference to adjudication panels whose unanimous decision is final and binding as is its non-unanimous but unappealed decision. There is a provision for ICC arbitration in London for issues surviving unresolved through the previous steps.

Pakistan In the context of the Pakistan government's encouragement of foreign private investment in the development of infrastructure projects, especially energy generation projects, the decision of the High Court of Punjab in the case of *Rupali v. Bunni*[5] has caused great concern to foreign investors. In the recent international construction boom in Pakistan, it had become common for the foreign party and the local partner to agree that the law of the contract should be that of Pakistan but that disputes should be settled by arbitration in a neutral country, often in Singapore, under international rules such as those of the ICC with the intention that speedy enforcement should be possible. In

---

[5]   PLD (1994) Lahore 525; Con L Yb (1995) 155.

Rupali, the Lahore High Court asserted jurisdiction over the award in an international arbitration where the law governing the contract was that of Pakistan but the seat of the arbitration was in London. It was held on appeal that the award of the ICC Tribunal in London was a Pakistani domestic award, despite the choice of the parties as to a neutral venue and the assumption that the award would be enforceable as a foreign award in Pakistan.

China Two developments in China affecting the construction industry are of particular importance. The Electric Power Law, which came into force on 1 April 1996, sets the general framework for the construction of electric power plants and production of electricity. The State Planning Commission has created a BOT (Build Operate Transfer) Investment Development Corporation to facilitate private infrastructure investment. China is set to announce a number of road, bridge, water and power supply projects where foreign ownership will be permitted under the BOT formula and newly created regulations. The first batch of limited pilot projects will test the water, both for the Chinese government and for foreign investors uncertain about the risks and the basis of operation of such projects.

Hong Kong has developed experience in the construction and operation of BOT schemes. Individual Ordinances are passed for each project, there being no general governing legislation. The concept has worked well so fat with a number of successful projects including cross-harbour tunnels. Investors must now await any effect of the change of sovereignty. Hong Kong is also a well-established centre for international arbitration. Although, the China International Economic and Trade Arbitration Commission (CIETAC) is most commonly used in Chinese trade and investment contracts, Hong Kong has also been widely used as a centre. There was reciprocal enforcement under New York Convention provisions between China and Hong Kong prior to the change of sovereignty. Following the change, a Hong Kong award will may be treated as a domestic award and there remains concern about the attitude of the Chinese courts to enforcement.

Conclusion The links between UK Society of Construction Law and the other European societies provides a useful channel for comparative study and for working towards co-operation and harmonisation where this is appropriate. Links should, where possible, be extended to jurisdictions beyond Europe, especially those where construction activity is expanding. It is apparent from a brief and necessarily selective review of recent developments in a range of countries that certain trends can be discerned:

- substantive legal principles in difficult areas of law remain divergent. Even in countries with a similar legal tradition difference persist and in some areas widen.

- a number of countries are tackling the need to codify important procedures such as those for public procurement; the European Union provides a regime which the Commission and Courts attempt to enforce.

- standard form construction and civil engineering contracts continue to be revised and developed with the benefit of comparative study.

- China is starting to show interest in foreign investment for the development of its infrastructure, with particular interest in BOT projects.

- large construction projects provide the vehicle for the development of new procedures for dispute resolution, the refinement of which benefits from international experience.

- international concern continues in respect of the uncertainty of enforcement of international arbitration awards, especially in the rapidly developing economies of Asia.

The Official Referees

Given the major expansion in the legal and economic importance of construction law, as well as the sheer volume of cases, it remains a serious judicial and procedural anomaly that Official Referees, since the Courts Act 1970, have continued to rank as no more than circuit judges. They generate practically the whole of the new areas of construction law at first instance. Their decisions are now widely reported and are frequently cited abroad. It remains the case, however, that in England their judgements are no more than technically persuasive, and no other Court of first instance is bound by them. At least their decisions can now be cited up to the House of Lords and are treated with the respect that they should command. But their position remains an anomaly considering the importance of the cases they transact, both in terms of their legal content and their commercial importance compared e.g. to the commercial Court.

Lord Justice Steyn, as he then was, in *Darlington v. Wiltshier Northern*[6] identified part of the problem when paying tribute to the late senior Official Referee in the following terms:

> *"I differ from his Honour Judge Newey QC, who died recently, with great diffidence. He was an outstanding judge and did more than any other judge to build up a modern Construction Court in the Queen's Bench Division. His experience was that some users found the name Official Referees quaint and others found it confusing. He preferred the name Construction Court. So does almost everybody."*

The campaign to elevate Official Referees to full High Court status has been spasmodic and has experienced a temporary halt more than once when faced with seemingly implacable opposition. The campaign will certainly continue and should be vigorously supported by the new range of construction industry bodies which have emerged under the umbrella of the Construction Industry Board.

While the Official Referees exercise full High Court jurisdiction, there is no doubt that the authorities are well aware of their limited status. This appears in a number of ways. First, the judge immediately responsible for Official Referee matters is not the Senior Official Referee, as might be expected, but a High Court judge appointed for that purpose. Secondly, one of the Official Referees has recently been "promoted" to the High Court bench (the first during the present century), so emphasising the absence of any supposed parity of status. Third, it was announced in May 1998 that, as from October 1998, the Judge in charge, Mr Justice Dyson, would hear Official Referees' business. A change of name for both the courts and the judges has been signalled. The effect of these measures will remain to be seen.

Historically, Official Referees were seen as tribunals to whom "real" judges sent the minutiae work, after the real judge had decided the important principles. A good example would be a case where a partnership had broken up. The principal disputes between the partners would be resolved by a High Court judge; and the taking of an account sent to a Master or an Official Referee. Thus, Official Referees were seen as inferior to High Court judges. The assumption that the position

---

[6]   (1994) 69 BLR 1

of Official Referee is inferior to that of the High Court judge is re-enforced by the fact that they do not enjoy the same trappings – the knighthood, the shorter pension term, and the salary. Yet Official Referees dispose of an annual list as heavy as any first instance High Court judge, outside the Commercial Court, and heavier than that of most of them.

There is thought to be a variability in the quality of the decisions emanating from the different Official Referees. While it must be true that no two judges are likely to reach identical conclusion in anything but the simplest case, let alone a complicated matter, there is some belief that the variability in the quality of decision emanating from Official Referees in this country goes further than that. Although perhaps not typical, the approach of Official Referees to appeals from, and other applications in connection with, arbitrations is seen to vary considerably according to which Official Referee hears the matter. Also Official Referees as a body, are seen to vary considerably from the approach of the Commercial Court, in that the Official Referees appear far more ready to intervene in arbitration matters.

There is, perhaps more importantly, a perception of great variability in procedure. An anecdotal example illustrates the point. In a fairly heavy case, Judge A approached the matter in a traditional way, ordered a series of trials, and estimated the length of those trials by reference to the usual time likely to be taken by extensive factual and expert evidence given orally. Given the diary problems of Court and counsel, the resultant time- table stretched out a long way into the future. This no doubt upset the Plaintiff and pleased the Defendants. A year or more later, Judge B heard a lengthy summons to review the case, and revised the procedure, imposing tight limits on the time to be taken in cross examination of witnesses, and limited time for the hearings. The consequence was a very different look to the calendar. This no doubt pleased the Plaintiff and upset the Defendants. Subsequently, Judge A reviewed things at a later summons, and indicated that he would be unlikely to enforce these stringent time limits if he happened to be the judge who actually heard the trials or any of them. This left everybody in limbo. While it is quite understandable how the situation occurred, it is equally understandable that such a situation does nothing for customer satisfaction, or reputation.

Proposed reforms

What course then can sensibly be followed to realise the great potential both of the Official Referees' Court and of the judges that sit in it? The following are the elements which have a role in any reorganisation of the Court which may take place in the future.

The Court should ultimately consist of a mix of High Court judges (not just one) and circuit judges, all sitting regularly but not exclusively on Official Referee business. Both High Court judges and circuit judges should have the opportunity to sit in other Courts, just as High Court judges already sit in the Divisional Court and in the Court of Appeal. This would widen the experience of the judges, and also ensure that they, both High Court and circuit were known to and appreciated by a wider audience than is at present the case. It would also potentially widen the catchment area of recruitment, since more of the legal professions would have been exposed to judges from the Official Referees Court. Official Referees should be promoted from circuit to High Court judge regularly.

One of the judges should have responsibility to overseeing the smooth running of the Court, including dealing with consistency in procedure. As this would involve specifically administrative skills, it could be either a High Court judge or a circuit judge. It should depend on who has the relevant skill.

The Court should be prepared to offer the parties difference procedures. There should be a choice between those involving the ultra-abbreviation of time in Court and those offering a much fuller exploration by oral hearing. Parties opting for the latter by agreement should expect to pay for the extra time. Where parties disagree, the Court should usually impose a shorter style of procedure. A handy rule of thumb would be to link the time limit to the sum at issue. Where shorter style procedures are involved, judges, of whatever kind, will require appropriately lengthy periods for both preparation and judgment writing. It should not be assumed that such work will be done at home, in what other trades would regard as social time. Once a particular procedure is adopted for a particular case, it should be adhered to, unless the parties agree to change it, or good cause is shown for a change.

There was once an idea that the judge who heard the interlocutory applications would be the best person to hear the trial. In the interests of "efficiency" this is not always achieved. It would be a good idea if it was achieved. Even in shorter cases, after taking into account the reforms suggested above, it might still not be possible to achieve this in all cases. But it should be possible more often and this would be beneficial.

A step which would greatly enhance their status would be for senior Official Referees to be invited to sit with the Court of Appeal, as is presently the case with circuit judges in criminal matters. In due time this practice could lead to consideration of promotion direct from Official Referee to Lord Justice of Appeal, a step which would do much to restore the supposed parity with High Court judges. This would necessarily entail widening of the areas of work undertaken by the judges as already suggested.

It will be obvious that what is involved is a long term task which cannot be achieved overnight. The aim is to enhance the reputation of the Court to a very high level, which will necessarily take time. The present Lord Chancellor, more than any of his recent predecessors, has direct experience of Official Referees business and should need no persuasion that their true status ought to be recognised by the application of new and fresh ideas.

The teaching of construction law

It is increasingly evident that a knowledge of law is an essential part of construction management and of any training programme for construction professionals. Like the church, the law has a grim history of self-protection and exclusivism, restricting both the dissemination of knowledge and its practice. Although professionally qualified lawyers still maintain a closed shop in the case of litigation, arbitration and other means of dispute resolution have always been open to person not formally qualified as barristers or solicitors.[7] Traditionally these have been referred to as "lay" advocates or arbitrators. But this term today means anything but "unqualified". Most people involved in construction disputes and indeed construction contracts generally have some form of legal knowledge and many of them now have formal legal qualifications.

The Centre of Construction Law, throughout its first decade, has endeavoured to pursue the ideal of construction law as a mixed-discipline subject, drawing from both legal and construction-based sources. In excess of 50 per cent. of graduates from the Centre of Construction Law are non-lawyers by original training and all of these have acquired a basic working knowledge of legal principles which they have then applied in a variety of construction situations.

Similarly, in the role of a learned society, the UK Society of Construction Law has been responsible for lawyers acquiring knowledge of and contact with the construction professionals, and they with lawyers, thus permitting construction professionals to acquire a working familiarity with legal issues. At both points, the centre and the society can claim some success in the de-mystification of law and the progressive breaking down of the interface between construction and law. What was once no-man's land is becoming increasingly familiar territory to those who have climbed out of the trenches on both sides.

When the Centre of Construction Law was first set up, the possibility of teaching construction law at first degree level was a very real option. For reasons which are largely historical, this was not pursued and the courses run by the centre have so far been at postgraduate masters degree level. Other institutions have considered joint honours courses involving law and construction subjects, and this remains a possible area of expansion of construction law. Given that many construction professionals who qualify originally in engineering subjects gravitate towards management, the addition of legal studies at first degree level is a logical and desirable combination of qualifications.

---

[7] But this is not the case in many jurisdictions, particularly those throughout the commonwealth where there is in force a "Legal Profession Act" or similar, having the effect of restricting the right to practise law. In such jurisdictions, there are a number of notable decisions to the effect that acting on behalf of a party to arbitration constitutes legal practise; see Construction Law Yearbook (1995) p3 and *Lawler & Matusky v. AG of Barbados* at p. 117.

Construction law as a specialist subject, is, however, naturally a post-graduate area of study. As the subject has developed at King's College, London and elsewhere, it has been taught as a self-contained Master degree aimed both at those in the construction industry and the legal industry. However, clear linkages exist with other areas of commercial law and major opportunities will exist for the expansion of the subject in the broader context of commercial law studies, possibly linked to the modular LLM degree at London University. This potential is clearly demonstrated by arbitration, hardly a recognised academic field two decades ago, yet now ranking as a major subject in its own right, including International Arbitration and other dispute resolution subjects. As taught at the Centre of Construction Law, arbitration clearly has appeal in a wider context than construction.

It is wise also to keep an open mind as to what constitutes "construction" and "construction law". The definition contained in the Housing Grants, Construction and Regeneration Act, 1996, Part II excludes some notable areas, such as oil and gas and electrical plant, which should on any view form part of the subject. In terms of the ambit of construction law, when the Centre of Construction Law was founded, the areas outside law proper were seen as embracing primarily management subjects. In the intervening decade, the emphasis has shifted and it would now be more appropriate to regard the activities of the King's College Centre as linking more naturally into other areas of commercial law, including banking and project finance, which are increasingly vital elements of any construction package. Indeed, the latest movements of the construction industry towards the Private Finance Initiative will tend to render whole projects dependent on the predicted financial out-turn, with correspondingly major feedback into the planning, design and construction phases of the project. It is perhaps too soon to judge where this initiative will lead the construction industry, but it already presents a picture recognisably different from the canvas on which Sir Michael Latham drew his conclusions in 1994.[8]

---

[8] Constructing the Team, HMSO, 1994.

Conclusions

This composite paper has sought to review some of the issues currently affecting construction and construction law, particularly through the institutions in which it is developed and promoted. The UK Society of Construction Law, while not the first in Europe, has played an increasingly prominent role in the development and co-ordination of construction law activities throughout Europe and is undoubtedly seen as a major source of professional expertise world-wide. The Society has also played a vital role in linking the different academic institutions now offering construction law and related subjects within the UK.

Internationally, construction law and the resolution of construction disputes plays an ever more prominent role in economic life, given the huge levels of investment which construction now represents. While harmonisation is, perhaps an even more distant goal than it once appeared, mutual understanding and appreciation between construction professionals and lawyers in different jurisdictions is increasingly vital, including for this purpose those involved in accountancy and auditing, where an international approach is more to be expected. Those involved in international arbitration must take account of the need for continuing business relationships and effective business communication, in addition to legal accuracy.

The list of construction law activities and developments in other jurisdictions is impressive indeed. Communication between national construction law societies offers a unique platform for comparative studies, as well as co-operation and harmonisation where this might be appropriate. At least, an awareness of major developments in other jurisdictions allows the opportunity to profit from experience.

In terms of the evolution and teaching of construction law as an academic discipline, the developments, past and future within the Centre of Construction Law show the importance of a flexible approach to a subject still awaiting a firm definition. Links can be seen in many directions and the closer integration of construction law with other areas of commercial law will become a viable option particularly at King's College, London.

Part I

The Place of Construction in Commercial Law

4. The Contribution of Construction to the Common Law

Sir Philip Otton[†]

Synopsis

This paper takes as its broad theme the substantial contribution which construction has made to the development of the common law. It considers the ways in which the practical problems and issues raised by the construction industry have come before the Courts as matters of great legal, technical and factual complexity; resolution of which has, in turn, challenged, changed and, in some cases, transformed, English common law.

Introduction

There is considerable (and increasing) technical and commercial complexity involved in the business of construction; and in order to fulfil their wider purpose, the Courts must (as always) consider and grapple with and assimilate the complexities thrown up by particular cases in the light of legal principle.[1] This process has a double-sided aspect which is, in one sense, precisely the special quality of the common law. On the one hand, technical and commercial realities (as they are argued on specific facts before the Courts) place established ideas and concepts under new pressures to adapt and accommodate. On the other hand, there are watershed moments in legal decision-making (some planned, others not planned), and these 'watersheds' have a profound influence upon the way

---

[†] I wish to acknowledge the invaluable contribution of Simon Hughes of Keating Chambers, 10 Essex Street. He undertook the burden of research and the more onerous task of marshalling my thoughts.

[1] *"...We are constantly being surprised, in our own work, by the new problems which are born of the complexity of life..."* For an interesting description of this complex process, see the lecture of Lord Goff of Chieveley (as he now is) entitled "The Search for Principle" (Maccabean Lecture in Jurisprudence, read 5th May 1983) published in the *Proceedings of the British Academy* (1984).

in which those involved in the business of construction plan and carry out their work.[2]

The Influence *upon* the Common Law

The many and varied ways in which the complexity of modern construction practice has pushed traditional common law principles to their boundaries is immediately apparent from a glimpse at recently decided cases. Recent construction cases have raised (to take a few examples) questions relating to the basis upon the Court should reward work performed in the absence of a contract (*Laserbore v Morrison Biggs Wall*;[3] *Banque Paribas v Venaglass*;[4] the question of what counts as consideration (*Williams v Roffey Bros*);[5] the basic assessment of damages (*Ruxley v Forsyth*);[6] the remoteness of particular operational losses (*T & S Construction v Architectural Design*;[7] *Balfour Beatty v Scottish Power*);[8] the effect of provision for liquidated damages in circumstances of sectional completion (*Bramall & Ogden v Sheffield City Council*;[9] *Philips Hong Kong v Attorney-General for Hong Kong*;[10] *J F*

---

[2] The idea of a judicial 'sea-change' is permitted, as a matter of jurisprudence, by the practice statement of 1966 *Practice Statement (Judicial Precedent)* [1966] 1 WLR 1234 which is discussed by Sir Rupert Cross in "The House of Lords and the Rules of Precedent", in Hacker and Raz (eds.) *Law, Morality and Society* (chapter 8); also Cross and Harris, *Precedent in English Law* (4th edition, 1991) page 102 *et seq.*

[3] (1993) CILL 896.

[4] (1994) CILL 918 (CA).

[5] [1991] 1 QB 1

[6] [1996] 1 AC 344

[7] (1993) CILL 842 where His Honour Judge Rich QC (after a review of the authorities) held that provided something was a "serious possibility" it would not fail for remoteness.

[8] The Times, March 23, 1994; (1994) CILL 925.

[9] (1983) 29 BLR 73 where His Honour Judge Hawser QC accepted what he described as a "very technical...but... correct" argument that the provisions for liquidated damages had to be interpreted *contra proferentum* against the Council.

[10] (1993) 61 BLR 41 where the Privy Council upheld provisions for liquidated damages in circumstances of sectional completion on a typical modern construction project. This important decision should, however, be read in the light of the particular way in which the appeal was formulated (ie on the basis of a series of hypothetical situations); per Lord Woolf at 54 (second paragraph).

Finnegan v Community Housing;[11] the scope and application of developing restitutionary principles (*Regalian Properties v LDDC*).[12]

In certain instances, the realities of construction practice have required the Courts to take a pragmatic attitude to established principles in resolving the disputes and novel fact-situations which come before them.

Williams v Roffey Bros is a good example here. The plaintiff entered into a sub-contract with the defendants to carry out carpentry work to a block of flats for a fixed price of £20,000. The plaintiff under-priced for the work, and began to experience financial problems, whilst the defendant became concerned that non-completion by the plaintiff would operate as a trigger for the time penalty clause in the main contract. The defendant made an oral agreement with the plaintiff to pay the plaintiff £575 for each flat on which the carpentry work was completed (being a total additional sum of £10,300). At first instance Mr Recorder Rupert Jackson Q.C. held that the oral agreement was enforceable and did not fail for want of consideration. The Court of Appeal dismissed an appeal by the defendant, and Glidewell LJ said:

> "...*Mr Evans accepts that in the present case by promising to pay the extra £10,300 his client secured benefits. There is no finding, and no suggestion, that in this case the promise was given as a result of fraud or duress. If it be objected that the propositions*

---

[11] (1993) 65 BLR 103 where His Honour Judge Carr upheld provisions for liquidated damages which produced a genuine pre-estimate of loss, notwithstanding that the LADs were the product of a formula required of the employer by a third part funder. It is also worth noting that in this case, unlike in *Philips*, the court heard evidence to justify the amount of the LADs.

[12] (1995) 11 Const LJ 127, where Mr Justice Rattee rejected Regalian's claim in restitution (in the absence of a contract) against LDDC for repayment of disbursements of £2.9 million which Regalian had paid in respect of a proposed development in circumstances where the parties had entered into negotiations expressly 'Subject to Contract' and thus on terms that each party was free to withdraw from the negotiations at any time. The approach of Rattee J. is likely to be preferred in this area of the law to that adopted by His Honour Judge Bowsher QC in *Marston Construction v Kigass Limited* (1989) 46 BLR 109 where the learned Judge found as a fact that: (i) there was no contract; and (ii) there was no express request that works be carried out prior to any future contract being entered into, and yet went on to allow Marston to recover for preliminary works.

above contravene the principle in Stilk v Myrick,[13] *I answer that in my view they do not; they refine, and limit the application of that priciple, but they leave the principle unscathed e.g. where B secures no benefit by his promise. It is not in my view surprising that a principle enunciated in relation to the rigours of seafaring life during the Napoleonic wars should be subjected during the succeeding 180 years to a process of refinement and limitation in its application in the present day...*"[14]

In other recent construction cases, the Courts have taken the opportunity to confirm and clarify long-established practice which is of wide application.

The decision of the House of Lords in *Ruxley v Forsyth* is a good example. This was a case in which Mr Forsyth entered into a contract with the builder for the construction of a swimming pool, for which the specification provided that the pool should be 7 feet and 6 inches at its deepest point. The pool was built so that it was only 6 feet and 9 inches at its deepest point. The claim by the builder on the unpaid account was met by Mr Forsyth's counterclaim for the cost of reconstructing the pool. The trial judge found as a fact that the only way of increasing the depth of the pool was to demolish and start again, at a cost of £21,560. The counterclaim was rejected by His Honour Judge Diamond Q.C., who awarded £2,500 general damages for loss of pleasure and amenity. The Court of Appeal allowed Mr Forsyth's appeal, awarding £21,560 in damages.

In reversing the decision of the Court of Appeal, the House of Lords re-affirmed the established position[15] on the *measure of damages* to be applied,[16] and the important role which the test of reasonableness has to

---

[13] (1809) 2 Camp 317; 170 ER 1168

[14] [1991] 1 QB 1 at 16 B-C

[15] See for example, *McGregor on Damages* (15th edition, 1988) paragraph 1091-92; and *Keating on Construction Contracts* (5th edition, 1991) page 202. Both passages were referred to by Dillon LJ (dissenting) in the Court of Appeal, see: [1994] 3 All ER 801 at 812-j to 813-b.

[16] For a recent discussion of the decision in the wider context of damages for breach of contract see Stephen Furst QC, "Damages for Breach of Contract: The Compensatory Principle" [1997] 3 Con. L. Yb. 17.

play in that assessment. As Lord Mustill said:

> *"In some cases the loss cannot be fairly measured except by reference to the full cost of repairing the deficiency in performance. In others, and in particular those where the contract is designed to fulfil a purely commercial purpose, the loss will very often consist only of the monetary detriment brought about by the breach of contract. But these remedies are not exhaustive, for the law must cater for those occasions where the value of the promise to the promisee exceeds the financial enhancement of his position which full performance will secure...as my Lords have shown, the test of reasonableness plays a central role in determining the basis of recovery, and will indeed be decisive in a case such as the present when the cost of reinstatement would be wholly disproportionate to the non-monetary loss suffered by the employer..."*[17]

Finally, there have been many recent cases in which the Courts have had to grapple with the technical complexities of advanced construction processes, before considering how, and with what consequences, established principles should be applied to complex facts and processes.

A good example here is the decision of the House of Lords in the Scottish appeal of *Balfour Beatty Construction (Scotland) Limited v Scottish Power plc*. Balfour Beatty were main contractors for the construction of parts of the Edinburgh bypass. In order to carry out this work, they established a concrete batching plant nearby and entered into an agreement for the temporary supply of electricity to the batching plant with the South of Scotland Electricity Board. Part of the work being undertaken by Balfour Beatty comprised the construction of an aqueduct by continuous concrete pour. A power failure occurred (caused by the rupturing of certain fuses provided by the Board in their supply system. The power failure meant that the construction of the aqueduct by single pour had to be demolished and begun again. Balfour Beatty claimed the cost of doing so as damages.

---

[17] [1996] 1 AC 344 at 360-G to 361-C

As pointed out in the judgment of Lord Jauncey (with which Lord Keith, Lord Bridge, Lord Brown-Wilkinson and Lord Nolan agreed), no point was taken on appeal as to the applicable legal principles (since the Lord Ordinary, at first instance, had referred to the test set out in *Hadley v Baxendale*[18]). The issue between the parties related to the decision on the facts, where the Lord Ordinary had said:

> "*The defenders could certainly contemplate that if the supply failed the plant would not operate and that if it was operating at the time the manufacture of concrete would be interrupted. What they did not know was the necessity of preserving a continuous pour for the purposes of the particular operation...It may be that the technique of a continuous pour for certain concrete structures may be a regular part of industrial practice, and it may be that the fact that if concrete is poured into position it will harden is within common knowledge, but the fact that an interruption of the pour could lead to a condemnation of the whole operation seems to me to be beyond the defenders' reasonable contemplation...*"[19]

In agreeing with this analysis, and allowing Scottish Power's appeal, the House of Lords demonstrated the critical importance of an understanding of the factual and technical detail in construction cases.

The Influence *of* the Common Law

Having briefly considered some of the ways in which construction practice can have an impact upon our understanding of legal principles, I now propose to consider the converse situation. In particular, in what ways (and how effectively) has the practice of the construction industry responded to changes in judicial attitude? I am thinking of one especially dramatic judicial 'sea-change', namely: that which culminated in the decision of the House of Lords in *Murphy v Brentwood District Council.*[20]

---

[18] (1854) 9 Exch 341

[19] The Times, March 23, 1994; (1994) CILL 925, extract taken from Times Law Reports bound volume p.164

[20] [1991] AC 398

It is instructive to consider what might be termed the construction lawyer's response to *Murphy* for two reasons: firstly, it points out the skill, innovation and creativity which has been applied to the complex problem of how make good the lacuna in liability created by *Murphy*. Secondly, however, it moves from the descriptive to the prescriptive, and suggests a consideration of change and reform, in an area which is as important commercially as it is complex from a legal point of view.

Murphy and its Legacy

In *Murphy v Brentwood* Lord Oliver said:

"The infliction of physical injury to the person or property of another universally requires to be justified. The causing of economic loss does not. If it is to be categorised as wrongful it is necessary to find some factor beyond the mere occurrence of the loss and the fact that its occurrence could be foreseen. Thus the categorisation of damage as economic serves at least the useful purpose of indicating that something more is required and it is one of the unfortunate features of Anns that it resulted initially in this essential distinction being lost sight of."[21]

Following this decision of the House of Lords (and that in *D & F Estates v Church Commissioners*), there is no longer the wide 'safety-net' of a claim in negligence for those involved in construction and construction contracts.[22] Indeed, the basic rule governing liability for economic loss can be expressed in this way: if, but only if, the defect in a building causes personal injury or damage to property other than the defective building, then damages for such injury or damage may be recovered in a tort action.[23] Again, although neither *D & F Estates* nor *Murphy* dealt

---

[21] *Ibid*

[22] See Anthony May's comments in "Extending and Curtailing Liability" in Uff & Capper (eds) *Construction Contract Policy – Improved Procedures and Practice* (Centre of Construction Law, 1991) in relation to the then two-month old decision in *D & F Estates v Church Commissioners*.

[23] This statement requires qualification in relation to the liability of local authorities exercising regulatory functions: their liability will depend upon the proper interpretation of the statutory provisions under which they operate, whilst the question of which local authorities would be liable for personal injury or damage

with the position of others involved in the construction of buildings, such as fabricators, architects and consulting engineers, it is implicit[24] that these must be treated in the same manner as builders: this reasoning has now been accepted in a number of decisions at first instance.[25]

The Contract/Tort Relationship

Prior to the decisions in *D & F Estates* and *Murphy*, some academic commentators had sought to explain the rise of tort after *Anns* by reference to the supposed rigidity of the English law of contract, seen, for instance, in the strict interpretation of the privity rule.[26]

As I see it, the interesting idea here is the suggestion of what might be termed an equilibrium of function between tort and contract. How has this equilibrium altered in the light of *Murphy*? In particular, how have those involved in construction and construction law sought in their *contracts* to distribute risks, identify the parameters of duties and liabilities and 'plug the gaps' which 15 years ago would have been left to the 'catch-all' claim in negligence?

---

to 'other property' was not decided in *Murphy v Brentwood* [1991] 1 AC 398 at 457 per Lord Mackay; 463 per Lord Keith; 479 per Lord Bridge; and 492 per Lord Jauncey. A detailed consideration of the position is to be found in Peter Cane, *Tort Law and Economic Interests* (2nd edition, 1996) page 207 *et seq.*

[24] It is notable, for instance, that in the decision in *Murphy* (at 466-G) Lord Keith explains the decision in *Pirelli General Cable Works Limited v Oscar Faber & Partners* [1983] 2 AC 1 on the basis of a special relationship based on reliance: *"...It would seem that in a case such as* Pirelli, *where the tortious liability arose out of a contractual relationship with professional people, the duty extended to take reasonable care not to cause economic loss to the client by the advice given. The plaintiffs built the chimney as they did in reliance on that advice..."*

[25] Application to an architect in *Lancashire and Chester Association of Baptist Churches Inc v Howard & Seddon Partnership* [1993] 3 All ER 467; to an architect and an engineer in *Wessex Regional H.A. v HLM Design* (1994) 10 Con. L.J. 165; to a do-it-yourself builder and vendor of garden sheds in *Willis v Castelstein* [1993] 3 N.Z.L.R. 103.

[26] Markesinis, "An Expanding Tort Law – The Price of a Rigid Contract Law" (1987) 103 LQR 354. More recently, the idea that the rise of tort is explicable by reference to the deficiences in contract law has been explicitly stated by the Law Commission: see Law Commission Report No 242: Privity of Contract: Contracts for the Benefit of Third Parties (July 1996) paragraph 3.14.

In exploring these questions, I propose to touch briefly on loss and third parties and the role of statute.

Loss and Third Parties

The status of third parties to contracts is a subject of immediate and practical significance to those involved in construction. The relationship between the parties typically involved in a construction project (developer/employer, main contractor, sub-contractor(s), the professional team) and the subsequent purchaser of the building is complex, and not least on the question of which party is to bear the particular risks of defects and structural failure. Restrictions in the ability to establish liability in tort have placed those involved in the construction industry under particular pressure to achieve greater flexibility of approach in contract law – particularly in areas such as privity, assignment and the recoverability of substantial damages.

It is no surprise, then, that two of the most recent and important decisions in this area are construction cases: the decision of the House of Lords in *Linden Gardens Trust Limited v Lenesta Sludge Disposals Limited* and *St Martin's Corporation Limited v Sir Robert McAlpine & Sons Limited*;[27] and the decision of the Court of Appeal in *Darlington Borough Council v Wiltshier Northern Limited and Another.*[28] Both of these decisions suggest ways in which a flexible and pragmatic approach to contract law can provide ways of compensating, at least in part, for the curtailment of tortious liability for pure economic loss in *D & F Estates* and *Murphy.*[29]

The Appeals in Linden Gardens and St Martin's Corporation

In both the *Linden Gardens* and *St Martin's* cases, the building owner which had been the original party to a construction contract had purported to assign the contract in breach of the clause which provided: "... *The* [Building Owner] *shall not without written consent of the*

---

[27] [1994] 1 AC 85

[28] [1995] 1 WLR 68

[29] For a more detailed discussion see, A.G.J. Berg, "Assignment Prohibitions and the Right to Recover Damages for Another's Loss" (1994) J.B.L. 129; and A. Tettenborn, "Loss, Damage and the Meaning of Assignment" [1994] C.L.J. 53.

Contractor assign this Contract." In the *Linden Gardens* case, the builder was sued by the purported assignee alone; in the *St Martin's* case, the proceedings were brought by the original party to the contract, as well as the purported assignee. On the question of the assignment, the House of Lords held that a clause in a contract that prohibits a party from assigning the contract will usually render any purported assignment ineffective to vest rights in an assignee; and whether the particular clause has this effect is a matter of construction.[30]

It was then in the *St Martin's* case that the question arose whether, if an assignment is prohibited, the original party, A, can nevertheless recover damages for a breach of contract which is committed by the builder after A sold the property to C, and where the breaches cause loss to C, not A.[31]

Lord Browne-Wilkinson gave the judgment in the *St Martin's* appeal with which Lord Keith and Lord Bridge agreed, deciding that in certain situations, A may be entitled to recover damages from B in connection with loss suffered by C as a result of a breach of contract which was committed by B after A had sold the property in question to C.

From the point of view of the present discussion, the following passage from Lord Browne-Wilkinson's judgment is particularly interesting:

> *"In my judgment the present case falls within the rationale of the exceptions to the general rule that a plaintiff can only recover damages for his own loss. The contract was for a large development*

---

[30] Lord Browne-Wilkinson at 108-F to 109-C.

[31] St Martins Corporation were originally the owner of the property at King Street, Hammersmith, and were the original party to the construction contract with McAlpine. The property was subsequently transferred to St Martin's Investments, following which the podium deck was found to be leaking due to breaches of contract by McAlpine. The losses were suffered by St Martin's Investments which owned the property and had to meet the cost of remedying the defective work. However, Investments could not sue since the assignment to it of the right of action was invalid. St Martin's Corporation could sue as the original party to the construction contract, since the assignment by it to St Martin's Investments was invalid. McAlpine then argued that St Martin's Corporation could only recover nominal damages since, at the date of the breaches by McAlpine, St Martin's Corporation no longer owned the property, and it had therefore suffered no loss.

of property which, to the knowledge of both the Corporation and McAlpine, was going to be occupied, and possibly purchased, by third parties and not by the Corporation itself. Therefore it could be foreseen that damage caused by a breach of contract would cause loss to a later owner and not merely to the original contracting party, Corporation. As in contracts for the carriage of goods by land, there would be no automatic vesting in the occupier or owners of the property for the time being who sustained the loss of any right of suit against McAlpine. On the contrary, McAlpine had specifically contracted that the rights of action under the building contract **could** *not without McAlpine's consent be transferred to third parties who became owners or occupiers and might suffer loss. In such a case, it seems to me proper, as in the case of the carriage of goods by land, to treat the parties as having entered into the contract on the footing that Corporation would be entitled to enforce contractual rights for the benefit of those who suffered from defective performance but who, under the terms of the contract, could not acquire any right to hold McAlpine liable for breach. It is truly a case in which the rule provides "a remedy where no other would be available to a person sustaining loss which under a rational legal system ought to be compensated by the person who has caused it."*[32]

Mr Fernyhough submitted that it would be wrong to distort the law in order to meet what he described as being an exceptional case...I am far from satisfied that this is a one off or exceptional case. We are concerned with standard forms of building contracts which prohibit the assignment of the benefit of building contracts to the ultimate purchaser...I would therefore hold that Corporation are entitled to substantial damages for any breach by McAlpine of the building contract..."

---

[32] This is a reference to the speech of Lord Diplock in *The Albazero* [1977] AC 774 at 847-B, referring to the decision in *Dunlop v Lambert* (1839) 6 Cl & F 600 *per* Lord Cottenham L.C.

In the light of the decisions in *D & F Estates* and *Murphy* this passage has some very interesting features:

(i)   prior to the 'sea-change' in tort, St Martin's Corporation would have had an immediate right of recovery against McAlpine for the costs of remedying McAlpine's defective work. Following the decisions in *D & F Estates* and *Murphy*, the House of Lords in the *St Martin's* appeal were directly confronted with the vacuum created by the irrecoverability of pure economic loss.

(ii) in the *St Martin's* appeal, therefore, the House of Lords were faced with a practical problem related to a fundamental aspect of the way in which the construction industry operates: the discovery of defects by a subsequent purchaser where there is a prohibition on assignment in the construction contract.[33]

(iii) in referring to the speech of Lord Diplock in *The Albazero* (*"...a remedy where no other would be available to a person sustaining loss which under a rational legal system ought to be compensated by the person who has caused it..."*) Lord Brown-Wilkinson recognised the *practical need* to permit recovery by St Martin's Corporation. In the context of the present discussion, it is interesting to identify the *reasoning* by which Lord Browne-Wilkinson achieved the practical result. As I see it, the following words are critical:

> *"The contract was for a large development of property which, to the knowledge of both Corporation and McAlpine, was going to be occupied, and possibly purchased, by third parties and not by the Corporation itself. Therefore it could be foreseen that damage caused by a breach would cause loss to a later owner and not merely to the original contracting party..."* (emphasis added).

The language (and, in part, the reasoning) applied here contain echoes of the language of negligence, and are applied to broaden traditional contractual categories, in a way which strives to reconcile the curtailment of tortious liability with the need to recognise, and give force to, complex

---

[33]   Lord Browne-Wilkinson at 115 C-G.

realities within the construction industry. Of course, the judgment of Lord Browne-Wilkinson is also full of challenges and questions:

- the discussion in *St Martin's* was confined to the question of whether the original building owner could recovery damages for loss suffered by a subsequent purchaser of the property. Where, rather than selling the property, the original owner grants leases, would such losses be recoverable, provided the entry into leases was foreseeable at the time of the conclusion of the construction contract? Such a case would seem to fall within the decision in *St Martin's*.[34]

- given the rather special position of the original owner in claiming damages for loss suffered by the subsequent purchaser, would this claim against the builder be subject to the set-offs which the builder may have against the original owner under the construction contract? Where the set-offs are immediately bound up with the construction contract, then there would seem to be no reason to prevent them. In order to 'ensure fair dealing between the parties'[35], then it would seem that an equitable set-off would be permissible if there is a cross-claim 'flowing out and inseparably connected with dealings and transactions which also give rise to the claim'.[36]

- since the decision in *St. Martin's* is based upon an exceptional situation – *"providing a remedy where no other would be available"* – the precise scope of application of the decision is uncertain.

---

[34] By way of contrast, in *D & F Estates v Church Commissioners* [1989] AC 177 it was held that a lessee could not recover from the builder in tort the pure economic loss represented by the costs of repairs; and see also *Department of the Environment v Thomas Bates* [1991] AC 499 for non-recovery by an underlessee.

[35] This is the broad principle stated by Lord Denning in *Federal Commerce & Navigation Company Limited v Molena Alpha Inc* [1978] 1 QB 927 at 974. It is relevant is this way: if a builder were not able to set-off claims which were inseparably connected with the construction contract, then the subsequent owner would be in a better   position than if it had taken an assignment of the construction contract.

[36] Per Lord Denning in *Federal Commerce* (*op cit.*) at 297 and see the decision of the House of Lords in *Bank of Boston Connecticut v European Grain and Shipping Limited* [1989] 1 AC 1056 at 1102-3 and 1110-1111. For an interesting discussion of the recent decisions on equitable set-off see, Derham *Set-Off* (2nd edition, 1996) page 47 *et seq*.

Darlington v Wiltshier

In *Darlington v Wiltshier*[37] Wiltshier, a construction company, entered into two construction contracts with Morgan Grenfell, to construct the Dolphin (recreation) Centre for Darlington Borough Council. In accordance with an agreement entered into with the Council, Morgan Grenfell assigned to the Council all rights and causes of action against Wiltshier to which Morgan Grenfell was entitled under the contracts. The Council claimed that there were serious defects in the Dolphin Centre due to bad workmanship or other breaches of provisions of the two contracts. In action an action brought by the Council against Wiltshier (the contractor) the Official Referee held, on a preliminary issue, that the Council as assignee was not entitled to more than nominal damages for breach of the contracts.

In allowing the appeal, and holding that the Council could recover substantial damages for loss caused by Wiltshier's breaches, the Court of Appeal referred to the following matters:

(i)   At 74-B *et seq* Dillon LJ referred to that part of Lord Browne-Wilkinson's speech in the appeal in *St Martin's* to which I hae already referred above, repeating the reference made by Lord Browne-Wilkinson to the words of Lord Diplock in *The Albazero*: (*"...It is truly a case in which the rule provides 'a remedy where no other would be available to a person sustaining loss which under a rational legal system ought to be compensated by the person who caused it'."*);

(ii) Following the reasoning adopted by the House of Lords in the appeal in *St Martin's* Dillon LJ also said:

> *"Mr Blackburn also sought to distinguish the decision in the* McAlpine *case on the ground that in the present case Morgan Grenfell never acquired or transmitted to the council any proprietary interest in the Dolphin Centre. I do not see that that matters as the council had the ownership of the site of the Dolphin Centre all along.* **It was plainly obvious to Wiltshier**

---

[37]   (1993) CILL 893 [OR]; [1995] 1 WLR 68 [CA].

throughout that the Dolphin Centre was being constructed for the benefit of the council on the council's land. Accordingly, I would allow this appeal by direct application of the rule in Dunlop v Lambert *as recognised in a building contract context in Lord Browne-Wilkinson's speech in the* McAlpine *case...*"[38] (emphasis added).

Interestingly here, following the reasoning of Lord Brown-Wilkinson in the *St Martin's* appeal, Dillon LJ considered the closeness of the relationship between the parties and the practical purpose of the construction contract, in deciding the question of which party may recover substantial damages for breach: the reasoning (and the language) used bears interesting resemblances to the language of duty of care.[39]

(iii) Whatever else may be said about the decision in *Darlington v Wilshier*, this much is clear: as with the decision in *St Martin's*, the problem which the decision confronts (in different and innovative ways) would not have arisen prior to the curtailment of tortious liability for pure economic loss. The decision in *Darlington v Wiltshier* must be seen, in any event, as an innovative response in the construction field to problems brought into sharper focus by *D & F Estates* and *Murphy.*

Of course, although the decision in *Darlington* does clarify and broaden the basis of the decision in the *St Martin's* appeal on the right of the

---

[38] [1995] 1 WLR 68, 75-76

[39] Steyn LJ approached the question from the perspective of a more fundamental analysis of contractual principles:
*"In order lawfully to avoid the financial constraints of the Local Government Act 1972 Morgan Grenfell acted as financier to the council in connection with the construction of the Dolphin Centre in Darlington. Morgan Grenfell entered into construction contracts with Wiltshier for the benefit of the council. **That is how the transaction was structured and that is how all three parties saw it**. And it is, of course, manifest that the council, as the third party, accepted the benefit of the construction contract. But for the rule of privity of contract the council could simply have sued on the contract made for its benefit.*
The case for recognising a contract for the benefit of a third party is simple and straightforward. The autonomy of the will of the parties should be respected *... "* (emphases added).

original owner to claim substantial damages for loss incurred by a third part to the construction contract,[40] there are important limitations upon the kinds of situations in which these decisions will assist in overcoming privity. For instance, the identity/exstence of a subsequent purchaser or tenant is very frequently unclear (or not contemplated) at the time of the construction contract, and so *Darlington* would seem not apply.

The Role of Statute

On the face of it, it is curious that any discussion of the important contribution made by construction law since *D & F Estates* and *Murphy* to the common law should involve a consideration of the role of statute. However, the curtailment of tortious liability and the response of construction law, does raise the following points of interest:

- How far has the 'sea-change' in tort led to a re-visiting of existing statutory remedies?
- Given the emphasis in the reasoning and decisions in *D & F Estates* and *Murphy* upon statutory remedies and the statutory power to create remedies, how far further can the common law go towards 'filling the gaps' left by the curtailment of tortious liability?
- Is it possible to suggest the route which further change might take?

Existing Statute – the Defective Premises Act 1972

In allowing the appeal in *Murphy*, each of their Lordships considered it relevant to have regard to the kind and extent of liability provided for by Parliament in the Defective Premises Act 1972.[41] The reasoning here

---

[40] In the light of *Darlington* (and in particular per Dillon LJ at 75-B, rejecting the submission that *St Martin's* did not apply because Morgan Grenfell never transmittted or acquired to the council any proprietary interest) the scope of the new principle appears to be broader that first thought. See John Cartwright, "Remedies in Respect of Defective Constructions after *Linden Gardens* " (1993) 9 Const LJ 281.

[41] See: Lord Mackay L.C. at 457-C; Lord Keith at 472-E; Lord Bridge at 480-H to 481-B; Lord Oliver at 491-G; and Lord Jauncey at 498-E.

was twofold: firstly, their Lordships drew the inference that, if Parliament had wished to extend the scope of liability, then such extension would be contained in the 1972 Act (or other legislation); and secondly in the face of legislation on the subject, extensions of liability were (by inference) a matter of policy to be dealt with by Parliament.[42]

A corollary to the reasoning of the House of Lords in *Murphy* is the increased interest in a 1972 Act[43] whose function might have been hard to place in the climate of *Anns*. Section 1(1) of the Act provides:

> *"A person taking on work for or in connection with the provision of a dwelling (whether the dwelling is provided by the erection or by the conversion or enlargement of a building) owes a duty -*
>
>> *(a) if the dwelling is provided to the order of any person, to that person; and*
>> *(b) without prejudice to paragraph (a) above, to every person who acquires an interest (whether legal or equitable) in the dwelling;*
>
> *to see that the work which he takes on is done in a workmanlike manner or, as the case may be, professional manner, with proper materials and so that as regards that work the dwelling will be fit for habitation when completed."*

Although the Act is limited to the provision of new dwellings[44] and has a 'fit for habitation' requirement which has been interpreted in a rigorous way[45], it has a number of advantages over the common law which has led to increased interest in its provisions amongst those involved in construction: (i) it allows damages to be recovered before anyone suffers

---

[42] For a discussion of the relationship between common law and statute in the broad context of the protection of 'economic interests' see Peter Cane, *Tort Law and Economic Interests* (2nd edition, 1996) page 186 *et seq.*

[43] The Defective Premises Act 1972 came into force on 1st January 1974. For a discussion of its origins, see: *D & F Estates v Church Commissioners* [1989] AC 177 at 193 *et seq.*

[44] See: *Jacobs v Morton and Partners* (1994) 72 BLR 92 per Mr Recorder Rupert Jackson QC at 105-C *et seq.*

[45] See: *Thompson v Clive Alexander & Partners* (1992) 59 BLR 77.

illness or injury; (ii) it permits an action to be brought against anyone who takes on work for or in connection with the provision of a dwelling (including a vendor or lessor who is involved in building on his land) and there are no problems of establishing proximity here; (iii) not only can the person who does the work be sued, but also anyone who employed that person to carry out the work (such as a main contractor or developer), whereas at common law an employer is not generally liable for the negligence of its independent contractor;[46] and (iv) the duty owed under section 1 of the Act cannot be excluded by contract.[47]

Perhaps most importantly, the Defective Premises Act 1972 is interesting and perhaps useful as a guide to future directions in the imposition of liabilities in that it has a particular *product* and a particular *consumer* in mind.[48] Rather than establishing very broad principles of liability, the Defective Premises Act 1972 takes as its starting point and its focus a particular part of market and consumers activity. In this way, it addresses very particular problems and fact-situations without the potential confusion of unnecessarily sweeping principle. As a model of liability, therefore, imposed upon contractors outside contract by reason of their entry into a particular kind of contract (the provision of a dwelling), the Defective Premises Act 1972 has its attractions. It will be interesting to see whether, in the future, the scope of its application is expanded, or whether, even, its basic structure will be the pattern for further legislation.[49]

'Filling the Gaps'

As discussed in this paper, the decisions in *D & F Estates* and *Murphy* marked radical changes in patterns of liability in many areas of commercial life. For those involved in construction law, these changes have had a great impact upon the crucial question of the relief available in respect of defective buildings and other property.

---

[46] *D & F Estates v Church Commissioners* [1989] AC 177.

[47] Defective Premises Act 1972, section 6(3).

[48] A judicial tendency to identify and earmark particular *kinds* of consumer can be detected in decisions and as *Smith v Eric Bush* [1990] 1 AC 831 with its focus upon the remedies available to the owners of modest dwellings.

[49] On this see: Simon Whittaker, "Privity of Contract and the Tort of Negligence: Future Directions" (1996) 16 O.J.L.S. 191 at 228-229.

In this paper, I have sought to highlight some of the important and innovative contributions which construction cases heard in the Official Referees' Court have made to the development of new patterns of liability. These changes have, in turn, been the occasion for the elaboration and refinement of some of the most deep-rooted of common law principles. At this point two questions must surely be asked: (i) what direction might we expect future changes to take place; and (ii) will those changes be a matter for the common law or for Parliament?

Reform – Third Party Rule

One particular legal issue which was returned recently to prominence partly because of the curtailment of tortious liability (and the decisions in *Linden Gardens* and *Darlington v. Wiltshier*) which is of especial interest to those involved in construction law is the third party rule in contract. There can be little doubt that the decisions in *D & F Estates* and *Murphy* have certainly sharpened the focus of the long-standing dissatisfaction felt in many quarters about the position of third party beneficiaries to contracts in English law.[50] This is a dissatisfaction most recently expressed at the judicial level by Steyn LJ (as he then was) in *Darlington Borough Council v Wiltshier.*[51] His words now form the 'opening shot' of the Law Commission, which has proposed a *Draft Contract (Rights of Third Parties) Bill.*[52] Again, it is of interest that, in showing how the third part rule continues to create problems in commercial life, the Law Commission draw out for special mention the problems of the construction industry. So, in their Report No 242 the Law Commisioners state that:

> *"3.12 In complex construction projects, there will be a web of agreements between the participants in the project, allocating responsibilities and liabilities between the client (and sometimes its*

---

[50] For a full account of this process, beginning with the 1937 Law Revision Committee, see Jack Beatson, "Reforming the Law of Contracts for the Benefit of Third Parties -A Second Bite at the Cherry" (1992) 45 *Current Legal Problems* 1.

[51] [1995] 1 WLR 68 at 76-D *et seq.* For further judicial criticism of the privity rule, see: *Swain v Law Society* [1983] 1 AC 598 at 611 per Lord Diplock; *The Pioneer Container* [1994] 1 AC 324 at 355 per Lord Goff; *White v Jones* [1995] 1 AC 207 at 262-263 per Lord Goff.

[52] Law Commission Report No 242 (July 1996), "Privity of Contract: Contracts for the Benefit of Third Parties".

financiers), the main contractor, specialist sub-contractors and consultants (architects, engineers, and surveyors). Most significant construction projects in the UK are carried out under one of three major contractual procurement routes, and so the documentation used is often very highly standardised.

3.13 The third party rule means that only the parties within each contractual relationship can sue each other. The unfortunate result is that one cannot in the 'main' contracts simply extend the benefit of the architect's and engineer's duties of care and skill, and the contractor's duties to build according to the specifications, to subsequent purchasers or tenants of the development, or to funding institutions who might suffer loss as a result of the defective exceution of the works. This cannot be achieved under the present third party rule without either joining the third party in question into the contract which contains these obligations, which in the case of a subsequent purchaser or tenant is impractical, since their identity may be unknown at the commencement of the works, or even for a long time afterwards, or executing a separate document – a "collateral warranty" – extending the benefit of the duties in question."

The practical, day-to-day effect of the privity rule upon construction planning and disputes is very considerable indeed: although it is said that sophisticated collateral warranties; the *Darlington v Wiltshier* exception; and the constructive trust reduce the harsher consequences of the third party rule, the the continued instances of complexity, unfairness and uncertainty in most important areas of commercial life cannot be ignored.[53]

The insurance industry ties in very closely with construction in very many ways, and the effect of the third party rule upon insurance should therefore be borne in mind. At present, a life insurance policy take out for the benefit of certain dependents (such as a co-habitee or stepchild) is unenforceable by those dependants. If a company takes out liability

---

[53] For a discussion of the issues see in particular: Professor Andrew Burrows, "Reforming Privity of Contract: Law Commission Report No. 242" (1996) L.M.C.L.Q. 467; *Law Commission Thirty-First Annual Report 1996* (Law Com No. 244) page 15 *et seq.*

insurance covering the liability of its subsidiary company, and its contractors and sub-contractors, only the company itself would have the right to enforce the insurance contract.[54] And again, if an employer takes out private health insurance to cover medical expenses on behalf of employees, the employees would have no right to enforce the insurance contract so as to ensure reimbursement of their health expenses.

Construction and the Question of Reform

In the face of a clear acknowledgement by judges and academics that some change to the third party rule is required – essentially for the benefit of the users or consumers of the legal system – then the question becomes one of how change is best achieved. The question of how change should be achieved is a complex and critical issue, and one which confronts judges and lawyers all the time. Can the common law arrive at sufficient uniformity and certainty of change? Can statute be sufficiently flexible to admit of changing facts, and the myriad of excepional circumstances?

Viewed from the point of view of the construction industry, the question of the third party rule and reform throws up special problems of how the construction industry operates; how the industry views itself; and the relationship between construction and the common law.[55]

The approach adopted by the Law Commissioners is a conceptual approach to the idea of the third party rule in general, whilst identifying particular problems in particular areas of commercial and consumer activity. This approach is summed up by Professor Burrows as follows:

> *"Linked to this is that reforming such a central doctrine of contract law not only potentially has far-reaching knock-on effects, but also requires the reformer to be confident of his ground across the full gamut of contracts. While the issues raised are essentially ones of*

---

[54] Compare: *Trident General Insurance Company Limited v McNiece Bros Pty Limited* (1988) 165 CLR 107.

[55] I am grateful to Professor Philip Capper for a lecture which he gave for the Society of Construction Law on 3rd December 1996 entitled, "Are the Law Commission right that their final Priviy/Third Party recommendations 'will not be opposed by the construction industry'?".

> *general principle, we found ourselves dealing with specialist questions relating to bills of exchange, carriage of goods by sea, arbitration agreements, the international carriage of cargo by air, construction contracts, and so on.* "[56]

The question is whether this approach (which intrinsically suggests legislation-led change) is too general and/or theoretical to meet the particular needs of the construction industry: should particular (third party) rights be extended by reference to particular products, rather than by reference to more generalised processes? This would be achieved either by common law developments such as those seen in *Linden Gardens* and *Darlington v Wiltshier*, or by legislation which was expressed to apply to very particular products or transactions, possibly in a similar way to the Defective Premises Act 1972, or the Unfair Contract Terms Act 1977.

The approach which one takes on these complex questions is ultimately bound up with how one views the relationship between construction and the law. Specialisation in construction law naturally reflects the increasing complexity of the construction industry, and a strong and confident body of practitioners and Courts have emerged over the last 15 to 20 years. However, the message of the earlier part of this lecture is that construction law has both contributed to, and benefitted from, its relationship with the general law, by which I refer both to the common law and to Statute.

The Bill proposed by the Law Commission – Contracts (Rights of Third Parties) – addresses what is a practical problem in so many areas of commercial and consumer activity. However, the Law Commission are right to identify a point of principle of general application – whether the will of two contracting parties should be respected if they wish (or it can be inferred that they wished) to confer a contractual benefit on another.[57] This is not generalised abstraction, but rather a reflection on what

---

[56] (1996) L.M.C.L.Q. 467 at 467.

[57] This is the way in which Steyn L.J. put the issue in *Darlington v Wiltshier* [1995] 1 WLR 68 at 76-E:- *"...The case for recognising a contract for the benefit of a third party is simple and straightforward. The autonomy of the will of the parties should be respected. The law of contract should give effect to the reasonable expectations of contracting parties."*

contracting parties should be permitted to achieve in their agreements.

The acceptance of third party rights is such a deep-rooted matter that general reform, by means of Statute, is really the only acceptable way forward. The particular experience of the construction industry would be acknowledged and accommodated by the Courts, whereas particular legislation for the construction industry would add a complexity and a sense of marginalisation which would be unwelcome and unhelpful.

Conclusion

The contribution of the construction industry to the development of the common law has indeed been impressive; equally, construction law has often been innovative and dynamic in its responses to wider changes in the law. The question of third party rights is an issue of potentially major impact for the construction industry, and is an issue on which the construction industry has had, and will continue to have, a very significant contribution. The question of reform also raises very interesting issues of self-image: is construction so specialist in its agenda that general legal principle quickly threatens to become mere abstraction, or is construction law (give the economic might of the industry) better placed than ever to be a driving force behind the continued development of the common-law...?

5. Judicial Review and the Construction Industry

Jeremy Winter

Synopsis

This paper examines how the application of judicial review to construction contracts is limited, how contract law may be extended to impose a duty of good faith, and how the rule in *Crouch* has been eroded.

Introduction

Most will be aware of the official doctrine that the courts do not have the power to question the decisions of certifiers under construction contracts.[1] Courts concern themselves with the interpretation of contracts and will not become involved in their operation or decision making under them.

While this argument may still be a controversial one in the construction industry, the apparent reluctance of the judiciary to become involved in the decision-making process is one that has become very familiar in the realm of public law. However, as yet, no one seems to have investigated the relationship between them. This paper will attempt to do that by examining:

1. Where one of the parties to a construction contract is a public body, whether judicial review can be employed by the other party, as an alternative legal mechanism to a private law challenge to the decisions taken by the public body with regard to the contract.

2. Whether there is any cross-fertilisation between public and private law in the possible existence of a duty to act in good faith in contractual situations.

3. The extent to which EC Public Procurement rules may provide the means to challenge the decisions of public bodies.

---

[1]   *Northern Regional Health Authority v. Crouch* [1984] QB 644

Consider the following three examples:

a.   A local or central government employer capriciously excludes from consideration an otherwise perfectly valid tender by a contractor.

b.   A local or central government employer withdraws a project (on grounds that there are insufficient funds available) prior to acceptance of any tender, but after various tenderers have incurred thousands of pounds in preparing their tenders.

c.   A local or central government employer under a construction contract that has no independent Engineer, and which has completely excluded all remedies to challenge the actions of the employer. The employer acts in an irrational way in refusing to grant any remedy such as extension of time or payment of additional costs, despite clear "moral" if not contractual right to such remedies. Is the contractor to be left completely without a remedy? Or may administrative law possibly offer him an alternative?

Then consider the same examples again, replacing in each case "a local or central government employer" with "a recently privatised public sector company". Consider each example again where the employer is a private company or consortium of companies under the UK Government's Private Finance Initiative. All of these examples have actually occurred or are likely to occur, in all their permutations. There will be many variations. This paper will not slavishly analyse each permutation in turn, but the examples will be used throughout to illustrate various points.

Administrative Law

The English courts have an inherent jurisdiction to review the exercise of statutory powers by public bodies. Powers must be exercised lawfully, reasonably, fairly and must not be exceeded or used for extraneous purposes. Judicial review is the process by which the High Court supervises the decision making of public bodies. The grounds on which judicial review can be granted (for the purpose of quashing the decision and requiring its reconsideration) can be summarised briefly as follows:

- want or excess of jurisdiction;

- where there is an error of law on the face of the record. This extends to the reasons given by the decision maker for his decision;

- abuse of discretion. These are decisions taken by public bodies that no such body properly directing themselves on their relevant legal role and acting reasonably could have reasonably taken. This is known as the Wednesbury Rule, after the case of *Associated Provincial Picture Houses Ltd v. Wednesbury Corporation*[2] in which it was formulated. Even where the legal position/discretion is defined widely, the English courts are reluctant to recognise any intention on the part of the legislature to confer an absolute discretion on the Executive such as to exclude its powers of review; and

- failure to comply with the rules of natural justice. Broadly the rules of natural justice embody a duty to act fairly and without bias.

Judicial review is a developing area of law.[3] Opportunities abound to seek judicial review of decisions by bodies exercising governmental powers or public law functions and non-governmental powers. The Courts are increasingly willing to review commercial decisions made by governmental bodies and to consider whether Councils have complied with statutory requirements governing the tendering process. Examples are given below.

On an application for judicial review the court is empowered to quash the decision or compel the decision-maker to re-consider its decision. However, in order to obtain a remedy in damages, it is necessary for the applicant to establish an independent private law action such as misfeasance/wrongdoing in public office (which requires proof of bad faith on the part of the decision maker), negligence or breach of statutory duty. In the absence of such a claim, there is no basis for awarding damages for public law wrongs.[4]

---

[2]   [1948] 1 KB 223

[3]   Those who think that construction law is hard to keep up to date with and understand developments should try monitoring administrative law.

[4]   See below for procedural difficulties involved in mixing a claim for judicial review with a claim for damages

In principle therefore, any decision taken by a public body will be liable to be quashed in judicial review proceedings, where the court concludes that one of the grounds detailed above is breached. This general principle is however subject to important exceptions, detailed below.

Who can apply for Judicial Review

The court may not grant leave to apply for judicial review unless it considers that the applicant *"has a sufficient interest in the matter"*.[5] The "sufficient interest" test is a generous one which includes some consideration of the merits of the case. If an applicant has a direct personal interest in the relief which he is seeking, it is likely that he will be considered as having a sufficient interest in the matter. Personal interest has to be more than personal concern; for example, a group of archaeologists seeking to preserve the remains of the Rose Theatre in Southwark, London, were held not to have a sufficient interest to challenge the decision of the Secretary of State for the Environment not to schedule the site as a site of national importance.[6]

Which bodies are subject to Judicial Review

As a general rule, judicial review applies to the acts or decisions taken by a government body. A government body has been described as a body performing a "public function" when it seeks to achieve some benefit on behalf of all or part of the public. This covers a wide range of bodies including those providing health, education, social services and procuring public works. However, public functions cannot be described as the exclusive domain of the State. Professional associations, independent regulatory bodies, utilities and many educational institutions have been considered as public bodies by the Courts.[7] Not all decisions taken by such bodies will be considered public law matters; only those which effect the public in a governmental manner. In order, therefore, to determine the nature of a body performing an action, it is necessary to consider the following:

---

[5]   Supreme Court Act 1981 and Rules of the Supreme Court Order 53, Rule 3(7)

[6]   *R   v. Secretary of State for the Environment ex p. Rose Theatre Trust Co.* [1990] 1 All ER 754

[7]   Recent examples include the Advertising Standards Authority, the Takeover and Mergers Panel and the Football Association (but not the Jockey Club).

- the principles of judicial review *prima facie* govern the activities of bodies performing public functions;

- the test of whether a body is performing a public function and hence amenable to judicial review, may not simply depend upon the source of its power or whether the body is ostensibly a "public" or a "private" body;

- not all decisions taken by bodies in the course of their public functions can be the subject matter of judicial review. In the following two situations, judicial review will not normally be appropriate, even though the body will be performing a public function:

  a. where some branch of the law more appropriately governs the dispute between the parties. In such a case, that branch of the law and its remedies should and normally will be applied; and

  b. where there is a contract between the litigants. In such a case, the express or implied terms of the agreement should normally govern the matter. This reflects the normal approach of English law, namely, that the terms of the contract will normally govern the transaction, or other relationship between the parties rather than the general law. A contractual nexus is not necessarily fatal to a claim for judicial review, but if the source of the power is contractual, that is consensual, this can be.[8] Where a special method of resolving disputes (such as arbitration) has been agreed by the parties (expressly or by necessary implication), that regime, and not judicial review, will normally govern the dispute. (However, City self-regulatory organisations (e.g. IMRO, SFA) are governed by contract which the members have "chosen" to enter into and have yet been held capable of review by the Courts. Likewise in *R. v. Chief Rabbi ex parte Wachmann*[9] the Court held that judicial review was not excluded simply because the applicant had consensually submitted to the Chief Rabbi's jurisdiction.)

---

[8] *R. v. Insurance Ombudsman, ex p. Aegon Life Insurance Limited* [1994] C.O.D. 426

[9] [1992] 1 WLR 1036

In what is a very important case for the purposes of this paper, *R. v. Lord Chancellor ex p. Hibbit and Saunders (A Firm)*,[10] the Lord Chancellor's Department invited tenders for Court reporting services and the four lowest tenderers of the seven who replied were invited to submit lower tenders. The applicants, who were excluded from this invitation, applied for judicial review of the decision to award the contract to the successful firm on the grounds of procedural unfairness by the LCD, (*i.e.* that they had a legitimate expectation that, although discussions might be held with tenderers to clarify a bid, discussions would not be held with some tenderers to enable them to submit lower bids).

The Court held that notwithstanding the fact that the procedures followed by the LCD were in part unfair to the applicants, the decision was not amenable to judicial review because it lacked a sufficient public law element. The Court stated that if a government body carrying out its governmental functions enters into a contract with a third party, the obligations that it owes will be under the contract, unless there also exists some other element that gives rise in addition to a public law obligation. A governmental body is free to negotiate contracts, and it would need something additional to the simple fact that the governmental body is negotiating the contract to impose on that authority any public law obligation in addition to any private law duties there might be. In particular, it was made clear:

- An invitation to tender attendant on a common law right to contract cannot be characterised as a statement of policy or practice equated with policy decisions by governmental bodies.

- The fact that the decision sought to be reviewed was the placing of a contract with a particular firm added force to the contention that there was unlikely to be any public law element in their decisions.

- The aspect which might have injected a public law element into the process was a possible distinction between a government department's aim in carrying out a tender procedure as compared with a commercial organisation, but the complaints here were not directed at that aspect, instead being directed at the failure to carry out the procedure adopted.

---

[10] [1993] C.O.D. 326. This is not a full report; a transcript of the judgment was obtained.

- There was insufficient "statutory underpinning" of the tendering process to make the decision a public law one. If a government body has a statutory obligation to negotiate a contract in a particular way with particular terms and fails to perform that statutory obligation, this would be a public law obligation which was subject to judicial review, *i.e.* the applicant would need to show not merely that the authority was acting by reference to certain statutory provisions but it was those provisions which imposed the obligations which were broken.

- However, it was said *obiter* that the position might have been different if bad faith or malice had been alleged.

Similarly, in *Mercury Energy Limited v. Electricity Corporation of New Zealand* [11] (discussed further below) the Privy Council was of the view that "*it does not seem likely that a decision by a state enterprise to enter into or determine a commercial contract... will ever be the subject of judicial review in the absence of fraud, corruption or bad faith*".

On the other hand, in *R. v. Cleveland County Council ex p. Cleveland Care Homes Association,* [12] judicial review was granted of the Council's specification of requirements for tenders and draft contracts for the provision of residential care, on the basis that the terms of the proposed contracts were unreasonable within the *Wednesbury* principles, even though the relevant legislation which allowed local authorities to enter into contracts with the private sector (for the provision of care facilities) did not restrict the Council's discretion as to what contractual terms to impose. The court considered that the effect of the Council's decision on existing residential homes was sufficiently related to the purposes of the legislation to provide the necessary "statutory underpinning".

These cases indicate an illogical dichotomy between the way in each the courts treat the decision-taking of local government bodies on the one hand and central government on the other. There is a reluctance to interfere with central government (as indicated by the *Lord Chancellor's* case) but a readiness to intervene with local government, as indicated by

---

[11] [1994] 1 WLR 521
[12] [1994] C.O.D. 221

the *Cleveland* case and many others[13]. The ostensible justification for the difference in treatment is that the acts of local authorities always derive from a statutory authority, whereas the acts of central government do not (what statutory power does the Lord Chancellor have to contract out shorthand-writing services, for example?). It is submitted that the lack of statutory underpinning to the acts of central government should increase rather than decrease the court's willingness to intervene in its decision-making process.

Are privatised industries susceptible to Judicial Review?

In the UK in the past 15 years or so, there has been an enormous move towards privatisation of industries that were once state-owned. This raises the question as to whether those bodies in their new private form are still susceptible to judicial review.

The answer may be different in relation to each privatised body, depending on the particular way in which the privatisation has occurred. Some guidance can be obtained from the decision of the Privy Council in the *Mercury* case.[14] This was an appeal from the Court of Appeal of New Zealand. The Electricity Corporation of New Zealand Limited was a company registered under the New Zealand Companies Act, but its shares were held by Government Ministers. It was set up under the State-Owned Enterprise Act 1986. Under that Act its principal objective was stated to be:

> "*to operate as a successful business and, to this end, to be:*
> *(a) as profitable and efficient as comparable businesses that are not owned by the Crown; and*
> *(b) a good employer; and*
> *(c) an organisation that exhibits a sense of social responsibility by having regarding to the interests of the community in which it operates and by endeavouring to accommodate or encourage these when able to do so.*"

---

[13] For example: *R. v. Derbyshire CC ex p Times Supplements* [1990] Admin LR 241, *Ridge v. Baldwin* [1964] AC 40

[14] *Mercury Energy Limited v. Electricity Corporation of New Zealand* [1994] 1 WLR 521

The Privy Council concluded that the Electricity Corporation was a public body as its shares were held by Ministers who were responsible to parliament and accountable to the electorate. The Electricity Corporation carried on its business in the interest of the public. Decisions made in the public interest by the Electricity Corporation might adversely affect the rights and liabilities of private individuals without affording them any redress. In these circumstances the Privy Council concluded that the decisions of the Electricity Corporation were amenable to judicial review not only under the specific New Zealand legislation, but also under common law.

There is of course a clear distinction between the New Zealand Electricity Corporation and the UK regional electricity companies ("REC's") in that the shares in the latter are held privately, rather than by Ministers as in the case of the New Zealand company. Nevertheless, the RECs are under a strict statutory regime[15] and answerable to an industry regulator, the Director General of Electricity Supply, on whom they depend for the renewal of their required Public Electricity Supply licences. It can clearly be argued that the RECs "carry on their business in the interest of the public", and that REC's decisions "might adversely affect the rights and liabilities of private individuals without otherwise affording them any redress". The same can be said of most other privatised industries (to a greater or lesser degree). It is suggested therefore that in principle decisions of most privatised industries in the UK would be susceptible to judicial review.[16]

Another decision which indirectly helps to define whether or not privatised industries would be susceptible to judicial review is *R v. Panel on Takeovers & Mergers, ex parte Datafin.*[17] In that case, the Court of Appeal held that a body need not itself be public, nor did its powers need to originate in statute or prerogative, provided that it had a "public element" or was under some "public duty". It could be said that there was a "public element" in the supply of the service for which that utility

---

[15] *Electricity Act 1989* and see Morais, K '*Regulation and Procurement of Independent Power Projects*' *infra* p. 225.

[16] Note however that where the enabling legislation provides its own dispute resolution procedure (e.g reference to the regulator and/or arbitration under s.23 *Electricity Act 1989*), then that procedure should be followed, rather than an application for judicial review.

[17] [1987] 2 WLR 699

existed. Thus the provision of a telephone service could be said to be the performance of a "public duty". However, that then raises the question as to whether new companies entering into the market for the supply of a particular service should be similarly subjected to judicial review, even though they have never had any connection with the public sector. The position of British Telecom (a former publicly owned company) and Mercury Telecommunications (a private company whose parent went from private ownership to public ownership and then back to the private sector) comes immediately to mind.

In *R v. Insurance Ombudsman Bureau ex P. Aegon Life Insurance Limited*,[18] the Divisional Court held that judicial review would not lie against voluntary bodies like the Insurance Ombudsman Bureau unless they were "public bodies". A body whose birth and constitution owed nothing to any exercise of governmental power could be classed as a public body only if it had been woven into the fabric of public regulation, or into a system of governmental control, or was integrated into a system of statutory regulation, or, but for its existence, a governmental body would assume control. Although in this case and in the case on the Panel on Takeovers and Mergers referred to above, the Court was really looking at a different question (namely the susceptibility of non-governmental *regulatory* bodies), this test as to what is or is not a public body could well be applied to privatised industries. Applying the tests outlined above might help to justify British Telecom being susceptible to judicial review, but Mercury not being so. The comments of Bingham MR (noted below in the section on good faith in contracts) in considering British Telecom's position in a private law context support this.

Applying for Judicial Review

It is important to remember that, under the Rules of the Supreme Court, which govern the judicial review procedure, an application for judicial review must be made in two stages. First, it is necessary to apply for and obtain leave to seek judicial review and only if leave is granted will the court proceed to hear the substantive application for judicial review. The relevant court for such applications is the Divisional Court, the particular section of the High Court that is responsible for judicial review. Under the Rules of the Supreme Court, an application for leave to apply for

---

[18]   [1994] COD 426

judicial review must be made promptly and in any event within three months from the date when grounds for the application first arose. Even if the application is made within three months, leave can be refused, if the applicant has not acted promptly and/or the rights of third persons would be prejudiced by the delay.

The application for leave to move for judicial review is made in the appropriate form and supported with affidavit evidence. The application for leave may be made by way of written application or orally to a judge. If leave is granted the applicant must serve an originating motion and the affidavit in support on all parties directly affected. The respondent has to file an affidavit in reply, which should explain the reasons for the decision challenged, if he has not sufficiently done so in the decision itself. A public authority has a duty to conduct its case with "all the cards face upwards on the table".

The court has a discretion in regards to who will pay the costs of the application for leave and the substantive hearing. Costs will usually be granted to the winning party.

The particular requirements of the Rules of the Supreme Court in relation to judicial review have given rise to some serious procedural complications as to the extent to which applicants can mix claims for public law and private law remedies in the same action. The starting point for this is the House of Lords' decision in *O'Reilly v. Mackman*,[19] in which the principle was laid down that where a person seeks to establish that a decision of a person or body infringes rights which are entitled to protection under public law, he must, as a general rule, proceed by way of judicial review and not by way of an ordinary action whether for a declaration or an injunction or otherwise.[20]

The strictness of this decision has been alleviated in some subsequent cases. For example, in *Davy v. Spelthorne Borough Council* [21] the Plaintiff commenced ordinary proceedings by writ against the defendant council alleging that it had negligently advised him as to his rights under the Town & Country Planning Act 1971 and he claimed:

---

[19] [1983] 2 AC 237
[20] This and the following summary is taken from the notes to the White Book Ord 53
[21] [1984] AC 262

(1) an injunction restraining the council from implementing an enforcement notice which it had served;

(2) damages; and

(3) an order that the enforcement notice be set aside.

The Court of Appeal held that claims (1) and (3) (but not (2)) should be struck out applying the rule in *O'Reilly v. Mackman*. The House of Lords upheld the decision of the Court of Appeal that claim (2) should not be struck out because it was an ordinary common law action in tort concerning his private rights and not rights protected under public law.

The scope of the rule in *O'Reilly v. Mackman* is still a matter of debate. There are two main approaches which have been canvassed. The broad approach is that the rule does not apply to actions brought to vindicate private law rights even though involving a challenge to a public law act or decision. If the broad approach is adopted, the aggrieved person will be forced to proceed by way of judicial review only in a case where private law rights are not at stake. The narrower approach is that the rule in *O'Reilly v. Mackman* generally applies to all cases where it is sought to challenge a public law act or decision, subject to some exceptions when private rights arc being invoked. In the case of *Roy v. Kensington & Chelsea & Westminster Family Practitioner Committee*,[22] the House of Lords left open the question which of these approaches should be adopted, but indicated a preference for the broad approach.

In the *Mercury* case (discussed above), the Privy Council did not appear to be troubled by the fact that the Plaintiff's action in that case clearly involved a mixture of private and public law remedies. The Privy Council struck out the Plaintiff's claim not because of any procedural irregularity, but because the Court took the view that there was nothing in the Statement of Claim or the Particulars that had been provided of the pleading which supported a claim for judicial review (Lord Templeman said that "*the general and vague assertions of impropriety... are not supported by any reference to a single alleged fact*").

---

[22] [1992] 1 AC 624

Legitimate Expectation

One of the examples given at the beginning of this paper is the currently topical one of where, after intending tenderers have spent hundreds of thousands of pounds on preparing tenders, a government department has withdrawn a project, so that the costs incurred by the tenderers are entirely wasted.

The Court's decision in the case of *R v. Lord Chancellor ex parte Hibbit and Saunders* referred to above does not bode well for tenderers who may be considering their legal rights to recover their wasted expenditure. There does, however, exist a faint possibility that tenderers might recover these costs under the administrative law principle of "legitimate expectation". This is a fairly recent development of administrative law, and it has at its roots the constitutional principle of the rule of law, which requires regularity, predictability and certainty in government's dealings with the public. Since it is a public law principle, a legitimate expectation may justify an entitlement to some form of procedural protection, even in the absence of a right in private law.

Legitimate expectation is more difficult to define than to apply. One attempt was made by Lord Diplock in *Council of Civil Service Unions v. Minister for the Civil Service*,[23] who said that, for a legitimate expectation to arise, the decision complained of:

> *"must affect [the] other person... by depriving him of some benefit or advantage which either*
>
> *(i) he had in the past been permitted by the decision maker to enjoy and which he can legitimately expect to be permitted to continue to do until there has been communicated to him some rational grounds for withdrawing it on which he has been given an opportunity to comment; or*
>
> *(ii) he has received assurance from the decision maker will not be withdrawn without giving him first an opportunity of advancing reasons for contending that they should not be withdrawn."*

---

[23] [1985] AC 374

Commentators consider that this definition is too narrow in referring only to **past advantage or benefit**. The expectation must also surely extend to a benefit in the future which has not yet been enjoyed but which has been promised.[24] From this it will be seen that there are two different kinds of legitimate expectation:

- that a hearing or other appropriate procedures will be afforded before a decision is made;

- that a benefit of a substantive nature will be granted; or if the person is already in receipt of the benefit, that it will be continued and not substantially varied.

An example of the latter is the case of *R v. Enfield LBC ex parte T.F. Unwin (Royden) Limited*,[25] where contractors on a Council's list of approved contractors had a legitimate expectation that they would not be removed from the list without a hearing. A legitimate expectation must be induced by the conduct of the decision-maker. The expectation will be derived from either an express promise or representation or a representation implied from established practice based upon the past actions or the settled conduct of the decision-maker. The representation must be "clear, unambiguous, and devoid of relevant qualification".[26] The representation need not be made to the applicant personally or directly; a general policy which affects that class of applicant is sufficient.

Applying all this to the situation where a government body such as the Highways Agency invites tenders for a particular project and then withdraws the scheme before tenders have been submitted, it will be seen immediately that there are serious difficulties in establishing the necessary representation. The dissatisfied tenderers would have to satisfy the court that on the particular facts of the case, the government department had made a clear, unambiguous and unqualified representation that the road scheme would go ahead. Given the recent propensity of the Government to change its mind about investment in infrastructure projects, it would seem to be difficult to establish the necessary representation.

---

[24] de Smith, Woolf & Jowell, *Judicial Review of Administrative Action* Fifth Edition, Sweet & Maxwell, London 1995, p.419

[25] (1989) 1 Admin LR 51

[26] *R v. Inland Revenue Commissioners ex parte MFK Underwriting Agencies Limited* [1990] 1 WLR 1545

Recent press comments have suggested that the Highways Agency may have taken a decision to drop the scheme in the original format, and to invite new tenders on a new basis some considerable time before they actually notified the tenderers of the decision to abandon the original procurement method. If legitimate expectation is not available to dissatisfied tenderers to grant them a remedy in relation to the withdrawal of the scheme, is there a lesser remedy based on the legitimate expectation that the relevant department would notify tenderers **as soon as** it made its decision to change the procurement method, to avoid tenderers wasting time and money on continuing to prepare bids? Even that would appear to have its difficulties in the light of the legal requirements outlined above.

Application of Judicial Review to Construction Contracts

It will be seen from the above that where there is a contract between the litigants, the express or implied terms of the agreement should normally govern the matter, and not judicial review. Not only does private law govern intra-contractual conduct, but also pre-contract conduct in the case of central government, if not local government.[27]

Notwithstanding the above, it is apparent from the cases cited that the courts have reserved their position where bad faith or malice can be established. Bad faith and malice are amongst the areas with which this paper is concerned (see the examples at the beginning), so the conclusion is somewhat circular—*prima facie* public bodies are susceptible to judicial review (except where there is a contract), but that exception in turn does not apply where there is bad faith or malice. There is a difficulty in determining precisely what is meant by the courts when they say that bad faith and malice is excluded as there is very little authority on the point. Perhaps this is because the type of case in which the courts might lay down guidelines as to what constitutes bad faith or malice would be likely to be settled before it reached the court.

Generally, contracts made by public bodies in the construction industry are subject to the same law that governs contracts between private persons. There is no separate body of law governing administrative contracts as there is in France and Germany. There are, however, certain

---

[27]   *R. v. Lord Chancellor ex parte Hibbit & Saunders* [1993] C.O.D. 326

qualifications which must be placed upon this statement. Contracts made on behalf of the Crown are affected by the relevant provisions of the Crown Proceedings Act 1947, which established the right to sue the Crown. Contracts made by statutory bodies such as local authorities are subject to the rules of *ultra vires*, procedural propriety (which includes good faith) and rationality (reasonableness). A contract made by a public body can also be challenged if it fetters the future exercise of its discretionary powers. In *Stringer v. Minister of Housing,*.[28] where a local planning authority in Cheshire agreed with Manchester University to discourage new development within the vicinity of the Jodrell Bank radio telescope, the purported agreement was without legal effect. Both nationalised and privatised utilities are subject to statutory duties regarding the terms on which they provide their services. Local authorities are bound to follow particular statutory procedures for statutory particular purposes when contracting with third parties.

These additional criteria govern the validity and creation of contracts with public bodies; however, public law also affects the performance of these contracts. As discussed, the Court will interfere with decisions made under the contracts where the decision reveals bad faith on the part of the public body or motives contrary to the statutory purpose for which the contract was created.

In summary, judicial review ought to be considered when the contractor suspects bad faith on the part of a public body or former public body in the performance of a contract, notwithstanding that the bad faith does not amount to a breach of contract. The view expressed by the Privy Council in the *Mercury* case, that "*it does not seem likely that a decision by a state enterprise to enter into or determine a commercial contract... will ever be the subject of judicial review in the absence of fraud, corruption or bad faith*" is, with respect, too sweeping a statement. There is a widely accepted academic view that it is difficult if not impossible to set out principles of universal application for judicial review.

One has only to consider the following statement of the Master of the Rolls, Lord Woolf, made as long ago as 1986 to realise that the frontiers of administrative law are capable of being expanded greatly beyond their current limits:

---

[28]   [1971] 1 All ER 65

"The interests of the public are as capable of being adversely affected by the decision of large corporations and large associations, be they employers or employees, and should they not be subject to challenge on Wednesbury grounds if their decision relates to activities which can damage the public interest?".[29]

Duty of Fairness in Contracts

In a situation where the conduct of the public body complained of is inappropriate conduct in the administration of a contract, it will be seen from the principles stated above that it may be difficult under current law to persuade the court to intervene to grant a public law remedy. The issue that will be considered in this part of the paper is the extent to which the absence of a public law remedy matters, in the light of developments in English private law of contract.

The extent to which a court can review independent decisions taken under a construction contract is ostensibly limited. The decision in *Crouch* can be seen as consistent with the principles of administrative law described above (even though derived from a different branch of the law), under which the courts will not generally exercise control over contractual decisions. *Crouch* of course applies to those contracts where the decision-taking on extensions of time etc is taken by an independent certifier. The more recent case of *Balfour Beatty Civil Engineering Ltd v. Docklands Light Railway Ltd.*,[30] deals with the situation where there is no independent certifier, and the employer himself takes decisions about extensions of time and such like. Balfour Beatty were engaged by the DLR under a contract which was essentially the ICE 5th Edition, with the following significant changes: there was no independent Engineer, so the decisions that he would have taken under the standard form (on unforeseen ground conditions, extensions of time etc) were to be taken by the Employer himself, and clause 66 (the arbitration clause) was deleted altogether.

Balfour Beatty submitted claims for a longer extension of time than the Employer had granted, and for disruption costs. It took its claims to

---

[29] *Public Law - Private Law: Why the Divide? A Personal View* [1986] P.L 220
[30] (1996) 78 BLR 42

court. The Employer contended that the court did not have the power to open up, review and revise its decisions, and so said Balfour Beatty were bound by the decisions taken at the time. The trial judge agreed with the Employer, so Balfour Beatty appealed to the Court of Appeal.

The Court of Appeal agreed with the judge on grounds essentially the same as those in the *Crouch* case, even though there was no arbitration clause in the DLR/Balfour Beatty contract. The Court said that the only circumstances in which it could interfere were when the Employer breached the contract in making its decisions (for example, by legal misdirection, dishonesty, unfairness or unreasonableness). Balfour Beatty had accepted in the contract that their entitlement to, for example, an extension of time was to depend on the Employer's judgment, and it was not for the court to decide whether Balfour Beatty had made a bad bargain or a good one.

The Court said it would be concerned if this left a contractor without any effective means of challenging partial, self-interested or unreasonable decisions by the Employer. The DLR's counsel countered this by accepting that the Employer was bound to act fairly and reasonably, even though this was not expressly stated in the contract.

In making this concession, the DLR's counsel made it unnecessary for the Court of Appeal to come to any conclusions about "*whether an employer, invested (albeit by contract) with the power to rule on his own and a contractor's rights and obligations, was not subject to a duty of good faith substantially more demanding than that customarily recognised in English contract law*". The quoted words are those of the then Master of the Rolls (Sir Thomas Bingham MR) from his judgment (he gave the only judgment in the case) who was clearly very tempted to extend the frontiers of good faith in contract law.

This is not the first time that Bingham MR, as he then was, has expressed views on the subject of good faith in contract. In *Timeload Limited v. British Telecommunications*,[31] Timeload had a contract with BT for the allocation of a specific telephone number. BT, pursuant to the terms of the agreement, purported to terminate the contract alleging that the contract had been obtained as a result of corruption on behalf of its own employees. However, Sir Thomas Bingham MR (on an appeal against the

---

[31] [1995] EMLR 459

grant of an interlocutory injunction restraining BT from terminating the contract) was unwilling to allow BT to escape their contractual obligations by such a narrow construction of their contractual rights (he described BT's counsel's argument that BT should be able to rely on the express terms of the contract as "an old-fashioned classical argument"). He felt that although it was now a privatised supplier and no longer a monopoly holder, it was nevertheless in a very dominant position as a supplier. He further indicated that the Court could use the clear intentions underlying Unfair Contract Terms Act 1977 as a platform for invalidating the use of restrictive contractual provisions of the kind in this case, even if the letter of the statute did not apply.

Bingham, MR has echoed his *Timeload* judgment in *Philips Electronique Grand Publique SA v. British Sky Broadcasting Limited.*[32] He stated that had it been material, he would have implied into the relevant contract a term that one party (BSkyB) should act in good faith in the performance of the contract. (That implication was not, as things turned out, in issue as there was no evidence that BSkyB had acted in bad faith).

While both *Timeload* and *Philips* involved a detailed commercial contract concluded between parties who were arguably acting to some degree at arms' length, those facts did not deter Bingham MR, from imposing good faith or reasonableness obligations. He was prepared to make the implication despite the historical preference of the courts to treat elaborate or complex commercial contracts as exhaustive codes, and to be reluctant to imply into such contracts terms which the parties did not see fit to introduce expressly (the "old-fashioned classical" approach). In addition, in the *Timeload* case the Master of the Rolls indicated a desire not only to impose limits on the freedom of parties to contract on such terms as they think fit, but also to move away from the age-old English legal tradition of interpreting statutes on their strict wording. He wished to move to the purposive or teleological approach of interpreting statutes in accordance with their stated or inferred aim. The purposive approach is of course becoming increasingly familiar in the UK as a result of it being the express manner in which the European Court interprets EU legislation, but nevertheless, to have it applied to purely domestic legislation comes as something of a shock to old-fashioned classical lawyers.

---

[32] [1995] EMLR 472, [1997] Info TLR 89.

Sir Thomas Bingham has now been appointed Lord Chief Justice, in which position he is unlikely to have much influence on the development of contract law for the next few years. There are however other reforming judges who could easily take up where he has left off. For example, Lord Steyn (now in the House of Lords but then in the Court of Appeal) has indicated his impatience with the traditional English law of privity of contract in the case of *Darlington Borough Council v. Wiltshier.*[33] With his Romano-Dutch law roots, he could conceivably be responsible for introducing a degree of obligation to act in good faith in contracts. Lord Woolf's reputation as a reformer (see his comments on the extension of judicial review to private companies above as an illustration) could lead him in the same direction, with more opportunities than the Lords in his new position as Master of the Rolls (in charge of the Court of Appeal) to put new ideas into practice.

These dicta of Lord Bingham put the focus on the question of whether any such duties of good faith in contract (if they did exist) would be different depending on whether the party to the contract whose conduct is complained of is a public or a private body. There is nothing in the *Balfour Beatty* judgment to indicate the answer to the question (and anyway, there would probably have been interesting arguments as to whether the DLR, as a private limited company, wholly owned by the LDDC, a non-governmental public body, was a private or a public body). However, the comments in the *Timeload* decision would seem to suggest that parties to contracts might be treated differently and be under different obligations depending on whether they are (or were) in the public sector. In the case of *Blackpool and Fylde Aero Club v. Blackpool Borough Council,*[34] discussed in more detail below, the fact that the party inviting the tenders was a public rather than a private body did not seem to be a relevant consideration.

Contractual rights of tenderers

One of the examples given at the beginning of this paper is where an employer capriciously excludes from consideration an otherwise perfectly valid tender by a contractor. It has quite recently been established that the tenderer does have a contractual remedy in this

---

[33]   [1995] 1 WLR 68

[34]   [1990] 1 WLR 1195

situation, and it will be seen that this remedy exists irrespective of whether the employer is a public or a private body. In the *Fylde Aero Club* case the Defendant local authority wrongly excluded the Plaintiff's tender from consideration. The Court of Appeal held that an invitation to tender was normally no more than an offer to receive bids, but circumstances could exist whereby it gave rise to binding contractual obligations; that although the defendant's form of tender did not explicitly state that they would consider timely and conforming tenders, and although contractors were not to be likely implied, an examination of what the parties said and did established a clear intention to create a contractual obligation on the part of the Defendants to consider the Plaintiff's tender in conjunction with all other conforming tenders or at least that the Plaintiff's tender would be considered if others were; and that, accordingly, the Defendant's failure rendered them contractually liable to the Plaintiff.

This finding does not depend on the fact that the Defendant was a local authority. It is also a finding based on the facts of the particular case. However, it is likely that the similar contractual obligation would be found in most tender situations. To revert to the example, if therefore the Employer (whether he was local or central governmental, a newly privatised body, or a PFI Concession Holder) capriciously excluded a tender, he would be in breach of contract. This would give the injured party a right in damages.

It is an undecided question as to what the measure of damages would be. In the subsequent but slightly similar case of *Fairclough Building Limited v. Port Talbot Borough Council*,[35] Parker LJ said:

> *"By way of post script I should add that I find great difficulty in seeing what damage the Plaintiff could have suffered even if there had been a breach of obligation. The most that could be said was that there was a loss of a chance that had it remained on the list something might have emerged to change its mind. In the light of the situation and the decision to which the Council have come, it seems to me that chance would have been worth precious little."*

For the "chance" to materialise, the rejected tenderer would have to show that, had his tender been considered, he would have been awarded the

---

[35] (1992) 33 Con LR 25

contract. If his tender was higher than other tenderers, then it could not be said that the failure to consider the tender has caused the tenderer any loss whatsoever. The expenditure on the tender would have been incurred and would have gained the tenderer little or nothing.

Since the *Fylde Aero Club* and *Port Talbot* cases are dependent on an implied contractual term, it would clearly be feasible (and should probably be good practice on the part of employers) expressly to exclude any rights and remedies on the part of tenderers for any acts or defaults on the part of the employer in the tender process.

The conclusion to be drawn from this section is that we may well see within a very few years a radical change in the law of contract to include an obligation on the parties to act in good faith towards each other. Whether that is done under the auspices of the Unfair Contracts Terms Act or under the common law remains to be seen. It seems possible that higher burdens of fairness will be imposed on public sector or privatised former government bodies. The result of that would be that the barriers that exist making it difficult to obtain judicial review (in the strict sense of Order 53) of actions under a contract (because of the reluctance of the courts to use judicial review in a contract situation) may be less of a problem than under the old orthodoxy.

It must also be remembered that the first time the 2nd Edition of the New Engineering Contract comes before the courts, we are likely to have judicial views on the meaning and effectiveness of the term requiring the parties to act in good faith towards each other. Scepticism was poured on this term by commentators who felt that such a duty was too vague, uncertain and evidentially too hard to prove. Nor was it clear what the measure of damages would be for breach. These commentators forget that French courts have managed such concepts for around 200 years.[36]

Statutory Remedies for Tenderers

To a considerable extent, statute now provides a remedy to dissatisfied tenderers for failure to follow proper tender procedures. There is both UK domestic and European legislation on this subject. The European legislation is analysed in the final section of this paper.

---

[36] Art 1305 of the Civil Code requires contracts to be performed "en bonne foi".

Under the Local Government Act 1988, local authorities are prohibited from exercising their functions in relation to public supply and works contracts by reference to "non-commercial matters". This would prohibit for example a local authority selecting its tender list on the basis of the proportion of the staff of potential tenderers that came from ethnic minorities. Under Section 19 of the Local Government Act 1988, the remedy of damages is available to any person who, in consequence of the authority's breach of duty, suffers loss or damage. This is in contrast to the traditional remedy of judicial review, under which damages are not generally available.

The Local Government Act 1988, as well as prohibiting local authority employers from taking into account "non-commercial matters" in the award of contracts, also sets up the regime for compulsory competitive tendering of a wide range of contracts for the supply of goods and services on behalf of the local authority[37]. In this respect the Act does not contain any specific remedy for dissatisfied parties who contend that they have been prejudiced by non-compliance with the CCT regime. However, the Act says that a local authority **may not** enter into a contract for the provision of such supply of goods or services unless it complies with the required procedures for CCT. To the extent therefore that the local authority awards a contract in breach of the CCT Rules, the contract itself will be *ultra vires*, the local authority will therefore be susceptible to challenge by judicial review, and for the improper decision to be set aside.

The Problem of Crouch

The decision of the Court of Appeal in *Crouch* remains an obstruction to the new willingness of the courts to review the conduct of parties to contracts to determine whether they have acted in good faith. The *Crouch* decision states that the role of an arbitrator under the typically worded construction contract is not the same as that of a court and, in particular, that the Court does not have the powers which the arbitrator enjoys under the contract. Where certain rights and obligations are to be determined by

---

[37] Since this paper was written and presented, the new administration has announced (but not yet implemented) its intention to abolish CCT, and replace it with a non-statutory "Best Value" procurement system.

the certificate or opinion of the Architect or Engineer, the Court cannot interfere with those decisions. It merely has the power to enforce the terms of an agreement; it has no power to modify them in any way.

If they survive appeal, two very recent cases indicate that *Crouch* may be a problem in name only. In *John Barker Construction Limited v. London Portman Hotel Limited*,[38] the arbitration clause in a standard JCT form had been replaced with the following words:

> *"The proper law of the agreement shall be English law and the English Courts shall have jurisdiction".*

Mr Recorder Roger Toulson QC (now Toulson J) conducted a lengthy analysis of *Crouch* and made the following comments:

> *"Nor would I agree, on the other hand, with the Defendant's argument that the grounds on which a decision of the Architect under Clause 25 may be challenged are limited to bad faith or manifest excess of jurisdiction. I find it quite unacceptable the suggestion that the parties can have intended that a decision on a matter of such potential importance should be entrusted to a third person, who was himself an agent of one party, without that person being under any obligation to act fairly. It seems to me to go without saying that the parties must have intended the decision maker to be under such an obligation, the imposition of which is necessary to give efficacy to the contract."*

> *"If the grounds of challenge to a decision under Clause 25 were intended to be so limited [to cases of bad faith or excessive powers] as to exclude challenge in the case of an aberrant, uninformed or unfair decision, provided that there was no fraud or patent excess of powers, I would expect the contract to say so."*

> *"I would hold that it was an implied requirement of a valid decision under Clause 25 that the Architect should act fairly and lawfully. Such a duty is consistent with the Architect's quasi-arbitral position, and the Courts are used to applying a fairness test when reviewing a decision of a person with quasi-arbitral powers.*

---

[38]   (1997) 83 BLR 31, 50 Con LR 43

If a decision was invalid, it would then be necessary to decide whether the appropriate course would be merely to declare the decision invalid, or whether the Contractor machinery had broken down to the point that justice required the court to determine the substantive question what was a fair and reasonable extension."[39]

The Judge then went on to consider the Contractor's individual events of delay and the extensions awarded by the Architect. On completing this consideration, he concluded that, although there was no bad faith or excess of jurisdiction on the part of the Architect, his determination of the extension of time due to the Plaintiffs was not a fair determination, nor was it based on a proper application of the provisions of the contract, and it was accordingly invalid. The judge considered whether to remit the decision to the Architect for his fresh consideration, but concluded that the Architect's memory was seriously awry. In those circumstances he did not see how the Architect could now arrive at a satisfactory determination. From this he concluded that:

"... this is a case in which the contractual machinery established by the parties has become frustrated or, put in other words, has broken down to a such an extent that it would not now be practicable or just for the matter to be remitted to the Architect for re-determination; and that in those circumstances the Court must determine on the present evidence what was a fair and reasonable extension of time."

Thus, while purporting to comply with the strictures of *Crouch*, the Judge found himself able to conduct a complete analysis of the Architect's decision making process, and to substitute his own views, even though there was acknowledged to be no bad faith or excessive jurisdiction on the part of the Architect.

Regrettably (at least for those that regard *Crouch* as an unnecessary restriction on the powers of the court) the decision in this case does not sit happily with that of the Court of Appeal in *Balfour Beatty v. DLR*. The latter preceded the *John Barker* case by only a very few days,[40] and

---

[39] The judge's analysis of his powers (that he could review the decision-making process if not the decision itself) has clear echoes of judicial mythology in administrative law cases, where judges insist that they do not substitute their own views for those of the executive.

[40] 3 April 1996 as against 16 April 1996.

it seems most unlikely from the judgment that counsel or the judge were aware of the decision. It has been seen that the Court in *Balfour Beatty* said that the only circumstances in which it could interfere were when the Employer (absent an independent Engineer in that contract) breached the contract in making its decisions (e.g by legal misdirection, dishonesty, unfairness or unreasonableness), whereas the judge in the *John Barker* case felt that he was not so limited.

The second case is *Tarmac Construction Limited v. Esso Petroleum Company Limited*,[41] a decision of His Honour Judge Humphrey Lloyd, QC. The contract in that case was essentially the ICE 5th Edition, but instead of deleting the arbitration clause in total as was done in the *Balfour Beatty v. DLR* case, the Employer had (in essence) just inserted the word "litigation" wherever the word "arbitration" appears in the standard form of the ICE 5th. So for example, the amended Clause 66 provided that the Engineer's decisions "*shall be final and binding upon the Contractor and the Employer unless either of them shall require that the matter be referred to litigation as hereinafter provided*", and that in the case of dissatisfaction with an Engineer's decision either party might "*require that the matter be determined by litigation by serving notice to the other party to the Contract of the intention to proceed to litigation*".

Judge Lloyd, in a lengthy judgment, reached the very sensible conclusion that in the contract the parties had expressed a clear intention that the Court could review and revise the Engineer's decisions, just in the same way as an arbitrator could. The Judge rejected the Employer's reliance on both *Crouch* and *Balfour Beatty v. DLR*, concluding that "*Esso's approach assumes that certain decisions of the Court of Appeal established principles which override or qualify what would otherwise be the natural interpretation of a contract*". He distinguished this case from *Balfour Beatty v. DLR* on the basis that in the latter, the Court of Appeal was satisfied that there was no agreed means of challenging the primary decisions of the Employer e.g. under Clause 44 (extension of time). In this case, there was a clear mechanism. In response to Esso's counsel's submissions that the Court only had the power to review the Engineer's decision making process and not the decision itself, the Judge commented that the amended Clause 66 was "*not apt to describe a process by which the Court's role is to enquire into whether the Engineer*

---

[41] (1997) 83 BLR 31, 50 Con LR 43

asked himself the right questions... the usual reason for dissatisfaction would be that the dispute was not resolved by the Engineer to that party's liking, not that the party was dissatisfied with the manner in which the Engineer decided the dispute. It would be artificial and unnatural to read it as requiring dissatisfaction on the grounds set out in Esso's formulation". For all these reasons the Judge concluded that *"Clause 66 clearly expresses an intention that the Engineer's decision is not final and may be revised by court".*

It is very hard to criticise Judge Lloyd's decision as a matter of simple interpretation of the Contract in question. The judgment forcefully rejects the commonly held view that the effect of *Crouch* was that parties could not, even if they wanted to, grant to the Court the power to open up, review and revise an Engineer's decision.[42]

Both the *John Barker* and the *Tarmac* cases are first instance decisions and contain aspects that might not survive appeal, but they nevertheless represent the removal of still more bricks from the *Crouch* wall, along with the other bricks that have been removed by previous decisions.[43]

Public Procurement Remedies for the Breach of EC Procurement Rules

The following is a summary of the remedies available for breach of the EU Public procurement rules. It is beyond the scope of the paper to analyse the circumstances in which these procurement rules apply, but delegates will be aware of the general scope of their application. This section of the paper deals with what happens when a contracting authority does not comply with these rules.

---

[42] This is referred to as "the third view" in the analysis of Crouch in May, *Keating on Building Contracts*, 6th Ed, (London, Sweet & Maxwell, 1995) page 430-1.

[43] For example, *Davy Offshore v. Emerald Field Contracting* (1991) 55 BLR 1, *Rapid Building v. Ealing Family Housing* (1984) 1 Con LR 1 and *Benstrete Construction v. Hill* (1987) 38 BLR 115.

An aggrieved person has three avenues in the event of a breach of the procurement rules:

- Intervention by the European Commission

- Reliance on the Remedies Directives (embodied in the UK in the relevant public works and utilities procurement regulations)
- Reliance on the common law in the UK or other embodied system of law elsewhere for the breach of a procurement procedure

The first two are available Europe-wide. The availability of the third is dependent on the applicable law of the procurement procedure. I turn to deal with these three remedies in turn.

Intervention by the European Commission

Article 169 of the EEC Treaty gives the Commission the role of European watchdog for implementation of Directives by Member States and their compliance with them. Although the defendant to an action brought by the Commission is always named as the Member State, the watchdog role of the Commission is not limited only to compliance by the central government with the procurement Directives. The definition of "State" in the Directives has been interpreted very widely to include health authorities, constabularies, local authorities, etc, the relevant common factor being an element of State control. The Commission may find out about infringement of the Directives in many ways. One of those ways includes an aggrieved person approaching the Commission and notifying it of an alleged infringement.

Complaints Procedure

An aggrieved person can make a complaint to the Commission about non-compliance although there is no formalised procedure. Although not a condition of it taking on a matter, the Commission will generally need to be satisfied that remedies under national law have been exhausted. This general rule will probably be observed more frequently in the light of the implementation of the Remedies Directives throughout the EU Member States. If the Commission decides that it will not take up the matter for the reason that in its view there is no breach, there is little that a complainant can do other than continue to lobby the Commission to take on the matter.

A complainant may give formal or informal notice to the Commission. An informal approach permits a degree of anonymity to be retained by simply alerting the Commission to a practice which may be in breach. However, if the infringement relates to a specific incident it would usually be unsatisfactory. To increase the likelihood of the Commission taking on a matter, the complaint should be in writing with basic information about the complainant and complete facts of the case. The complainant should provide proof of claims made and that genuine difficulties are being faced in the absence of the Commission's intervention (all with supporting documentation).

If the Commission adopts a complaint it will generally follow the procedure set out in Article 169 of the EEC Treaty,[44] as follows:

(1) The Commission contacts the member state and raises the infringement;

(2) The Member State usually replies to the Commission's submissions;

(3) If the Commission is not satisfied with the response it will issue a reasoned opinion setting out a full statement of the facts, the infringements and calling for the infringement to be brought to an end within a certain time (usually 2 months);

(4) If the Member State does not comply within the time limit set the matter will be brought before the Court of Justice (the procedure takes approximately 2½ years).

a) Advantages:

- Potential for anonymity; and
- the involvement of the Commission may very quickly get results through a change in the infringing procedure.

---

[44] Trepte P-A, *Public Procurement in the EC*, CCH, London, 1993, p 208 - 212.

b) Disadvantages:

- It is dependent on the Commission being willing to take up the cause, and it is unlikely to be willing to become involved in the assessment of a tender. There needs to be a significant issue to attract the Commission's attention:

  (i)   patent discrimination on nationality
  (ii) rejection by a member that the rules apply
  (iii) the proceedings will provide clarification of the Directives. [45]

- It is potentially very slow; and

- Relief can only be granted to the Commission, not the aggrieved party. However, this can be mitigated by the indirect impact of the Commission's prosecution on the infringing member, for example the Great Belt Bridge case,[46] where, shortly before proceedings for interim measures brought by the Commission were to commence, the matter settled with the Danish Government acknowledging its specifications were in breach and agreeing to remove offending provisions in future contracts. It offered compensation to disappointed tenderers.

Reliance on the Remedies Directives

The Remedies Directives set a minimum standard of remedies throughout the EU, and avoid previously inconsistent or non-existent remedies in Member States. There are separate Directives for public procurement and utilities procurement, as follows:

- The Public Remedies Directive—Directive 89/665 [1989] OJ L395/33.
- The Utilities Remedies Directive—Directive 92/13 [1992] OJ L76/14

---

[45] For example, Case C-87/94 *Commission v. Belgium*, 25 April 1996
[46] *Commission v. Denmark* Case C-243/89

These have been implemented in the UK through the incorporation of relevant regulations reflecting the Directives in the procurement regulations. The forum for determining complaints of non-compliance in the UK is the High Court (England/Wales/Northern Ireland) and the Court of Session (Scotland). There are very few reported cases.[47]

a) Who can avail themselves of the remedies (by reference to the UK Regs)?

The remedies are probably available only to persons who are nationals of and established in a Member State (plus EEA members in the case of a contract falling within the Public Supply Regulations). They are possibly also available to suppliers who are nationals of or resident in states which are not EU or EEA members but are GATT contracting states.[48]

Non-compliance is actionable by any contractor/supplier/service provider (as the case may be) who suffers, or risks suffering, loss or damage. This extends to non-tenderers since *"contractor"* in the procurement regulations is defined as *"a person who sought, or who seeks, or would have wished to be the person to whom a ... contract ... is awarded"*—the breach may arise from their wrongful exclusion from a pre-qualification list under the restrictive procedure.

b) Preconditions to the Remedies

Proceedings can only be brought if:

- The complainant has informed the contracting authority of the breach or apprehended breach and of its intention to commence proceedings;
  AND

- Proceedings are brought promptly and within 3 months from the date when the grounds for bringing the proceedings first arose (unless the Court considers there is good reason for an extension of time).

---

[47] An example of which is: *General Building & Maintenance plc v. Greenwich Borough Council* (1993) 65 BLR 57.

[48] Trepte P-A, Public Procurement in the EC, p 220, N.B. the consideration of GATT is not relevant to the Works, Services or Utilities Directives

c) Remedies available

The remedies that are available are dependent on whether or not the contract to which the alleged breach relates has been entered into.

Pre-contract, a complainant can seek any or all of the following orders:

- An interim injunction to suspend the procedure leading to an award or the implementation of any decision to award;
- An order setting aside a decision or action;
- An order that the contracting authority amends any document (e.g an infringing specification); and
- An award of damages to a complainant for loss or damage suffered as a consequence of the breach.

Post-contract, a complainant can seek only damages. This will be of little benefit to a complainant who was not a tenderer. The remedies of an injunction and damages are further considered below:

Injunction

From a practical viewpoint, the most important remedy to a complainant will be interim injunctive relief. This can only be obtained **prior** to the contract which is the subject of the procedure at issue being entered into. This means there is some potential for dispute as to when the contract was entered into. There is no reason to think that the usual criteria applied by the courts when injunctive relief is sought will not be applied here, *i.e*:

- the complainant would need to show that there is a serious case to answer;
- the complainant would need to demonstrate that damages would not be a sufficient remedy to the complainant; and
- the complainant would be required to give an undertaking to pay damages to the contracting authority if the court finds that an injunction should not have been granted.

An additional element that will need to be considered by a complainant seeking an injunction in the UK is the balancing of interests. Article 2(4) of the Remedies Directives provides that Member States may provide that the body responsible for making interim orders can take into account the probable consequences of the measures for all interests likely to be harmed, as well as the public interest, and may decide not to grant such measures where the negative consequences could exceed the benefits. The UK has not chosen expressly to provide for such a measure but the courts themselves have adopted such a balancing exercise where (as frequently will be the case) damages will not be an adequate remedy to the contracting authority.[49] If the complainant is to have any chance of tipping the scales in its favour, the complainant should demonstrate that it would have had a good prospect of winning the tender if it were not for the alleged breach.

Damages

To recover damages the complainant must prove:

- the alleged breach of the rules; and
- the damages sought.

Surprisingly, there is no guidance in the Regulations on the assessment of damages. Assessment of quantum will be dependent on the existing national laws which may lead to inconsistencies in standards of proof and levels of compensation throughout the EU. In the UK the assessment of damages will be dependent on the framing of the cause of action.

a) Breach of statutory duty

The most obvious cause of action would be tortious breach of statutory duty. Loss recoverable would most probably be limited to **tender costs and associated expenses** as damages for tort are generally limited to that which would put the complainant into the position that it would have been in if the tort had not been committed.

The difficulty a complainant faces in recovering more substantial damages, such as loss of profit, is in satisfying the court that on the

---

[49] *Factortame Ltd v. Secretary for State for Transport (No. 2)* [1991] 1 All ER 70

balance of probabilities it would have been the successful tenderer. This is not so difficult where the award of tenders was for the lowest price and the complainant had the lowest price, but it could be particularly hard to do where the contract is awarded on the basis of the most economically advantageous tender. It would generally be more difficult for a complainant to prove that it would have been the successful tenderer the earlier in the procedure that the alleged breach occurred (eg absence of contract notice).

Under the Utilities Contracts Regulations 1996,[50] ("the Utilities Contracts Regulations"), which implement the Utilities Remedies Directive in the UK, the difficulty in proof is eased through the lowering of the standard of proof. By Regulation 32(7), the supplier, contractor or services provider need only show that it would have had a "real chance" of winning, as follows:

> *"Where, in proceedings under this regulation the Court is satisfied that a provider would have had a real chance of being awarded a contract if that chance had not been adversely affected by a breach of the duty owed to him ... the provider shall be entitled to damages amounting to his costs in preparing his tender and in participating in the procedure leading to the award of the contract."*

b) Breach of an implied contract

It may also be possible to allege breach of an implied contract relying on the reasoning in the *Fylde Aero Club* case,[51] (although this would not be available to a complainant who did not tender)—*i.e.* where an invitation to tender prescribes a clear, orderly and familiar procedure and the tenderer submits a conforming tender, the tenderer is entitled to have its tender opened and considered in conformance with that procedure.

The damages recoverable would include **tender costs and associated expenses** although recovery would be subject to the complainant proving that it would have recovered these costs if it had been successful. It may also be possible to recover **lost profit** as damages for breach of contract

---

[50] SI 1996/2911
[51] [1990] 1 WLR 1195

are intended to put the plaintiff in the same position as it would have been had the contract been performed. The complainant would have to satisfy the court that it would have won the contract and that it would have made a profit.

There is some doubt whether a claim based on implied contract would succeed, because of the argument that a promise to perform something which the promisor was already bound to perform by law is not good consideration.

c) Additional remedies attaching to procurement by utilities

The Utilities Remedies Directive contains a further three remedies that a Member State may, at its election, provide for in its implementing legislation. However, only the third has been implemented in the UK:

- **Dissuasive payments**: A Member State may provide for orders imposing administrative penalties if infringements have not been corrected. The penalty must be of a sufficient level to dissuade the utility from infringing.

- **Attestation**: A Member State may provide for the independent assessment and attestation that a utilities procurement procedure complies with EC law and the implementing legislation. There is no provision dealing with the effect of attestation other than that the fact that attestation has been given may be included in an Official Journal notice.

- **Conciliation**: A complainant may ask for a dispute to be resolved through the conciliation procedure prescribed in the Utilities Remedies Directive. This optional remedy has been implemented in the UK in Regulation 33 of the Utilities Contracts Regulations but may be of limited use as the conciliation procedure can only commence with the consent of the utility.

Conclusion

From the above brief summary it will be seen that the EU public procurement regime and associated Remedies Directives would provide a remedy of sorts for the types of procurement "misbehaviour" given in the examples at the beginning of this paper. Despite the limits on the scope of recovery, this may provide the best avenue to disgruntled tenderers, given the limited extent to which the English courts will be prepared to use administrative law to interfere with private law arrangements. On the other hand, it seems quite likely that English law will soon allow a greater application of the principles of good faith in the conduct of parties to contracts. That would give greater discretion to the courts to use the private law of contract to control the conduct of contracting parties.

6. Litigation Law Reform: A Sheep in Woolf's Clothing ?[†]

H.H. Judge Anthony Thornton, QC

Synopsis

This paper analyses the nature and deployment of litigation in the construction sector by reference to its historical roots. Conclusions are made as to how present reforms may achieve a better result in terms of time and cost.

Introduction

It is conceivable that legal historians of the future will describe 1996 as having been a watershed for litigation. The "Access to Justice" reform initiated by Lord Woolf's monumental report, the Arbitration Act 1996, the Civil Evidence Act 1995 and the legal aid reform proposals will, if successfully implemented, transform litigation. The key words are "successfully implemented". Since 1851 there have been 60 reports on aspects of civil procedure and the organisation of the courts of England and Wales. Despite that, the former Master of the Rolls, Sir Thomas Bingham, has described the fundamental problems of the civil justice system, problems of cost, delay, inaccessibility and procedural unfairness, as "a cancer eating at the heart of the administration of justice".

It must be remembered, however, that reformers are confronted with a Morton's fork. To the extent that reforms provide partial solutions to the four cancerous pillars of civil justice, the same reforms will encourage the greater use of a system which, in consequence, could leave a greater number of litigants using an improved system that is as subject to delay, cost and inaccessibility as is the unreformed system.

[†] This paper has been developed from the 1996 Michael Brown Foundation lecture entitled 'Litigation Reform – an Impossibility?'. The lecture was first published at (1997) Const LJ 166, and is reproduced with kind permission.

This is the Morton's fork or "M25" effect. The system, as reformed, encourages greater use of its resources with, ultimately, no substantial improvement to the users.

This should not, however, deter reformers. The present system grossly misuses the available resources and, at the very least, litigators should be striving to make the best possible use of such scarce resources as the state is prepared to allocate to dispute resolution. I am primarily concerned with the efficient use of the resources needed to resolve complex technical disputes. These are disputes which defy mediation, are not capable of being compromised at an early stage and which involve factual and technical issues of some complexity. These disputes may be dealt with by courts or arbitrators. The Arbitration Act 1996 vests in arbitrators great flexibility, largely unsupervised by the courts, to run and resolve disputes referred to them. However, the rules of court introduced following the Woolf final report will give judges similar flexibility. Both processes will have, in common, the power to require litigants to follow procedures that are determined by the tribunal, to inflict a binding and enforceable decision on the parties and to compel the attendance of witnesses and the production of documents. It follows that the underlying principles governing the litigation process, principles that must walk a tight-rope between efficiency and fairness, are the same for both systems.

In this paper I propose to examine these principles. A good starting point is to ask why 60 committees have failed to eliminate the cancerous growth from the system. Historical insight can be instructive. Since technical disputes involve the use of scientific methods and conclusions, it is also instructive to consider how effectively the legal process grapples with technical questions. My inquiry is concerned with both history and the use of scientific method in a legal context, an appropriate way, I believe, to remember Michael Brown in this third Michael Brown Foundation lecture. The Foundation, based here at King's College, aims to provide instruction and research in construction law and management. Michael Brown himself, before his tragically early and untimely death, had already shown how engineering and law can be effectively combined to eradicate and resolve engineering disputes.

Brunel: The Father of Construction Litigation?

My examination focuses first on Kingdom Isambard Brunel. Brunel is regarded by many as the father of the industrial age, particularly because of his railway projects and his work on two steam ships, the *Great Britain* and the *Great Eastern*. But he was a flawed genius, if his management skills and his ability to ferment disputes are taken into account. I am concerned only with the Great Western Railway, built between Paddington and Bristol between 1836 and 1841. This line really was Brunel's. The range of his talents and achievements is remarkable. He persuaded the newly-formed Great Western Railway Company to engage him as the surveyor for the proposed railway in 1833 when he was only 26. His formal education had ended when he was 14. However Brunel fils had, in his father Marc Brunel, a formidable teacher of engineering skills. Isambard worked alongside Marc on the Thames tunnel project and he also gained much practical experience undertaking an apprenticeship with a renowned machine-tool craftsman, Henry Maudslay. Brunel is the ideal example of the utility of vocational training.

After he was appointed surveyor to the line, Brunel single-handedly directed the project in all respects. He surveyed the whole route, produced most of the engineering drawings needed for the private bill, chose the gauge, designed the locomotives, drafted all the many contracts, negotiated many of the land purchases and chose and negotiated with each of the contractors. One of his most remarkable achievements was to pioneer the Great Western Railway Bill almost single-handedly through the House of Commons in April 1834 and, then, through the House of Lords. In the Commons, he was cross-examined by Serjeant Merewether with considerable ferocity. Throughout, Brunel remained unruffled. He was able to identify from memory each landowner along the route and the depth and length of each cutting and embankment. In the House of Lords his performance was even more remarkable. The first bill was lost but was re-presented in 1835. Merewether again led for the opposition and he cross-examined Brunel for 11 of the 40 days in committee. When Brunel emerged from his ordeal, he replied to a question as to how he had remained so cool and collected in the face of the leading Parliamentary advocate of the day with the laconic answer: "Merewether could not possibly know as much about engineering as I do".

That answer highlighted the other side of Brunel. He was stubborn, difficult and domineering. He also had to build a railway that cost three times it original budget. Throughout, funds were tight and Brunel, as the almost imperial engineer, kept all the contractors starved of funds. He was the certifier and, if any dispute arose, the arbitrator as well. In consequence, the construction of this line gave rise to two of the most important nineteenth century building disputes.

The first dispute was with William Ranger. He had been let four contracts near Bristol which involved cutting four tunnels and constructing the Avon Bridge. Brunel required each contractor to lodge a bond of £5,000 in cash for each contract at the outset. That, and the lack of certification, meant that Ranger was unable to complete these contracts. Brunel made him an offer whereby he could have kept the Sonning Cutting work whilst relinquishing the rest. However, Ranger was a proud man and he refused. His contracts were terminated. The ensuing dispute was argued in equity before the Vice-Chancellor. Ranger had little success and, in consequence, he appealed to the House of Lords. The case was argued twice. On the first occasion, after the conclusion of the argument, Lord Chancellor Cottenham died. The case was then re-argued before Lord Cranworth four years later. The appeal took 10 days and the Lord Chancellor then gave an extempore speech which covers nearly 30 pages in the law reports.[1] The appeal was partly successful. The case, having taken 16 years to be concluded, is still cited in the current edition of Keating for no fewer than five different propositions of law. One is that a contractor may not accept a repudiation and then sue for a quantum meruit. This settled a controversy which has rumbled on to this day because many commentators have overlooked Ranger's case in favour of a contrary decision of the Privy Council in 1904.[2]

---

[1]   *Ranger v G.W.R.* (1854) 5 H.L.C.71, 10 E.R. 824. As was customary in House of Lords' Appeals from the Vice-Chancellor, the appeal was heard by two Lords. Lord Brougham sat with the Lord Chancellor.

[2]   *Lodder v Slowey* [1904] AC 442.

The other dispute was even more remarkable Ranger's successors on three of his contracts were Hugh McIntosh and his son. They were formidable Scots engineers who were nearly, but not quite, defeated by the Great Western Railway and its engineer. Conditions were appalling and 20 men were killed during the construction of the Twerton tunnel alone. This tunnel also nearly killed the McIntoshes financially since two of Brunel's financial tricks occurred there. Firstly, he made the contractor cut the stone facings with such precision that the work was turned into ashlar work. However, Brunel would still only pay for the work at ordinary coarse item rates. Secondly, the contractor uncovered a Roman masonry floor. It was lifted and preserved without damage but all at the McIntoshes' expense.

The McIntoshes brought proceedings in Chancery. Their case is cited today for two principal reasons. The case confirmed the ability of a contractor to recover interest as damages in equity and also to recover without a certificate. The case took from 1838 until 1865 when, exhausted, the executors of both father and son decided against an appeal to the Court of Appeal. By then they had recovered £100,000 as well as interest over a 28-year period. Had they appealed, they could have argued for a further £100,000 with some prospects of success. The case is reported in 8 separate law reports at different stages of its progress to trial. Every possible procedural manoeuvre was attempted by the GWR and Brunel. Eventually, an account was ordered and accounts were taken in the Vice-Chancellor's chambers by the Chief Clerk in Chancery over a five-year period since 900 items were disputed, the smallest being for less that £1. The reference back to the Vice-Chancellor, Sir John Stewart, was argued for 23 days. His judgment is restrained, particularly as it was argued both that he had no jurisdiction to entertain the suit, then in its 28th year and, also, that there should be a new trial. He rejected both submissions with these words: "If I am wrong in this view, the correction of it will, I hope, extract some luminous exposition of principle on which such cases should be treated".[3] These 19th-century vignettes set the scene for a consideration of equally complex contemporary litigation.

---

[3] *McKintosh v G.W.R.* (1865) 4 Giff. 881. The references to all the earlier decisions in the litigation may be obtained from the index of cases in the English Reports.

Inherent Qualities of the Present System

Before considering whether reform is possible, I believe it important to consider whether there are any essential features of the present system. This is an empirical question. It cannot be said that any features of a dispute resolution system are necessary. However, the inherent qualities of our legal system have developed unabated since at least the Norman Conquest. We ceased to be directly influenced by the Holy Roman Empire centuries ago and we have never been subject to the desire to codify and standardise our substantive or procedural law. Moreover, we have always allowed our law to develop pragmatically and in a piecemeal fashion. Lord Woolf and the draftsman of the Arbitration Act 1996 are not latter-day Dr. Panglosses and all of us must take our history as we find it.

I suggest that there are at least four essential and unassailable features of our system. These may be summarised in four catchwords: approach, autonomy, disclosure and probity. Clearly, I must elaborate each of these.

Approach

We have all grown up with the common-law truism that a party presenting a case has the burden of proving it. In other words, a tribunal must decide a case, to the appropriate standard of proof, by reference to, and only to, the evidence and arguments produced to it. This is very different to the civilian systems. These systems start from an importantly different standpoint, namely from the question: what is the truth of the matter? This approach does not regard a tribunal as being bound by the admitted evidence but requires the tribunal, in the light of all materials that have been received and any other materials that it chooses to consult, to draw its conclusion as to where the truth lies. Thus, although the adduced materials are relevant, they are not regarded as the exclusive fount from which the tribunal draws its knowledge.

This difference of approach is usually characterised by describing our system as adversarial and the civilian systems as inquisitorial. These terms describe the two different procedural approaches to litigation.

However, they also describe a much more significant difference, a difference that I have characterised as autonomy. There is no civil law equivalent to the peculiarly common-law doctrines that a tribunal is ignorant of the law and does not itself gather in the facts. Take knowledge of the law first. A civilian tribunal is subject to the well-known principle: *jura novit curia*, which, in a loose but fair translation, means that it is for the court to know the law. However, any tribunal in the English system is entitled to work on the basis that it will be informed of the law by the parties who bear the responsibility of submitting the law to the tribunal. No common law judge or arbitrator knows the law. The pages of the Journal of the Chartered Institute of Arbitrators have from time to time been filled with a discussion as to whether or not it is the duty of an advocate appearing before an arbitrator to bring to the arbitrator's attention any decision adverse to the party for whom the advocate is appearing. This is a duty imposed on all advocates in all courts and one which is a consequence of the absence of a principle of *jura novit curia*. A clear answer, at least for barristers, is that there is such a duty. Paragraph 610(c) of the current 5th Edition of the Code of Conduct is unequivocal in imposing a duty on a barrister to inform "the court" (which is defined in the Code to include any tribunal in which a barrister may appear as an advocate) of all relevant decisions and legislative provisions of which he or she is aware whether they be favourable or unfavourable to the contention for which he or she is arguing.

Autonomy

The autonomy of which I speak is particularly marked in the factual sphere. The tribunal in England has always had a limited power to call for documents, summon witnesses and take judicial notice of facts not formally proved. But these powers are rarely used. This is not merely a philosophical approach that the common law has adopted. It is a highly practical one too. If a tribunal is to participate in the investigation and preparation of a case, it needs both time and resources to undertake such a task and the English system gives it neither.

Consider the French system as an alternative. A full statement in writing is required from each party at the outset of its respective case. These statements set out the evidence, both in terms of the facts relied on and how those facts are intended to be proved. Relevant documents are annexed to the statements. These materials form the basis of the dossier which the tribunal then opens. In many courts in France and elsewhere, even at first instance, there is a banc of three judges but this is not an essential feature of the civilian system. What is essential to the system is that all further investigations are in the hands of the tribunal. The judge will call on one party or the other to produce further material or instruct the greffier, or clerk of the court, to obtain it. The judge will commission expert evidence and supervise its production and elaboration. These experts' reports will be added to the dossier. Any interrogation of witnesses will be undertaken by, or at the direction of, the judge and the planning and programming of the trial will lie exclusively in the judge's hands. Finally, the dossier is summarised and the judgment is settled and published.

This is, to some extent, a caricature of a French civil trial but it does not, I believe, do undue injustice to the civilian system, a system that is not inherently defective but which is very labour intensive. In England, there are about 2,000 judicial officers including all judges, district judges and full-time chairmen of tribunals and stipendiary magistrates. In Germany, there are currently well over 20,000 judicial officers and in France at least 10,000. A further feature of the civilian system is that there are a significantly greater number of disputes actually decided by the courts and there is no requirement that there be an oral, public hearing. Furthermore, the hearing need not be continuous. Undoubtedly, these features of the civilian system are, in part, culturally-based but, nonetheless, they are the consequence of a lack of what I have called autonomy. Any significant departure from English principles of autonomy could have profound effects on the resources required by this system and could also have profound effects on the number of disputes coming into the system. Furthermore, none of the participants in the system, be they judges, arbitrators, advocates, litigators or court staff, have been trained or acclimatised to a system that is, literally, tribunal-led.

Disclosure

In turning to examine the disclosure principle, I bring to your attention the report of Sir Richard Scott[4] into the circumstances surrounding the sales of arms to Iraq and the prosecution of four people involved in a related criminal trial. Much of that report is concerned with public interest immunity and the extent to which it is legitimate for the state to withhold relevant documents from litigants, particularly but not exclusively criminal defendants, because their disclosure is contrary to the public interest in allowing policy documents of the executive to remain confidential. This ongoing debate highlights the fundamental approach of the English common law that all parties in civil litigation have a duty to disclose to other parties all relevant materials. The civil law does not impose a similar duty on litigants since the tribunal has the ultimate duty of obtaining all materials. .

In speaking of disclosure, I am not merely speaking of disclosure of documents, although that is an important part of the process. I am also speaking of the basic approach adopted by our system to the litigation process. Parties must disclose all aspects of their case long before trial and may not easily amend it near to, or during, the trial itself. Parties must tender their evidence for critical examination. This examination may be oral, by way of cross-examination. It may be on oath but in writing, by way of interrogatories and affidavits verifying the accuracy and full extent of discovery. Expert witnesses must meet and produce written agreements as to the extent of technical disagreements between them and any report that is tendered is to be the evidence and opinion of the expert uninfluenced by the exigencies of litigation or the gloss and interpretation of lawyers.

Probity

This leads directly to my final principle, that of probity. I refer to the ethical rules governing the professional behaviour of judges, arbitrators, advocates and litigants. These rules place high standards of behaviour upon the participants. In the case of lawyers, whether case-

---

[4] *Report of the Inquiry into the Export of Defence Equipment and Dual-Use Goods to Iraq and Related Prosecutions* 1995-1996 HC.

presenters or case-preparers, they are bound by three duties—to justice, to the tribunal and to the client. At times, the first two over-ride the third and litigants from other countries, even those with a common law tradition, are often surprised at the way that their interests are potentially over-ridden by the duty of the advocate not to mislead and of the litigator to disclose prejudicial materials. There are many further duties owed to a tribunal. For example, a barrister must return, unused, privileged material obtained by mistake, must withdraw from a case if the client instructs the barrister not to disclose materials that the barrister becomes aware of that should be disclosed, and must not devise facts, ask scandalous questions or impugn witnesses who the barrister has had the opportunity to cross examine but who have not been given the opportunity to answer the allegations. I suggest that the extent of the pre-trial deposition process and discovery motions in American litigation result, in part, from professional standards that are neither as extensive nor as well observed and enforced as are their English counterparts.

Duties and Standards

The duties to which I have referred above have been developed over seven centuries for barristers and over four centuries for solicitors and their forebears, the attorneys and the proctors. An advocate was one who addressed the court on behalf of another who then swore the truth of what had been said on his behalf. In the ensuing centuries, largely due to the influence of training exercises in the Inns of Court and of the judges acting as Visitors to those Inns, the ingrained professional duties that I have referred to were developed. The attorney, who had the authority of his client to enter his case on the court rolls, had to be licensed by the court in question by also being entered on its rolls. That process made him an officer of the court, he had to observe the strict requirements of the court and could be summarily punished by the judge and have his name struck from the rolls for any transgression.

These high ethical standards depend, in part, on a balance having been struck. If each party must disclose its case in full, warts and all, the tribunal in return must be capable of being relied upon to decide the case on the evidence it has heard and not on evidence that it has received by its own initiative, particularly evidence which is unanswered or not commented upon, otherwise the advocate or the litigator cannot and will not observe the same duties to the court and to justice as are currently expected of them.

The system also places duties on the tribunal. I will refer to one of these duties, owed by judges and arbitrators alike. This is the duty to be free of prejudice and partiality. Of course, no tribunal in any system can fairly have a pecuniary interest in the outcome. But, in our system, the tribunal must not provide assistance or advantage to one party not afforded to the other. This duty is enforced, for judges, by three requirements, those of public justice, reasoned decisions and a ready avenue of appeal. An arbitrator may be released from these requirements, but only by the decision, or autonomy, of the parties. If the parties wish to have the hearing in public, obtain a reasoned award or appeal on questions of law, the arbitrator is bound to comply. Those who advocate that there should be a mandatory limitation on the ability to appeal questions of law raised by an arbitrator's award give, I suggest, insufficient weight to the discipline imposed on an arbitrator by the potential of an appeal.

The result of all these principles taken together is that the system is perceived as one in which disputes will be determined by neutral tribunals relying only on the materials the parties have placed before them. The parties can be relied upon to have revealed all relevant materials. The weight and reliability of these materials will have been tested and the decision-making process will be transparent, impartial and open to correction where abuse is detectable. Any reform of the system and any working within it should seek to maintain that balance. I stress again that this arrangement of the spokes of the wheel is not immutable. I merely draw attention to the fact that the pattern of the spokes must always be examined as a whole.

Procedural Details of the Present System

These procedural details flesh out the requirements of fairness or natural justice and procedural regularity. The recent growth of public law has, incidentally, led to a much clearer articulation of these requirements. In summary, any tribunal whose decision is susceptible to judicial review must, in fulfilling its duty to comply with the rules of natural justice, also comply with a number of essential procedural steps. These steps must also be complied with by arbitrators and no judge who departed from them would find his judgment upheld on appeal. In general terms, a tribunal may not be a judge in its own cause and may not condemn a party who has been unheard. This latter principle was enshrined by Fortescue J. when condemning the Chancellor of Cambridge University in 1723: "No man shall be condemned unless he has been given prior notice of the allegations against him and a fair opportunity to be heard".[5] These requirements are buttressed by requirements of procedural fairness before and during the hearing and as to the manner in which the decision is structured. The touchstone of procedural fairness is this: did the hearing allow each party to obtain fairness of the sort referred to by Fortescue J.?

English civil trials currently provide six procedural means of securing fairness. These are pleadings, discovery, expert evidence, factual evidence, cross-examination and both written and oral submissions. What Lord Woolf and the Arbitration Act 1996 are, essentially, striving for is the means whereby the time and expense involved in deploying these six processes can be reduced without undermining the principles that I have already outlined. The six are closely inter-related and any trial or pre-trial procedure must carefully blend each with the other five.

Agenda for Trial

It is worth, at this point, pausing to consider the way in which the English process sets the agenda for the trial. I deliberately use that phrase to highlight a further feature of the English litigation process. This is that the process has a clearly defined focus culminating in a

---

[5] *R v Chancellor of Cambridge University* (1723) 1 Stra. 557 at 567.

contentious hearing. The hearing need not, in fact, be an oral process. A "documents only hearing" may be an oxymoron but it is a well-recognised procedure in arbitration and, to some extent, in smaller court cases. What is required, however, is a concluding part of the dispute-resolution process when all the materials are gathered together and considered together in the round in a continuous process. When part of the procedure is oral, this process, or trial, takes place on successive working days and the agenda is carefully prepared and strictly followed. This process is very different in a civil system. The dossier is completed by irregular and disjunctive steps, is reviewed piecemeal and the focus of the process is the decision which may have been preceded by a hearing but not necessarily by a lengthy hearing nor by one which is a culmination of the process. The "continuous hearing" is a process which is deeply ingrained into our procedure and is one which the six procedural parts that I have referred to must be tailored to meet.

The trial or hearing is strictly structured because it is, in truth, a process of deciding issues. The jury, when it was habitually used as a means of resolving factual disputes in civil cases, answered a series of questions posed by the judge. Many of the procedures now followed have, as their origins, the attempts by lawyers to focus the trial by identifying the issues to be decided or by attempts to prevent the case getting to the jury at all. This was achieved by devising complex rules about demurrer, pleas in bar and the like and by setting up alternative courts whether of equity, common pleas or exchequer. My own title of Official Referee refers to the office set up in 1875 as a means whereby businessmen could remove their complex factual disputes from the jury without having to have them arbitrated since arbitration was reviled in late-Victorian England. My forebears, non-practising barristers who were not judges, had referred to them by the court disputes for a report which was then referred back to the court. Since these individuals were full-time officeholders, they were not only referees but official referees.

I digress. Our pre-trial procedures have been devised to identify what is in dispute. This is done by segregating out issues or questions which must be answered by the tribunal when travelling along the critical path to a decision. The process seeks to identify the issues that are agreed so that the agenda at the trial can be focused on the disputed issues and their resolution. I turn now to examine each of the six parts of the process in turn.

Pleadings

The present form and function of pleadings is comparatively recent and only goes back to the great Victorian reforms, whereby the forms of action were abolished and law and equity were fused. Before 1852 and the reforms of the Common Law Procedure Act, a plaintiff had to lodge with the court a writ or plea which identified the precise form of action relied upon. The writ did not disclose the evidence to be adduced and the parties would usually engage in repetitive pre-hearing jousting by which the defendant sought to exclude the action as disclosing no cause of action and as one located in the wrong court whereas the plaintiff sought, usually with the assistance of bills filed in equity, to obtain the documents and evidence needed to support his writ.

When the modern rules of court were introduced in 1875, these procedural complexities were, in theory, swept away. Instead, the plaintiff had to set out his claim in a statement which "in summary form set out the material facts on which he relies but not the evidence by which those facts are to be proved". What has gone wrong is that the distinction between the facts and the evidence by which those facts are to be proved has become blurred. Even Sir Jack Jacob, the doyen of civil procedure and the long-standing Chief Editor of the White Book, has described the distinction as one which requires great skill to maintain and is frequently unattainable. This has led to pleadings that suffer from two inter-related features, they rarely define the issues and they paraphrase the available evidence at great and often unread length. These problems are to be swept away by the Woolf reforms. In principle, short statements of principle will define the rules of pleading. They will require a document which succinctly states the facts entitling a remedy, the actual remedy claimed and any matters of law and principle needed to establish that remedy.

This approach was, however, adopted by the Victorian draftsman of the 1875 Rules of Court. He was sufficiently confident of the correctness of his technique that he had his rules annexed to the Judicature Act

1875 as a schedule. What went wrong? I ask that question because those who operate the new procedures will be seeking to avoid the same mistakes. I can only offer three partial answers to the question.

The first is that the pleadings are the documents that set the scene at the outset of the procedural process. That process is protean. As the facts, documents and issues unfold, so the pleadings become dated. Yet, the parties may only present their pleaded cases at trial. In consequence, the pleadings seek to keep open all avenues so that, at trial months or years later and after many subsequent developments, a party is not procedurally wrong-footed. There is a need, at least in complex cases, for relatively short initial pleadings to be up-dated, at little cost, just before the trial or for a party to be able to rely on subsequent materials without being held to the initial pleadings. It will be necessary for there to be a sanction, by way of exclusion or costs, if evidence or facts are put forward which bear no obvious relationship to any reasonable development of the initial pleading.

The second problem is that the principle has developed whereby each side should know the other side's case before it reveals its own. Of course, taken to the limit, this is a logical impossibility. However, lists of documents, statements, reports and submissions are usually exchanged. This leads to each side pressing the other for greater and greater particularity in its pleaded case so as to minimise the perceived but usually imaginary risk that the exchanged material will unfairly prejudice the party proffering it. If, in principle, a party can always be required to lead at any stage of the proceedings, there is less need to deploy a case in detail at the outset. Preparation for trial can, instead, develop organically.

The final problem is that the statement of claim is required to identify a cause of action and the defence to traverse every allegation and advance every feature of a positive case in reply. Unparticularised "pregnant negatives" may not be pleaded. These requirements can and should be relaxed. They are only needed to enable the striking out procedure to be operated and to prevent embarrassment by one side of the other. However, if the control procedures that are to be operated by the tribunal at each stage are effective, the pleadings need only identify the salient features of a party's case.

If these principles are observed, it is to be hoped that a modern feature of complex technical disputes will be avoided. An extreme example of this is a case where the detail is set out six times: firstly in the pleadings, then in particulars, then in schedules, then in the witness statements, then in the experts' reports and finally in skeleton arguments. Ideally, each part of a case should be set out once with, possibly, a final composite document which can be prepared towards the end of the process and which would be part pleading, part schedule and part submission.

Discovery

The process whereby a party must make available documents adverse to its case or which "lead to a train of inquiry" is, historically, part of a wider process which allows one party to interrogate the other party. Both procedures were developed in equity to mitigate the rigours imposed on litigants by the common law that required strict proof by litigants who often lacked the means to achieve this because the relevant deed or conveyance was in the hands of the opposing party. The Bill of Discovery was developed in equity and, by the nineteenth century, it enabled documents and evidence to be obtained in order to supply vital evidence or to prevent expense and delay.

Clearly, as Lord Woolf recognises, the discovery process must be curtailed. Since I am concerned with technical litigation, I will concentrate on the proposals for multi-track litigation. The case management procedures being evolved will require detailed consideration of what discovery should be ordered, in addition to the discovery to be provided by the standard discovery process. In making the relevant decisions about what discovery should be given, it may be useful to bear a number of factors in mind about the current rules and practices.

The first is that the current rule, known as the Peruvian Guano rule, is often misunderstood and misapplied. The only material that that 1883 Court of Appeal decision requires to be disclosed is:

- documents which directly or indirectly advanced the opposing party's case or damages his own; and

- documents which might fairly lead an opposing party on a train of inquiry which might have either of these consequences.

The relevant limitations are "directly" and "train of inquiry". The narrowness of these limitations can be seen from the *Peruvian Guano* case itself.[6] In that case it was alleged by the plaintiff that an agreement, compromising a dispute, had been broken by the defendant. The defendant's case was that there never had been a concluded agreement, that negotiations for that purpose had continued throughout the relevant period and that there was, therefore, no breach of contract. The documents in question were minutes of board meetings of the plaintiff subsequent to the alleged agreement. Clearly, what was said at those meetings might well indicate whether, at the time, the plaintiff was in fact proceeding on the basis that no concluded agreement had been reached. However, in a passage that is not usually referred to, Brett LJ. stated that if the documents showed that there had been attempts to negotiate a settlement, such documents need not be disclosed. This shows that the test of relevance was, in Brett LJ's mind, a narrow test. If the documents did no more than support the plaintiff's case, the plaintiff need not disclose them. They only became disclosable if they tended to show the opposite. No litigator today would conclude that a plaintiff's documents, which merely supported its case, were not disclosable because they were irrelevant.

What has happened is that, since the photocopier was invented, commercial documentation has multiplied and the limiting factors I have referred to have been relaxed. However, a document which advances or damages a case is, broadly, one which, but for the hearsay rules, would prove or disprove an issue in the case by reference to its own contents. A document only puts a litigator on a train of inquiry if its contents point to a source of evidence which will prove or disprove an issue. Unfortunately, when the documentation is vast, the task of

---

6   *Compagnie Financiere du Pacifique v Peruvian Guano Company* (1882) 11 QBD 55

sifting the documentation defeats even the most conscientious and the result is to over-disclose. This can be seen from an examination of trial bundles. It is invariably the case that only one-hundredth of the contents of trial bundles are referred to at the trial. This is because those who prepare trial bundles are doing so from an excessive mass of documentation. Thornton's Law of Documentation states that ten times too many documents are disclosed and a hundred times too many documents are placed in trial bundles. The irrationality of the present system is shown by the rule that a core bundle of documents should be prepared for the trial containing particularly relevant documents. This process would be unnecessary if only relevant documents had been put into the trial bundles in the first place.

Thus, even if the multi-track approach to discovery is adopted, a means of speedy and economical filleting is required. I suggest that these rules might assist:

1.   No document passing between two parties need be disclosed to the opposing party. Any notation or addition to a party's copy should, however, if known about, be disclosed.
2.   Relevance should be better defined so as to clearly identify its true scope.
3.   The use of document search techniques and protocols for computer-assisted discovery should be developed.
4.   The only issues for which discovery should be provided should be those identified in the initial pleadings

Evidence

I turn now to evidence. This is adduced through witness statements. At present, most witness statements contain lengthy and inadmissible paraphrases of contemporary documents and the system of preparing them is much in need of change. It is first worth noticing the Civil Evidence Act 1995 which, I believe, can transform civil litigation since, in effect, it abolishes the hearsay rule. Section 1 of the Act provides that evidence shall not be excluded on the grounds that it is hearsay. The Act is now in force.[7] The effect is that, in practical terms, that the contents of any document are capable of proving themselves unless the contrary is established by cross-examination or by other evidence. If the juridical rules are used to devise effective working practises, witness statements can be reduced in scope enormously. This is because a witness need only put into a statement any fact not gleaned from a contemporaneous document. What will be required is for each party to identify its evidence as follows:

- To highlight which parts of which document it relies upon. This could be done by listing the facts relied upon and by cross-referring those facts to the relevant document.
- Serving witness statements which plug the few evidential gaps.
- Serve further documents or witness statements which identify the facts in an opposing party's documents and statements which are challenged.

This procedure could be linked to rules and practices which limit both the content of, and time allowed for, cross-examination, both being determined by reference to the evidence that a party has already identified as being challenged.

Expert evidence

This type of evidence is more problematical. Much discussion of this topic is obscured by a failure to appreciate an ambiguity in modern practice as to what is meant by expert evidence. Originally, expert evidence was evidence of opinion. It was admitted as an exception to the exclusionary rule that the tribunal decided the issues and, hence, the witnesses' opinions as to such issues were irrelevant. Lord Mansfield set the stage in a civil engineering dispute concerned with whether an embankment had caused the silting of a harbour in a judgment in 1782 which included the following statement: "Mr.Smeaton understands the construction of harbours, the causes of

---

[7]   The relevant Rules of Court are set out in RSC O.38, r.3A.

their destruction and how they are remedied. In matters of science no other witnesses can be called."[8]

However, nowadays, the admission of the evidence of expert witnesses has been extended to cover the evidence, whether factual or opinion, of any witness which is relevant and which depends, in part, on the technical or specialist knowledge or training of a particular witness for its content or veracity. There are at least five categories of expert evidence:

1. Primary evidence, usually produced by forensic means. Any laboratory testing, statistical data or evidence dependent upon observation requiring training or experience to assimilate falls into this category.

2. Background evidence needed to set the scene which requires technical expertise or knowledge. A description of how a piece of software is programmed, how a machine is designed or how a relevant tendering exercise is performed are examples of this category of expert evidence.

3. Valuation and accounting evidence. Such evidence is part factual, part forensic investigation and part opinion evidence, usually of a very subjective kind.

4. Evidence of causation. This evidence seeks to explain why an event in issue occurred or the link between breach and damage or the causal connection between events in issue. This is evidence of both fact and opinion.

5. Opinion evidence, usually of professional standards, current practices or of what could reasonably have been expected of an individual given the actual or presumed facts in issue.

I have omitted evidence of claims consultants and quantity surveyors, particularly in construction disputes. A tendency has grown up to adduce evidence from such persons, in the guise of opinion evidence, when the evidence is, in truth, second-hand factual hearsay. The

---

[8] *Folkes v Chado* (1782) 3 Doug KB 157

witness will read the contemporaneous documents and then express an opinion on whether delay has been caused, expense incurred or a breach of contract perpetrated. Such evidence is inadmissible and construction litigation would be enormously simplified and reduced in scope and expense if it was rigorously excluded. This exclusion would not eliminate so-called planning evidence, often supported by computerised analyses. The analyses fall into my first category, being primary evidence, and the commentary is, or can be confined to, opinion evidence.

The reason for labouring this analysis of expert evidence is two-fold. Firstly, any issue-identification process should take into account these different features of expert evidence. Questions concerned with admissibility, the sequence and timing of meetings, reports, supplementary reports, agreements as to disputed and agreed issues and as to whether to allow cross-examination and, if so, when and for how long need to be addressed in relation to each category of expert evidence separately. Secondly, it helps to consider the potential use of court-appointed experts. These could usefully provide some primary, background and evaluation evidence but are less obviously capable of being used in relation to questions of causation and opinion.

This leads me to consider two particular categories, those concerned with causation and opinion. They involve evidence containing detailed scientific evidence yet the legal process does not readily accommodate itself to scientific methods. For example, it makes no sense to a medical witness to ask whether, on the balance of probabilities, whooping-cough vaccine caused a paralysing spasm within the brain. Scientists search for certainty, not for probability.

We owe much to Sir Karl Popper for our understanding of scientific methods. It was he who explained that scientific knowledge is provisional. What is known cannot be proved to be true and it may turn out to be false. What a scientist seeks to do is to justify his preference for one theory over another. A scientifically true statement is one which has the least insecure foundation available. The truth must be tested against all available data. The better a proposition stands up to these comparison tests, the more confident will the scientist be that the relevant statement is true, that is, is one that is incapable of being demonstrated to be false.

This understanding of scientific method is important when scientists are concerned with causation. For example, whether or not clay heave or structural instability, or both, caused cracking in a particular building will depend, in an engineer's view, upon inspections, empirical data, soils investigations, and whether or not the primary facts appear to correspond with current codes of practice, experience, local knowledge and the ascertained opinions of others in what appear to be comparable situations. These opinions will be gathered from many sources including technical papers and publications, journals, ad hoc notifications, local experience and unrecorded data.

However, as long as a scientist's approach to scientific inquiry is appreciated, the common law can grapple with the problems of causation and opinion particularly if recourse is made to a much over-looked but important judgment of the then Bingham J. in the Schering Chemicals case in 1983.[9] In that case, the issue was whether a pregnancy testing drug caused birth defects. The plaintiff wanted to adduce much background technical data and relevant papers as the means of proving certain primary facts. The plaintiff sought to use a combination of the Civil Evidence Act 1968 and the rule of court that allows the court to direct how evidence is to be adduced at trial. The judge ruled that neither procedure was available to the plaintiff but he then ruled as follows, in a short extempore passage of great force:

> "*The articles can be referred to by experts as part of the general corpus of medical knowledge falling within the expertise of an expert in this field. That of course means that an expert who says ..... 'I consider there is a causal connection between the taking of the drug and the resulting deformity' can fortify his opinion by referring to learned articles, publications, letters as reinforcing the view to which he has come. In doing so, he can make reference to papers in which the contrary opinion may be expressed but in which figures are set out which he regards as supporting his contention. In such a situation one asks: are the figures and*

---

[9] *H. v. Schering Chemicals Ltd.* [1983] 1 WLR 143

statistics set out in such an article strictly true? And I think the answer is no. I think that they are nonetheless of probative value when referred to and relied on by an expert in the manner in which I have indicated. If an expert refers to the results of research published by a reputable authority in a reputable journal the court would, I think, ordinarily regard those results as supporting inferences fairly to be drawn from them unless and until a different approach was shown to be proper."[10]

What is needed then is an approach to expert evidence which carefully identifies the issues to which that evidence is to be adduced. Where the evidence consists of materials of the kind addressed by Bingham J., these should be listed out at an early stage. Throughout the process of gathering and preparing evidence, sequential service is better than mutual exchange so that each expert can answer the opposing expert's points of view. The final statement agreed by the experts, currently under Order 38 Rule 38, is the vital last link in this process since, if that statement fairly and accurately lists all relevant technical issues that are agreed and disagreed, with brief reasons for any disagreements, the scope and extent of cross-examination and argument at trial can be reduced enormously or, often, can be eliminated altogether.

There are three further inter-related features of expert evidence which should be considered. The first is the rule of both law and professional ethics that provides that the evidence of an expert should be, as Lord Wilberforce put it, untainted by the exigencies of litigation.[11] The effect of this rule is that neither an advocate nor a litigator should play any part in the drafting of, or even, strictly, the layout and content of, an expert's report. This can and does create great difficulties for litigants on occasion. Clearly, the substantive content of an expert's report should be that of the expert. However, the issues that should be covered, the way that the evidence on those issues should be laid out, the topics to be covered in "without prejudice" meetings with other experts and other presentational matters cannot fairly be left exclusively to an expert witness. Moreover, many experts are not as

---

[10]   *Ibid* at 148

[11]   See Lord Wilberforce's speech in *Whitehouse v Jordan* [1981] 1 WLR 246 at 256

used to expressing their views in a formal context as lawyers are and assistance in the drafting of passages of the report so that they accurately reflect the expert's real meaning is often helpful. In my view the rules should be relaxed so as to allow input in relation to these matters without, in any way, compromising the independence and impartiality of the expert so far as his opinions are concerned.

My other two comments relate to current suggestions that the courts should appoint experts, possibly on occasions to the exclusion of parties relying on their own experts, and that any communication with an expert should not be subject to "without prejudice" privilege. A court-appointed expert may be appropriate to deal with purely factual and forensic matters. I cannot see that fairness to the parties can be provided if a court-appointed expert is allowed to deal with opinion evidence or causation. Equally, I think that any breach of the "without prejudice" privilege rules associated with the preparation for, and conduct of, litigation, even if confined to expert evidence, would be a very dangerous step. Although these proposals are put forward as a means of economising and saving resources, there is, as I see it, a grave danger that the principles upon which our system of litigation is based, that I have sought to identify already, could be seriously compromised if these proposals were introduced to any significant extent. An advocate or litigator's duties to justice and to the tribunal are difficult enough to achieve. It would be placing potentially insuperable burdens on lawyers if their present ethical duties have to be fulfilled with the "without prejudice" privilege having been partially abrogated and if a party cannot rely, to any significant extent, on an expert witness that it wishes to appoint.

Cross-examination

This feature of procedure fulfils two vital functions. It enables a party to explore and expose an opposing party's weaknesses, particularly when the evidence that has been tendered is tempered or even untrue. Nothing is more likely to expose the liar than a short but effective cross-examination. The second purpose is to put specific aspects of a party's case to an opposing party so that these can be tested by extracting the evidence and comments of the opposing party. This is particularly helpful when a party may not, deliberately or inadvertently, have dealt with part of the opposing case. Cross-examination is often regarded as an integral part of the adversarial process not found in the inquisitorial process. This masks the fact that, in an inquisitorial process, the tribunal conducts its own questioning of a party's case and, therefore, cross-examination is shifted from the representatives of the parties to the tribunal. In my view the ability to cross-examine in appropriate circumstances is an essential ingredient of a fair trial. Undoubtedly the extent of cross-examination and the time to be allowed for cross-examination can be carefully controlled. If pre-trial management is carefully handled, the need for cross-examination can be significantly reduced. At the trial, once the issues have been identified and all the evidence and supporting materials have been marshalled, the tribunal both can and should be provided with the means of testing the evidence and exploring each side's weaknesses. Without cross-examination, these tasks can only be fulfilled, if at all, by the tribunal entering into the arena itself.

Submissions

In the last 10 years, all advocates have become familiar with written submissions. These tend to take one of three forms although I am, in reality, identifying three points on a spectrum. The document produced by an advocate can be a full written speech, it can be a summary which, in particular, identifies the propositions of law and the factual material relied upon or it can be a skeleton index of the submission to be advanced. Unfortunately, no uniform practice has yet developed as to which kind of written material is appropriate for any particular occasion, nor as to how an advocate should make use of written material in a subsequent oral address. In general terms, a skeleton is appropriate to open a case, a summary is appropriate in relation to any argument or submission that does not involve reliance upon oral evidence and a closing speech is best dealt with with a full written document to supplement it. An advocate, armed with a written adjunct to an oral submission should use that document as an aide memoire rather than as a text to be read, like this lecture, to a captive audience.

Conclusion

I have sought to deal, albeit briefly, with the salient features of the litigation process. I now return, in conclusion, to three themes that I have already dealt with. First and foremost, I stress that the litigation process is to be regarded as a dynamic whole. Each part of the process should be considered, and operated, in conjunction with each other part of the process. Those concerned with complex cases need, for example, when settling the pleadings to have thought out how those pleadings will assist, and be used in, each subsequent stage of the litigation. Equally, any move to curtail discovery may lead to the need for more extensive cross-examination and too restrictive an approach as to expert evidence may lead to unnecessarily lengthy submissions at trial. If, however, each part of the process is adapted and used with each other part of the process in mind, there is clearly scope for considerable economies of both resources and costs in comparison with our existing procedures.

The second point I would stress is that the system that is being reformed is a common law system which is based on an adversarial approach in the sense that I have described this evening. Unless and until it can be seen quite clearly that the system is incapable of being reformed, it would be both premature and foolhardy to seek to jettison this approach for what are perceived to be the advantages to be gained from a civil law system. Our own system has sufficient strengths to enable it to be developed rather than jettisoned.

Thirdly, and finally, I turn back to Brunel and the litigation that he engineered. When one considers how inadequate the resources of the nineteenth-century litigator were compared with our own, it is remarkable that cases of such complexity were decided and concluded at all. Even in a modern stream-lined system, a suit involving 900 items with all the factual and technical complexities that were involved would take an enormous amount of time and effort to resolve. The system can be reformed and, given the will and a measure of good fortune, I believe that Brunel's twenty-first century counterparts can be made to submit to judgment in a timescale and at a cost that does not cause the latter-day equivalent of the McIntoshes' executors to give up exhausted before the litigation process has been concluded.

Part II

Procurement and Project Strategy

7. The Economic Realities of Construction

John Uff, QC & Edmund Ryan

Synopsis

The paper examines current views on the issues of efficiency and reform in construction contracts and procurement. It is suggested that treatment of these issues at all levels has exhibited a reluctance to recognise the true economic interests of the parties and the consequences of those interests. Other influences on forms of contract and procurement methods are examined and proposals made for a fresh approach to efficiency in construction.

Introduction

There is a striking similarity between proposals currently in circulation for the reform of construction contract procedures[1] and those for the reform of civil procedure.[2] They have at least the following in common:

- present procedures are perceived to be inefficient;
- cost savings are demanded to produce better value for money;
- the development of a more rapid and efficient means of dispute resolution is regarded as a key factor;
- many reports on the same theme have been produced over the past half century; and
- at the heart of the problem is an entrenched system, based on established professional structures, which has shown itself to be highly resistant to change.

The last proposition would readily be accepted in the case of civil procedure but perhaps less so in relation to construction. It will be

---

1 Sir Michael Latham, *Constructing the Team*, HMSO, London, 1994
2 Lord Woolf, *Access to Justice – Interim Report*, HMSO, London, June 1995

suggested that the entrenched position of the professional bodies within the UK construction industry bears a major segment of responsibility for the seeming inability to effect changes in procurement methods as well as management techniques in construction. In this sense, Sir Michael Latham and Lord Woolf have been fighting the same battle.

The objective of reform, both in construction and in civil procedure is to realise the massive potential for cost saving. In the cause of construction, domestic costs are significantly higher than those of competitors, particularly competitors within the European Community.

Any serious analysis of the operation of the construction industry must identify self-interest and take into account the true goal of commercial organisations. Latham has attempted this in relation to the main Contracting parties suggesting that the avoidance of Conflict is an overriding interest to contractors. But the interests of professional bodies and their members were not considered. There seems to be a tacit assumption that construction professionals stand aloof, independent and untouched by self-interest. This makes it appropriate for them to promulgate standard forms of contract in which their interests are prominently represented. This situation calls for reconsideration. It is, therefore, suggested that professionals should be regarded in the same light, and with the same degree of critical analysis, as any other producer within the construction process.

The most convenient vehicle for reform is the construction contract coupled with the procurement system, including the chain of obligations and rights thereby created. A subsidiary but relevant factor in the process of reform is to identify the party who should initiate the reform. There is a strong traditional bias in favour of the professional bodies, with the major employers also taking a prominent role. Of lesser prominence, historically, has been the contractor, yet he is the party required to take the major part of the risk and to carry out the bulk of the physical work. There are grounds to suggest that the most appropriate party to produce contract forms should be the party who is to carry out the project and bear the risks inherent in the work.

Competition

Procurement methods are inevitably influenced by competition, which is an inescapable requirement of projects involving major expenditure, whether private or public finance is involved. While competition on price is essential to maintain a healthy market, it is suggested that incentives must also exist to produce quality and thus best value. In relation to professional services it has been recognised that competition based purely on price involves potentially serious disadvantages, not least in tending to stifle innovation. In terms of construction work, however, the present professional-dominated procurement systems mean that the principal areas of competition must be in the unit price for carrying out fully specified work, the contract being awarded to the tenderer who prepared to reduce these prices to the lowest aggregated level. It is notorious that, in some cases at least, low tenders are submitted in the expectation of enhanced recovery through claims. There can therefore be no assumption that the lowest tender represents the best value in overall terms and there is much evidence to suggest that this is often not so. No procedures exist for determining the "best value" tender and an attempt to do so would negate the whole system of competition.

In order to achieve true and meaningful competition between producers in the construction industry a new approach to procurement is needed to enable producers to mobilise all viable means of competition. These should include management and application of design skills in the same manner as would apply in any other major supply industry. The professional structure of the UK construction industry can be seen as depriving producers of these major elements of competition. The Latham Report declared major cost reductions of up to 30 per cent. were possible. The way in which these savings could be achieved was not explained in the Report but the idea is by no means new. The essential element which could unlock savings at this level is the opportunity for true and full competition. Unfortunately this was not an option developed in the Latham Report. This option is discussed further below.

Latham and self-interest

Long before the inception of the Latham Report there was a widespread feeling in the UK construction industry that major reforms were needed. Many of the recommendation for reform contained in the Report have been applauded as positive steps towards better organisation within construction. However, implementation of the recommendations has been slow particularly when seen against the speed with which the Report was produced. There has been a tendency to accept protracted debate as a substitute for action. Why should there be such difficulty in putting the recommendations into effect? One reason it is suggested is that the Latham Report fails to address or to identify the real driving force of self-interest.

The pursuit of self-interest is a normal consequence of economic activity in a commercial market. Self-interest would usually manifest itself in profit maximisation. Although this proposition is over-simplified it is sufficiently accurate for the present discussion. The call by Latham for "fair dealing" has obvious commercial limitations and the question must be asked how self-interest is to be reconciled with fair dealing. To have any substance, all players in the market must openly support fair dealings, for to do otherwise might damage their market position. This appears to have occurred at least at the level of debate. But there is scant evidence of anyone having changed their intended course of action because of a desire to deal "fairly". It would be wrong to say that bad faith otherwise determines commercial behaviour, but self-interest necessarily requires examination of economic consequences. Where dealing "fairly" would result in loss of some benefit an economic agent will be motivated to deal less than fairly, certainly if the chance of discovery was remote. The moral hazard, prevalent particularly in the insurance industry, is a testimony of this particular phenomenon.

Self-interest v. fair dealing

Latham has placed much emphasis on what is termed "win-win" as a solution to certain problems of the construction industry. "Win-win" generally appears to have the same meaning as "partnering" where the firms organising themselves for a construction project, should openly transact so as to achieve mutual respect for each other's trading position and interests.

Partnering has its roots in the "relational" contracts generated by the manufacturing industry[3] and has also been in evidence in construction as between contractor and subcontractors. It is a mechanism for aligning the interests of the parties. However, it is clear that self-interest remains the main dynamic because both parties achieve benefit through co-operation; the client pays promptly and with a minimum of investigation, gaining quality work without protracted negotiation; the contractor resists any temptation to maximise on opportunities, to pursue claims or otherwise, in return for ensuring future work from the client. An example of these kinds of arrangements can be found where some of the major retailers have a continuing programme of construction.

For partnering, as for relational contracts, the best chance of success is maximised in long term relationships. Construction is different from manufacturing in that the relationship with clients is often limited and not ongoing. While there are major clients who are capable of giving and obtaining benefits from partnering it cannot be regarded as a general panacea for construction. Furthermore, if partnering became widespread the benefits of competition would be lost. Competition regulates the market through prices. Without competition it would become impossible to define prices without independent and costly information gathering and co-ordination.

Value for money

Another concept highlighted by Latham as of major importance to the construction industry is "value for money". This principle indicates that the client requires the best quality at the least price. Such an aspiration is not surprising but it serves the interest of the client only. How is such a concept to be reconciled with self-interest? Competition on price only, will give the correct market price and is necessary as a regulating mechanism. The control of quality is a separate issue.

---

3   Macneil, I R., '*Economic analysis of contractual relations*' in Burrows, P. & Veljanovski, C., *Economic Approach to the Law*, 1981.

It is generally accepted that UK construction prices are too high and give poor value for money. To produce economic efficiency the total value of the transaction for construction should be maximised to all parties as a whole. Value maximisation for economic organisation is important to all transactions taking place in any commercial market, since it gives maximum benefit to society in allocating resources most efficiently. Construction projects should be organised so as to maximise the value as a whole, that is the best quality at the lowest cost to all parties to the transaction. It is suggested above that the means of increasing economic efficiency is through widening the ambit of competitive tendering thus reorganising the construction market.

Although the Latham Report has provoked much debate about the organisation of construction the conclusions evidently owe much to the members of the industry whose opinions were solicited of proffered. This may be seen as a proper way in which to define the problems of the industry. But given the unavoidable self-interest of the parties concerned, the conclusions as to remedies must be questioned. This is particularly so in regard to achievement of economically efficient industry.

The professions and self-interest

Many commercial transactions are simple and discrete and thus give rise to few problems in their completion. The ordinary sale of goods is a familiar process involving many millions of transactions that take place each day. As the sums of money involved become greater there may be more problems but again disputes are often resolved with little difficulty. The Latham Report gave some interesting comparisons in Table 1 between the motor industry, housing and general construction and posed the question as to why construction was such a poor performer.[4] The answer lies in the nature of the transaction. In the motor industry the contract is an entire contract for a finished product. The same often applies in the case of housing, although it may be more complex to execute. In these cases the consumer can inspect the

4 Rimmer, B., Conference organised by "Contracts Journal" and CASEC, London 15 December 1993.

finished product for suitability and quality before any transaction takes place.

General construction does not operate in this way. Design and construction are usually split into two separate contracts and the costs of co-ordination are considerable. The construction product cannot be manufactured in advance awaiting a buyer as in the examples given above. But the question should be asked whether the separation of design and construction is necessary. Traditionally, at the start of a construction project the client has sought advice from the professional. The professionals will then undertake services, including design but will not participate directly in providing the finished product.

The professional has been in an enviable position of being able to advise a client, who is often relatively ignorant of the construction process. Professionals as economic agents must act in their self-interest. It is not suggested that there exist any elements of bad faith in the professionals seeking to make the best of this situation. The professional has merely picked out those parts of the construction process which suits his commercial purposes best and offered this service to the client. The result is that the designer has up to quite recently avoided the risks involved in construction. In this dual role of designer and main adviser to the client, he has tended to give the professional the opportunity to protect himself from economic risk, which must result in increased risk for the client and others. A construction industry operating on this split basis, necessarily entails increased costs: a clear situation of economic inefficiency.

The special relationship between the professional and the client has led to the professional also assuming the administrative role in construction, a further opportunity to his advantage. Such a situation compounds the problem and it is now being openly recognised that the professional has often to be the judge of his own errors,[5] a difficult role for a self-interested agent. From the economic standpoint the construction professional is no different from all the other players in the construction market. Any artificial prominence or protection

---

5   Highways Agency, Trunk Roads and Motorways: Review of Contractual Arrangements, Consultation Document, January 1996

afforded to one player will have adverse economic consequences for the project and for the client.

Elements of economic construction

There have not been many attempts to analyse the construction organisation using economic theory and little interest seems to have been given to these attempts. The most notable was by Winch in 1989 when he reviewed a number of different theories and related them to construction.[6] Winch concentrated on transaction cost as a means of analysis and concluded that construction was a failed market. He called for more integration of design and the construction phase and in this respect blamed the professional institutions for prolonging the status quo. Others had used the transaction cost approach previously to analyse particular aspects of construction organisation.[7]

Over the past two decades transaction costs have been used to analyse industrial organisations[8] and also the law controlling the transactions. The main thrust of this type of analysis has been in intra-organisation, dealing with such questions as "make or buy", that is whether production should be organised within the firm or within the market. In construction, production is organised on an inter-firm relationship where the client goes to the market and buys the design and the construction from various firms, these relationships being controlled by contracts. It is the attributes of transaction costs in the inter-firm relationship that are of greatest interest in the present context and which should be considered for both organisational design and the design of the contract itself.

Because construction is complex and the design is usually incomplete at the start of building process the opportunity to renegotiate the price

---

6 Winch, G. '*Construction firm and construction project: a transaction cost approach*', **Construction Management and Economics**. 7. 331-347, (1989).
7 Reve, T and Levitt, R E., '*Organisation and Governance in Construction*' **Project Management** Vol. 2 No 1 Feb 17-25.
8 Williamson, O E., *Markets and Hierarchies: Analysis and Antitrust Implications*, Free Press, New York, 1975; Williamson, O. E. '*Transaction-cost economics: the governance of contractual relations*', **Journal of Law and Economics**, **22** 233-261, (1979); Williamson, O. E., *The Economic Institutions of Capitalism*, Free Press, New York, 1986.

exists post formal conclusion of the contract. In most market transactions, all price bargaining takes place before the transaction is completed so that if the bargaining is unsuccessful, the parties can withdraw at minimum cost. Such a situation does not exist in traditional construction contracts where much of the bargaining takes place after the transaction has been concluded and often after construction has taken place. In this environment opportunistic behaviour will dominate since both parties are locked-in and know that neither of them can withdraw without considerable cost. Put in an exaggerated form, the parties complete the work and then bargain for the prices afterwards.

Bargaining for the final price would be acceptable giving perfect information, as when both parties have full knowledge of the value that other party places on the transaction. However, such a situation rarely exists in any market and in construction information is usually incomplete or asymmetric. For example, contractors are often accused of tendering at a low price and seeking to make their profit on the claims; but the contractors will reply that claims are only a request for their fair entitlement. Which is correct?

All disagreements and disputes are manifestations of information-related problems. Most traditional forms of contract make it an employer liability where there are inconsistencies or ambiguities in the contract documents. If the contractor notices an inconsistency at tender stage he may be tempted not to reveal this and perhaps capitalise on this post-tender. If the contractor does not notice the inconsistency at tender stage and is faced with a clarification by the employer's agent, will he reveal that he used the more expensive alternative in his tender? Unfortunately when the contractor uses the least expensive alternative in his tender and reveals this fact to the employer's agent, he is unlikely to be believed. These are problems related to asymmetric information, which tend to suppress openness and trust.

Problems of incomplete information are even more prevalent. The best example of this exists in extension of time claims where the contractor has problems defining the extent of delay. To establish what has happened does not present too much of a problem. However, to ascertain the scope of delay necessarily requires not only the establishment of what has in fact taken place, but also what would have occurred had the delayed event not manifested. It is fair to say that the question of what would have occurred had the delaying event not manifested is impossible to establish with any degree of certainty. The effect of the delay and disruption to the contractors programme is equally uncertain. The difficulty involved in proof or negotiation of claims is immense.

Current traditional forms of contract produce an environment that promotes opportunistic behaviour where information is scarce. The result is that completion of the bargain is protracted and often requires a third party decision-maker to resolve disputes. The excess of bargaining leads to high transaction costs and increases the overall cost of the construction product.

An added factor in the present standard forms of contract which exacerbates protracted bargaining is the presence of a named client's agent. The client's agent has a limited remit which only allows him to bargain within the terms of the contract. Where information is incomplete it may be more efficient to seek a commercial settlement. But the client's agent cannot involve himself in such a settlement and bargaining continues for a long period on the contractual rights of the parties and the ascertainment of hard fact which does not exist. The client himself is the best party to reach settlement on commercial terms but many public agencies will not communicate with the contractor until a reference is made to arbitration.

Appropriate forms of contract

For more than thirty years there has been a call for a unified standard form of contract for the construction industry,[9] a call which was renewed in the Latham Report. The underlying rationale is that the unified form would be beneficial. Far from achieving this aim the past decade has seen a proliferation of standard forms. However, there has also been an increase in the number of different procurement methods available.

---

9 Banwell, H. The Placing and Management of Contracts for Building and Civil Engineering Work, Ministry of Public Building and Works. HMSO, London, 1964.

Why should a common form of contract be considered beneficial? The use of a common form will go some way to resolve the informational problems. With usage, the duties and liabilities will become well known to all parties engaged in construction and this should reduce the arguments about interpretation. Of much greater importance is the issue of what should be the basis of a unified form of contract? The Latham Report contains recommendations for good practice but gives little further direction apart from recommending NEC for common use. A DOE publication issued shortly after the Latham Report entitled "Fair Construction Contracts"[10] gave further indications. However, nowhere in this later document was there to be found clear guidance on what was considered a "fair" contract. Did "fair" mean an equitable allocation of risk? A fair contract could equally be interpreted as one, however onerous, in which the parties are fully enlightened as to the liabilities they are to incur and have ample opportunity to submit a tender to reflect these liabilities.

The preponderance of academic study has been towards the allocating of risk in a balanced way.[11] Research has produced principles for the balancing of risk.[12] The main theme running through risk allocation was controllability of the risk. Allocating the risk to the party that can best control events prior to and after the risk occurs is claimed to facilitate good management on the basis that it allows the party concerned to control his costs, usually by keeping them to a minimum in order to maximise profits. Although risk is important to the management of the internal organisation in construction there is no justification for regarding this factor as having over-riding significance in drafting the substance of the contract particularly in relation to market exchange between organisations. Given that it is good management practice to identify and control risk, it remains the case that efficient ascertainment of the final price it is vital to the economic interest of both parties. It is necessary to look to the economic elements of the bargain made, in order to seek to achieve efficiency in the process of contract, to facilitate proper market exchange. Whatever the

10 Department of the Environment. *Fair Construction Contracts: a Consultation Paper*, May 1995.
11 Abrahamson, M. '*Contract Risks in Tunnelling*', Tunnels and Tunnelling, 1973.
12 Perry, J G and Hayes, R W. '*Risk and its management in construction projects*', Proc. Institution of Civil Engineers, June 1985.

arrangement of risk allocation the reduction of transaction cost will produce a more efficient market exchange. When drafting a construction contract, therefore, it becomes important to generate terms which will reduce prolonged bargaining. It will not be possible to reduce transaction cost to the level of a simple transaction since the product in construction is complex. Informational difficulties need to be removed from the market and placed within the internal organisation where they can be dealt with more efficiently. The result will be to negate opportunistic behaviour and lead to less disagreement and disputes. Such changes in construction contracts may result in terms being more onerous on the contractor. But until the contractor is placed in a position where he has to price properly without relying on post tender gains, by including risk premium within the price, improvements are unlikely.

It must be concluded that the form of contract recommended in the Latham Report, the New Engineering Contract, does not satisfy these criteria. This form claims to be based on good management principles which will assist the internal organisation to operate better. It is suggested also that some of the terms of the NEC go some way to reducing opportunistic behaviour. But these affects will be marginal only. No proposals currently exist for the creation of any alternative unified form for the construction industry.

Demands for reform

In addition to calls for greater efficiency and reduction of disputes and conflict in the UK construction industry, demands for reform now include a substantial reduction in cost. Comparison with performance in other countries suggests that cost reductions are both possible and long overdue. But the means of achieving this have proved as elusive in the construction industry as in the legal industry.

Traditional and well-tried reform methods include the refinement of management techniques and re-assessment of risk placement. More recently the Latham Report has suggested a new concept of "fairness" in construction management which is suggested as leading to harmony and dispute reduction. None of these factors has yet produced hard evidence of any change, let alone increased efficiency and cost savings.

A fundamental re-appraisal of the basis of production in the construction field is justified by the enormous financial gains which could be produced by serious reform. Such a review should start with an appreciation of what is suggested as the major drivers, namely self-interest and opportunistic behaviour. Many markets outside construction have managed to control opportunistic behaviour through reputation and normal market forces, which is fully in accordance with self-interest. For historical reasons, the organisation within the construction industry has proved resistant to such controls and reaction.

Short of re-organising the UK construction industry, the most convenient vehicle to achieve reform is through construction contracts and their associated procurement systems. A key factor here is to identify the party which should initiate such reforms. Traditionally this has been the province of or at least heavily influenced by, the professional institutions. There are a number of serious objections to this however, including the fact that contrary to popular conception, the professional institutions are also driven by self-interest. Their influence within the construction industry has been waning for many decades and the present generation of standard forms could by seen as an attempt to buttress their interests at the expense of other players in the construction process.

Furthermore, the New Engineering Contract (or NECC), with production costs estimated at around £½ million must demonstrate the sheer impossibility of seeking to produce yet another industry-wide standard form, whatever may be the merits of such documents. In fact the NECC embodies comparatively modest changes to the existing family of standard form contracts. These are not sufficient to justify the cost of, or the prominence given to, the form which, like all other current forms, fails to address the question of self-interest and opportunistic behaviour. The espousal of NECC by the Latham Report, seen by many as justification of the enormous production costs, could as well be seen as confirmation of the lack of any radical ideas emanating from Latham.

In economic terms the key to efficient market organisation and resulting cost reduction is in control of the transaction costs. This generally represents the difference between efficiency and inefficiency, profit and loss. Current standard forms, including NECC, make no attempt to control transaction costs and, through the mechanism of claims, virtually ensure a high level of such costs in any situation involving uncertainty of overall recovery.

The solution suggested is to encourage producer-designed construction packages incorporating such combinations of risk, management, certainty and contingency as the offerer feels commercially prudent. The neutral term "producer" is favoured to avoid any pre-conception as to whether such packages should be initiated by the traditional "contractors" or "professionals". As part of the package on offer, decisions will be needed as to the necessary input of design services and all other elements of the construction process. Overall, it is inevitable that successful packages will be those which find means of reducing transaction costs. But this can be left to be determined by market forces.

The effect of these suggestions would be the "privatisation" of construction projects, not through any public sale of assets but through the removal of artificial (and frequently government-sponsored) constraints. If these proposals lead to a re-shaping or re-alignment of the UK construction industry, it is entirely appropriate that should be as a reaction to market forces and not in response to any "grand plan" or yet further government-inspired report.

In recent decades the UK construction industry has been used as an economic regulator and has had to demonstrate tremendous resilience merely to survive. This particular shackle shows distinct signs of loosening through the development of Private Finance Initiatives. There should be no doubt that the industry, or at least the contractors, possess the ability and will to realise the potential huge cost savings. They should be permitted and encouraged to pursue this on their own agenda.

Conclusion

A remedy must be sought to overcome the reluctance to change. This reluctance has existed in the construction industry for a number of years. Without change, the construction market will remain inefficient. Any future report on the industry will repeat the recommendations of both Banwell and Latham. Change should be achieved by commercial decisions by contractors and not forced through by the client. Contractors should accept more onerous conditions. The contractor in this situation should be in a position to control the risks he would be taking and to organise and manage his business accordingly.

There are a number of UK contractors with substantial resources who would be likely to thrive in such a re-organised market. But the clients would have to accept apparently increased tender prices in order to benefit from ultimate reduction in the final price. It will take courage by both parties to achieve these objectives.

8. Infrastructure Procurement: Practical Implications

Bruce Claxton

Synopsis

This paper examines the means by which decisions were made as to the procurement route on a major water supply scheme in Africa.

Introduction

The extent and rate of growth of the population of Gaborone, the capital of the Botswana, required the augmentation of its water supply. A number of feasibility studies identified the North South Carrier Water Project as the desired route. Water was to be collected in reservoirs to be built in the north of the country by damming rivers. The water was to be transferred to the capital by pipeline. Before the project got off the drawing board, the Botswana Ministry of Mineral Resources and Water Affairs, required a comprehensive review of project procurement and implementation including not only the construction phase but also the operational phase.

Procurement Options

The basic procurement options were classified into; traditional, design and build, build operate transfer, and build own operate transfer. Within these categories, a number of variants in respect of time, cost and quality were identified and examined. For each of the options and several of their sub-options, a detailed analysis of time and cost were made. As far as was possible the various options were assessed on the basis of a "level playing field" in respect of both time and cost. The quality requirements remained constant over the full range of options. A number of international contractors were invited to give indications of both the time period that they would require for tendering for the primary options as well as the cost of preparing the tender. The tenders were compared, the findings of which are set out in tabular form, below:

Procurement Option	Contract Type	Cost[1]	Period
Traditional	Single contract	0.25% - 0.50%	15 weeks
	Multiple contracts	0.25% - 0.50%	12 weeks
Design & Build	Single contract	0.35% - 0.75%	15 weeks
	Turnkey	0.50%-1.00%	36 weeks
B.O.T.	Engineer Design	0.50%-1.00%	24 weeks
	Design & Build	0.75%-1.50%	36 weeks
	Turnkey	1.00% - 5.00%	1 year
B.O.O.T.	Concession	5.00% - 1500%	2 years

Programme

Another aspect which is always difficult to assess in a project of this genus, is the programme for construction. Given the pipe requirements, in terms of the range of flow characteristics, several manufacturers of either the same material or different materials could supply the total needs over a shorter period. However price and interface control may suffer. Likewise, the laying of the pipe could be on a few concurrent fronts or a large number of shorter lengths. In order to permit a realistic participation of local labour the pipe laying was programmed to be carried out on several fronts, but only as the project devloped. One length was to have a high level of expert control to act as a training front from which trained teams could then move on to new lengths. Thus, one length would be started and, when underway, this would provide two new teams to start new lengths in due course. Two new trainee teams would then start at the training length and in time become the teams for subsequent

---

[1] Cost is defined as the direct cost to the Tenderer as a percentage of the value of the facilities as built.

lengths. To make fair comparisons between the procurement options these type of assumptions had to be assumed as constant.

The time constraints for the basic options could be summarised as:

- preparation of pre-qualification documentation—variable time scale dependent on option;
- enabling arrangements, including legislative, institutional and financial—variable time scale;
- contractors' required tender periods—variable time scale;
- post-tender, pre-construction review and negotiation period—variable time scale;
- contractor's design, and its approval period—variable between traditional and all design & build options; and
- start of manufacture of supplies and equipment, especially pipe.

A basic cost for the facilities "as built" was estimated. Weighted factors were then applied to that basic cost to represent the variable scope of responsibility and also risk. The cost to the Client was also assessed for each of these scenarios. The client's own direct costs were variable as well as his expenditure in respect of the Engineer, Project Manager, and Banker (dependent on source and nature of funding). It was assumed that the costs of technical audit and independent inspection (in manufacturers, works as well as at site) would be constant because the work content would be similar.

Risk Analysis

The risks associated with achieving the project objectives, particularly the more dominant objectives were analysed and their influence was taken into account in the recommended strategy. The risks were analysed and the time objective of having the pipeline operational by 1st January 1999 was predominant. Only the traditional procurement route could safely bring in such timely completion without handing the initiative to contractors to find ways of beating the time estimates under the design and build option, which would suggest a much higher import (plant, materials, labour, supervision etc.) content. Furthermore the potential for delays under design & build, BOT and BOOT increased since the lead times assumed in the models, before invitations to tenders could be issued, were to some extent optimistic. For example, the lead time for the enabling legislation for the BOOT option was two years. However, since this would have been the first time the process may well have taken very much longer.

The risks of time and costs overruns were constrained by the structure of the recommended strategy of multiple construction contracts. This coupled with the objective of involving local contractors and local labour wherever feasible without prejudicing quality or time, led to the choice of eight separate construction contracts. As mentioned above, the pipe laying programme assumptions were based on sequential start up on several lengths, so too the various structures were packaged into types. Thus the water treatment works were a separate package; experience could be gained on the first and the same team move sequentially to the other. Likewise the pumping stations and break pressure tanks.

Costs could be controlled quite closely for these contracts because their definition could be finalised after the three early contracts had been placed. In the context of the whole project a 100 per cent. variation in the out-turn costs of the preliminary works contract was found. This suggested that this contract really needed to be defined 'on the ground'. As work progressed, only one half of one per cent. variation to the project cost was, in fact, experienced. Similarly, as two thirds of the cost of the project represented the pipe supply contract, it made sense if the delivery condition could properly be specified and thus controlled. Isolating this from the construction work was effected in order to prevent the obscuring of causes of delay, changes and other aspects which lead to "claims" opportunities.

Recommended Procurement Option

The study concluded that the project should be procured by traditional means using eight separate construction contracts. These construction contracts were based on FIDIC, and the client was to have a dedicated project management team, specialist advisors, a design auditor and an independent inspection agency. The construction contracts comprised:

1. Preliminary Works;
2. Pipe Supply;
3. Pipe Laying;
4. Water Treatment Works;
5. Pumping Stations;
6. Break Pressure Tanks;
7. Reception Reservoir; and
8. Infrastructure Works.

This traditional procurement route enabled the areas which were suitable for local contractors to be separated out. Cost control was able to be exercised by separating the more sophisticated structures from the lower cost but quantity variable aspects such as the preliminary works and infrastructure works contracts.

Conclusion

This project established that the optimum procurement strategy is dependent on the dominance of identifiable project objectives, the particular project's circumstances, and the sensitivity of pertinent variable factors. It is submitted that studies of this nature and depth should be carried out more often, since the appropriate procurement strategy is not always obvious even after rigorous risk analysis, and the project objectives themselves can be tested to confirm their relevance and importance ranking.

9. Private Finance Initiative: Emerging Principles

Geoff Haley

Synopsis

Since its emergence, the Private Finance Initiative ("PFI") has seen radical changes in both practice and principle. This paper discusses the significance of the most recent changes in practice brought about by the New Labour Government before considering some major PFI contractual principles in detail.

Introduction

PFI starts where the Conservative Government's policy of privatisation ends. It was intended in 1992 by the then Chancellor of the Exchequer Norman Lamont to inject private sector innovation and business skills into a public sector thought to be administratively over-populated and lacking commercial negotiation experience. The scheme is founded upon the premise of procurement of a high capital value asset being passed to the private sector together with the attendant risks.

The PFI contract itself is a "design build finance operate and maintain" contract ("DBFOM") with the high capital value asset being transferred to the balance sheet of the private sector (usually a special purpose vehicle ("SPV") owned by consortium members/financiers). This was intended to lower the Public Sector Borrowing Requirement in the longer term as the public sector would be paying for the servicing of the asset out of revenue, rather than by procuring its construction through capital expenditure. Payments under the contract consist of at least two different streams: services (directly attributable to the services provided) and availability (linked to the building being available for use).

Thus an NHS Trust wishing to procure a new district general hospital would, having evaluated the necessity and cost of the various options available to it, and having established that a new hospital was necessary, publish an advertisement in the Official Journal of the EC asking for expressions of interest. Documents setting out the Trust's output specifications (*i.e.* an assessment of their needs in terms of building and service specifications, couched in terms which allow the private sector to devise their own solutions to the problem) are then distributed to interested parties. After an often long procurement process, the number of tenderers is whittled down. A Preferred Bidder is ultimately selected, being one who in the opinion of the public sector offers the best value for money and optimum risk transfer whilst remaining affordable.

The concept of risk transfer is central to the PFI – the risk of public sector construction contracts over-running is notoriously high. The Thames Barrier and the British Library projects are but two well-known examples. Initially the public sector's aim appeared to be to transfer all risks to the private sector. This proved both commercially and financially unacceptable in such a long-term contract (of at least 25-30 years). The Conservatives clarified the aim as meaning "optimum" risk transfer. As a result risks are currently transferred to those best equipped to deal with them so that the public sector often shoulders some of the burden.

Value for money and affordability, the other two cornerstones of the PFI concept, are inextricably linked. A value for money calculation assesses the risks to the public sector under normal and PFI procurements; at its most simple, if the PFI calculation is approximately equal to or less than the cost of a standard procurement value for money can be shown. Whether a project is affordable is a matter for internal discussion, however the cost of services is often prohibitively high either because the specifications are also high, or because the public sector has not provided the bidders with sufficient detail to make an informed bid.

New Labour – New PFI?

The months before the General Election in May 1997 were an uneasy time in the PFI market. Not knowing what steps a new Government would take, many projects either stalled progress, or were expedited to achieve financial close before the election was called. The new Labour Government very swiftly stamped its authority on the process. Roads projects and NHS projects have been ruthlessly and objectively streamlined with only those most likely to succeed being allowed to continue. It has enacted new legislation (see discussion *post*) and published the results of a review addressing the institutional structure, the process itself, guidance and dissemination of know-how as well as attacking the problem of bid costs.[1] The proposals themselves set out many of the trends for PFI in the future. These include:

- standardisation (as far as is possible) of both OJEC adverts and PFI documentation, which will cut down on the time and costs incurred in the bidding and negotiation process, and make contract pricing easier.

- the grouping of smaller projects in the Local Authority, Health and Education sectors. This proposal recognises that due to the project finance techniques used in PFI, professional and bidding costs tend to be too high to sustain projects of less than £10 million capital cost. At least until the sector matures this concept allows small PFI's to take off. It also indicates that perhaps securitisation techniques will come into play in the future. My firm is currently advising the public sector on a fast-track 'grouped' project in the Higher Education sector, bundling 3 projects into one worth around £10 million in capital terms and have consequently seen how successful this attitude can be.

- the signing off of commercial viability by a new Government Taskforce before the procurement procedure commences. This means that more work will have to be accomplished at the initial stage, which will also mean that affordability and potential value for money calculations will have to be

---

[1] The Bates Review 23 June 1997.

finalised at this stage. This will be vital in achieving a smooth well-run process and prevent the public sector from issuing OJEC notices without a fully-formed idea of their requirements and the level of services they require, as is still seen at the moment. A further implication will be to promote a more realistic timetable for the full process.

Case Law to Date

Two decisions with similar circumstances in the course of 1996 proved an obstacle to the PFI's progress.

Credit Suisse v. Waltham Forest LBC[2]

The Council formed a company to purchase housing for the purpose of providing accommodation for homeless persons. The Company was to lease the housing to the Council for a three-year period and then resell it. The Council guaranteed the punctual payment of all sums payable by the Company to the Bank, and undertook to pay the Bank any sum which the Company failed to pay on its due date. The Council also indemnified the Company for any shortfall between the loan monies and eventual sale proceeds. Although it was anticipated that the properties would be sold at the end of the three-year period at a profit, in 1990 the property market collapsed and in 1993 the Company was put into administrative receivership. The Bank and the Company sought to enforce the guarantee and the indemnity against the Council. At first instance the claims were upheld on the grounds that the giving of the guarantee and the indemnity was a necessary condition of the scheme, which was designed to fulfil the Council's duty under section 65 of the Housing Act 1985 to house homeless persons, and was within the powers conferred on the Council by section 111 of the Local Government Act 1972.

The case went to the Court of Appeal where it was held that the Council had no express statutory power either to guarantee the obligation of the Company under the loan agreement or to indemnify it

---

[2]   [1996] 3 WLR 943

against losses suffered as a result of the scheme. The implied powers of the local authority were then considered and it was stated that under section 111 of the Local Government Act 1972 it was necessary to identify the relevant statutory functions and to examine the context in which such powers were to be exercised. It was held that the arrangement did not entitle a local housing authority to discharge any of its functions by means of a partly owned company. It was held that there was no scope for implying the existence of additional powers outside the statutory code, as detailed provisions had been made by Parliament in relation to certain statutory functions. In addition section 111(3) of the Local Government Act 1972 clearly stated that the power to enter into financial obligations was subject to the imposition of statutory controls. It was held that *Credit Suisse v. Allerdale*[3] applied.

Credit Suisse v. Borough Council of Allerdale

This case concerned the creation of a development company to assist the Council specifically in financing projects outside the government limits. The Council wished to provide a swimming pool in its area, the Company was therefore to build a pool and time-share units the sale of which was to be set against the pool construction costs. A guarantee of £6m was given by the Council to the Company stating payment to be on demand and that such guarantee only became effective in the event of the development company's insolvency. Credit Suisse granted a facility to the Company of £6 million in total. The time-share units proved difficult to sell and the development company went into liquidation. The bank demanded repayment of the entire loan and claimed under the guarantee.

A central point of the Council's denial of liability concerned the *vires* surrounding entry into the guarantee. It was argued that the Council had no statutory powers to enter into the document, and if it otherwise did, it was purporting to use the guarantee to facilitate a scheme which the Council itself could not do because it was:

- outside the Council's borrowing and spending limits; and
- for an improper purpose (i.e. carrying on a trade in timeshare accommodation for profit).

---

[3]   [1996] 3 WLR 894

It was concluded at first instance that the Council had no statutory powers to give the guarantee due to an impermissible means of providing such facilities, it was for a purpose outside the Council's functions (namely the time share purpose) and the Council's decision was based on irrelevant and impermissible considerations. Judge Colman presiding commented that banks and other credit-providing institutions are exposed to a major risk when dealing with local authorities, that of discovering the documents are *ultra vires* the powers of that local authority, and they have little opportunity of assessing the local authority's exercise of decision making in this regard.

The Court of Appeal affirmed the decision at first instance, stating time-share accommodation not to constitute the provision of recreational facilities and the establishment of the Company and guarantee to be *ultra vires* the express and implied powers of the Council.

Comment

The decisions in these cases caused the financial community great concern, the field of PFI being a new concept to them with no repayment track record. Third party revenue often forms part of the payment stream, reducing the ultimate cost to the public sector, and of course provision of the asset itself is by the private sector with indirect reimbursement by the public sector. Either of these aspects it was felt could prove fatal to the public sector's *vires* in executing such a contract. Although these cases are easily distinguishable from PFI contracts, and the guarantees in question are never given by the procuring authority in PFI structures, it was felt that the risk of contracts being *ultra vires* was too great. This concern also spread to the NHS sector which has similarly prescribed powers.[4]

---

[4] At a public/private partnerships forum in June 1997 Adair Turner, Director-General of CBI stated that the *vires* issue for health *"has also brought the same issues into sharp relief in education.... [and local government]"*. The local government problem is addressed by way of a new statute, but education problems specifically in the schools and further education sectors, still need

The *Süzen* Case[5]

This case has potentially far reaching consequences for many PFI contracts which are of course as stated earlier, a complicated form of services contract in which the consideration of TUPE costs and implications plays a very significant part. Where the public sector engages a contractor to provide it with a service such as catering or cleaning, it was previously thought that the Transfer of Undertakings Regulations applied. This would usually mean that on the engagement of the contractor, the public sector employees would become the employees of the contractor and on each and every occasion when the contractor was changed, the liability for the employees would continue to pass to the new operator of the service.

The Süzen case makes a radical change. This case questioned the application of the Acquired Rights Directive[6] (and therefore the equivalent UK legislation[7]) to second generation contracting out. It provided that where there is no simultaneous transfer of tangible or intangible assets (i.e. property, equipment or goodwill) and where the major part of the work force (calculated by reference to numbers or skills) are not employed by the new contractor, the work force do not automatically become the employees of the new contractor. The *Süzen* case applied where one contractor was changed for another but it is possible that the principle established has been further extended to the first time contracting out of services.[8]

---

clarification. The higher education sector is not at the moment seen to be a problem, universities possessing a wide degree of autonomy.

[5] *Ayse Süzen v. Zehnacker Gebaudereingung GMBH Krankenhausservice & Le Fohrt GMB* Case C-12/98, [1997] IRLR 255

[6] 77/187/EC

[7] Being the *Transfer of Undertakings (Protection of Employment) Regulations* 1981 SI 1981/1794 as amended by the Trade Union Reform and Employment Rights Act 1993.

[8] In the case of *Betts and Others v. Brintel and KLM* the Court of Appeal stated that there was no difference in principle between first and second generation contracting out. The Court's view was that the Süzen principles would apply equally on a first generation case.

Specific indemnities must now be acquired to cover this situation and the potential costs stemming from it. PFI contracts, being long term and potentially involving several changes of service operator, will we predict, be in the vanguard of TUPE cases, expanding on the *Betts v Brintel* statement.

Recently the government launched a consultation process in response to the European Commission's amended proposal for a reviewed Business Transfer Directive.[9] It has had the opportunity to invite views as to whether the "transfer of undertakings" definition should be enlarged, so as to cover assignment and reassignment of a contract for the provision of contracted out services. This would remove the uncertainty caused by the *Süzen* case. The Government is very keen on this initiative and stated that it intends to use its presidency of the EU Council during the first half of the year to push this Directive through. It has however also indicated that it would be possible to widen the Transfer of Undertakings Regulations on a national basis.

Recent Statutory Changes

PFI has encountered some practical and perceived legislatory problems since its first incarnation. Many of these problems have been raised by financiers who when dealing with a statutory body wish its powers to be made clear, and having frequently encountered insolvency in limited companies wish public sector bodies' procedures to be equally clear.

- Residual Liabilities (National Health Service) Act 1996

  This Act was rushed through Parliament when it became clear that the financial community were concerned that upon insolvency or merger of an NHS Trust, it was not clear whether existing contractual arrangements would be honoured. If for example, such an insolvency terminated the Concession Agreement, the bank may not have been recompensed. All remaining concerns at the legislation now appear to be allayed by comfort letters distributed for each particular project.

---

[9] See IRLB 567, p.15.

- Local Government (Contracts) Act 1998

This Act is intended to pre-empt the difficulties encountered in the NHS sector and of course, in different circumstances in the *Allerdale* and *Waltham Forest* cases and for the first time indicates an increasing Governmental awareness that in this field it must be seen to be proactive rather than reactive. It confirms already existing powers to enter these contracts, and provides for certification of an *intra vires* project. This certification prevents either party from seeking to escape its obligations by pleading the Act to be *ultra vires*. Once issued, the certificate is considered valid and can only be overturned in public law proceedings. The Act also allows funders to agree terms prior to commercial/financial close which subsist after and despite any *ultra vires* ruling. Therefore compensation terms can be agreed with funders should a contract be *ultra vires*. This Act is an encouraging stance taken by the Labour administration and it is to be hoped, one which shall continue.

- National Health Service (Private Finance) Act 1997

As a response to the reluctance of the financial markets to become involved in NHS Trust PFI projects to enter into PFI deals, again due to perceived *vires* problems, this Act was passed as soon as possible after the election. The Secretary of State for Health certifies an agreement as being externally financed and subject to such certification the NHS Trust may enter into it. The Act also clarifies the ability of Trusts to enter into direct agreements with the financiers allowing the financiers to step-in to the contract in place of the SPV should an SPV default endanger the contract.

- Local Authorities (Capital Finance) Regulations 1997

  These regulations are the consolidation of a number of earlier provisions designed to relax controls over Local Authority expenditure to specifically facilitate the ability of Local Authorities to enter project transactions under the PFI.

  Controls over Local Authority expenditure were set up under the Local Government and Housing Act 1989 prior to the development of the PFI. These restrictions would neutralise many of the advantages gained through structuring a project in the manner subsequently promoted under the initiative. Under the controls, a PFI scheme would have been treated as the procurement of an asset under a credit arrangement. The project would therefore be unable to proceed without a Local Authority embarking on an approval procedure with the Central Government unless it could finance the project from Central Government grants or the sale of existing assets. Furthermore, the project would be accounted for in its entirety as capital expenditure in the initial year of contract substantially reducing the Authority's capital resources in that year. In other words, the PFI process was treated no differently to a normal construction procurement.

  The regulations principally recognise the fact that the capital expenditure made under a PFI transaction, where sufficient risk is transferred, is essentially private rather than public and that therefore the restrictions on public capital expenditure are inappropriate. The risk transfer requirement is made clear in the definition of "Private Finance Transaction", the phraseology used by the regulations, and is the essence of the characterisation of the project as being privately financed.

  The regulations define three classifications of project which, depending upon the nature of and degree to which risks are transferred, eliminate or reduce the need for credit approval or public capital input; and reduce or remove entirely the full value of the project from the Authorities' balance sheet for the initial year.

Contractual Principles

Although no PFI contract can ever be standardised, there are several key issues, the treatment of which has become well-known. This reduces negotiation time and therefore bidding costs. Three of these issues are set out below. Also indicated, where possible, are the current approaches being adopted.

Force Majeure

Force majeure is the circumstance under which the party suffering from a non-default incident, unforeseen and outside the control of the parties (i.e. usually the private sector partner) can be excused from further performance of the contract.

The Law Reform (Frustrated Contracts) Act 1943 (the "Act") will apply unless the contract incorporates a provision dealing with the possible events of *force majeure* and their effect upon the performance and termination of the contract. The contract will be deemed "frustrated", i.e. incapable of performance, however there will be no contractual provision stating how long an event has to persist , before the contract can be deemed frustrated. A widely drafted *force majeure* clause eradicates, to a large extent, the uncertainty of the Act, and also gives the respective parties control over the circumstances surrounding an event.

As a public/private partnership, it is important that the parties to a PFI contract know as clearly as possible what will happen at any given point in the contract period. Building an effective working relationship over the span of the contract is also imperative, which is aided at the outset by a recognition of the private sector's need for certainty in this respect. It is equally important for bankers to be able to quantify the extent and circumstances of loss. This is much easier if an express contractual term sets out all the likely *force majeure* events.

The aim of a *force majeure* clause should therefore be to address risks which cannot be economically insured and to specify how those risks should best be managed. The events outside the bidder's control which the bidder might wish to include would be as follows:

1   War (whether war is declared or not), invasion, act of foreign enemy, armed conflict, hostilities, civil war, terrorism, general or partial mobilisation in each case within and involving the United Kingdom;

2   Rebellion, civil disorder or disturbance , riot, conflagration, terrorism or insurrection which causes physical damage and long term disruption, in each case within the United Kingdom;

3   Blockade or embargo;

4   Nuclear explosion, radioactive or chemical contamination, epidemic or ionising radiation unless the source of the contamination or radiation is brought to or near the site, the Project Facilities or the Equipment by the Special Purpose Vehicle ("SPV") or the public sector or any other persons for whom the SPV or the public sector is responsible or any other person for whom the SPV is responsible;

5   Effects of weather, flood, drought, windstorm, tempest, fire, explosion, corrosion, earthquake, lightning, volcanic eruption, or other natural disaster of overwhelming proportions;

6   Failure, shortage or delay of power, fuel or transport;

7   Any accident at sea in the air or on land and any pressure waves caused by aircraft or other aerial devices travelling at sonic or supersonic speeds, or damage caused by articles falling from aircraft or the impact of satellites;

8   Official or unofficial strikes, lockouts, go-slows or other labour disputes which apply generally to the industry or activity concerned;

9   Save for circumstances or events for which responsibility is allocated to either party pursuant to the agreement, any circumstances which are beyond the reasonable control of either of the parties and which could not have been foreseen and avoided by an experienced contractor or an experienced facilities operator, as the case may be, and having regard to the parties' state of knowledge.

Possible consequences of the above events of *force majeure* in relation to the proposed project include inability to maintain minimum safety requirements, inability to operate on or around the site, possibility that the site may be rendered permanently unusable, or that buildings may be destroyed.

The Position of the Treasury

Under the 'Basic Contractual Terms' published by the Private Finance Panel Executive and HM Treasury,[10] *force majeure* events are limited to:

(a) war, civil war, armed conflict or terrorist attack arising within and affecting the United Kingdom; or

(b) nuclear, chemical or biological contamination of the Contractor's *(i.e. SPV's)* property arising from any of the events at (a) above.

The Treasury's proposed definition of *force majeure* is extremely narrow. The Treasury envisages that other circumstances which have previously come under *force majeure* will be dealt with separately under specific provisions within the contract.

An example of how this approach can be implemented can be seen in the way in which the issue of extension to the concession duration was dealt with in the two completed PFI prison projects. The contracts provided that if the opening of the facility was delayed by events such as strikes by third parties, civil commotion or exceptionally adverse weather conditions then the concession period would be extended, rather than the event in question giving rise to both parties being fully released from their obligations under the contract.

The *Force majeure* events should at this juncture be limited as far as possible to those of the Treasury, as standard PFI practice. The consequences of *force majeure* should also be considered:

---

[10] 21st October 1996.

a) Length of time before contract is terminated. A relatively short "cure period" should be granted – perhaps 6 months, which is a reasonable mid-position and has been acceptable to bankers on other projects.

b) Possible payment to private sector on the occurrence of a *force majeure* event.

c) Suspension of performance regime in respect *ONLY* of services that cannot be made due to the occurrence of an event of *force majeure*.

d) Suspension of availability payment to the extent the event has rendered the premises unavailable.

e) The party suffering the *force majeure* event (i.e. usually the SPV) to use best endeavours to remedy the situation.

Uninsured Risks

The Treasury approach to *force majeure* appears to work perfectly well for the eventualities described. However, for other events often included under the *force majeure* head but excluded by the Treasury definition, this approach may not work. Examples of such events are natural disasters (e.g. earthquake, volcanic eruption etc.) and damage caused by articles falling from aircraft or the impact of satellites. Events such as these have the potential to be equally as devastating as the events included in the Treasury's definition of *force majeure*. If the latter definition of *force majeure* is to be used then the contract must recognise some other forms of cataclysmic events beyond the control of both parties and provide for a method of releasing the parties from their contractual obligations, or for events of a less cataclysmic nature a method for adjusting the parties' obligations in a just and equitable manner.

One possible method of achieving this would be to classify such risks as "Uninsurable Risks". Such a title is a slight misnomer as, in fact, some of these risks may actually be insurable, albeit at a disproportionate cost. The consequences of an event of "Uninsurable Risk" could be fixed by the contract to be less final and absolute as the consequences of an event of *force majeure*. For example, it could be provided that the obligations of the parties are suspended for the period while the risk operates, subject to negotiation between the parties as to how any resulting additional costs will be shared.

The contractual consequences of an "Uninsurable Risk" event occurring may vary depending on whether it occurs during the construction phase of the project or its operating phase. For example, long delays during the construction phase could be compensated for by an adjustment to the availability payment over the remaining term of the agreement and/or an extension to the concession period. In the case of such events occurring during operation then another possible solution would be to suspend any monitoring and performance requirements.

If any bidder is forced to shoulder a high level of risk by a very narrow definition of *force majeure* then this will be reflected in the overall pricing of the bid. Extra insurance costs and/or contingency sums will have to be built into the pricing structure.

Compensation on Termination

Why should the public sector pay the private sector compensation at all on termination of the Concession Agreement? This is a question often asked, and with reason. The theory behind compensation on termination is that:

1   On termination of the Concession Agreement, everything falls away and ownership of the buildings reverts to the public sector.

2   This would mean that if no payment is made, the public sector obtains the buildings free of charge (apart from the previous Unitary Service Charge payments), and would therefore receive a 'windfall'.[11]

3   Therefore, it is usual for senior debt providers to require repayment on termination.

---

[11]   This is expressly not recommended in the Private Finance Panel's publication entitled "Further Contractual Issues", published in January 1997.

A counter argument to the concept is that senior debt providers have an opportunity to 'step in' to the shoes of SPV before termination occurs, and if they do not do so, they should not expect to be kept whole by a repayment of SPV's borrowings. At the moment however and certainly until the PFI sector matures, this argument merely renders the project unfinanceable.

Three scenarios can be envisaged in which the Concession Agreement could be terminated:

(a) fundamental breach of contract by the public sector

(b) fundamental breach of contract by the SPV

(c) non-default termination, e.g. *force majeure* events (see *ante*) or a change in law (*post*) which produces substantial increase in costs

In the event of contract termination, the key issue is to provide a mechanism to ensure that the SPV is compensated for the value of the project assets plus other liabilities and expenses. In general, the SPV will suffer more loss on termination than the public sector, as the facility which it designs and builds using its own and bank finance will revert to the public sector on termination.

The SPV is likely to request compensation for:

- its cost in developing and constructing the project (where termination occurs during construction);
- outstanding borrowings, including interest and commission, and third party liabilities (where termination occurs during the operational phase);
- financing costs, interest and finance charges (for example breakage costs); and
- a return on equity

However, the public sector will wish to limit the above by:

- limiting compensation to the SPV in the event of SPV default and in the event of *force majeure*
- deducting losses suffered by the public sector

Debt repayment

Until the PFI market matures, debt providers will always push to be kept whole on termination. In the future, this will no doubt change but debt returns are at present not seen to be sufficiently high for a significant risk as this to be taken on by the banks.

Reimbursement of equity investment

The private sector view is usually that where termination is not caused by SPV default, the compensation payable should also include reimbursement of the equity investment in the SPV (sometimes including liabilities incurred towards third parties or breakage costs and the costs of demobilisation). This is often calculated on the basis of the deemed fair market value of the equity share capital in the SPV, taking into account the value of the contract **before** termination. However, the public sector would wish to exclude return on equity and limit demobilisation/third party costs in the event of SPV default and *force majeure.*

Deducting losses

In compensating the SPV for equity and/or loan repayments, the public sector will wish to ensure it is in turn compensated for its losses. However, the public sector should avoid deducting its losses from debt repayments, as the key aim in termination provisions is to facilitate repayment of principal debt, in order to improve the project's bankability. Accordingly, any compensation provisions should not impinge on debt repayment.

Force majeure

The SPV may argue that risk of *force majeure* events (for which commercially viable insurance is not available) cannot rest with the SPV because banks will not lend to the SPV unless they are confident that their debt will be discharged in full if the contract fails due to *force majeure*. Accordingly, debt repayments must be made, however beyond that mutual liabilities should be minimised. This means that the SPV should take on the risk of losing equity, and any further compensation provisions should be limited to direct losses only.

Changes in Law

Changes in law which would have an impact on the project range from increases in taxation; to changes in health and safety regulations which require a change to the building; to changes to a specific law or regulation regarding the relevant sector e.g. student accommodation, in the case of a university, or specific PFI project discriminatory legislation – for example windfall tax on PFI concessionaires. The impact of a change in law will vary not simply with the type of change but also with the phase of the project affected by the change.

As an example, during the construction phase the effect is likely to be limited to the cost to SPV of making changes to the design, specification or quality etc. of the building. A change in VAT amounts or minimum wage legislation, however, may affect the payments which the SPV has to make to its sub-contractors (in either phase). During the operational period, a change in law could have a number of consequences including increasing operating costs or reducing usage. In either scenario, this might prejudice the SPV's ability to cover its running costs and debt service.

SPV should be prepared to accept a significant proportion of the risk of a change in law. SPV should have considered the risk in preparing their bid. Usual business risks for example a change in corporation tax should not be passed back to the public sector. The public sector should consider offering a compensation payment to SPV should the change incur costs exceeding an agreed figure. Furthermore, any increase in costs over a prescribed ceiling figure would permit either party to terminate the Agreement.

Procedure in the event of a change in law is summarised below:

- Where a change in law is likely to cause an increase in construction, operation and maintenance costs, SPV must supply full written details of the anticipated effects of the change on their costs.

- Agreement must then be reached between the parties on the percentage increase in costs the change will cause.
- If agreement is not reached, the percentage increase will be determined by the disputes resolution procedure.
- No compensation will be given to SPV where the increase in costs falls below a prescribed limit.
- Compensation will be given where the costs exceed the lower limit but do not exceed a prescribed upper limit.
- Compensation will be calculated in accordance with a formula set out in a Schedule to the Concession Agreement.
- Should the increase in costs exceed the prescribed upper limit, either party may terminate the agreement.
- Unless the agreement is terminated, SPV will be expected to carry out all its obligations under the terms of the Concession Agreement irrespective of whether or not agreement has been reached on the percentage increase figure or if a compensation payment is to be made.

Finance-led Contractual Principles

Although to a great extent the concerns of the SPV and the financial community are at one with each other, in certain respects the latter's voice is heard particularly clearly. In relation to issues affecting the payment stream for reasons which are too obvious to relate, certain clauses are at the moment being inserted as a result of financial pressure. Ultimately of course once the PFI market can be tracked, concerns such as these particular ones will be allayed.

Set off, Deductions and Withholdings

In any commercial agreement the area of set off allows healthy debate, but never more so than in this sphere. The public sector wish for unlimited rights however it has been clear from early in the PFI's growth that this is entirely unacceptable to financiers. The financial community therefore press for no right of set off deductions or withholding. Again this is unpalatable for the other side, who invariably feel that if SPV has done something creating a set off situation, in any normal situation set off would be permitted.

A suitable compromise may be to limit the right of set off to a financial cap permitting SPV (essentially the equity providers) pain to be felt, but allowing debt service to continue. Additionally, a "time" cap can be instituted allowing set off etc. to a financial cap per month, but with the full amount payable (with interest, again the rate to be applied will be a subject of debate). A further question arises if termination occurs and full set off has not been made – the public sector will quite rightly wish to make any compensation payment subject to their rightful set off requirements.

Tax Gross-Up

This clause is inserted in an attempt to subvert a problem arising in the course of a long concession term. If a PFI tax is imposed on the receipt of PFI Unitary Service Charge Payments in the hands of SPV, the payment stream reverting to the financial community will similarly diminish. Even if SPV can continue with debt repayment, the equity will no doubt be affected.

Payment Deduction

Without doubt these provisions will need exhaustively to be negotiated. They often incorporate pain layers in accordance with the importance of the service at fault or the area unavailable. Principles banks inevitably wish to inspect will include:

- adequate cure periods prior to deductions
- no deductions for an area's lack of availability if the public sector use such area anyway
- indexation of payments annually
- clear procedures for establishing service performance levels

Future Trends

The PFI market is still nascent. It celebrates its sixth anniversary this year, however it is only in the last 6 months that we have seen tangible progress and significant contracts (particularly in the health sector) reaching commercial agreement and financial close. In a further 5 years we expect the market to have matured, with the provision of debt to PFI projects of common occurrence, banks and other credit institutions being familiar with the particular problems posed by such a contract.

There has already been developments in the bonds market for PFI projects – recent PFI projects which use bonds included the A1(M)/A417-A419 road project. The bond issue for the Greenwich Rail Link was snapped up by the pensions sector showing that the appetite for these deals is there, if it can be fed. This particular bonds issue is significant in that no insurance was used – previously Monoline Bond Insurance has been utilised to ensure a AAA credit rating. As the sector grows in familiarity such bond issues will become more common, and of course will make for a totally liquid asset. It will be interesting in the future to see what ratings are given by for example Standard and Poors to PFI projects.

We are increasingly seeing the use of EC and lottery Grants within PFI projects. Again this may be an area requiring specific legislation to clarify the position in some areas as both EC Grants and lottery funds tend to be geared towards a public sector recipient which at the moment creates ill-needed complications and ring fencing.

A further development which has occurred in the past 5 years is the setting up of specific funds for equity investment in PFI projects. Funds currently available in the UK market have been set up by Charterhouse, CIBC Wood Gundy, Innisfree and BZW; and 3i has an earmarked sum for PFI projects. There is still a significant equity gap, and a lot of potential for a PFI market in the future – PFI equity is relatively long term and forms an interesting possibility for portfolio diversification.

Conclusion

This paper highlights the progress made in the doctrine and practice of PFI in the short space of half a decade. In the next few years as the market settles and major PFI groups emerge, the corporate market in PFI special purpose vehicles will grow – flotations and securitisation will increase as will Management Buy-Outs. Just as the MBO structure emerged and developed in the 1980s into various forms – MBI's, BIMBO's – so do we fully expect creators of acronyms to be at work for many years to come on variations on the theme of PFI.

Annex I
Private Finance Initiative – Progress Chart

- **Throughout 1980's and early 1990's**

  Growth of infrastructure projects using private finance, for example the Dartford River crossing and Skye Bridge projects.

- **November 1992**

  Norman Lamont announces the Private Finance Initiative.

- **December 1993**

  Private Finance Panel has its first meeting (having been formed with the aim of promoting the PFI, and assisting with the resolution of problems in reaching a satisfactory agreement between the public and private sectors).

- **November 1994**

  The Chancellor of the Exchequer states that "The Treasury will not approve any capital projects in future unless the private finance options have been explored".

- **31 October 1995**

  New rules were announced to allow LEAs to retain a larger proportion of the proceeds from sale of surplus assets from April 1996 for two years. The set-aside requirement will be 25 per cent. for debt redemption, compared with the previous figure of 50 per cent.

- **December 1995/January 1996**

  Contracts signed for the DBFOM of two new prisons at Bridgend, South Wales, and Fazakerley, Liverpool.

- **January 1996**

  Hermes Investment Management and AMP Asset Management each invests £25 million in the Innisfree PFI private equity fund targeting schemes worth £25-300 million.

- **March 1996**

  Launch of A1(M)/A419-A417 Bond given a AAA rating by Standards and Poors

- **9 May 1996**

  The Court of Appeal ruled that Allerdale District Council had exceeded its powers in giving a guarantee of a development company to Credit Suisse, causing ripples of alarm amongst funders and prospective PFI partners that after signature of a contract, the local authority could avoid their obligations and argue that they had exceeded their powers.

- **22 May 1996**

  National Health Services (Residual Liabilities) Act 1996 passed.

- **June 1996**

  Charterhouse launch a £50 million Equity Fund to invest in PFI.

- **September 1996**

  £165 million bond issue for the City Greenwich Lewisham Rail Link (mostly bought by UK pension funds and insurance companies), without any third party guarantee, and given a single-A rating.

- **6 December 1996**

  Stephen Dorrell, the then Health Secretary agrees to provide written assurances on funding in relation to NHS hospital projects.

- **March 1997**

  New Labour elected to power, and promise a review of the PFI.

- **23 June 1997**

  Paymaster General Geoffrey Robinson accepts the 29 recommendations set out in Malcolm Bates' (Chairman of Pearl Group) review of PFI.

- **June/July 1997**

  Local Government (Contracts) Bill receives first and second readings, reaches committee stage and is submitted to the Lords. The Bill allays the fears of banks following their perception of the Allerdale and Waltham Forest cases.

- **3 July 1997**

  The Minister of State for Health announces prioritisation of 14 major acute hospital PFI schemes, chosen according to service need, PFI-ability and status. Twenty-nine other PFI schemes are halted and their appeals all prove unsuccessful.

- **15 July 1997**

  The National Health Service (Private Finance) Act 1997 receive Royal Assent clarifying the *vires* of NHS Trusts in entering contracts such as PFI concessions.

- **18 August 1997**

  City Heavyweight appointed as head of the New PFI taskforce. Adrian Montague formerly Co-Head of Global Project Finance at Dresdner Kleinwort Benson will now be the Chief Executive of the new Treasury Private Finance Taskforce.

- **19 November 1997**

  Public-private partnerships in Local Government get a big boost – with the announcement of a doubling of the level of investment that can receive Government support in 1998/99, Government support will now be available for up to £500 million of new PFI.

- **27 November 1997**

  Local Government (Contract) Act received Royal assent. This Act allays the fears of banks following their perception of the *Allerdale* and *Waltham Forest* cases.

- **22 December 1997**

  PFI Conference programme launched.

- **10 February 1998**

  A Significant Project List was published heralding a change in PFI project quality. Around 50 PFI projects deemed as significant, are benefitting from the Treasury Private Finance Taskforce input to help ensure their commercial viability. A List of nearly 30 projects signed since 1 May 1998 was published.

- **13 February 1998**

  The first Welsh PFI Hospital contract was signed at Glan Hafren. This contract will provide the Glan Hafren NHS trust with a new £10mn community hospital in Chepstow.

Annex II
PFI Projects signed since 1 May 1998

Defence

Army Personnel IT System	£150 million
Defence Fixed Telecoms	£70 million
Helicopter Simulator	£100 million

DfEE (PFI/PPPs)

Clarendon	£16 million
Colfox	£15 million
Falmouth	£3 million
UCL	£14 million
King's/UMDS	£142 million

DETR

Harrow (IT)(LA)	£1 million
Isle of Wight waste management (LA)	£13 million

Foreign & Commonwealth Office

2 small vehicle service contracts	£3 million

Northern Ireland

Medical equipment	£3 million
Belfast Hospital Renal Unit	£3 million
Planning Services IT	£3 million

Health

Carlisle	£63 million
Dartford	£115 million
Norfolk and Norwich	£214 million
South Bucks	£39 million

Home Office

2 Passport Agency contracts each worth	£15 million

Inland Revenue

Edinburgh	£9 million
Glasgow	£9 million

Lord Chancellor's Department

ARAMIS	£30 million

Scotland

Baldovie Waste to Energy	£43 million
Bowhouse Prison	£80 million
Stirling FE Centre	£4 million

Department of Social Security

Longbenton	£120 million
Prime	£350 million

Serious Fraud Office

Document management IT	£4 million

10. Risk and Reality in Private Infrastructure Development

Chris Head

Synopsis

This paper examines the difficulties in securing private finance for infrastructure projects, with a high civil engineering content, which, prior to widescale privatisation, were in the public domain.

Introduction

In the past most civil engineering contracts for infrastructure development were in the public sector. They were usually promoted by utilities whose primary purpose was the implementation and operation of such projects. These organisations generally knew their business well; they might have been slow and bureaucratic, but they understood the project cycle and retained control of it through a well tried contractual framework in which the role of each party was clearly understood.

Within the last few years much has changed. The bushfires of privatisation that swept the old order away have brought in a cast of new players. Developers, bankers, investors and lawyers have come tumbling into the previously staid world of infrastructure development. It is now an altogether more exciting place to work in, but at times one cannot avoid the thought that we are making up the script as we go along.

The Allocation of Risk

The financing of any project is all about the management of risk. Various risks are present irrespective of the type of project, for example country risk, currency risk, etc., but it has to be admitted that most large civil engineering works also have an inherently high completion, that is construction, risk. Quite simply they are prone to cost and time overruns, which, with the best will in the world, are not always avoidable if one starts with ambitious targets. Needless to say, the risk can be greatly reduced by lowering the targets but this generally does not satisfy the developer who invariably demands the best of both worlds.

Participants in the construction process are generally aware of the complex web of agreements that surround any private infrastructure project. They cover everything from the concession itself to the financing, construction, operation, and maintenance of the works, and the selling of the product itself be it water, electricity or the right of passage on a toll road. A large number of parties are involved in these agreements, and the risk has to be allocated between them for the duration of the concession which may be 20 years or more.

When it comes to the allocation of risk it is the financier who decides what is acceptable in the market.[1] For the construction contract this is likely to include the following conditions:

- Contractor to assume all construction risk, probably on the basis of a fixed price, lump sum contract with heavy penalties for under-performance or late delivery; and/or
- Single point responsibility with the contractor held responsible for the engineering design, procurement and construction of the complete project. In short, an EPC or turnkey contract.

Similar conditions have been extensively applied in project financing in the past, but usually in the context of schemes dominated by equipment supply which, although technically complex, are relatively predictable in their outcome. For example, a typical gas-fired thermal power station involves the erection of largely standardised, factory made equipment; it can be sited virtually anywhere and constructed quickly. This is a very different situation for projects like hydroelectric power stations which are highly site specific and typically involve

---

[1] For a detailed exposition on this subject, see Scriven, J. ' *A Funder's View of Risk in Construction*' in Uff, J. & Odams, A.M. *Risk, Management and Procurement in Construction*, Centre of Construction Law and Management, King's College London, 1995.

heavy civil engineering works such as dams, tunnel and underground caverns in remote locations.

Private Hydropower Projects

In terms of project financing, greenfield hydropower developments can be seen to be at the challenging end of the spectrum. It is not only the nature of the works that cause the bankers concern, but also the fact that once they are completed their output is vulnerable to the vicissitudes of rainfall. The new challenge in construction law for this type of project is to develop a contract framework that makes it possible.

Despite the problems the potential rewards of hydropower are such that a significant number of BOOT (build-own-operate-transfer) schemes are now actively being promoted. Included amongst these are some very large projects involving investments of $1 billion or more. Overall private hydro is probably five years behind comparable thermal initiatives, and so to date few have reached financial closure. However, and for a number of reasons, including fuel diversification and the pressure for renewable energy and reduced greenhouse gas emissions, it is inevitable that we shall see more private hydro projects in the future; and an examination of the implication of the financing conditions therefore becomes more germane.

Construction Risk

To appreciate how significant the recent changes have been it is worth recalling how large infrastructure projects were developed in the past. The utility took responsibility for the design which was tendered on the basis of standard documentation such as FIDIC. To achieve the best price the works were usually split into a number of separate contract packages, each containing work of a similar type that would be within the scope of a single contractor. In the case of the civil works the tenderers invariably had available to them the results of extensive site investigations, and furthermore they had the reassurance that if quantities changed payment was on remeasurement.

The contractor was not required to price in great uncertainty, and in consequence the bid was usually competitively low. In return for this price advantage the utility assumed wide responsibility—for the design, for project management, for unforeseen ground conditions, and ultimately for the successful performance of the project. Both they and their financiers from the international lending agencies like World Bank understood the risks and accepted them, presumably because it was in their interest to do so.

Under the private development scenario the opposite seems to be the norm. The pressure is to push all risk onto the contractor, and wherever possible he in turn passes it down to his subcontractors. The theory that risk should rest with the party best able to control and cover it has tended to give way to the harsher realities of the market place, with risk being passed down to those least able to resist. This sometimes appears to be happening with complete disregard for the realities of the situation. For example on more than one occasion the author has had to argue that whereas it is reasonable for a contractor bidding a hydro scheme to assume the short-term hydrological risk of floods, which is anyway normally insurable, it is quite illogical to extend this into expecting him to assume responsibility for the long-term hydrology (i.e. the output of the scheme).

Fixed Price and Risk Sharing

Difficulties are particularly evident when the owner demands fixed price, lump sum contracts for works that have not been fully investigated or designed. It is interesting to reflect that under the previous system of remeasurable contracts the utility had generally carried out extensive site investigations and design studies before inviting bids, so that the contractor not only assumed less risk but he also bid with the advantage of much greater knowledge of the project.

The motivations of a private developer at the same stage of the project cycle are different. His primary concern is to establish a price on which he can base the negotiation of the power purchase agreement, and until that is secured he is understandably reluctant to spend any more than absolutely necessary on site investigation and design studies. Hence there is a tendency to arrive at a project cost on the basis of a sketchy definition, and at a later stage when everybody finds that they are bound by the price the project has to be configured to suit. With such an approach there is no guarantee that one eventually ends up with the most suitable or profitable configuration.

Obviously the contractor's price must reflect uncertainty. There is a strong body of opinion which upholds the notion that any contractor has to bid on something like a worst case scenario, particularly if he is required to assume the risk of unforeseen ground conditions when there has been inadequate site investigation. If the owner pushes this position too hard there is a danger that he will end up paying for site conditions that do not materialise and in the extreme this could render the scheme non-viable. On projects where the owner is secure, it would generally be in his interests to pre-invest more in site investigation and design development at the tender stage to ensure a tighter and more competitively priced construction contract.

Where the pressure is for a fixed price contract against inadequate site data, a more constructive approach might be to allow remeasurement of a few key quantities which cannot be determined with any certainty at the time of contract award. This allows at least some measure of risk sharing. For example, in the case of a dam where the principal uncertainty hinges around the ground contact situation, the remeasurable items might be grouting, excavation and fill; everything else could be covered by a lump sum.

Obviously as soon as the contract is structured in a way that apportions any construction risk to the owner, it implies that he has to have contingency funding available. This worries the bankers because they consider any relaxation of pressure on the contractor to be wrong, and they fear an uncertain final price. In practice there are many ways of sharing construction risk between the owner and the contractor and one can play tunes to limit the owner's exposure and maintain contractor motivation. Each situation needs to be structured to ensure that the parties are encouraged to work together to achieve the optimum design, acceptable quality of construction and timely completion. In this context the question of design responsibility is of key importance.

Design Responsibility

The requirement that the contractor should assume responsibility for design has obvious attractions because it avoids the possibility of divided responsibility in the event of things going wrong. It works well for projects where the end product can be accurately defined in advance through a performance specification, and it has the advantage of allowing the contractor a design to suit his construction methods. The difficulty with applying this approach to certain types of civil engineering project lies in two important facts, the significance of which is not always appreciated, namely:

- that for most large civil engineering works the bulk of the design takes place after contract award; and
- a performance specification alone is not always sufficient to adequately define the quality of the end product.

Whilst neither of these is a problem in the context of a conventional remeasurable contract in which the owner retains control of the design, they are of considerable importance under a fixed price turnkey arrangement in which the contractor has design responsibility. The difficulty arises because there is an element of judgement and preference engineering in the design of most civil works, mainly directed towards long term durability and operational ease. For example, one river intake might apparently work as well as the next but in the fullness of time become plagued by siltation problems. It is probable that the better intake will cost more to build, and if it is not defined in some detail in advance there will be strong inclination for the contractor to adopt the cheaper of the two or the one his designer first thought of.

In an ideal situation the design will be sufficiently advanced at the time of signing the contract that the owner will know beyond doubt what he is getting. In practice this seldom happens for the reason already noted. Design requirements in a narrow structural sense can be made specific through reference to the appropriate codes and standards, but there is no similar way in which the more fundamental aspects of the design can be precisely specified in advance. In consequence there is a tendency to rely on generalised expressions (e.g. "to internationally accepted standards") which leave a lot of room for interpretation.

The owner may not like what he sees coming forward but once the contract is signed he will be in a contractually weak position when it comes to enforcing changes. One partial solution to this problem is to adopt a staged design approval process, under which the owner's influence diminishes as the design evolves. One can be confident that the contractor will resist any interference in the design on the grounds of cost and delay, but it will be harder for him to object if it is written in from the outset. A typical three stage approval process might be as follows:

Stage 1:   Concept designs are tabled by the contractor for the approval of the owner who can either enforce changes where there are obvious failures to comply with the contract, or seek to negotiate them.

Stage 2:   General arrangement layout drawings are submitted for checking that they follow the concept already agreed. They would normally be accompanied by Design Briefs setting out the assumed loading conditions and design philosophy.

Stage 3:   Detailed designs are submitted for inspection before construction to ensure that they conform the General Arrangements already agreed, and with the specification and relevant codes and standards in the contract.

In practice the question of the contractor assuming design responsibility is much less of a problem if the contract is remeasurable, but then the owner worries that he is paying excessively for over-design. In either case there is a need for checks and balances, and an clear understanding of the implications of placing responsibility for an evolving design in one camp or the other.

Resource Risk (Hydrology and Reservoir Operation)

The subject of resource risk as applied to water resources projects is largely unexplored territory in contractual terms. Again we find a situation which is now in sharp contrast to that which prevailed previously. A private company makes a commitment to deliver a product, and if it fails to do so it may suffer loss of revenue and possibly other penalties.

In the case of private hydropower schemes there are a number of key questions that arise:

- Who is assuming the hydrological risk?
- With what confidence can we predict the scheme's output?
- Who will operate any reservoirs, and to what criteria?
- What else in the catchment that could affect water availability?

Hydrological uncertainty manifests in two forms. First there is the inevitable question of the confidence that can be placed on the assessment of future river flows; this tends to be directly related to the quality of the historic record. Secondly, even when the long-term average flow has been accurately established, there remains the fact that one cannot predict short-term variations in hydrology.

Like any other risk, hydrological risk has to be allocated. Although there is often a presumption that it falls on the developer this need not necessarily be the case, particularly when he has inherited from the purchaser a feasibility study giving the estimated scheme output. In this circumstance the concessionaire might reasonably argue for compensation if the scheme failed to produce the revenue expected through lack of water, but it could take some years to establish whether the shortfall was due to an unusually dry sequence of years or an error in the original flow estimate. Another device is to bias the tariff very heavily towards capacity charges as opposed to energy, which reflects the fact that the marginal cost of hydro generation is effectively zero.

With hydropower it is important to distinguish between average and firm energy. There are varying definitions of firm energy but it is typically taken as the output of the scheme having a 95 per cent. probability of exceedence in any year. Firm energy sometimes regarded for contractual purposes as a "guaranteed output" but one has to be very careful about this because, unlike similar guarantees on thermal stations, it is an obligation over which the owner/operator has very little control.

Where the revenue is related to energy generated, equity returns may be calculated on the basis of average energy, but when it comes to debt servicing one cannot assume a constant output each year and it is necessary to recognise the possibility of a series of dry years in succession. In this eventuality it may be necessary to resort to contingency funding such as an escrow account. Clearly any scheme is most vulnerable to this problem in the early years after commissioning, when the debt service burden is at its highest but before any significant reserves can be established. The hydrological probability of this coinciding with a period of low flow has to be carefully analysed, and the impact assessed under a series of downside scenarios.

The presence of a reservoir on the system raises some further interesting issues. Quite apart from the question of ownership, the way in which a reservoir is operated can materially influence the revenue from hydropower schemes and other projects downstream. There may well be conflicting interests in the waters stored by the reservoir with, for example, the irrigation or water supply sectors wanting an operating regime which curtails hydropower generation under certain conditions. Even where there are not conflicting water users, there may well be limitations imposed on the operation of a reservoir for environmental reasons so that it is constrained to low value, base-load operation instead of earning higher revenue as a peaking scheme.

Finally it will be necessary to secure the long-term security of the hydrology by addressing the subject of water rights and possible future developments in the catchment, which could impact on the future revenue stream for the private project. All of these issues will need to be covered in the various agreements.

Conclusions

The implementation of heavy civil engineering projects under private financing poses a particular challenge in terms of establishing a contractual framework which will satisfy the requirements of the financiers and yet, at the same time, produce the best project at the most competitive price. There appears to be some way to go before we have an established template which meets the requirements of the situation.

Specifically one has to recognise that it is often counter-productive to try to place all construction risk on to the contractor when the site has been inadequately investigated. One has to be careful about the allocation of design responsibility when there is a lack of clear project definition. And where hydrology is concerned there is a particular need for the parties to understand the complexities and the extent of their liabilities.

There is scope for closer co-operation on these matters between the lawyers, financiers and engineers concerned. It is important that these professionals have sufficient common ground between themselves to be able to offer sound advice based upon a balanced understanding of all the issues. This is indeed a new challenge for us all.

11. 'Institutional Economics' and Partnering in the Construction Industry†

James Barlow

Synopsis

This paper explores the extent to which 'institutional economics' can help to explain the emergence and forms of partnering in the British construction industry. The background to partnering and the forms it can take is then discussed, following which the findings from case studies of five partnering arrangements are examined to discuss how far institutional economics can help to explain the nature of these relationships.

Introduction

There is a growing interest on the part of the government and industry in the way collaborative relationships can improve the poor performance of the construction industry. Construction clients, contractors and suppliers have all sought ways of reducing the waste of resources associated with competitive tendering by making more use of 'partnering' and supply agreements.

To some extent, this interest mirrors the increased attention in organisational theory to new forms of 'hybrid' and 'virtual' enterprises,[1] and in institutional economics to uncertainty-reducing

† An earlier version of this paper was delivered to the AEA Conference on Construction Econometrics, Neuchâtel, 20-21 February 1997. The paper is based on research funded by the Economics and Social Research Council's Innovation Programme.

[1] Miles, R. & Snow, C. 'Network organisations: new concepts for new forms'. *California Management Review* 28 pp.62-73 (1987); Powell, W. 'Neither market nor hierarchy: network forms of organisation' in Staw, B. and Cummings, L. (eds.) *Research in Organisational Behaviour. Volume 12*, JAI Press, Greenwich, CT, 1990; Thompson, G., Frances, J., Levacic, R. & Mitchell, J. (eds.) *Markets, Hierarchies and Networks. The Co-ordination of Social Life*, Sage, London, 1991; and Williamson, O., 'Transaction cost economics and organisational theory'. *Industrial and Corporate Change* 2(2), pp.107-156 (1993).

arrangements, such as 'obligational contracting' and supply agreements.[2]

Concepts from institutional economics are potentially useful because of their focus on transaction costs as a key factor behind the emergence of non-market models of organising production. The emphasis is on the **environmental setting** of organisational behaviour and the **contractual arrangements** which govern the flow of resources between actors. Supply agreements, obligational contracting and partnering can all be seen in these terms as examples of non-market exchange designed to reduce uncertainty and minimise transaction costs.

The emergence of partnering in the UK construction industry

The impetus towards partnering

Although labour costs in Britain's construction industry are low, its out-turn construction costs are amongst the highest in the European Union. This is partly a result of poor labour productivity, but more fundamentally many commentators blame the industry's organisational structure and culture. Construction industries in all countries tend to be fragmented. However, what marks Britain (and the USA) out is the high degree of adversity in the inter-firm relationships in the industry. Claims, counter-claims and litigation frequently continue long after a project has been finished. The emphasis on competitive tendering sets up a 'my gain – your loss' ethos; unsuccessful bids result in costs which are absorbed by the industry as a whole.

The adversarial environment is regarded as a major hindrance to improvements in efficiency – the Latham Committee emphasised the importance of greater collaboration between clients and suppliers in helping to reduce the level of disputes. Many commentators feel that improving the performance of the industry will require new forms of

---

2   Williamson, O., *Markets and Hierarchies*, Free Press, New York, 1975; Kregel, J., 'Markets and institutions as features of a capitalistic production system'. *Journal of Post-Keynsian Economics*, 3(1): 32-48 (1980); Hodgson, G., *Economics and Institutions* Polity Press, Cambridge, 1988; and Imrie, R. & Morris, J., 'A review of recent changes in buyer-supplier relations'. *OMEGA International Journal of Management Science*, 20 (5/6): 641-652 (1992)

collaborative association, even though the industry has to some extent always combined forms of functional and market-based relationships.[3]

A more fundamental push towards construction industry partnering is the view, held by many important clients, that the current framework for managing the construction process in certain types of project is inadequate.[4] Traditional models view the construction process as the purchase of a product, governed by legal contracts. There is minimal uncertainty in the project ends, while any uncertainty in the means by which it is implemented is passed on to the contractors or sub-contractors as risk. The production process is managed by dividing the work into discrete packages which are purchased and completed according to a logical, planned set of phases.

This type of model can work – within current productivity standards – for relatively simple, slow and certain projects. When this is not the case, when projects are more complex or uncertain, or need to be completed rapidly, it becomes harder to co-ordinate the large number of specialist participants that are often involved. Under the circumstances construction tends to resemble a prototyping process, whereby the ends and means of the project are continuously negotiated by the various parties involved. This necessitates a blurring of the traditional boundaries between construction phases and activities, leading to more complex, non-hierarchical systems of communications. Although the transactions between parties are still governed by commercial contracts, more important for success is the way in which the values held by each party are accommodated to ensure no one set of values dominates the outcome of the project.

---

[3]   Bresnen, M., 'Construction contracting in theory and practice: a case study'. *Construction Management and Economics*, 9: 247-63 (1991); Eccles, R., 'The quasi-firm in the construction industry'. *Journal of Economic Behaviour and Organisation*, 2: 335-57 (1981); and Langford, D., Kennedy, P. & Somerville, P., 'Contingency management of conflict: analysis of contract interfaces' in Fenn, P. & Gameson, R. (eds.) *Construction Conflict Management and Resolution*, E & F Spon, London, 1992.

[4]   Howell, G., Miles, R., Fehlig, C. & Ballard, G. 'Beyond partnering: towards a new approach to project management' *Proceedings of the Fourth Annual Conference of the International Group for Lean Construction*. University of Birmingham 1996.

Howell *et al* argue that the partnering movement is evidence that the current framework for managing the construction process in complex, quick and uncertain projects is inadequate. Partnering represents an attempt to re-conceive the construction process, moving towards the right hand side of Table 1 but maintaining the best elements of traditional approaches.

'Traditional' model	➜➜➜	'Partnering' model
Construction as the purchase of a product	Underlying philosophy	Construction as a prototyping process
Fixed – minimal uncertainty in ends but uncertainty in means passed on as a risk	Project ends and means	Evolving – negotiation between owners, contractors and suppliers
Commercial contracts	Transactions governed by	Values of participants
Construction phases	Project management emphasis	Supply chain management
Within contractors	Project management activities	Between contractors – the 'virtual organisation'
Hierarchical	Communications	Multiple levels
Contract failure, excessive optimism, low performance	Disputes arise from	Inappropriate allocation of risk, stifling of innovation

Table 1 – Models of the construction process
Source – adapted from Howell et al.

Partnering forms

There is nor accepted definition of 'partnering' – some long-standing traditional client/contractor relationships are described in this way and there are probably as many definitions of partnering as there are firms engaged in it. Broadly, partnering refers to a variety of working relationships that enhance and maintain collaboration. However, a difference between partnering and more conventional arrangements – such as joint ventures – is that the latter involve a *legal* partnership. Organisations involved in partnering tend to be held together because of perceived mutual benefits. Partnering can therefore be seen more as a *process*, with the legal contract simply a feature of the relationship between the participants.[5] This suggests that it may be possible to identify different 'degrees' of partnering according to the nature of the relationship between the partners. These will range from situations where clients simply work with potential partners to develop their tenders, but with procurement by competitive tendering, through sequential tendering to more formalised arrangements, possibly with some form of partnering 'agreement'.

In management science there are three main perspectives on partnering.[6] First, most commentators see it as a tool for improving the performance of the construction process, emphasising the way partnering helps to create synergy and maximise the effectiveness of each participants' resources. A major benefit of partnering is its ability to influence project cost by bringing participants together at an earlier stage. Even though the initial design and planning costs may be higher in a partnered project, this should be offset by savings made by improved efficiency and a reduction in disputes. In the longer term, the existence of a partnering relationship can reduce the time spent by participants in learning how to work together, making them more responsive to any problems that might arise.

Second, partnering has been seen as a management process, for example a form of strategic planning or a variant of Total Quality Management (TQM). Finally, other commentators have focussed on the

---

5   *C.f.* Slowinski, G., Farris, G. & Jones, D. 'Strategic Partnering: process instead of event', *Research Technology Management*, May/June 1993, pp. 22-25.
6   Barlow, J., Cohen, M., Jashapara, A. & Simpson, Y. *Towards Positive Partnering*, Policy Press, 1997.

contractual and relationship implications of partnering, seeing it as a way of 'putting the handshake back into business'.

Minimally it is useful to distinguish between long-term partnering relationships, lasting the duration of several projects, and one-off relationships for a single project. *Long-term partnering* covers a broad range of strategic alliances between organisations or between different departments in the same organisation. While it can involve highly-structured agreements providing for a high level of cooperation between partners, long term partnering stops short of a true merger and allows each participant the latitude to pursue independent objectives and obligations.

Project partnering generally refers to a much narrower range of cooperative arrangements for the duration of a specific project. These can involve the entire construction project, with the relationship embracing the whole process from conceptualisation to finished product, or merely the early design and planning stages of a project. The distinguishing feature of project partnering is that its arrangements are of limited duration and generally end with the completion of the project.

Evidence from other industries (for example automotive, electronics) suggests that partnering is most appropriate where the value of the product or service is high or critical to a client's business, or the type of project is complex, but the number of contractors able to carry out the work is limited. Where there are few suppliers and the value of the product is low, there can be insufficient business for suppliers to build up a relationship with a single client and 'global resourcing' strategies, drawing from as wide a pool of suppliers as possible, may be more appropriate. Nor would clients be wise to enter a long term partnering agreement where a high value product or service is involved and there are numerous suppliers, since the client may lose the advantage of competitive tendering. This does not, of course, preclude the client from working with an exclusive group of suppliers ('local resourcing').

Understanding partnering – institutional economics approaches

Economists have increasingly turned to such issues as transaction costs, property rights and other contractual mechanisms to explain forms of economic organisation.[7] To what extent can this improve on existing management science approaches to partnering, which emphasise its organisational and cultural features, and research on supply chain management, which sheds light on the circumstances when partnering is most appropriate?

Institutional economics incorporates elements neglected or excluded in neo-classical perspectives directly on the frictions in transactions between firms to explain the choice between market and non-market models of organising production. Markets are seen as the most efficient mode of economic organisation until transaction costs rise to unacceptable levels, generally under conditions of high uncertainty or market failure. In competitive environments incentives therefore exist to develop organisational forms which best economise on transaction costs.[8] Williamson[9] outlines four different sub-disciplines which all stem from a common 'institutionalist' perspective – public choice theory, property rights approaches, agency theory, transaction cost economics. All four are distinguished by their stress on the contractual, rather than the technological, arrangements which govern and structure the flow of resources.

Transactional economics has been seen as useful for understanding partnering in the construction industry.[10] Alsagoff argues that in the

[7]   See Eggertson, T. *Economic Behaviour and Institutions* Cambridge University Press, 1990, for a general discussion and survey of institutional economics.

[8]   Milgrom, P. & Roberts, J. *Economics, Organization and Management*, Prentice Hall, Englewood Cliffs, 1992, and Veljanovski, C., *The New Law and Economics: a research review*, Centre for Socio-Legal Studies, Oxford, 1982.

[9]   Williamson, O., 'A comparison of alternative approaches to economic organization', *Journal of Institutional and Theoretical Economics* 146 (1990), pp.61-71.

[10] Alsagoff, A. & McDermott, P., 'Relational contracting: a prognosis for the UK construction industry' *Proceedings of CIB W92 Procurement Systems – East Meets West* University of Hong Kong, 1994, and McDermott, P. & Green, C., 'An inside-out approach to partnering' in *Partnering in Construction*.

construction context market inefficiency arises from imperfect knowledge of the financial risks at the time contracts are negotiated, the level of uncertainty over product definition and standards, and the 'locked' nature of the contract. Under these circumstances there is a tendency for parties to behave opportunistically – once a contract has been signed, power relationships change and contractors are able to exploit clients through additional claims.[11]

There has, however, been criticism of analytical attempts to emphasise transaction costs. Recent researchers have attempted to model transaction costs with a neo-institutionalist framework.[12] Bresnen argues[13] that there is a need to escape the power-dependency framework of held by much of the existing research on inter-organisational relations, whereby the nature of relations is determined by the comparative market and organisational power of the contractual parties. This arises from an over-emphasis on the economics and contractual mechanics of relationships. Focusing on the terms and conditions of specific transactions can result in researchers ignoring the strategic choices and tactical manoeuvring by actors to cope with conditions of dependency.

It is therefore critical to explore the factors which encourage or inhibit different forms of partnerships and the inter- and intra-organisational processes involved. A recognition of the diversity between and within

---

Proceedings of a One-Day Conference, University of Westminster and University of Salford, 1996.

[11] *Ibid* and Buckley, P. & Enderwick, P., 'Manpower management' in Hillebrant, P. & Cannon, J. (eds.) *The Management of Construction Firms*, MacMillan, London, 1989.

[12] Barzel, Y., 'Transaction costs: are they just costs?' *Journal of Institutional and Theoretical Economics* 141 (1985) pp.4-16 and Wohar, M., 'Alternative versions of the Coase theorem and the definitions of transaction costs' (1988) *Quarterly Journal of Business and Economics* pp.3-19. See Cooter, R. 'The cost of Coase' (1982) 11 *Journal of Legal Studies* 1 and Schlag, P., 'The problem of transaction costs' *Southern California Law Review* 62 (1989), 1661-1700 for criticism.

[13] Bresnen, M., 'An organisational perspective on changing buyer-supplier relations: a critical review of the evidence' (1996) *Organisation* 3(1): 1221-146 and Bresnen, M., 'Cultural change in the construction industry: developing the client's management role to improve project performance' in *Partnering in Construction Proceedings of a One-Day Conference*, University of Westminster and University of Salford, 1996.

organisations is also essential.[14] Furthermore, Robins argues[15] that researchers should avoid implying causality in the relationship between transactions and organisational structure, and situate transaction costs within more general organisation theory. This leads one to the conclusion that qualitative research on organisational culture and individual behaviour is an essential aspect of research in this field.[16]

I turn now to consider the ways transaction economics can help to assimilate the preliminary findings from a major research project on partnering.[17]

Evidence from the case studies

The research primarily involved a series of case studies of existing and emerging partnering agreements in different construction sectors (see Table 2). In-depth semi-structured interviews have been conducted with around 62 key staff in 36 companies involved in five partnering arrangements. These staff were responsible for both setting-up and the day-to-day management of the partnering arrangements. The interviews examined such areas as the direction of, and motives for, the particular strategies that were adopted, the ways in which personnel adjusted to change by making trade-offs or restructuring work relationships, and the evolution of partnering in response to unexpected events or crises. A series of interviews was also carried out with contractors who are actively seeking partnering relationships with potential clients, to explore their experiences in the current construction market.

---

[14] Winch, G., *Managing Production. Engineering Change and Stability*, Clarendon Press, Oxford, 1994.

[15] Robins, J., 'Organisational economics – notes on the use of transaction cost theory in the study of organisations', *Administrative Science Quarterly*, 32: 68-86 (1987).

[16] McDermott, P. & Green, C., 'An inside-out approach to partnering' in *Partnering in Construction. Proceedings of a One-Day Conference*, University of Westminster and University of Salford, 1996

[17] Funded by the Economic and Social Research Council and carried out by James Barlow, Michael Cohen, Ashok Jashapara and Yvonne Simpson. The results are published under the title *Towards Positive Partnering* (Policy Press, 1997).

	Refurbishment	*New Build*
One-off projects	*Selfridges:* Five contracts for refurbishment of Oxford Street store totalling £10m (part of £65m programme) 10 partner firms	*British Petroleum:* The 'Andrew Alliance', construction of a North Sea oil platform for an economically marginal field. 8 partner firms
Continuing construction programme	*NatWest Bank (London Region):* Redesign of bank branches; increase in construction work from c.40 to 60-100 projects a year. Selection from pool of 6 main contractors, 6 M&E contractors, 4 QS, 8 architects. Aim to further reduce the pool	*Safeway:* Long term build programme of new supermarkets, c. £200m pa. 2 main contractors (+others on occasional basis), 2 steel frame firms, 1 tiling firm, 6-10 store equipment firms, 2 refrigeration firms. *McDonald's:* Building 100 free standing drive-through restaurants p.a. across the UK. 2 modular building suppliers.

Table 2 – Details of case study partnerships

Clients' and contractors' reasons for partnering

Transactional approaches suggest that imperfect knowledge and the rigid nature of contracts are key factors behind the growth of collaborative relationships in the construction industry. To some extent this was reflected in the reasons why the case study clients had chosen partnering – generally this was because they needed to carry out projects with specific requirements which could not be fulfilled using traditional procurement methods. A concern to reduce cost and overcome previous negative experiences of traditional competitive procurement approaches, especially the escalation of cost, was the common factor behind the decision to partner by all clients. Interestingly, though, disputes avoidance appears *not* to have been a major impetus for clients, although an outcome of partnering was a far less confrontational atmosphere in the various projects.

The degree to which clients and their suppliers faced significant risk problems arising from project uncertainty varied between case studies. The large and complex BP and Selfridges projects both involved high degrees of risk, as well as considerable uncertainty over project ends and means. To some extent these were evolving through a process of negotiation between client, contractor and other suppliers. Construction in these examples could be described as prototyping process.[18] There were also relatively few suppliers which could fulfil the project requirements, making the careful selection of partners critical for project success. NatWest's programme of bank refurbishment also involved an element of uncertainty since many of the individual projects were in old and historically important buildings. Here, however, there was a far larger pool of contractors and suppliers on which the client could call.

In other cases, especially McDonald's and Safeway, the construction programme essentially involved the purchase of a standardised product, which was delivered on a repetitive basis and used a large proportion of prefabricated components. For McDonald's though, there were very few suppliers in the UK or elsewhere in Europe who could provide them with the modularised components they required for their buildings.

Clients also had other reasons for partnering. In particular, Safeway and NatWest wished to rationalise their supplier base, having learnt lessons from supply chain management processes in their retail business. Also important for some retailers was the need to ensure that trusted contractors and suppliers adequately represented them or their brand to their public customers or other internal clients.

---

[18] See Table 1, *supra*, p. 182.

In most cases partnering was suggested by the client and *contractors and suppliers* were generally unaware of the concept before involvement in the projects. A degree of scepticism within the contractors and suppliers was quite common, making it necessary for key personnel to 'sell' the concept internally. Some smaller firms felt they had no choice about the type of relationship with their client. In other cases firms had been working for the client for several years and felt the current arrangements were simply a development of this relationship. Some of the firms argued that although they were involved in informal partnering in which work was negotiated, they were nevertheless working under a competitive framework and had to tender for specific jobs.

Selecting partners

Only British Petroleum and NatWest could be said to have developed rigorous procedures for selecting potential partners. BP's approach partly emphasised the degree of commitment shown by possible partners to work with them to drive down cost and seek efficiency improvements. NatWest's selection process was more iterative, with the number of contractors and suppliers being honed down over three year on the basis of past performance. Safeway, on the other hand, had not attempted to rationalise its supplier base in the same way as NatWest. Long term relationships – informal partnering – were no guarantee of selection for specific schemes.

Some clients were concerned about maintaining competitiveness by selecting several suppliers or sub-contracts. For NatWest there was also a feeling that not only would a smaller supplier base lead to increased flexibility, but a firm's knowledge that it was on a chosen list would make it more likely to perform well. Safeway brought in other main contractors – which themselves had existing relationships with suppliers – in order to increase the pool of sub-contractors. McDonald's, which did not tell their initial supplier of modular buildings that they were going to introduce another firm, felt that the presence of two firms had 'made a tremendous difference' to each other's outlook.

Contractual relationships

The form of contract and mode of remuneration varied considerably, reflecting the different types of project, degrees of risk and internal attitudes. BP and Selfridges had established a partnering 'charter', signed by all parties. In other cases, it was felt that the lack of guarantees over future workloads made this impossible. In the case of McDonald's, there were no formal contracts at all..

As to remuneration, in the cases involving repeat projects, rates tended to be up to 30 per cent. below the going market rate, to reflect the benefits of longer term business. However, only the BP project structure contained a formal gain-sharing mechanism which provided explicit incentives to promote enhanced performance. In other cases the incentive for contractors and suppliers to perform was more indirect. On-time payment arising from reductions in the level of conflict, learning new approaches, and technical innovation were all outcomes from the partnering relationships, with possible longer term financial benefits.

The 'balance of power'

It has been noted that it is important to avoid over-emphasising the comparative market and organisational power of the contractual parties in shaping the nature of the relationship. Nevertheless, it was clear that there was great variety in the forms of relationship between the partners and the balance of power between them. It was also evident that a degree of dependency characterised some of the relationships. This was not simply an outcome of the recession in the construction industry and/or desperation on the part of smaller suppliers to take work under any contractual arrangement. An imbalance in power also emerged from the partnering process itself. Attempts to simplify information flows and develop new communications structures were a common feature in all the case studies, generally either by excising a chain of command or by allowing key people in each organisation to talk directly to one another. This helped to break down formalised, hierarchical systems of communication and create a flatter structure. However, some partners felt that there had been a disproportionate increase in the amount of time spent in communications. The number of points of contact between organisations had grown and many interviewees agreed that this had meant more meetings. Some partners therefore felt there was an uneven balance of power in terms of time spent on communications – clients were able to demand more of partners than in traditional types of relationship. Several contractors and suppliers complained that partnering was consequently an expensive approach to procurement, with an uncertain pay-off.

Conclusions

The major problems of the British construction industry are related to high transaction costs and market failure. These arise from the level of uncertainty surrounding may types of project and forms of contract which lock the parties into overly restrictive relationships. This environment is the result of the industry's organisational structure and its historically adversarial culture.

Transaction cost economics can help explain the *basis* for partnering as a form of organising production. A major benefit of partnering is the way it can reduce construction costs and improve performance by encouraging collaboration between participants at an earlier stage. In the longer term, partnering can result in technical and business innovation. Broadly, partnering serves to reduce the inter- and intra-organisational transaction costs in the construction industry.

Such an approach can only take us so far, however. In particular it cannot explain the subtleties of different partnering forms, nor can it explain the precise circumstances under which it may emerge. To a large extent, the impetus for partnering in the research case studies could be described as a desire to reduce transaction costs arising from the current poor performance of the construction industry. Essentially, clients believed that their construction programmes could not be fulfilled using standard procurement approaches, which were seen as too unpredictable or costly in terms of staffing, time and money. Also some clients had learnt lessons from procurement practices in their core business, partnering being seen a tool to rationalise the supplier base and thereby improve construction performance. However, 'soft' issues also featured as an important reason for some of the clients, who were keen to develop links with trusted contractors who could act as their public face and represent their brand image.

It has been noted that it is important not to assume that there is some sort of causality in the relationship between transactions and organisational structure. However, the balance of power in the partnering relationships cannot be discounted as a factor underpinning their evolution. Despite the importance of mutual trust and gain, stressed by a number of clients, power frequently remained on the client's side. This can be seen in three ways.

First, competitive tendering still dominated the procurement practices, backed by a continuous performance assessment of partners. Other clients maintained a pool of preferred suppliers which had increased in size in order to inject an element of competition into their construction programme. Second, the relative power of clients was evident from the systems of remuneration, where, to account for the benefits of a longer term relationship, specific tasks were costed at 30 per cent. below the market price. Only the BP Andrew Project had a formal gain-sharing mechanism with incentives for partners to improve their performance. In other cases the incentive for contractors and suppliers to perform was more indirect, relating to vague promises as to future work. Finally, an imbalance in power could be seen in terms of the increased amount of time spent in communicating with clients and other partners. This was seen as a particular problem by smaller firms.

Institutionalist approaches cannot shed much light on the process involved in making partnering work. Raising the level of mutual trust – as partnering implies – is potentially problematic in an industry which has been dominated by traditional procurement methods involving rigid inter-firm contract, hierarchically organised project partners, and highly competitive relationships.

The case study research suggests that two essential elements of successful partnering are the selection of personnel and openness of communications within and between organisations. There is evidence that clients and contractors recognise this, with several examples of the strategic movement of key individuals to achieve an optimum mix of personalities and attempts to build more flexible structures for communication. Trust emerges as a result of these features. This does not mean that *organisational culture* is unimportant, as it is this which plays a major part in clients' preparedness to engage in the partnering in the first place, in their choice of partners, and in the ease with which these features can be established. However, theoretical approaches which over-emphasise the contractual and economic features of relationships fail to reflect the behavioural processes involved in partnering.

So, to what extent can institutional economics improve on our existing understanding of partnering? Management science perspectives emphasise the role of partnering as a tool for maximising the effectiveness of each participants' resources. This tells us little about the conditions for the emergence of partnering, as it essentially views partnering as a management process. Institutional economics, on the other hand, can help shed light on these conditions, although it is important to place such an explanation in the context of their environment – how many potential suppliers of the particular construction product exist, how critical is the product to the client?

While it cannot explain the subtleties of the partnering process and the variety of forms it may take, institutionalist perspectives on economic theory are nevertheless important because of their focus on elements neglected in other approaches. The challenge is to find ways of including such issues as environmental setting and organisational culture and behaviour in economic models of construction markets. In the longer term such a process may lead to a growing convergence between economic theory and theories of organisational behaviour.

12. Partnering: Problems and Pitfalls in Practice†

John Dorter

Synopsis

This paper examines some fundamental conceptual differences between partnering agreements and traditional construction contracts in the context of seeking to mesh the legal liabilities, rights and obligations arising thereunder with the project itself. In conclusion, an illustration of the dangers which may arise when the conceptual differences are not fully realised by the drafsman, or are overridden by commercial imperative, is given.

Introduction

Experience to date with partnering in the construction and engineering sector has demonstrated that an essential issue has been the failure adequately to recognise whether it is the parties' relationships and conduct, as distinct from contract, which has been "partnered". The proponents of partnering have glibly claimed that partnering:

- "puts the handshake back into business";
- "is the way we used to do business"; and
- "is common sense".

Be that as it may (or may not be), the bald fact is that not one project has been done on a handshake, trust or "a person's word being their bond" to the abandonment of the normal contract. Fundamental and finally fatal is the failure to relate the "philosophy", "mind set" and

---

† This paper has been developed from the author's two previously published papers entitled *Implications of Partnering for Mining and Construction* and *Partnering — Think it Through* published at (1996) 12 BCL 176 and (1997) 13 BCL 23 (reprinted (1997) 63 JCIArb. 210), respectively. The kind permission of **Building and Construction Law Journal,** The Law Book Company, Sydney and the Chartered Institute of Arbitrators, is gratefully acknowledged.

"process" of partnering to the benefits, rights, obligations and liabilities of the parties under their contract. Captains of commerce have been quick to proclaim that "Partnering is not a contractual agreement nor does it create any legally enforceable rights or duties". However, some slippage, and even cracks, are now appearing. Other champions of partnering assert that it is "a process of establishing a moral contract or charter". Such "moral contracts" and "gentlemen's agreements" raise the spectre of those Claytons contracts, whereby each party hoped that the arrangement was a contract binding on the other party but not upon themselves.

Structure and application of partnering — good faith

The quintessence of successfully meshing the obligations and liabilities of the parties is the bringing together of conduct and contract. True it is that one or two judges, following black letter law, are biased against doing so. In fairness, there is the highest authority that the main bridge (in the form of a good faith clause) cannot be implied. Compare no less than Lord Ackner:[1]

> "*The concept of a duty to carry on negotiations in good faith is inherently repugnant to the adversarial position of the parties when involved in negotiations. Each party to the negotiations is entitled to pursue his (or her) own interest, so long as he avoids making misrepresentations. To advance that interest he must be entitled, if he thinks it appropriate, to threaten to withdraw from further negotiations or to withdraw in fact, in the hope that the opposite party may seek to reopen the negotiations by offering him improved terms.*"[2]

An alternative view may be that there are, in fact, some answers. First, in that case, Lord Ackner was speaking of negotiations. Secondly, Lord Mansfield said, as early as in 1766, that good faith was "applicable to all contracts and dealings",[3] which would seem to be a common theme of that age:

---

[1]   *Walford v Miles* [1992] 2 AC 128

[2]   *Ibid* at 138

[3]   *Carter v Boehm* (1766) 97 ER 1162 at 1164

"in contracts of all kinds, it is of the highest importance that courts of law should compel the observance of honesty and good faith."[4]

For example the doctrine of good faith is powerfully employed in the United States of America:

*"Every contract imposes upon each party a duty of **good faith and fair dealing**[5] in its performance and its enforcement."*[6] (Emphasis supplied.)

In fundamental form, such a contractual bridge is simply building upon fundamental implied terms of long standing, for example:

- in all things, to act reasonably, honestly and fairly;
- to do all things necessary so as to co-operate in achieving the contractual aim; and
- not to prevent, impede, fetter or hinder the other party in the performance of the contract.

Of course, in order to prevent developments in a vacuum, such fundamental issues must be followed through. The drafting team must remove or reduce "adversarial" clauses, such as time bars and Draconian forfeiture and "non-constructive" provisions. What must, however, be recognised by the construction professionals is that the twin towers of specification writing and drafting of contracts are not their forte. It is all very well for them to plead in defence that this was not their motive in becoming architects, engineers or surveyors, but that does not excuse them from the duties owed under their contract of appointment. Were it not for the fact that in practice very many documentation defects are rectified during the execution of the project,

---

[4]   *Mellish v. Motteux* (1792) 170 ER 113 *per* Lord Kenyon at 113-114.

[5]   Significant is the reference to both good faith and fair dealing. Whatever the readiness or reluctance of Australia's judges to hold that the doctrine has arrived in Australia (perhaps even in a compromise form similar to Canada's), Parliament has already done it – in respect of both good faith and fair dealing. If those involved in the failed or distressed partnered projects can resort to the Trade Practices Act and the Fair Trading Acts, why should not those drafting contracts?

[6]   Restatement of the Law, Contract (1981) § 5205

they would suffer much more claims in negligence and breach of contract. As it is, if the client does not thereafter enter a claim against his professionals, they still can suffer the trauma of cross-examination and other criticism when a forensic tribunal, such as in court or at arbitration, reviews their documentation (and administration).

Without such consultants having to be lawyers, the bare fact is that simply a cut and paste exercise with the historically relevant documents and correspondence, produces a confusing, contradictory collation of paper conducive to the evolution of disputes. To take just one illustration:

> *"I must say that the departure from traditional terminology in amending the well known clause ... is not only anomalous but deplorable. It is like tipping an entirely gratuitous truck load of manure into this already sufficiently muddied stream."*[7]

Is it really too much to ask of those involved in the preparation of tenders and contract documentation that they address their minds to the fundamental concepts involved in the transmission of risk and liability. Good faith and fair dealing provision are not lightly to be tampered with—the consequences can be absolutely disastrous.

General conditions of construction contracts

I turn now to consider some of the factors in a construction contract that do not sit easily with a partnering agreement, and which present significant obstacles to the drafstman.

A fundamental factor to be kept in mind is the contractual background of mutuality in reciprocal rights and obligations. I take as the respective bases the generally accepted principle that a construction contract is an exchange of promises to produce a project for a price within a given period, and that a partnering agreement, or charter, is a pro-active co-operation which co-joins disparate entities who share a common goal.

---

[7]　*In the Matter of an Arbitration between Taylor Woodrow International Limited and the Minister of Health* (1978) 19 SASR 1

Implied Terms

The *Mackay v Dick* [8] implied term is basic to nearly every construction contract, that is to say the parties have each promised the other that he will do all that is necessary to be done on his part for the carrying out and achievement of the contractual aim. This principle has been given judicial support by the High Court of Australia in *Electronic Industries Limited v David Jones Limited* [9] and by Macfarlan J in *Perini Corporation v Commonwealth of Australia* [10] (the Redfern Mail Exchange case). In that case, Macfarlan J attached considerable importance to the basic aim of a construction contract:

> *"It must in my opinion be assumed that the parties entered into this agreement and it must be assumed that when they did so they intended to achieve something. The definition of what they intended to achieve is to be found in the agreement itself."*
>
> ...
>
> *"In my opinion the plaintiff and the defendant, being the parties bound by this agreement, are bound to do all co-operative acts necessary to bring about the contractual result."*

In following the *Mackay v Dick* implied term Macfarlan J. went on to say:

> *"I think I may safely say as a general rule that where in a written contract it appears that both parties have agreed that something shall be done which cannot effectually be done unless both concur in doing it, the construction of the contract is that each agrees to do all that is necessary to be done on his part for the carrying out of that thing, though there may be no express words to that effect."*

A similar but different implied term is common in conveyancing contracts; *viz* "each party will do all such things as are necessary on his part to enable the other party to have the benefit of the contract".[11] This

---

[8]   (1881) 6 App Cas 251

[9]   (1954) 91 CLR 228 at 297-298

[10] [1969] 2 NSWR 530

[11] *Butt v McDonald* (1896) 7 QLJ 68, *per* Griffith CJ at 70-7; *Secured Income Real Estate (Australia) Ltd v St Martins Investments Pty Ltd* (1979) 144 CLR 596 *per* Mason J, as he then was, at 607.

implied term is somewhat of a higher order than the *Mackay v Dick* implied term and it may be too high for the sophisticated and detailed provisions of a construction contract, as distinct from the fairly standard provisions of conveyancing contracts for the sale of land. Implied terms readily accepted by the courts in respect of routine and consumer-type sale of goods transactions are not always readily imported into sophisticated construction contracts.

A promise to use one's best endeavours, albeit of a high order such that second best is not good enough, must still be construed reasonably. For example what is required is discharge of what the promisor can do to achieve the contractual aim within the bounds of reason, as distinct from acting in such a way that he is ruined.[12]

Like most long term contracts for major projects other than just construction (eg joint ventures), there is a need for some mechanism to make those mutual promises work. In short it is the function of the contract administrator. Against this contractual context and legal background the qualifications, or qualities, required of the contract administrator come close to professional ones. It is not without significance that most major construction contracts in Australia for some time until recently, and their antecedents in the United Kingdom, specifically contemplated "the engineer" or "the architect" as distinct from "the superintendent". Indeed, thereafter and until recently, "the superintendent" was prima facie to be an engineer or architect.

The contract administrator generally needs to be able to apply organised knowledge and ability in serving the rights, duties and interests of the principal and contractor—with integrity, honesty, fairness and usually reasonably. These qualities usually have to transcend commercial and monetary considerations. The contract administrator's role is an invidious and almost impossible one. Apart from these duties to both employer and contractor, the contract administrator has an overall duty to achieve the contractual aim. Although the principal and the contractor are supposed to be co-operating in that achievement, in practice they are very soon evidencing their competing commercial concerns; he or she is required to try to hold the balance between those contenders.

---

[12] *Hawkins v Pender Bros Pty Ltd* [1990] 1 Qd R 135

Commencement

It is generally a fundamental term of a construction contract that the site be made available in a time sufficient for the contractor to perform his obligations under the contract. Breach of this condition by the principal may entitle the contractor, at common law, to rescind on appropriate facts if these facts are such that the principal has repudiated the conditions. For example, a construction contract required the principal to excavate the site to a specified level and to give to the contractor possession of the site, duly excavated, not later than a specified date. The principal failed to excavate the site and did not give possession to the contractor by the specified date. The principal also gave to a third party a contract for the fabrication of steel work; notwithstanding a provision in the specification that such work was to be performed by the contractor. The contractor wrote to the employer advising that the contract was at an end. The High Court held that the principal by his conduct had evinced an intention no longer to be bound by the contract, so that the contractor was justified in acting as he did.[13]

Most major construction contracts, therefore, seek to reduce the owner's common law exposure by clearly expressing the contractor's remedy as an extension of time, together with, if the extent and degree of the delay becomes more serious, suspension or determination.

Progress, programming and performance

A similar philosophy applies to the contractor's obligations as to time in carrying out and completing the works. The obligation of the contractor is, at common law, to execute the work within a reasonable time. This obligation is generally expressed in construction contracts that the contractor is to, for example, 'execute the work regularly and diligently'. "Diligently" has been held to mean not only the individual industriousness of the builder but also his or her efficiency and the efficiency of all those who are working with him or her.[14] More recently, "regularly and diligently" has been held to mean that the

---

[13] *Carr v J A Berriman Pty Ltd* (1953) 89 CLR 327
[14] *Hooker Constructions Pty Ltd v Chris's Engineering Contracting Company* [1970] ALR 821 *per* Blackburn J at 822.

contractor must carry out the work in such a way as to achieve his or her contractual obligations, including planning, provision of sufficient and proper materials, employment of competent tradesmen, management of work force—all to the effect that he or she carries out his or her obligations under the contract to an acceptable standard and according to his or her time obligations.[15]

The contractor's obligation to proceed with the performance of the works regularly and diligently does not imply an obligation to programme his or her performance strictly so as, for example, to avoid delays.[16] Accordingly that further obligation has to be expressed: that is to say the contractor is not to be entitled to an extension of time unless he or she shall have taken proper and reasonable steps both to preclude the occurrence of the cause of delay and/or to avoid or minimise the con-sequences thereof; and the contractor is constantly to use his or her best endeavours to avoid delay and to do all that may be reasonably required to expedite completion.

On the contrary, the law is now fairly well settled that the programme is essentially the contractor's programme. It is suggested that the better view is that float belongs prima facie to the contractor; subject of course to clear and express provisions in the contract to the contrary. Accordingly some employers try to have the best of both worlds by placing all the usual time obligations upon the contractor yet dictating and monopolising the management of his or her programme Such contractual provisions need to be very carefully drawn because otherwise the consequences can be almost catastrophic for the principal by way of consequential claims for disruption, acceleration, prolongation etc.

The contractual linchpin of the programmesmanship strategy is the contractor's obligations, confirmed by the courts, to honour two basic obligations, viz: carrying out and completing the work in accordance with the contract documents; and carrying out and completing the work in accordance with the directions of the contract administrator.

---

[15] *West Faulkner Associates v London Borough of Newham* (1993) 61 BLR 81 (1992) 31 Con LR 105; affirmed by the Court of Appeal, and see Tolson, S., (1996) 62 JCIArb, 70(s).

[16] *Walter Lawrence & Son Ltd v Commercial Union Properties (UK)* (1986) 4 Con LR 37

It does not take a very astute draftsperson to remember that the reciprocal obligations under a contract render it a double-edged sword. Succinctly put, the obligation to perform in accordance with the contract administrator's directions can be turned around in order to use (or perhaps abuse) time and money. The critical link in the "programmesmanship strategy" (and therefore where it is most vulnerable) is whether the revised, optimistic programme is given contractual force.

Once the contractor is able to secure contractual force for the contract administrator, he or she can choose between a number of options. Most contracts give the contractor at least extra costs. Some are more generous with an express entitlement to delay and disruption. Yet again, some (albeit perhaps unwittingly) give an express entitlement to acceleration compensation. Even worse, very few contracts make such compensation exclusive and exhaustive; so that a claim for the more generous damages for breach of contract is often still available. How the contractor then exploits the situation is a matter for him or his advisers. Plainly this is fundamentally incompatible with a partnering agreement.

Extension of time

The combined effect of the principal's obligation to avoid infringing the contractor's rights in respect of his programme and the "penalties" which would otherwise be cast upon the contractor for failure to observe the time provisions is such that the principal is subject to what has been held to be a warranty, albeit impliedly, not to interfere with the progress of the work; for example by failing to obtain permits which the principal is required to obtain.[17]

The employer who does not, in fact, have clean hands will jeopardise his remedies including any provision for liquidated damages, unless the contract protects him with an appropriate provision for an extension of time. The legal basis of this bar to his or her right to liquidated damages is best known as the ' 'prevention principle'; its basis perhaps

---

[17] *Ellis-Don Ltd v Parking Authority (Toronto)* (1978) 28 BLR 99. Compare also the *Perini* duty to co-operate in achieving the contractual result.

also being an implied term.[18] Alternatively, either the basis can be said to be an implied supplemental contract,[19] or the basis can be said to be waiver.[20]

The tug-of-war between the prevention principle and risk allocation has caused considerable concern about concurrent or overlapping delays. One short, simple solution is provided by AS 4300:

> *"Where more than one event causes concurrent delays and the cause of at least one of those events, but not all of them, is not a cause of delay listed in Clause 35.5(a) or (b), then to the extent that the delays are concurrent, the Contractor shall not be entitled to an extension of time for Practical Completion."*

However, it is a valid observation that such a provision is not truly fair and balanced, and certainly does not accord with the essence of partnering. Perhaps a better way of dealing with the problem is to leave it to the contact administrator. However, this raises an issue as to whether it is appropriate to leave difficult questions of causation and contribution to the contract administrator. Those responsible for clearly identifying the risk and concisely allocating it have a duty to recognise the fundamental criterion of causation. Perhaps a better way is to give the contract administrator guidelines, for example:

> *"Notwithstanding the other provisions of his clause, in the event that concurrent delays occur to the work under the Contract the Superintendent shall determine the Contractor's entitlement, if any, to an extension of time by apportioning the resulting delay by*

---

[18] *C.f. Aurel Forras Pty Ltd v Graham Karp Developments Pty Ltd* [1975] VR 202 *per* Menhennitt J at 209; and *Southern Foundries (1926) Ltd v Shirlaw* [1940] AC 701 *per* Lord Atkin at 717
  "(The) *positive rule of the law of contract that conduct of either promiser or pomisee which can be said to amount to himself 'of his own motion' bringing about the impossibility of performance is in itself a breach*"
  Lord Atkin's principle has successfully been applied in *Commissioner for Main Roads v Reed & Stuart Pty Ltd* (1974) 48 ALJR 461 *per* Stephen J at 642.

[19] *Aurel Forras Pty Ltd v Graham Karp Developments Pty Ltd* [1975] VR 202 *per* Menhennitt J at 209

[20] *Dodd v Churton* [1897] 1 QB 562

the Contractor in reaching Practical Completion to the various causes of the delays to the work under the Contract on the basis of their respective contributions to the delay by the Contractor in reaching Practical Completion. The validity and enforceability of the Date for Practical Completion as so extended shall not be affected by any negation or reduction which has occurred as a consequence of the Superintendent's apportionment in the entitlement the Contractor would otherwise have had to an extension of time for any particular cause of delay, including but not limited to the causes of delay ... [set out above]."

This cumbersome clause underlines that mutuality and reciprocity in contracts should never be forgotten. There are often substantial and significant situations where it is in the employer's interests that there be an extension of time. Strategic interests of the contractor, on the other hand, may depend upon there not being an extension of time. On balance, the interests of the contract and the project may be such that it be available and considered.

Variations

Increased physical work under the contract is of course also another factor. Accordingly it needs to be dealt with by carefully crafted clauses. Such clauses should leave no doubt as to what is or is not a variation. Such clauses should also require early "alert" and ongoing communication, including early notification of the likely "impact" as to both money and time. Perhaps the best illustration of what can go wrong is the dreaded latent condition. Big claims and large amounts of money have been built on alleged latent conditions. Accordingly best practice in risk identification, risk allocation and risk management requires a good latent conditions clause.

As to variations, the basic proposition used to be that the principal was in a better position to know his own property than the contractor, who simply comes upon it for the first time and for the limited purpose of doing some work on it. Accordingly it was the principal who should bear the responsibility for any special difficulties of the site. Departing from that proposition there evolved the practice of drawing contracts so as to impose upon the contractor, who was after all more expert in such matters relating to construction, the liability for all investigations, tests etc necessary for the purpose of carrying out the works the subject of his or her promise in the contract. That in turn was seen to be going too far the other way, so that the "latent condition" proviso (sometimes together with equitable adjustment) was often added. The modern philosophy is not unlike that in respect of the latent defect in conveyancing developed from the old cases like *Flight v. Booth* [21] and *Torr v Harpur.*[22] Resources exploration and exploitation is probably the highest risk industry. The industry is not far behind it in terms of risk. When the risks of both come together in subsurface situations, parties to a contract need to work harder at the risk identification, risk allocation and risk management.

For too long there has been widespread and longstanding concern in the construction industry with the difficulties involved in the preparation and provision of geotechnical site information; let alone the high incidence of claims and disputes over latent conditions. These claims and disputes have become almost inevitable in the construction of bi-centennial highways, airports, earthworks reclamation, dams, shafts, tunnels, dredging wharves and other marine structures.

In summary, the industry would be guilty of perhaps the worst "tunnel vision" if it were to ignore the many facets and directions of the risks associated. Accordingly, the aim of the good contract should perhaps be:

(a) to provide bases for the realistic apportionment of responsibility and risk associated with subsurface soil/ground conditions between all relevant parties to the construction project;

(b) to establish and define broad categories of data for the purposes of disclosure in tender and contract documents, and to define the differences between them;

(c) in terms of these categories, to realise what data should be provided to tenderers and in what manner, if at all, they should be qualified;

---

[21] (1834) 1 Bing (NC) 370, (1834) 131 ER 1160
[22] (1940) 57 WN 195

(d) to establish principles and procedures in order to deal with conditions which vary significantly from those described, and especially for the apportionment of the consequences between the contractor and the principal;

(e) to minimise the risk to the contractor by enabling him

(f) to make as informed a decision as possible on construction methods, costs, rates of progress etc; and

(g) to minimise the risk to the principal, *ie* latent deemed variations, delays, ingenious claims from contractors for delay costs, prolongation, disruption, acceleration and equitable adjustment.

It is clear from the above that the allocation of responsibility in general terms is critical if a construction contract is adequately to mesh with a partnership agreement. The approaches to contractual allocation of responsibility for site investigations, let alone for differences therefrom, can and do differ significantly. The approach chosen will depend upon a number of factors including:

- the economic state of the industry and the resultant cost benefits, or lack thereof, to the principal, including provision for relief for latent ground conditions;
- the commercial bargaining power of the parties;
- attitudes, perceptions and policies; and
- the desire to set up the contract to avoid or at least reduce claims or actions about site investigations and latent conditions differing from them.

At one end of the spectrum there is the Utopian possibility that the principal may assume all of the responsibility in relation to the conditions encountered by the contractor. The logic behind this approach is of course that it is the principal's site and it is reasonable for the principal to assume responsibility in relation to the site's adequacy to support the design, or in relation to problems during construction. Furthermore, in many cases, the principal will have come to know the site well through the investigation programme and may know what to expect from other projects in the area. If the principal assumes such responsibility, he has an incentive to carry out the most appropriate level of investigation.

The advantage of this approach is that the principal will, at least in theory, pay for only the conditions actually encountered, rather than automatically pay for substantial contingencies included in the tender price which may not actually be encountered during construction. Difficulties can occur in this approach in determining whether a condition encountered was within the original, reasonable foreseeability of the parties at the time of contract, or whether there should be some deemed variation on the basis that the condition differs sufficiently from those which should reasonably have been anticipated and allowed for in the tender price. For this reason it is important that the parties agree about both the conditions expected and the reliability of the data provided at the date of the invitation to tender, not at the date of the claim.

At the other end of the spectrum, the competent contractor is expected to take total responsibility for the site conditions and must find a solution to all problems impacting upon his or her construction, at his own expense and without concessions from the principal. The rationale for this approach is that the contractor has been chosen for his or her competence and should best know, and be able to make allowance for, the conditions likely to be encountered; and therefore the construction resources and methods required. In some circumstances, the contractor may be in a better position to know what to expect in terms of ground conditions. It is trite that this approach leads to ingenious and complex claims, disputes and ill-will; especially if the market is tightly competitive at the time. The successful tenderer probably will not have included such contingencies in his or her price and may even have under-bid. Then the principal, in practice, often resists strenuously and emotionally, firmly feeling that the contractor should have taken the risk.

The latter generally represented the attitude of the courts until comparatively recent times. The fundamental doctrine of freedom of contract permitted the judges to assume that competent contractors made allowance in their tender prices for such risks. Even if the judge thought the contract was not a wise one, and one which he would not have entered into, then 'If that is the bed the parties made for them-selves, let them lie in it.'

Traditional contractual analysis has encouraged the contractor to plead the claim as an alleged warranty in the contract; albeit more often than not without success. For example, one contractor contracted with the City of London to take down an old bridge and build a new one. In inviting him to tender for that contract, the principal had supplied him with drawings and a specification prepared by the principal's engineer. When he was awarded the contract, he agreed to obey the directions of the engineer (contract administrator). Descriptions of the work were expressed to be "believed to be correct" but not to be guaranteed. The House of Lords held that such a warranty could not be implied into the contract.[23]

Similarly, site conditions relating to the elements and weather fared no better as the subject matter of alleged implied warranties. When a contractor alleged such an implied warranty to the effect that the seashore on which he was to carry out the proposed works would remain in the same condition as at the date of the contract, the House of Lords again held that no such warranty was to be implied.[24]

The precise terms of the contract are of course critical.[25] The plain fact that the principal generally seeks to keep the tenderer' price down is normally not reflected in the terms of the contract. Nevertheless, when one adds to that the principal's (usually by his or her consultants) desire to impress upon the contractor his or her particular wishes in respect of design, method of work etc, there are usually reflections of this in the terms of the contract.

Accordingly, the risk will often shift in contract documentation which tends to blur the strict demarcation between the respective roles of contractor, principal and principal's consultants. For example, when tenders were invited for a design and construct project, the principal's quantity surveyors told the successful tenderer that the design was to be prepared on the assumption that the soil conditions were as indicated on the bore hole data provided by the principal. On that assumption, the tenderer's design was adequate but, during the carrying out of the work, the presence of tufa was discovered and re-design of the

---

[23] *Thorn v City of London* [1876] 1 AC 120
[24] *Jackson v Eastbourne Local Board* (1886) Hudson's BC (4th ed) 81.
[25] *George Wimpey & Co Ltd v Territory Enterprises Pty Ltd* (1971) 45 ALJR 38

foundations, together with additional work, was necessary. In the circumstances the contractor alleged an implied term or warranty by the principal that the ground conditions would be in accordance with the assumption put to him. The court upheld the implied term or warranty, essentially because the contract was one for a comprehensive development, whereby the contractor had to know the soil conditions in order properly to plan his programme for the carrying out of the work and to assess the resources he would need.[26]

Ultimately the welfare of the contract, of the project and of the parties is best served by a balanced and equitable contract, and this is generally in concord with the philosophy of partnering.

Conclusion

In conclusion, I cite a painful example of what can go wrong when the fundaments of conduct and contract are blurred. This case revolves around a contract for the construction, maintenance and operation of a motorway let by an Australian Government Agency. The construction component was construct only and the general conditions of contract were based on AS 2124 (now AS 4000).[27]

After award of the contract the Government Agency, as principal to the contract, suggested to the contractor that the project be partnered. Two months later, a one day workshop was held. Most of the site personnel who were going to be "at the coal face" attended and generally got on very well—especially over the very lengthy post-workshop barbeque. Senior representatives of the principal and the contractor did not attend; and neither the contract administrator, nor the consultants attended.

At that workshop the principal's people said more than once that partnering would not change the legal relationships: rather it would

---

[26] *Bacal Construction (Midlands) Ltd v Northampton Development Corporation* (1975) 8 BLR 88 *per* Buckley LJ at 100.
[27] For a discussion of some of the provisions of the Australian Standard 2124:1992 contract, see my paper in Odams, A.M. (ed) *Comparative Studies in Construction Law: The Sweet Lectures*, Construction Law Press, London, 1995, p.49. A copy of the contract is included as an appendix to that collection.

'define the working relationships between the parties and the factors that would facilitate the successful completion of a successful project'. One of the more senior officers of the principal also said: "Partnering is not a legal procedure but a formal recognition that every contract should include an implied covenant of good faith and fair dealing." At the end of the workshop all present signed a "charter", which included statements such as:

> "*in partnership, we promise that we are committed to ...*
> *cooperation ...*
> *minimum extra cost ...*
> *maximising budget opportunities ...*
> *no delays ...*
> *no disruption ...*
> *all so as to bring the project in within time and price.*"

Two months later the contractor notified the contract administrator that it had been delayed for some four months in trying to obtain adequate resources for a specialist portion of the project' in that, despite the principal's and the contract administrator's insistence thereon, it was just not available in the industry. The principal intervened and told the contractor not to worry about it any more, in that the principal would now do that part of the contract work itself. The contract administrator did not issue a variation order to omit that work.

One month after that notfication (now three months down the line), the contractor encountered a latent condition. The contractor did comply with the contract in giving notice to the contract administrator. The principal intervened and told the contractor that the contractor might now use nearby borrow pits which were not previously to be available, thus (in the principal's opinion) solving the contractor's problem.

Six months further on (now nine months down the line), the contractor gave formal notice to the contract administrator that the compounding of the above events had caused disruption and delay. The contractor claimed adjustments to the contract sum by way of compensation. Again the principal intervened and told the contractor that a particular programme deviation put forward by the principal would solve the contractor's problem.

Three months further on (now a full year into the contract), the contractor made it clear to the principal and the contract administrator that it wished to commence litigation against the contract administrator. The contractor notified the principal that a cooperative compromise would be for the principal to remove and replace the contract administrator.

At one of the regular partnering review and evaluation meetings the principal's on-site champion said: "How come our last partnered project went so much better than this one? (You seem to have resourced down on this one.)" The situation continued to deteriorate. The contractor entered a formal claim, alleging, *inter alia*:

(a) a collateral contract, particularised as to the partnering charter;

(b) breaches of contract, particularised as to:
    i.   an implied term to cause the contract administrator to cooperate where difficulties were encountered;
    ii. latent conditions;
    iii. programme deviations and adjustments to the contract sum; and
    iv. variations;

(c) misrepresentation;

(d) misleading representations and misleading conduct, particularised (allegedly without limitation) as to the workshop and the "charter";

(e) frustration, particularised as to contradictions between the construction contract and the partnering relationship;

(f) waiver of the contractual provisions for the benefit of the principal, including especially time bars on claims; and

(g) estoppel, including its use as a sword.

The claim goes on to claim relief by way of:

- an order that the contract be set aside and the contractor be entitled on a quantum meruit basis; and
- in the alternative, damages.

In support of the claim the contractor argues, inter alia, that the principal (including those for whom the principal is responsible) used an inappropriate and misleading contract delivery method, *viz* Design & Construct would have been more appropriate; and partnering should have been suggested before tenders were invited or at least before the contractor's tender was accepted.

I leave you to consider whether partnering can in its present state of evolution form a contractual bridge between contract and conduct by simply building upon fundamental contractual provisions of long standing.

Part III

Construction and the Regulated Industries

13. Informal 'Contracts' in Regulated Industries

Peter Vass

Synopsis

This paper provides an introductory overview of what are termed 'contractual' issues which have arisen in the regulation of the privatised, network industries.

Introduction

The regulated industries referred to in the title cover the utilities and other network industries which, following privatisation, have been regulated by separate bodies from the sponsoring departments of state responsible for those industries. The industries were privatised by separate Acts of Parliament, but the companies themselves have plc status, shares in which were listed on the Stock Exchange at privatisation. There are many common features in contracting practice and the application of the law, therefore, as between the regulated industries and other commercial entities. There are, however, some distinctive 'contractual' issues which have arisen through the development of regulation – most of which are about informal 'contracts'. The question is whether they should be made more formal.

The introduction will set out the general framework, followed by a section which focuses on the investor and the customer with respect to these 'contractual' issues. The inverted commas around 'contractual' have been used simply to indicate that we are concerned with both formal and informal contracts; the latter often being referred to as understandings, bargains, expectations and other similar terms.

History and structure

The nationalised network industries have been progressively privatised since BT was sold by the Government in 1984. British Gas was floated in 1986, followed by BAA (formerly the British Airports Authority) in 1987. The ten water and sewerage companies in England and Wales were sold in 1989, and the UK electricity industry in a sequence from the 1990 to 1996, the latest being British Energy, the non-magnox nuclear generating sector. Railtrack was privatised in 1986, and most of the non-infrastructure components of British Rail have also been sold or are in the process of being franchised; most notably the passenger train services.

The structure of the industries established at privatisation has developed. BT, British Gas and BAA were sold in broadly the same form as when they were nationalised, so that BT and British Gas had strong, vertical integration. The complaint was that this inhibited the development of competition. Later privatisations involved restructuring of the industries such that it would facilitate the achievement of theobjectives behind privatisation and effective regulation. The key distinction is between natural monopoly businesses (such as the high voltage transmission networks) where competitive networks would be wasteful, and potentially competitive businesses, such as generation and supply. In effect, a distinction between the network as a transport medium and the products and services which need to utilise that network.

Unbundling has allowed regulation to focus on the natural monopoly services to ensure that non-discriminatory access is provided to all comers at a fair price; whilst at the same time promoting the introduction of competition in the other businesses with a view to achieving long run, self-sustaining competition. Where this can be achieved, deregulation can take place, leaving on-going regulation of the access prices and conditions applicable to third parties which wish to use the networks to reach their customers.

Regulators

The regulation of the companies is typically by licence; and the licence conditions are monitored and enforced by a specific statutory officer, the Director General (DG). The CAA is one exception at present. The powers are vested in the DG, but the DG has the resources to establish a regulatory office to enable him or her to carry out their duties.

Often, regulatory officers are referred to as 'economic' regulators to distinguish them from the 'quality' regulators, such as the Environment Agency. Such a separation of duties was one aspect of the restructuring of the water industry at privatisation. There is, of course, another dimension of public policy which is concerned with social and distributive justice. Some commentators have regarded the model of privatisation to date as a *tri-partite model.* Economic regulators concerned with efficiency and the control of monopoly power; quality regulators concerned with standards for public goods and the correction of market failures associated with various 'externalities' (unpriced transactions); and the government concerned with general responsibilities for ensuring universal access and affordability. In practice, the government has to take responsibility for the regulatory system overall because it appoints the 'economic' regulators and has to establish the various quality standards which are monitored and enforced by the quality regulators.

The intended sequence of events is best described, however, as one in which certain standards of service are established, which then provide a constraint on the economic regulator in regulating the companies [because the companies have to achieve the required standards of service]; from which the economic regulator sets the conditions within which efficient regulated companies can earn at least the minimum rate of return necessary to meet the output requirements and standards of service. Prices are assumed to be non-discriminatory and to be related to the cost of supply, and hence questions of affordability and equality of access to services which many judge to be public services (albeit privately provided) are left to government mechanisms such as income support. In practice, economic regulators have been progressively drawn into questions of distributive justice; in part because of weaknesses in the social security system, in part because the political focus of social problems is channelled through the economic regulation, and in part because the legislation establishes certain universal service obligations which have to be complied with. This may limit the regulators' ability to introduce competition (which in general will erode cross-subsidy) because new entrants would 'cherry pick' the remunerative services and leave the incumbent to pick up the cost of the loss-making social obligations.

Incentives

The primary legislation sets out the duties of each regulator. Typically these are general, and may be divided into primary and secondary duties. They may require the regulator to ensure the availability and continuity of supply; to see that the functions of the company are properly carried out; to enable the company to finance their business; and to protect the consumer. The structure of statutory duties has been of concern to some commentators, and particularly to consumer bodies such as the National Consumer Council, because the regulator is judged to have to balance the interests of the companies against the interests of consumers.

However, in practice, the focus of the regulators has been almost exclusively on customer protection, and the duties can be reconciled by interpreting the primary objective of regulation as consumer protection, subject to ensuring that the companies can finance themselves. It would not be in the long run interest of consumers if companies were only allowed prices which were less than the long run cost of supply. It is sufficient that the regulator should allow the minimum rate of return which is necessary to finance an efficient company.

The legislation does not usually state the detailed means by which economic regulation shall be achieved. However, the regulators were appointed with a view to imposing a system of 'incentive regulation'. The companies should be given incentives to improve their efficiency over and above that forecast by the regulator and built into the relevant financial controls. By introducing a system of maximum price controls (known generally as the RPI – X system) which operates for a fixed period (typically five years), the company has the incentive to improve efficiency further because – given the maximum allowable prices – these further improvements will be turned into increased profits. This contrasts with the cost-plus properties of rate of return regulation, which has little or no incentive to improve efficiency.

The *quid pro quo* for the consumer is that by improving efficiency beyond that forecast by the regulator, the company 'reveals' new information to the regulator, who takes it into account when setting the maximum allowed prices for the next period. Higher profits today are therefore a quid pro quo for lower prices for the consumer tomorrow – albeit a difficult political message to get across to the public because the high profits have to come first. The maximum allowable prices therefore enable regulators to control the potential abuse of monopoly power and ensure prices are no higher than the long run cost of supply, whilst the incentive element of the regulatory system gives the basis for a progressive reduction in the prevailing long run cost of supply.

The Regulatory 'Contracts'

The first point to make is that the system of regulation by licence gives great discretion to the regulator, and whilst there are mechanisms of appeal – most notably to the MMC if a company does not agree with the proposed licence change put forward by a regulator – the wide discretion is reflected in the difficulty of a company succeeding in arguing through judicial review that the regulator had acted beyond his or her powers.

The second point is that 'expectations' about the system have been very ill-formed, and this has contributed to the acrimony of debate. In part the ill-formed expectations are because of the intrinsic complexity of the practice of regulation;[1] in part because of preconceived ideas of the nature of profit (good or bad) and the role of companies in providing public services; and in part special pleading – deliberate obfuscation in order to try and create a better bargaining climate. The former has been compounded, however, by a failure of government, regulators and the companies to effectively communicate the objectives of the incentive system and how regulation is expected to work, explaining why it is not a zero sum game in the distribution between customers and shareholders, but potentially one in which both parties can gain due to the net improvement in efficiency.

---

[1] For example, financial models used to set X in the price cap.

Prospectus

The first problem began at privatisation. The government has one agenda at flotation, the regulators another the day after privatisation. If decisions which suit the former are incompatible with the effective achievement of the latter, then it is inevitable that tensions will arise and regulators will start to unwind what appeared to be the 'bargain' at privatisation. This has been most notable in the post – privatisation restructuring of the industries and the problems of carry-over of investors 'expectations' in resetting X at the periodic review.

In each case investors have argued that the government's regulatory bargain with them has been overturned by arbitrary action from the regulators. British Gas, for example, was privatised as a vertically integrated monopoly. The first regulator, Sir James McKinnon, argued that this militated against his ability to promote effective competition – particularly as British Gas continued to act, in his terms, as 'an unreconstructed monopolist'. The prospectus and the licence referred to a 25 year monopoly on its franchise market.[2] Nevertheless, a succession of inquiries and a new Act have swept that away within ten years of privatisation. British Gas is now in the process of demerging into a separate transportation company (TransCo) and a competitive gas supply company. From one point of view, unbundling is the culmination of an inexorable regulatory requirement that natural monopoly be separated from competitive businesses (and hence investors must have been on notice of this, knowing the objectives of regulation). From another, the 'Sids' feel betrayed because the prospectus did not prove sacrosanct.

Resetting X

The government, not the regulator, sets the price caps at privatisation. The basis of the calculations was not widely debated and even Sir James McKinnon was surprised to find when he inquired over the basis of the figures in the build up to first periodic review that whilst the final figures had been a judgment, they had also been designed 'to get the company off to a good start'. Regulators across the industries have been faced with having to manage public anger over the generous

---

[2] Less than 25,000 therms per annum.

privatisation settlements – with its consequences of large excess profits and rewards for directors through share options – something which has conditioned the regulators to try and redress the balance (which excites a response from the companies that there is a danger of expropriation of assets and claw-back of past earnings, which is in principle disallowed in an incentive regulatory system).

The five 'contractual' issues which have arisen in resetting X therefore, in which there is an implied – and statutory – obligation on the regulator to give sufficient allowable revenue to meet the forecast present value of costs, are:

(1) Does the cost of capital or the allowed revenue achieve a carry-over of expectations of return and dividend growth which was 'promised' at privatisation?

(2) Is the asset base treated correctly and rolled forward (ie preserved) from one regulatory period to another?

(3) Is claw-back occurring – either by setting impossible targets for the forthcoming period (which means an average return over the previous and the forthcoming period) or by re-opening a review once the bargain has been struck?[3]

(4) Can regulators move out of the generally accepted ambit of the regulatory system to which they were appointed (ie a periodic price capping system) to introduce new forms – which might include rate of return regulation, annual formula profit-sharing systems or agreements with the companies that if they 'accelerate' the return of benefits to customers from out-performance, then that will be taken into account in the next regulatory review in order to preserve the carry-over of economic profit and hence maintaining the incentives within the system?

(5) Should discretionary expenditure by the companies in this period automatically be added to the capital base by the regulator for calculating the rate of return in the next period?

---

[3] As Professor Littlechild, Office of Electricity Regulator, did for the Distribution Review in 1995 – even though this was not technically a re-opening because the initial changes had not been formally incorporated into a licence change.

Each of these questions has a common element, which is the need for a clearly articulated methodological framework. The debate would then be about the numbers that fit into the boxes – rather than whether the box should be there at all.

It is interesting to note that regulators (see water and electricity in particular) have indicated their willingness to set down the methodology in writing and to use that as a template for the bilateral negotiations. Such 'agreements' could feature in litigation in due course, but would be a significant improvement both for public understanding and consent for the system, and in creating the conditions for sensible bargaining between the company and the regulator in his or her role as surrogate competitor.

A similar need to codify the role of regulators has occurred in the relationship between the economic and the quality regulators. Rising environmental standards have been one reason for rising water bills, but Ian Byatt questioned whether the standards were either too high or being introduced too fast. In effect he considered that government had an obligation to carry out a cost-benefit test to ensure – as far as is reasonably possible – that standards are optimal in the sense of incremental cost equals incremental benefit. There is a major issue here, not only for product quality, but for design of capacity and reliability of supply. It does not necessarily make economic sense to be able to supply in all circumstances. Logic won the day; ministers agreed to carry out such tests and the obligation for cost-benefit analysis has been included in the recent Environment Act.

Customers

Regulated companies operate a tariff in their monopoly franchise; competition is the protection in the non-franchise markets, which are intended to cover the whole of the energy market by 1998. It quickly came to the attention of regulators that whilst price control is a key objective, price has no meaning without specifying the quality to which that price relates. The economic regulators have progressively become involved in the setting of standards of service and where a failure can be attributed to management, guaranteed compensation schemes have been introduced. A formal contract which might be triggered automatically or on application from the customer. The powers of the regulators have been harmonised and brought to the level of the regulator with the most powers by the Competition and Service (Utilities) Act 1992. There are obligations on the regulator to test consumer wishes and preferences in the specification of new standards.

The extent of compensation is being increased because of supply problems such as took place in the cold winter and drought of 1995. This has developed further, however, into a more formal penalty and claw-back system for companies. Take, for example, water. OFWAT announced on 4 August 1995 that customers must get the quality of service 'they pay for'. Ian Byatt stated "It is not sufficient for companies to assert that they will meet compliance by the due dates. We want to see solid evidence of moves towards compliance ... If companies have not delivered quality improvements, then that means customers have paid too much. This will be reclaimed for customers by lowering price limits and hence bills".

This is not just in the next periodic review. On 3 June 1996 OFWAT announced the completion of its enquiries into Yorkshire Water's performance. In effect the company was fined by reducing its maximum price cap. The Northern Ireland electricity regulator has also proposed to clawback revenue for capital underspend by the Northern Ireland Electricity Company.

Conclusion

A wide range of informal 'contracts' have developed in regulation. Public confidence, however, remains low and improved transparency of the regulatory process will probably require greater formality for what have previously been 'understandings'.

14. Regulation and Procurement of Independent Power Projects†

Kristine Morais

Synopsis

This paper reviews the structure of an Independent Power Project and considers the principal risks involved in the procurement and the implementation of such a project and to the ways in which sponsors may safeguard against such risks when analysing the major project documentation and suggestions made for the protection of the revenue stream. The nature of the regulatory environment is analysed and the 'global risks' inherent in such a highly regulated industry are outlined. Conclusions are made as to whether the current privatisation impetus can be sustained.

Introduction

Since privatisation of the electricity industry in 1990 there have been over 40 generation licences granted to Independent Power Projects ("IPPs") to commence operation in Britain. At the same time we are informed that there is an over supply in generating capacity in Britain. Market forces tell us that this must result in rapidly falling prices which will benefit the consumer, but what does this mean for the financiers and sponsors of an IPP? IPP's are formulated, built, owned and operated in the private sector and are only viable provided that they are able to generate revenue at a level that permits them to repay their financiers and return some benefit to their sponsors.

---

† This paper has been developed from the author's MSc thesis entitled '*A Competitive Market through Regulation? — A review of the structure and an analysis of the regulatory environment in which Independent Power Projects are procured and implemented*' submitted in part fulfillment of the MSc degree in Construction Law and Arbitration at King's College London.

In order to prepare a viable project and succeed in a highly competitive market an IPP must know the industry it is entering and be well informed of both the "elemental" and "global" risks inherent in that industry.[1] It is only with knowledge of these risks that it possible to ensure proper provisions are made in the project documentation; and where the risks are inherent in the regulatory environment determine in advance what measures may be taken to reduce a projects exposure to such global risks.

This paper will consider the factors relevant to undertaking an IPP in England and Wales. It will outline the structure of the privatised electricity industry introduced by the Electricity Act of 1989 (the "1989 Act"); consider the structure of an IPP, in particular the main project documentation with a view to addressing means by which the revenue stream may be protected. It goes on to consider the global risks inherent in undertaking such a venture in a highly regulated industry and questions whether regulation (although onerous) could benefit an IPP and could be used as a spur to promote competition.

The Scottish electricity industry has developed differently from the industry in England and Wales and for that reason the privatisation exercise had to be undertaken in a different form. Scottish Power PLC and Scottish Hydro-Electric PLC were privatised as vertically integrated units: that is to say, each company carried out the activities of generation, transmission, distribution and supply in Scotland, as opposed to the privatisation exercise undertaken in England and Wales which lead to the fragmentation of the industry and saw the formation of separate companies undertaking generation, transmission, and supply with competition in the areas of generation and supply. Whilst the issues relating to the structure, form and risk management of an IPP discussed below are equally applicable to Scottish IPP's, the regulatory framework considered in this paper will not cover Scotland.

---

[1]   The elemental risks are the project risks which must be identified and dealt with in the project documentation and the global risk are those factors outside the control of the parties.

The Nature of the Privatised Electricity Industry

During the 1980's, developed nations saw the need to combat two major problems: The first was the obvious budget deficits to meet the costs of maintaining its massive infra-structure and the second was to combat the inefficiency of State-owned companies.[2] Privatisation was introduced to relieve the financial and administrative burden of Government, reduce the size of the public sector, and raise efficiency and productivity.[3] The state owned utilities were principal targets.

Privatisation of the electricity industry ("EI") took place in 1990 and was facilitated by the introduction of the 1989 Act. There is no doubt that the electricity industry was in need of reform. Despite the introduction of a raft of legislation throughout the 1960's and 1970's to try and improve the economic regulation of the industry it was cumbersome inefficient and expensive to run. From 1979 with the advent of the Tory government greater competition was seen as the answer. The Government took its first step towards greater liberalisation of the industry with the Energy Act of 1983. The 1983 Act aimed to introduce competition in generation by removing statutory barriers erected against the entry of independent generators; as noted below it proved a failure. More radical steps would be required to combat the monopoly of the State-owned corporations.

In order to understand the privatised EI it is important first to understand the nationalised industry.

The Electricity Act 1989

The 1989 Act was the instrument that brought about the privatisation of the electricity industry in England, Scotland and Wales. The Act which is in three parts (supplemented by 18 Schedules): introduces the new regulatory regime; provides for the restructuring of the industry and for

---

2 Sir William Ryrie, '*Financing Infrastructure Facilities: the Role of the Private Investor*', in Proceedings of the European Investment Bank Forum 1995, pp. 104 - 106.

3 Mohamad Hanafiah Bin Omar: '*Malaysian Experience in Build Own Operate and Transfer Method of Privatisation*', Second International Construction Projects Conference, London, 5 - 6 June 1989, p. 1.

its transfer from public to private ownership; and retains residual powers for the Secretary of State to deal with such matters as civil emergencies and the decommissioning of nuclear installations.

The 1989 Act provided the framework not merely for the privatisation of the industry, but for its complete transformation. It is said that the restructured industry bears no real resemblance to any other electricity industry in the world and there is no other industry which has gone nearly so far in desegregation; the whole thrust of the new structure being to encourage competition in the areas of generation and supply.[4]

Section 4 of the 1989 Act sets out the requirement that a licence is required to generate, transmit and supply electricity—the salient elements of the regulatory regime are contained in these licences. All the newly privatised companies have licences issued pursuant to Section 6 of the 1989 Act.

The three entities, who assumed the role of the now defunct Central Electricity Generating Board ("CEGB"), National Power plc ("National Power), PowerGen plc ("PowerGen") and Nuclear Electric (which remains in public ownership) have generation licences for their generation activities. It is interesting to note that the generators were originally under no statutory obligation to invest in new generating capacity, to maintain existing capacity or (in general) to declare generating sets available to generate electricity. This is particularly surprising as the three companies account for the majority of electricity generated in England and Wales. If National Power or PowerGen were to close down facilities without reference to the Director General of Electricity Supply ("DGES") then the effect on supply and the price of electricity would be devastating (even today, although their market share has fallen substantially).

The National Grid Company plc ("NGC") currently has the only transmission licence. The charges levied by the NGC vary according to the area where the power stations are situated. It has been noted that

---

4   House of Commons, Session 1991-1992 Energy Committee, Second Report, *Consequences of Electricity Privatisation*. Report together with the Proceedings of the Committee, 26 February 1992, London HMSO (Introduction) p. xi.

the most important condition in the NGC licence is that it must provide a non-discriminatory service at regulated prices and in accordance with published terms for connections to and use of its "wires system".[5] Each Regional Electricity Company ("REC")[6] has a public electricity supply licence which permits them to supply to a particular area and they may also apply to generate a certain amount of electricity.[7]

In addition to generation, transmission or supply licences a "second tier licence" may also be granted. This licence is required by:

- generators engaging in direct sales to customers;
- RECs wishing to supply specified premises outside their authorised areas;
- brokers buying electricity from generators or other suppliers and selling to end users; and
- large consumers supplying their own premises.[8]

The Pool

The Pool is not a physical entity, although all electricity (for general sale) is deemed to flow through it. The Energy Committee[9] explained the general mechanism of the Pool as follows: it is a central feature of the new system. It is a half hour auction or spot market in electricity, designed to cope with the fact that electricity cannot be stored in large quantities and therefore supply and demand must always be in balance. The two main purposes of the Pool are to determine which generating stations run (based on bid prices) and to determine the cost and price of electricity traded. The need for the Pool arises from two special features of electricity generation; first, there is no way of

---

5   Winsor, T. '*The New Legal Regime for Regulation of the Electricity Industry*', *IBA Section on Business Law*, .Utilities Law Report, September 1991, p. 4

6   These companies evolved from the pre-privatisation Regional Boards.

7   The RECs also control the distribution system freedom of access to the distribution system is ensured by the inclusion of Condition 8 of the Public Electricity Supply Licence.

8   Bailey, S.K. & Tudway, R.H.,*Electricity Law and Practice*, Sweet & Maxwell, London, 1992, § 6.12 pp. 6-7. (Bailey & Tudway).

9   The Energy Committee, *op. cit.* pg. xiii

distinguishing electricity generated from any particular station, and, secondly, electricity cannot be stored.

Despite the presence of the Pool and its importance in price determination almost all electricity is sold by way of bilateral arrangements known as 'contracts for differences' which provide a degree of protection against the fluctuations in the Pool price. The contracts are not contracts to deliver electricity but are a means of determining the price paid for electricity. A simple form provides that the generator and purchaser agree to make electricity available at an agreed "strike price". If the Pool price goes up the generator will give the purchaser a refund, if the price falls below the strike price the purchaser will pay the generator the difference.

All suppliers and generators have to be members of the Pool. The core of the contractual framework is the Pooling and Settlement Agreement ("PSA") and Schedule 9 which together with the Grid Code and distribution codes define the method of operating the Pool. The PSA is between the generators, suppliers, the NGC as grid operator and provider of ancillary services, the two external interconnected parties and two subsidiaries of the NGC, NGC Settlement Limited (as Settlement Systems Administrator with responsibility for financial settlement within the Pool) and Energy Pool Funds Administration Limited (the Pool funds administrator).

The PSA provides for the creation of the Pool Executive Committee ("PEC"), which comprises of representatives of the generators, the REC's and interconnected parties; and the DGES has the power to appoint a member on behalf of small generators if they do not make their own appointment. The role of the PEC is to supervise the settlement system and its operations and while it does not have power over the actual management of the Pool, it does monitor the NGC as Grid Operator and Ancillary Services Provider, it also considers applications by new parties to be admitted as members of the Pool. Admission of new parties will be granted provided they have fulfilled the admission conditions which include the requirement that the new party has a generation licence or is exempted from the obligation to hold one and that it has in place connection agreements with a Pool member.

Structuring an Independent Power Project

While the issue of risk identification and management is beyond the scope of this paper an analysis of the issues relating to the undertaking of an IPP would not be complete without an attempt to identify the principal risks associated with such a project. The principal issue which must be determined when considering the project documentation is the identification and allocation of risk on the party who can best bear that risk. The purpose is to ensure that one has a "bankable" asset, as the size of infrastructure projects and their complexity necessitate substantial investment and borrowings.

The development of a private power project can be one of the most complex projects to structure.[10] It is an enormous venture and a high risk activity, which requires a detailed understanding of the regulatory framework within which the IPP has to operate as well as a thorough knowledge of the engineering and financial risks inherent in the undertaking. Failure particularly at a later stage of the project could result in financial ruin for a project's sponsors and their financiers.

Type of Power Station

One of the first issues to consider is the type of power station to be procured. To a certain extent the choice is pre-determined—the last five years[11] has seen the growing dominance of gas turbines which are seen as the cheapest option to build and maintain. The IPP considered in this paper will be a combined cycle gas turbine station ("CCGT").

Nuclear power stations and other non-fossil fuel sources such as water, wind, solar or waste are recognised as being substantially more expensive to build and operate than the fossil fuel (oil, gas, coal) generators. While the cost of building a nuclear power station can be prohibitive there is an incentive to build other non-fossil fuel stations There are statutory obligations on the RECs to secure a minimum

---

10 Payne, H., *'Principal Issues in Power Projects'*, Study Group Conference for International Commercial Contracts, 26 - 29 August 1996 p. 1.

11 Lewis, D. J., *'Gas Turbine Power Generation: A Developer's View'*, The Institute of Energy, Conference on Gas Turbine Power Generation, London, 4 May 1995 p. 1.

amount of non-fossil fuel generating capacity to encourage non-fossil fuel development and to ensure nuclear stations continue to operate. The additional costs of non fossil fuel generation is subsidised by the fossil fuel levy imposed on the RECs which is paid by electricity consumers through higher electricity charges.

Coal power stations, while technically the cheapest option as the supply of coal is cheap and plentiful (especially as the coal restrictions have been lifted) is actually a very expensive option as all emissions (sulphur oxides in particular) from coal stations have to be treated (desulphurisation after burning), in order to comply with environmental guidelines. The "dash for gas" therefore is an understandable reaction. Gas stations are quicker to build, are "environmentally friendly" and are believed to be cheaper to run.[12] The fear of a "pollution tax" also makes it sensible to consider the introduction of the most environmentally friendly option.

The identification of a purchaser and the needs of that purchaser will be a very important aspect in deciding what sort of power station a sponsor would wish to install. If a REC needs non fossil fuel generating capacity that may determine the issue even though it will be the more expensive option. The demand the station is required to meet will also be a determinative factor. The options are generally "base loading" or "peaking" stations. Base load stations are designed to operate at close to full capacity most of the time. A peaking plant is expected to generate at short notice infrequently. Base load stations though more expensive to build are more economical to run whereas the adverse is true of peaking stations. There are also "mid-merit" stations which may be set to operate as base load stations for set periods and peaking at others.

A failure to determine the requirements of the IPP at inception may lead to the wrong choice and therefore wrong usage of the plant which could give rise to severe operational and maintenance problems. The decision to build a CCGT station carries with it a number of advantages. The fact that the technology has been tried and tested means the construction period and the level of operating efficiency can be determined with a measure of confidence. Furthermore the rate of

---

[12] Bailey and Tudway *op.cit.* §. 3.04, p. 3.

conversion of fuel is generally more efficient than that of a coal-fired station.

Risks

Two rather trite statements relating to risk analysis are: no two projects are the same; and do not be complacent in assuming that familiar and similar are synonymous. A sponsor undertaking to set up two small combined cycle gas turbine stations in England may meet with completely different risks depending on the actual location of each station.

The risks associated with any major project can be analysed at two levels. There are the specific project or elemental risks, which must be identified and dealt with in the project documentation, and there are what have been refered to as "global risks";[13] these are factors outside the control of the parties and inherent in the political, legal, commercial, social and environmental fabric of the country[14] within which the project will be constructed. While one tends to view the global risks of constructing an IPP in England as being minimal, this is a complacent and wrong approach. A change of government with greater interests in protecting the consumer, or a Labour government with an agenda to protect the UK coal industry (and therefore reserve a substantial portion of the EI for coal-fired stations), tax increases, the power of the environmental lobby, European Community Directives, not to mention manipulation of the Pool or an unforeseen use by the Secretary of State of a discretionary powers could all change the commercial viability of a project.

The principal risks associated with an IPP[15] can be divided into two phases of pre-commissioning and post-completion.

---

[13] Payne, H.: *"An Analysis of the Risks Inherent in the Build-Own/Operate - Transfer ("BOT") Method of Infrastructure Procurement"*, 1994 Alfred Hudson Prize Paper, Society of Construction Law, London, p. 11.

[14] Merna, A. Payne, H. and Smith, N. J., *Benefits of a Structured Concession Agreement for Build -Own-Operate Transfer ("BOOT") Projects*, (1993) 10 ICLR 33.

[15] Freshfields: *Project Finance*, Guide prepared by the Freshfields International Project Finance Group, Second Edition, July 1993 p. 47.

Pre-commissioning Risks include:

- development period costs ;
- construction cost increases (technical problems and site conditions will be major areas of concern);
- procurement of consents and approvals (environmental and planning issues will be very relevant including obtaining rights of way);
- delay in completion (causing difficulties both for the Contract for Differences and the Fuel Supply Agreement);
- interest rate fluctuations;
- defective performance on completion; and
- failure to completion (in particular force majeure).

Post completion risks include:

- performance of the plant (defects would include not merely plant which cannot operate, but plant which is unable to operate at the level of efficiency considered economic);
- fuel supply deficiency or fuel price increases;
- O&M cost increases (this could be linked with plant defects which make the operation of the plant more expensive than anticipated);
- reliability and availability;
- grid/transmission system failure (including construction of the Pool system and merit order);
- changes in law or of the regulatory system;
- increase in taxes;
- interest rate increments;
- force majeure.

Bearing in mind these risks the financiers, sponsors and the regulators (who will not consider a licence application unless the sponsors can prove that the project is commercially viable); will wish to ensure that there are sufficient safeguards in place throughout the project documentation to protect as best as is possible the income revenue from the project, by effectively managing the risks.

Key Issues in Independent Power Projects

There is to date in Britain surplus generating capacity. For a new power station to be profitable it has to be able to be reliable in meeting demand and it has to be cheaper or at least as cheap as its competitors. To achieve that aim the project has to be well researched, structured, designed, built and operated. A failure to navigate successfully through the regulatory quagmire could delay the start of a project with knock on effects to construction start dates, completion of the project and considerable costs and reputation lost under a Power Purchase Agreement or a Fuel Supply Agreement. Whilst there are many competing issues which require consideration when reviewing the main project documents, ultimately the final consideration must be protection of cashflow and the revenue stream, and in reviewing these documents, reference will be made to this theme.

Financing

In project finance transactions the cashflows and revenue streams from the project will be used to repay loans to financiers and generate profit for the investors. For this reason the financiers will have to review all project documentation to ensure that income stream is feasible. Not just in respect of the immediate loan arrangements but that the project will continue to be feasible over a 15 to 20 year period.

Financiers' key considerations will be to ensure that they can take effective security over the project documents, and that if they have to enforce their rights under the project contracts, that those contracts will remain in place and that third parties will not exercise rights of termination. While the different methods of financing a project are beyond the scope of this paper it is worth considering briefly one of the principal methods in use – non-recourse or limited loans.[16]

In very general terms non-recourse or limited recourse loans provide the lender with security over the assets or revenue generated by those assets in order to be repaid their loan and interest. If the revenue is

---

[16] See further Scriven, J. '*A Funder's View of Risk in Construction*' in Uff, J. & Odams, A.M., *Risk, Management and Procurement in Construction*, Centre of Construction Law and Management, King's College London, 1995, p.71 *et seq.*

insufficient, then the financier may take enforcement action against the assets over which he has security.[17] The need for security is important, to ensure that other creditors are not permitted to take over the asset thereby effectively preventing the financier being repaid or in any event corrupting his security.

A non-recourse or limited recourse security, will only be of use if the financier on deciding to step into the shoes of the project company has a right to continue the project company's plan under the main project documents, (*i.e.*, the construction contract, the supply and purchase contracts) remain in place).

Project Supervision

The appointment of an independent expert or engineer is also vital in balancing the interests of the participants with those of the project goals and providing an unbiased view on the success of the project. The appointment of such an expert would in general be a pre-requisite to the involvement of the financiers. The role of the independent engineer may include:

- ensuring that the design or construction of the plant is not being compromised in order to achieve greater savings in construction costs or to meet unrealistic target dates;
- providing a view on the revenue stream the plant is able to generate and therefore the level of borrowing it could support;
- on completion of the project ensuring that the plant is being efficiently and responsibly run;
- acting as an impartial mediator between the parties in the event of disputes; and
- providing an external assessor who may provide an impartial view of the project for the benefit of the lender.

---

[17] Wood, P. and Vinter, G., *Project Finance*, Allen & Overy Publication, London, 1992, p. 17.

Sponsorship

Most IPP's are carried out by single purpose project companies. The composition of the sponsor company will therefore have a significant impact on the success of the project. While many Ipps are undertaken by large developers such as PowerGen or National Power, the smaller IPP's are being undertaken in joint ventures and consortia. Ideally the sponsor company should be composed of individuals who have a strong vested interest in the success of the project as their commitment is an important impetus to ensuring that partisan interests are subordinated for the good of the project.

It has been observed that constructors have entered the projects market and that the marrying of a constructor with an off-take purchaser has become quite common in such ventures.[18] Constructors have, therefore, become promoters of large infrastructure projects in order to obtain lucrative construction contracts, and have in general no interest in being long term equity investors in the venture. The purchaser's interest is in obtaining power at an advantageous and predictable price and obtaining a return on its own direct investment by receiving a share of the price received from electricity supplied to the Pool. Such a relationship is regarded as being potentially dangerous to the project, as the participants' loyalty is to their own deal rather than to the project as a whole. The potential end result being a reduction in the projects' revenue or a reduction in its contractual protection, as the presence of participants with dual roles (which is not uncommon) does give rise to potential conflicts of interest.

The introduction of a third participant in the venture is a helpful method of breaking down the polarised positions of the participants. A useful addition to a consortium would be the Operations and Maintenance Company. As a result of their function, they have an interest in balancing the competing claims of both constructor and off take purchaser thereby providing an in-built mediator. An independent and effective management of the project company would also be important in ensuring that contact with the project companies participants is not too one-sided.

---

[18] Montague, A., *Build-Own Transfer: A Re-Evaluation*, Linklaters and Paines, London, 1989, p. 11.

Purchasing the Power

The Agreement that governs the purchase of the electricity is the linchpin in the project documentation, as it will determine the revenue that will be generated by the IPP and hence whether the project is feasible and more importantly the rate of return that the sponsors will obtain from their investment. The need therefore is to ensure certainty of price and reliability of plant so that availability of electricity is "guaranteed" when it is required.

The Offtake Agreement or Power Purchase Agreement in England will generally take the form of a Contract for Differences ("CFD"). This is a hedging contract to off-set the fluctuations inherent in the Pool method of trading electricity. The issues which must be determined by that contract are; first, the definition of the price, and, secondly, the quantity of electricity the purchaser will undertake to purchase. These criteria can be effected in two main ways:

- take and/or pay whereby the purchaser will pay for a stated quantity of electricity whether or not he uses it; and
- the two-part tariff, whereby the purchaser will be required to pay a base price ("capacity charge") to cover fixed costs and a variable element ("energy charge") to cover such matters as fuel costs.

General considerations would be of concern to the sponsors are:

- The agreement must provide a sanction if the IPP is unable to perform its obligations under the CFD. The provision of liquidated damages will generally be included, although most such provisions include a cap on the maximum sum which can be recovered and the division of risk will have to be considered to accommodate unforeseen circumstances arising from a force majeure situation.
- A CFD for a defined period, which will reflect the time required to repay loan facilities (usually 15 years) although the design life of the IPP may be for a longer period than the contracted time.
- The parties have to determine the level at which the station will generate. Consideration must be given to whether the

station will operate for example as a baseload or peaking station and precisely how those terms are defined. The term baseload may sometimes mean generation at 80 per cent. of the stations net capacity though with other systems it may mean 60 per cent. For this reason, target availability figures must be agreed at inception (i.e., at project feasibility stage) although the CFD should provide for an ability to review this figure once the IPP is complete and adjustments should be permitted if the station is unable to meet its availability target (it has been suggested that this arises, for example, because of design defects or bad construction[19]).

• As the whole success of the project is dependent on this agreement the status of the purchaser is vital and checks must be undertaken to ensure its status and solvency.

Fuel Supplies

The aim of the Fuel Supply Agreement ("FSA") is to ensure that fuel of a certain quality and quantity is available for a given period at a specified price. [20] While reference is made here to "fuel supply" the term "feed stock" is generally preferred in the industry as the raw material necessary to generate power may derive from a non-fossil fuel for example, water, waste or wind. If the fuel supplier defaults there will be a drop in the availability of the power station unless alternative fuels are obtained, this will of course threaten the revenue stream and profitability of the project.

The principal issues are regarded to be to "guarantee" supply, though adequate provisions in initial requests for supply and in ensuring that proper back up facilities are in place, and to ensure that the allocation of risk of fuel price increases will pass straight through to the power purchaser. Consideration in the FSA must therefore be given to the following:

---

[19] Vinter, G., *Project Finance A Legal Guide*, Sweet and Maxwell, London, 1995, § 3.62, p. 41.

[20] Payne, H., *Principal Issues in Power Projects*, Study Group Conference for International Commercial Contracts, 26 - 29 August 1996, p. 10.

- the maximum quantities of gas that the sellers will be obliged to supply. This quantity will be broken down into the maximum amount in any half hour, then the daily and yearly maxima;

- a provision to indemnify the seller if the power station takes more than its allocated maximum quote. The seller will usually seek to ensure that their recourse if the buyer exceeds his contracted quantity is on a weekly or monthly basis rather than annual basis where the swings and roundabouts are likely to even out more easily. The seller may seek the right to suspend supply but such a draconian provision should be resisted;

- a take and pay provision requiring the IPP to purchase a minimum quantity of gas in each contract year. This obligation will be calculated on the basis of the power station's expected reliability and its scheduled maintenance programme (consideration will also have to be given to the maintenance programmes required by the gas supplier);

- the delivery point for the gas supply. As the gas will generally be piped in, at the delivery point responsibility for its proper despatch will be that of the power station;

- a provision including the field in order to "guarantee" supply. It is quite common for the seller to "ear mark" a particular gas field to meet the power stations demand and undertake not to enter into any contracts with third parties which could threaten the IPP's supply;

- a provision specifying the quality and pressure of the gas which must be supplied if the quality or pressure falls below a certain limit then the power station should not have to pay for the gas supplied;

- a provision that the seller will provide back-up supplies to ensure they are capable of meeting demand;

- sanctions if the seller fails to meet their gas obligations in the absence of force majeure. As with CFD the seller will be generally faced with a liquidated damages provision, such damages will take into account the lost price and availability suffered by the IPP;

- while a force majeure situation is likely to release a seller of his liability to provide gas, it will not release him of his obligation to provide back up supplies.

Constructing the Station

There are potentially any number of procurement strategies available for the tender of the construction works for an IPP as with any other major project. From the point of view of the financiers however, a single point of responsibility is an attractive option. If the construction works go wrong in a project of this complexity the cost of carrying out the forensic exercise to determine liability could be astronomical.

A turnkey form of contract is therefore very attractive as it provides relative certainty in respect of money, time and quality. The idea being that the contractor obtains his specifications, and the sponsors do not reappear until the completion date to metaphorically receive the keys to the station. By virtue of this fact the contract should be fixed in terms of specifications (performance requirements) price and time, however the complexity of the construction process does not permit so simplistic a solution. The banks and the sponsors will wish to check progress and quality and have a right to request variations, although the greater the degree of control exercised by them, the greater the responsibility they have to assume. The price will in general be fixed, but it is important to be aware of the standard price "re-openers",[21] including provisional sum items and prime cost items and the ability to price extra work (variations to the contract specifications).

The design of a CCGT station, has the benefit of being tried and tested. However, that factor alone is not sufficient for the sponsor not to look further at design issues. Design obligations are rarely carried out solely by the contractor. The sponsor would have prepared specifications, performance criteria, carried out initial reports and probably the preliminary design. This work is likely to have been undertaken by a third party engineer. While the constructor may be required to assume liability for this third party's design work, as the constructor is part of

---

[21] Vinter, G., *Project Finance A Legal Guide*, Sweet and Maxwell, London, 1995, § 3.29, p. 30.

the sponsor there may be more interest in pursuing the third party. A further consideration is whether the design has to be fit for purpose or merely be to the standard of the reasonable professional.

The sponsor and financiers may additionally wish to impose a strict obligation on the constructor, but as noted above this has to be balanced with the premium cost which the constructor will require. The imposition of an absolute standard may not provide the financiers with a cast iron case. The cause of performance deficiencies may be difficult to identify and a constructor may dispute that a performance deficiency is due to a design fault and allege that it is due to the method of operation.

In order to try and ensure the quality of the power station the independent engineers appointed by the sponsors will be required to inspect the site during the course of construction, and to attend and monitor the final tests on completion. The operator of the power station should also be encouraged to attend site during construction, not with a view to criticising the constructor's work but to co-operate with him to ensure the efficiency of the final product. The operator's role would be essentially twofold, he is in a good position to assist in uncovering any potential defects so that they can be rectified immediately and he is also able to familiarise himself with the plant so that once the station is completed he will be fully conversant with its method of operation.

The issue of constructor performance should also be considered, and the performance of the contract should be guaranteed. [22] This could be in the form of a parent company guarantee that will confirm that the project will be built in time, within budget and specification. Performance bonds should also be available from all major works and supply sub-contractors and the sponsors should be able to call upon these bonds if there is a failure in the execution of any of the constructors obligations.

---

[22] Payne, H., '*Principal Issues in Power Projects*', Study Group Conference for International Commercial Contracts, 26 - 29 August 1996, p. 12.

Time

While a penalty for non-completion is a clear incentive for the constructor to meet the completion date, an alternative is to provide him with incentives to achieve various stages of completion by pre-determined dates with the view to ensuring that the project proceeds smoothly. The method of including milestone or stage payments is quite common, the addition of bonuses for achieving the milestone date and penalties for a failure to do so, will act as additional incentives.

While payment incentives and penalties are a useful means to ensure performance the incorporation of a realistic programme which allows for float to deal with unforeseen circumstances, a well considered design and limited (or preferably no) variations is possibly a better guarantee that the date of completion will be met.

Completion and Performance Tests

The construction contract should specify that tests on completion and performance tests must be carried out prior to the work being taken over by the sponsors. The tests must prove that a minimum level of performance (as specified by the contract) can be attained. Performance will be usually defined in terms of output and fuel efficiency. Yet the issue of potential delays must also be considered. Delay in completion may arise as a result of: [23]

- default by the power purchaser; if the power purchaser has not complied with his part of the bargain to provide the facilities necessary for the transmission of electricity capable of being generated by the station;
- default by the fuel supplier in failing to complete the supply connection;
- default by the contractor; and
- force majeure.

---

[23] Freshfields: *"Project Finance"*, Guide prepared by the Freshfields International Project Finance Group, Second Edition, July 1993, p. 49.

While it is clear that liability for the failures of the purchaser and supplier should rest with them, and the constructor must assume liability for his defaults, the sponsors must decide how best to apportion the risk, if delay in completion is due to a force majeure event. Consideration should be given to the following:

- the constructor to assume the risk, but be encouraged to insure against it;
- the power purchaser to assume liability for the capacity charge (see above); or
- the sponsors to bear some or all of the risk.

Defects Liability

The liability for the constructor for defects and the length of the defects period is of importance to the sponsors and the financiers. A power station may under-perform in two areas:[24] poor availability; and/or high heat rate. If the under-performance is due to poor availability, this will result in a loss of generating capacity and the capacity payments will in general be reduced on a pro-rata basis. If the guaranteed heat rate (i.e., the amount of fuel required to generate a unit of electricity) cannot be met then, again, the power purchaser will be entitled to claim a reduction to the energy charge (as the fuel costs are a component of this charge).

Liquidated Damages

The construction contract should provide for payment by the constructor of liquidated and ascertained damages ("LAD") for failure to complete the works within the time for completion. As LAD's are a genuine pre-estimate of loss, calculation of the sums owing should be equal to "the capacity charge and the damages that will be payable to the power purchaser for the delay".[25] Although it should be noted that

---

[24] *Ibid*, pg. 51
[25] *Ibid*, pg. 49

in practice LAD's are widely viewed as a way of limiting the constructor's liability for consequential loss.[26]

Some commentators tend to concentrate on the issue of LAD's being inadequate to compensate the financiers especially if there is prolonged delay. Yet an alternative source of revenue which does not appear to be widely considered is the revenue generated by the plant during the commissioning period.

If completion has not been certified the station will remain in the constructor's possession, the cost of fuel and consumable for the commissioning tests is generally supplied by the sponsors, but the power generated will be supplied to the Pool and therefore payment will be received for its despatch. The sums generated over the commissioning period may amount to a considerable sum; unless the contract conditions clearly identify this revenue as belonging to the sponsors this revenue will be a "windfall" for the constructor and could be used to set off any claims for LAD's potentially resulting in no loss to the constructor.

Operations and Maintenance of the Station

Operation and Maintenance Agreements ("O&M") are generally regarded as the poor relations in the suite of project contracts.[27] It is often believed that if the construction contracts are well drafted and the station is built to the specified standards then the success of the project is guaranteed. In terms of the project life, the operating phase dwarfs the time taken in developing and constructing the project and yet very little thought is given to its terms.[28] Furthermore as the financiers will want to be satisfied on the key contractual documentation before they consider lending, the O&M Agreement is often drafted before the detailed design has even commenced.

---

[26] Scriven, J., *A Banking Perspective on Construction Risks in BOT Schemes*, (1994) 11 ICLR 313, 325.

[27] Vinter, *op. cit.* § 3.44, p. 36, and Pritchard, N., *"Operating and Maintenance Agreements - The Poor Relation Amongst Project Agreements"*, (1996) 13 ICLR 291.

[28] Pritchard (1996) 13 ICLR 291.

The principal issue for the financiers is to ensure that the O&M Agreement remains in place throughout the term of the loan and that costs will be fixed. They will also be keen to see early involvement of the operators in reviewing the plant design and construction which could be vital to the subsequent operation of that station. Consideration must be given to the operator's obligations to ensure not just the efficient, safe and economical operation and maintenance of the power station, but that the station is being run with a view to protecting the best interests of the sponsors. Their services will also have to be dovetailed with the CFD and FSA to ensure compliance with those agreements.

The sponsors should seek undertakings such as compliance with all Health and Safety Regulations, conformance with all the plant manufacturers' recommendations and insurance requirements. Operation of the plant should also be in a manner so as to minimise all wear and tear. In addition, the operator may be required to guarantee that the station will achieve the target energy availability levels set out in the CFD, that the operating levels and standards are maintained and that in general the operator will comply with good industry practice. Before accepting an obligation to guarantee the station's output the operator may seek a "back to back" undertaking from the sponsors that the station is capable of meeting its output.

Careful consideration needs to be given to the level at which any penalties are set. A failure to achieve the specified output may give rise to LAD's. Damages may often need to be capped, as the operator's profit margins are likely to be low and a small default may put them out of business which will ultimately adversely affect the sponsors. The threat induced by a performance bond may, however, be a good measure and provide financiers with some recourse in the event of default.

The financiers need certainty and will want to ensure that the operator's fee is fixed; if not fixed, the fees must be tightly controlled so that it is not open to subsequent exploitation by the operator.[29] However, a fixed fee at inception for the duration of the loan agreements would not be possible or practicable as it will be difficult

---

[29] *Ibid,* at 295

for the operator to get price offers from sub-contractors and suppliers and any figure will include a substantial profit element to insure against future contingencies. An alternative therefore would be to separate the fee issue from the agreement, and permit a re-negotiation of the fee on a regular basis. The fee proposal could be on an open-book basis calculated possibly on a cost-plus basis.

Incentive payments should be considered, but these may be harder to achieve as profit will be determined "by reference to the level of cash which the financing agreements permit to be distributed to the project sponsors".[30] Furthermore, as the profitability of the power station will be affected by Pool prices despite the efficient manning of the station, they may not be able to optimise their project revenue.

As with the operator's fees there is again a dichotomy between the desire for price certainty and the need to ensure costs are reasonable. While a similar system of a rolling fixed fee would be one solution, an alternative would be to introduce a system whereby costs incurred within the ambit of an approved budget will be reimbursed, while the penalty for a failure to keep the budget could be onerous. Provision of course would have to be made for extraordinary expenses.

Regulatory Environment

It has been demonstrated that the electricity industry is highly regulated. Thames Power, for example, when reporting to the Energy Committee in 1992[31] anticipated needing approximately 40 primary consents, approvals and licences from about 25 bodies for a single power station. It is, however, particularly important to note that the 1989 Act is not a code;[32] provisions regulating the industry are to be found in a number of different sources, including the Regulations made pursuant to the 1989 Act setting out guidelines for the implementation of the Act, EC Directives, Planning laws, the Environmental Protection

---

[30] *Ibid,* at 296

[31] Energy Committee, Second Report, *Consequences of Electricity Privatisation, op.cit.,* pg. xxii.

[32] In that it does not bring together all relevant legislation pertaining to the industry.

Act, Health and Safety legislation and Employment laws. Whilst EU, Environmental and planning issues are very significant, a detailed consideration of their impact on a proposed IPP is beyond the scope of this paper, but for the sake of completeness their importance has been highlighted below.

When considering whether to pursue a project, a sponsor must not only assess the contractual relations set out in a concession agreement and the contractual framework. There is a need to establish the approvals required by the various regulatory authorities and consideration must be given to circumstances which could lead to the withdrawal or alteration of those approvals; sponsors must understand the global risks with which an IPP has to contend.

The Licence

The licence is the crux of the whole IPP, without it one is not even permitted to construct the facility. The licence is an important part of the regulatory framework within which the IPP will operate. Although many of the substantive issues relating to the construction and operation of the IPP are found in a variety of pieces of legislation and in industry practice.

Terms of the Licence

The licence is granted by the DGES[33] and is a pre-requisite for any power station which will export more than 10 MW to the Grid. Criminal sanctions are imposed on a failure to have the requisite authorisation. A licence may be requested from the DGES in payment of a fee of £100 (although there is also an annual fee levied). Not all generators, for example those operating on single premises, require a Licence. Single premises has been defined by the DGES as not being restricted to a single building. If a number of buildings forming constituent parts of the same premises, are in single occupation and have a geographical connection the premises will be viewed as single premises and do not require a generation licence.[34]

---

[33] Electricity Act 1989, s.6

[34] The Electricity (Class Exemptions from the Requirements for a Licence) (Amendment) Order 1994 and the Electricity (Exemptions from the

The terms of the licence have been standardised and are based on the initial licences granted to National Power and PowerGen on privatisation. The DGES has to include these conditions in all licences he grants. The discretion to grant exceptions from the licensing requirements lies with the Secretary of State. As there is competition in generation the controls in a generation licence are less intrusive. In particular there are no direct price control mechanisms to determine the price of electricity sold by the generator, (although the Pool price is a determinative factor in price fixing).

All generators providing more than 100 MW to the transmission and distribution system have to be members of the Pool and comply with the Grid Codes and the distribution code (if the generator is to be connected directly to a distribution network of an REC). These Codes (together with the PSA) are the technical rules that govern the connection, operation, transmission and distribution of power within the EI. In order to comply with the Codes the IPP will have to comply with the planning code and the standards applicable within the EI to ensure that its power station is compatible with the Grid. Needless to say failure to link up with the Grid would mean that the generator will be unable to supply the Pool and (unless it is servicing for example single premises) this would lead to the failure of the IPP.

The DGES is required (although the Secretary of State has a discretionary right to vary these obligations) to include specified conditions requiring compliance with technical standards and with franchise restrictions. The licences may also provide the IPP with important ancillary rights and obligations such as statutory powers to dig up streets and acquire land through compulsory purchase so that they may operate without major disturbances. The simplicity of the licence is deceptive, as many of the legislative "teeth" are found not in the licence but in other statutory obligations.

Requirements for a Licence) (Amendment) (No. 2) Order 1994 have introduced modifications to this requirement to assist small generators.

Application for a Licence

Section 4 of the 1989 Act requires that any person who seeks to generate electricity must be licensed or exempted. The Electricity (Class Exemptions from the Requirement for a Licence) Order 1990 lists class exemptions although it is possible to make an application to the Secretary of State to obtain a specific exemption.

The Electricity (Applications for Licences and Extensions of Licences) Regulations 1990, prescribe the forms of application for licences required under Section 6 of the Act, and the documents and particulars to be contained in such applications. For example, application for a generating licence must include:[35]

- a current statement of accounts kept by the sponsor in respect of any undertaking carried out by them;
- an outline business plan for a forecasted five year period (including: particulars of the person or persons to whom the applicant intends to provide electricity including details of lines to be connected; the maximum power expected to be available from each generating station at any one time; the expected life of each generating station; annual forecasts of costs, sales and revenues and project financing, stating the assumptions underlying the figures provided);
- details of major expenditure including decommissioning costs;
- evidence of net annual cashflow to demonstrate the financial security and feasibility of the project.

The volume of information required is substantial, a sponsor must have fully conceptualised his project before approaching the DGES for a licence. There is therefore a very real risk that if the DGES considers the project to be ill-founded and not feasible that he will reject the application and the development cost incurred by the sponsor would be lost.

---

[35] Schedule 4 Part II of the Electricity (Applications for Licences and Extensions of Licences) Regulations 1990

The Powers of the Secretary of State and the DGES

The two principal individuals responsible for the regulation of the industry are the Secretary of State for Energy and the DGES. Their primary obligations under the 1989 Act[36] encapsulate the fundamental objectives of the government's privatisation exercise which are:

- ensuring that all reasonable demands for electricity are satisfied;
- ensuring that all licence holders are able to finance the carrying on of the activities which they are authorised by their licences to carry on; and
- promoting competition in the generation and supply of electricity.

In exercising their duties under the 1989 Act, the Secretary of State and the DGES should have in mind the promotion of their secondary obligations which include protection of consumer interests in respect of the price, quality and continuity of supply of electricity as well as safety and environmental considerations and the promotion of efficiency and economy on the part of the supply and grid licence holders.

Secretary of State

The 1989 Act confers on the Secretary of State fundamental and wide ranging powers. Despite the declared aim of the privatisation exercise to free the industry from centralised control, the 1989 Act does little to diminish the power of government.[37] Whilst the role of the Secretary of State is generally limited to the appointment of the DGES and the administration of wide powers within the 1989 Act to make regulations for the industry, the Act confers many ancillary powers to the Secretary of State which cover licensing functions, operational activities and reporting. The Secretary of State's powers include:

---

[36] Electricity Act 1989, s.3

[37] Bailey and Tudway *op. cit.* para 5.01, pg. 5/1.

- a right to veto any modifications to a licence, voluntarily negotiated and agreed between the DGES and a licence holder;[38]
- a right to veto any reference by the DGES to the Monopolies and Mergers Commission ("the Commission"), or conversely to refer to the Commission a matter which the DGES may not consider warrants that reference;[39]
- the need for his consent before the DGES can make requirements regarding individual standards of performance;[40]
- the right to direct that information he considers to be not just contrary to public interest but contrary to the commercial interest of any person to be excluded from the Register kept by the DGES.[41]

The Secretary of State's consent is also required for the construction, extension or operation of a generating station and to the installation of electric lines[42] and the acquisition of land and rights over land by compulsory purchase.

What is of greater concern to a sponsor of an IPP are the Secretary of State's powers under Sections 34 and 96 of the 1989 Act, as they could have significant impact on a sponsor's cashflows and affect the revenue stream. Section 34 of the Act, permits the Secretary of State, as his sole discretion, to direct generators to create and maintain minimum stocks of fuel at power stations and to give directions as to the operation of the power station. While it is envisaged that this power will only be used in extreme circumstances, the power itself is drafted in very wide terms and may be used at any time; there is nothing to prevent the Secretary of State from using this power "in contemplation of an event, to neutralise the effectiveness of an expected fuel supply dislocation".[43] Compensation is available for compliance with the

---

[38] Electricity Act 1989, s.11(4)

[39] *Ibid,*s.12(5).

[40] *Ibid,* s.39(1).

[41] *Ibid,* s.49(4).

[42] *Ibid,* ss. 36 and 37.

[43] Winsor, T., '*The New Legal Regime for Regulation of the Electricity Industry*' *IBA Section on Business Law*, Utilities Law Report, September 1991, p. 7.

exercise of this discretionary power,[44] yet it is unlikely that the compensation will be sufficient to cover the revenue lost if the power station had been operated on a commercial basis.[45]

Section 96 of the Act is even more wide ranging: the Secretary of State has power (which overrides all other obligations of the recipient) to give licencees or persons exempt from licences "such directions of a general character as appear to the Secretary of State to be requisite or expedient for the purpose of preserving the security of buildings or installations used for or for purposes connected with generation, transmission or supply of electricity, or mitigating the effects of any civil emergency which may occur". The wide definition of civil emergency does little to curtail the power.

Any direction issued pursuant to Section 96 has to be placed before Parliament, unless the Secretary of State believes that to do so would be contrary to "national security or the commercial interests of any person", when he would be permitted to keep the matter confidential and refrain from doing so. While national security reasons do present some valid basis for withholding information, any Section 96 direction would have a commercial impact on the recipient; if the Secretary of State wished to be capricious he would rarely need to disclose his directions. Once a direction is deemed to be confidential, that status will apply to any person affected by the Section 96 direction, and he will be prohibited from raising the matter. The net effect of this provision is that if the Secretary of State decided that a particular emergency is likely to disrupt electricity supplies[46] he could take over the entire electricity indsutry and run it on strategic rather than commercial lines.[47] This provision is particularly draconian; no formal arrangements have been included for the recovery of lost costs and profit.[48]

---

[44] Pursuant to Section 34 of the 1989 Act and the Fuel Security Code

[45] Directions pursuant to Section have been issued by the Secretary of State in relation to coal stocks held by National Power and PowerGen.

[46] A terrrorist attack could be such an example.

[47] Winsor *op. cit.* pg. 7.

[48] Although the DGES has said that he could consider compensating a generator for his costs expended in complying with the directions. Offer - Statement by

The DGES

Notwithstanding the considerable powers of the Secretary of State, the administration and regulation of the electricity industry is largely carried out by the DGES and OFFER. The focus of the DGES' role is consumer protection. The Energy Committee defined his tasks as being to "promote competition, oversee and protect customer interests in areas where there remains a monopoly".[49] The functions of the DGES under the Act require him to assume the role of investigator, judge, adviser, reporter and archivist.

The 1989 vests specific powers in the DGES, such as the right to modify licences with the agreement of the licence holder;[50] issue directions as to the administration of the licence;[51] and determine disputes referred to him by either an electricity supplier or customer regarding supply.[52]

The DGES had, until 1992,[53] far more powers than any other regulator to intervene in the industry he regulates. In addition to consumer protection he has responsibility for ensuring access on a competitive basis to the transmission and distribution systems, which will inevitably affect generation.

The statutory powers to promote competition allow the DGES to refer uncompetitive practices to the Commission for them to investigate and report, in particular as to whether the practice adversely effects public interest;[54] and to exercise concurrently with the Director General of Fair Trading (DGOFT) some of the latter's functions under the Fair

---

the Director General of Electricity Supply the Regulatory System and the Duties of the DGES, 17 October 1990, pg. 7.

[49] Energy Committee, *op. cit.* pg. xivii

[50] Electricity Act 1989, s.11

[51] *Ibid,* s.7

[52] *Ibid,* s. 23

[53] The *Competition and Service (Utilities) Act* 1992 was initially introduced to standardise the powers the regulations of the four major utilities, with respect to the area of customers services, the Act does go further and confer on the DGES additional powers in respect of standards of performance, provision of information, determination of disputes and powers of enforcement.

[54] Electricity Act 1989, ss. 12 to 14.

Trading Act 1973 and the Competition Act 1980.[55] These powers relate to courses of conduct detrimental to the interests of consumers, monopoly references and anti-competitive practices.[56]

Similarly the Restrictive Trade Practices Act 1976 ("RTPA") requires agreements in respect of goods or services which are restrictive and which might be harmful to the public interest, to be registered. Once registered the DGOFT may[57] refer the agreement to the Restrictive Trade Practices Court for a ruling on whether the agreements operate against the public interest. However the RTPA does not apply to certain types of agreements relating to the generation, transmission or supply of electricity.[58] Further the Deregulation and Contracting Out Act 1976 provides that where it appears to the DGES that a person is pursuing anti-competitive practice, he may seek legally enforceable undertakings or refer the matter to the Commission.

A principal aspect of the DGES's role as consumer champion is to ensure price control through promotion of competition. The rationale under the Act is that the greater the competition the greater the downward pressure on costs and prices. The DGES expressed his belief that "a competitive market, with efficient and financially sound participants, operating within a stable regulatory framework, is in the best interests of consumers, shareholders and the industry itself".[59]

The Energy Committee[60] perceived the need for full and effective competition in the areas where it had been introduced (i.e., generation),

---

[55] Bailey and Tudway, *op.cit.* § 12.04, p. 6 and refer to Fair Trading Act 1973, ss 44 and 45 and Electricity Act 1989, s.43.

[56] Under the Fair Trading Act 1973 a monopoly situation is said to exist where at least 25 per cent. of the goods of any description supplied in the UK are supplied by one and the same person (the Electricity Act 1989, s.100 deems electricity to be goods for the purpose of the competition and restrictive trade practices legislation.)

[57] Subject to the provisions of section 21 of the Restrictive Trade Practices Act 1976.

[58] The Electricity (Restrictive Trade Practices Act 1976) (Exemptions) Order 1990 and Electricity Act 1989, s.100(2).

[59] Offer - Statement by the Director General of Electricity Supply the Regulatory System and the Duties of the DGES, 17 October 1990, § 2, p.1.

[60] Energy Committee, *op. cit.* pg. xviii

they believe that for genuine competition to exist the market had to be "transparent" i.e., all participants and entrants had to have access to relevant information and where a level playing field did not exist rules had to be put in place to assist competition. A sponsor of an IPP therefore has to be aware of how the DGES intends to exercise his considerable powers to ensure competition and implement licence obligations and in particular whether it could be used to its benefit or detriment.

Ancillary legislation

EC Directives have a significant moment on IPP construction and operation. It is a declared aim of the EU that there be a central market for power within the Union. EC Directives cover a wide range of issues including competition law and funding,[61] procurement rules, design, health and safety and environmental issues. The effect of EC Directives cannot be underestimated as it is trite law that where a Directive is precise and unconditional it may be relied upon against a Member State once the date of transposition of the Directive into national law has passed and the Member State has failed to implement it.

Environmental and planning issues are also of importance both because they tend to be emotive and susceptible to public pressure which must be appreciated from inception. The planning process suffers from the NIMBY[62] phenomena not just for environmental reasons which one would consider "normal" but for other slightly more obscure reasons. There is a tendency to favour coal stations both for political reasons (i.e. support for the British coal industry) and also because there is greater job creation potential as coal stations take longer to construct and operation is more complex. [63]

Environmental considerations are wide ranging and include issues such as Sections 36 and 37 of the 1989 Act which require applications to build a station and/or install electric lines to be supported by an

---

[61] Articles 85 and 86 and 92 to 94 respectively of the Treaty of Rome.

[62] Not in my back yard !

[63] Lewis, D. J., '*Gas Turbine Power Generation: A Developer's View*', The Institute of Energy, Conference on Gas Turbine Power Generation, London, 4 May 1995, p. 2

environmental statement[64] and Section 3 and Schedule 9 of the 1989 Act (which require that consideration be given by the IPP to aspects of the natural or historical features of the site), The Environmental Act also requires that a system of Integrated Pollution Control be implemented and authorisations are required form Her Majesty's Inspectorate of Pollution which must be reviewed at least every four years and the IPP must demonstrate that Best Available Techniques Not Entailing Excessive Cost ("BATNEEC") have been implemented to prevent or minimise releases of prescribed substances and to render harmless any substances (whether or not prescribed) which may be released.[65]

Conclusion

Privatisation of the electricity industry in England and Wales was daring and innovative. The 1989 Act fragmented the Electricity Industry creating, through the formation of the new independent generating companies, the NGC and the RECs divisions in the generation, transmission and supply of electricity. The purpose was to create a dynamic competitive market in the areas of generation and (eventually) supply and provide an environment that would welcome new investors. Privatisation also created two dominant powers in generation: National Power and PowerGen while not colluding, were in fact a duopoly. They were intimately aware of each other's methods of operation and had a stranglehold on the generation market. This coupled by the fact that there was an over supply of generating capacity in the UK did not make the market particularly attractive to IPP's.

Despite this fact, IPP's are being undertaken and the numbers are increasing. To be successful in such a constricted market they have be able to be efficient and generate power at prices which are cheaper or at least as cheap as their competitors (or come within the non-fossil fuel quotas). The necessity to convince financiers and regulators from inception that they have a "bankable" project, requires the sponsors to have in place from inception all major project documentation. This is a

---

[64] Applications must comply with the provisions of the Electricity and Pipe-line Works (Assessment of Environmental Effects) Regulations 1990.

[65] Of particular concern is compliance with the Large Combustion Plants Directive and pollution of the waterways.

particularly onerous task as for example the Operation & Maintenance Agreement may have to be drawn up even before detailed design has been undertaken. The only method of ensuring success therefore is careful planning, the principal component being risk assessment and management.

The "elemental" risks which can and should be dealt with in the project documentation, must be considered with a view to identifying and allocating the risks on the party who can best bear them. Of particular importance will be protection of the revenue stream, as this will determine whether sponsors will obtain financing or a licence to generate from the DGES. The "global" risks being those inherent within the environment in which the IPP will operate may appear to be somewhat of a quagmire to navigate.

While the level of regulation could lead the cynical to query whether the heavy hand of government control has been lift from any part of the electricity industry apart from the costs, what has become apparent, in reviewing the way in which the DGES has exercised his powers to control the market dominance of National Power and PowerGen, is that regulation can be used as a spur to competition. The DGES in controlling Pool prices through the Pool price undertakings, in promoting greater transparency in the way National Power and PowerGen operate, in obtaining and ensuring that plant which they intend to mothball or close is made available for sale, and in particular in requiring the disposal of 6,000 MW of generating capacity has introduced a more level playing field for IPP's. The DGES's role has been crucial to providing IPP's with a niche in the generation market.

The result of the DGES's intervention can be seen in his 1995 Annual Report where he reports that there were reductions in average real electricity prices in 1995/96 compared with the previous year. The proportion of over 1 MW sites choosing second tier supply licences had risen 52 per cent. in 1995/96 and the proportion of sites between 100 kw and 1 MW had risen to 33 per cent. That over 2,500 MW of new independent generation capacity came on stream bringing total capacity of independent generators to over 5,800 MW. Over 2,000 MW of further independent capacity is under construction[66] and the effect of the sale of 6,000 MW of generating capacity will roughly double the extent of independent generation in England and Wales. The sales are a significant impetus to the development of competition in generation and it introduces Eastern Group plc as a new major player with 9 per cent. of the market share in generation.

The DGES is of the view that barely six years after privatisation the generation market in England and Wales is no longer vulnerable to the manipulation of the dominant forces.[67] For an IPP therefore regulation has been a benefit; the issue now for them to determine is whether they are well structured, cost effective and have the competitive edge to survive.

---

[66] Offer - Annual Report 1995 - A Summary of the main points of the Annual Report, pp. 1-2.

[67] Offer - Press Notice (R28/96) - Disposal of Plant, 25 June 1996, p. 1.

15. Power Generation and Control Systems

Geoffrey M Beresford Hartwell

Synopsis

This paper examines the complexities of a power station, the nature of the control systems required and what levels of co-operation are required in practice to effect continuous supply characteristics.

Introduction

A modern power station project is complex. Of course it is complex in the way that other major technical projects are complex, but it also has special complexity. It has the special technical complexity associated with the need to operate in synchronism with others in a supply network. It has the special commercial complexity associated with the commercial structure in which it is created and in which it has to operate.

A modern nuclear power station has other complications associated with regulation and the safety imperative. So-called thermal[1] or fossil fuel power stations have to contend with the environmental consequences of plant which has as its function to process huge amounts of energy. Smoke and sulphur in the air. Nitrogen oxides. There is regulation for thermal stations as well. Even the so-called renewable energy systems, wave, tidal and wind power, have environmental consequences, not all of which are seen universally as benign.

There a number of constraints on power station projects, both at the commercial and at the technical level, which require to be considered, some of which have an effect upon the creation and management of the project and some of which impinge upon the creation and execution of contracts for the work.

---

1   Although nuclear power stations are also thermal. Perhaps "combustion" power
     stations would be more correct.

Control of Power Generation

If there is one dominant technical feature, other than the sheer amount of energy to be handled, it is the need to control that energy very quickly and in response to a single external stimulus: the instantaneous demand for electricity, manifested at the power station as the grid frequency. I am going to digress sufficiently to explain the nature of that phenomenon, the control of power generation in a supply and distribution system.

To begin this digression, I would ask you to consider what might, until recent years, have been called a conventional power plant. A steam turbine generator, powered from a boiler fired by burning an oil fuel. Such a generator would be interconnected, through an electrical transformer, with many others throughout the country, by the National Grid. Similarly, all the users of electricity are connected to the same grid, a network of high-voltage cables covering the entire country, joining, as I say, generators and users of electricity.

For all practical purposes, it can be said that, at any time, all the generators connected to the grid are turning at the same speed. That speed is determined by the frequency of the grid. It is the frequency of the grid. 50 cycles per second is 3,000 revolutions per minute, or 1500 or 750 rpm., depending upon the pole arrangement of the machine, generator or motor, in question. At least that is how it appears when you look at our typical generator, our conventional generator, in a typical power station. In fact, the frequency of the grid is not as fixed as it seems, because it is determined by the settings and behaviour of the totality of the generators connected to it and by the totality of the loads upon the grid network.

It is hard to believe, but the frequency of the nations power supply, upon which we rely for light, heat and for a thousand and one other things, is albeit briefly under the consumers, control. When an electrical appliance, say a kettle, is switched on, the fifty cycles per second becomes infinitesimally slower, in fact, all the generators in all the power stations slow down by the same amount. Thus, when the kettle boils and switches itself off, the grid frequency becomes that degree faster again; and all the generators speed up again. Every light, every use of electrical energy, has the same effect. The ability for the generators to fluctuate in response to demand is the key to the whole operation of an electricity distribution system.

The Generator

I turn now to examine the operation of the generator. It is driven by a steam turbine which has a governor. If the machine was not connected to any grid, if it were running on no load, or if it were to be, say, a single generator supplying power to an island, the governor would simply regulate the speed of the turbine and hence the generator – they are connected by a common shaft. When the load on the machine was connected or increased, that would tend to require more work from the turbine and more torque in the shaft, consequently the turbine slows down. The reason is quite simple; energy is admitted to the machine at a more or less constant rate and the rate of use of energy in a rotating machine is found by multiplying the torque by the speed. More load, more torque, less speed.

The Governor

The governor of a steam turbine is a device which adjusts the opening of the steam throttle valve, the accelerator, if you like, in response to the speed of the shaft. Slow down and the throttle opens a little; speed up and it starts to close. If a typical turbine governor were set, as you might expect, to a speed corresponding to 50 cycles per second, the it would open the throttle fully, to its full load capacity, if the loading made the frequency fall to 49.5 cycles. Conversely, if all the load were released, the speed would increase to only 50.5 cycles before the throttle became almost completely closed at light load. There would be a change of one cycle per second in fifty corresponding to the full load range of the machine. That is what is known as a 'two per cent. governor droop'. The setting is adjustable. In the island scenario, adjusting the setting increases or decreases the actual speed at which the generator provides the power demanded, but the power demand itself remains more or less unaffected – or nearly so for all practical purposes.

When there is more than one generator, however, the picture is altogether different. The governors are the same, they depend upon the frequency just as they ever did, but, in a fairly complex and extensive system, one machine is not enough to disturb the frequency of the system significantly. Whereas altering the governor of the one machine meant that the frequency changed with a more or less constant load, doing so in a large system means that the frequency stays more or less the same while it is the load, that is to say the share of load, taken by the adjusted machine, that changes.

Nothing can be done at the power station to control the total load on the system and nothing about the frequency or the speed at which the generators run, but decisions can be made as to how much power will be contributed to the total. By turning the governor settings up, the power station contributes more, if turned down, less. If a substantial number of power stations make similar adjustments at the same time, the frequency be affected. That is what happens, several operators adjust the frequency of the National Grid overnight, to hit eight o'clock in the morning.

The integrated effect

This process has been examined at length for two reasons. One is that it and its effects dominate the performance of power stations and the financial returns available from them; technology meets money face to face. The other is that it makes electricity generation unique, or very nearly so, in that it is the provider, the producer, that has control of how much he sells. Because that is so, fairly complex rules and disciplines have to be in place to allow the system to work at all. That is nothing to do with the questions of ownership and privatisation, it is a simple fact arising from the nature of dealing with this kind of energy.

Speed, frequency and governor settings are, however, not the entire story. If a generating system is overloaded progressively then it will certainly slow down, but the load may also cause the excitation in the generator itself to collapse so that the generator simply stops working. Trip devices generally will disconnect it before that happens. Very sudden loss of load may over speed the machines; that also results in an immediate trip, shutting down the machine altogether.

This may not be the forum on which to go into further details, but the principles set out above explain, for example, how it comes about that the National Grid responds almost automatically to sudden storms or the extraordinary excursions of demand – millions of kettles, millions of washrooms – that follow a television weepy or an early morning title fight. They also explain what happened, I think it was in the late 1950s or early 1960s, when the whole of the North East American and South East Canadian Network collapsed completely, following an incident near a hydro station at the Border. The United States authorities were greatly concerned that such an extensive blackout could occur so quickly. They did not believe it to be accidental and the emergency and armed services were put on emergency alert.

Consequences of Power Generation

Before the former State-owned power generation enterprises "went public" – there was a recognised method for selecting which stations would run at or near full load, the so- called "base load" stations, which would run at part load to provide the balance of the demand, and which would be run to provide backup for high demand (known as "spinning spare"), and also to stabilise the system and reduce transmission losses by absorbing what is loosely termed "wattless power" or reactive power.

The former Central Electricity Generating Board, and the Central Electricity Authority before that, had a system based on "Merit Order", a measure of the overall efficiency of each station under their control. The decision as to whether to bring in or to load a plant was based, more or less, on that efficiency. Later, of course, it became more complex, there were other considerations, such as the use of energy from the channel link, the problems associated with shutting down the nuclear stations which may "poison out" for a period if shut down sharply, and the ever increasing size of single units. Larger turbines may be susceptible to thermal stresses if they are caused to change load over too great a range too rapidly. Nevertheless, Merit Order was a fairly simple concept and capable of administration according to a set of relatively straightforward rules. There were others on the system, the South of Scotland Electricity Board and the North of Scotland Hydro-Electric Board, but co-operation was relatively straightforward. Or so it seems now.

In the current arrangement, however, there is a market in electrical energy, operated by the National Grid.[2] Generators make bids for

---

[2]   For a more detailed analysis, see Morais, K.P. , *Regulation and Procurement of Independent Power Projects*, supra, p.225.

forward deals on the amount of energy they are to provide and they are paid according to those bids and according to their actual performance, as well as for providing a reserve source of energy – the "spinning spare". A complicated legal and commercial regime prevails, with its own internal arbitration system. It is all a little like a game of bridge, with contracts used in lieu of playing cards. The technical consequence is that the load control system of a modern power station may have to be sufficiently versatile to allow the station to operate efficiently and to adjust its load in a variety of different operational scenarios.

The Operating Environment

Power stations operate in a complex control environment, to which they are more or less rigidly tied. For the reasons outlined above, their control systems have to be flexible and have to be able to take account of changing external conditions. I have said that the dominating technical features of a power station are the sheer amount of energy involved and the speed with which the demand for energy may change. There is another major technical feature to be considered, however, and that is the complexity of the internal operating environment. A power station is a complex process plant combining many different processes, each often of different manufacture and each having its own operating parameters and requirements. The design is therefore complex and, moreover, the contractual environment is no less complex, I would suggest, than the plant itself. The prime concern is to ensure that appropriate information is exchanged between the myriad participants in the project without corrupting what might be called the clear stream of contractual responsibility. To demonstrate the technology behind this problem, which is a very real one, not confined to power stations but certainly there seen at its most extreme, I would take you through a typical modern combined-cycle power station on what will be a brief outline, or at least as close to a brief outline as I ever get.

A typical combined cycle power station combines gas turbine generators with steam turbine generators. The steam for the steam turbines is generated in boilers, waste heat boilers to give them the traditional name, heated by the exhaust gases from the gas turbines. Because the theoretical efficiency of a thermal system is determined by the difference between the maximum temperature at which energy enters the system and the temperature at which the heat is finally rejected, a combined-cycle power station is more efficient than either the gas turbine generators or the steam turbine generators.

Heat is finally rejected to the environment at two points; one, the exhaust gas leaving the boiler or heat exchangers; the other, by way of condensers in which the steam turbine exhaust is condensed, just as Watt suggested. The heat is then discharged either directly to the air, or to a cooling water system which itself may discharge the heat to the air, via a cooling tower, or directly to a body of water, if the power station is coastal or on an estuary. There are examples where the body of water is a lake, but not, I think, in this country.

Because gas turbines, even large gas turbines, are capable of changing load relatively quickly and because the steam turbines are a little smaller than the previous class of turbines used in conventional stations (typically 300MW against 1,000MW), the stations are also well suited to duty at varying load.

Response to Change

At this juncture it is apposite to examine how responsive such a situation is. Any change of demand has effects upon the whole system and there are limits to the rate at which various sections can accept change. There is a limit to how fast the gas turbines and steam turbines may change load, dictated by considerations of thermal change between mechanical parts. There is a limit to how fast the boilers will increase their output following an increase in the amount of hot gas available, because the water has to be heated and steam created. After each change, there is a delay in achieving thermal equilibrium at every stage, from the flames in the combustion chambers of the gas turbines to the condensers; fuel pumps, feedwater pumps, or boiler circulating pumps, for example, have their own characteristics in this regard.

Design of Power Generation Installations

The design of any power generation installation has to take account of these differences between the optimisation of output and the external criteria dictated by the operating environment, and how to integrate them so as to obtain the optimum performance. In practice that is done in two principal ways: so far as is practicable, the individual items of plant are themselves designed to integrate effectively with one another so as to be compatible over a wide range of duties; where that is not fully practicable, operating regimes are devised to cope with the differences. For example, many combined-cycle power stations have means of diverting the exhaust, in whole or in part, away from the heat exchange boilers and direct to the atmosphere. Others may have provision for steam to be dumped from the boiler direct to a condenser, sometimes separate, sometimes a part of the turbine condenser. Such operational techniques are less efficient, but they do facilitate start-up and part-load operation.

Design Translation between Plants

If I may be permitted to digress for a moment or so, I would like to touch upon a particular example of the problems of matching the design of different items of plant one to another. This example is not from a combined cycle power station, but from a nuclear power station. Many nuclear power stations have what are called "once-through" boilers. Instead of circulating water around arrays of tubes, the flow is direct and the water is evaporated and superheated in one pass through the system. Feedwater goes in, passes through the tubes which are progressively hotter and superheated steam leaves.

Optimum performance and corrosion resistance is achieved by using different steels at different stages, pipes of different materials being welded to make a single steam-raising pass. So far so good. The steels used at the high temperature end tend to be alloy steels whose main quality is resistance to creep at high temperatures. As it happens, those same steels, or some of them, are susceptible to corrosion cracking if they are exposed to damp; because their function is also to superheat steam which already is superheated and therefore dry, this does not presnet a problem. These steels must be used at the top end of the boiler, something different at the bottom. The actual situation is, of course, more complex, it is common to use three different materials, sometimes more.

A nuclear reactor operates within fairly narrow temperature ranges and for reasons associated with the cause of the Windscale fire, now nearly forty years ago, the inlet temperature of the heat exchange gas – in a gas-cooled reactor – has to be more or less fixed. That means that, at part load, the outlet temperature will be lower than it is at full load. How much lower depends upon decisions that are made about the arrangement of the reactor, the fuel, the level at which control rods normally sit and any changes to the cooling flow.

This raises the question as to what happens in the boiler. Because the temperature is lower, although the rate of flow of water and steam is less, the transition from water to wet steam and from wet steam to dry and eventually superheated steam may move higher or lower in the boiler, depending upon the exact relationship between the boiler and the reactor.

External design parameters

The modern combined cycle power station is required, as I have said, to follow the load demand of the Grid, within the commercial framework set up for it. The station is complex, and each piece of specialised plant within it has first to work with the other plant, then to follow the overall load demand, all with the minimum of human intervention. Indeed, many of the events which occur are simply too fast for human intervention. That is one reason for automatic control. Add to that a need to detect any failure and take action to correct it or to nullify its effect. Add further a need to monitor the performance of every item of plant so as to predict a need for maintenance and to review the efficiency of performance. There is a need also to monitor and switch the high voltage switches which connect the station to the Grid and to monitor the electrical transformers. Then add a further element to record the emission of smoke, sulphur, nitrogen oxides, carbon monoxide, unburned hydrocarbons and complex combustion products that may be harmful and, finally, records of imported gas and any oil fuel used. The corollary to this is that any power station has to be controlled by a very complex control system, usually based on at least two computers with communications to every quarter of the installation.

Integration and Control of the Design

The control system described above will be the product of a specialist manufacturer. Although it controls everything, it does not control everything itself. For example, the gas turbine and steam turbine governors come with the turbine. Usually they come complete with their own systems of monitoring and protection, probably developed over a period of years. Manufacturers do not like to let other people interfere with their proprietary systems, because their systems are part of the safety arrangements. No one who has seen the consequences of a burst turbine would wish to argue with them about that. But they have to be integrated with the station control system at the right level of hierarchy and with the correct degree of autonomy.

The design of all this is a kind of iterative process. The overall designer, the builder's system designer, starts by putting together a scheme, using the knowledge he has. The suppliers of the component plant are contacted and they comment on the design from their own point of view. They exchange information and the overall design is amended or adjusted in the light of it. Usually the system designer, the builder or perhaps the engineer, if there is a main contract and it is of the once traditional type, will have in his team a complete portfolio, so to speak, of mechanical, electrical, civil and structural engineers, but it is the systems engineer who has the problem of resolving the technical interplay.

Not only is the development of a power station system design an iterative process, it is an iterative process that continues throughout the period of construction of the station and often beyond. It may not be until attempts are made to operate the plant that incompatibilities are observed. That will lead to changes. There may be a change in the so-called "fine tuning" of the control systems, whether the overall system or the control system of a particular plant. There may be a change in the operating regime, although in a competitive environment, operational limitations generally are unwelcome. There may have to be changes in the physical plant, usually the least attractive area to change, because of the costs and delays that may result.

Legal consequences

Now the legal problems emerge, where a number of individual suppliers exist, each contributing to a whole. Each is in contract with a central authority, usually a main contractor. There is tension between the final buyer and the main contractor. Of course, one wants the most for his money, the other wants to see an end to his work at a profitable price. The same is true at each level. Design information has to flow up and down the contractual chain, but it also has to flow between people who have no contractual links. People who elsewhere may be in competition (and some of this design information is clever stuff that gives one or another a competitive edge). Design information goes on flowing long after the deals have been done and the contracts made.

The practice in the industry is to pass the design responsibility down the chain wherever possible. That may mean that more than one sub-contractor or supplier is left with a responsibility wider than his own scope of work, involving the acquisition of information from others with whom he has no contract. Moreover, this approach to delegation may hamstring the main contractor or the end user. Having delegated the design, they are in difficulty if they don't like it. Approval or disapproval is a very blunt instrument to use for design adjustment and involves a significant risk of creating variation which may be costly.

In past years the power industry was not noted for its litigiousness. There was extensive co-operation. Manufacturers repaired their equipment long after it was out of the defects liability period. The originators of the IEE/IMechE model forms of contract could say, with some pride, that their words had rarely, if ever, fallen to be construed by the courts. The principal specialist Institutions were asked to appoint arbitrators once in a blue moon. And even then the references settled.

Conclusion

In conclusion I pause to reflect on the happy (but not very busy) days. In the United Kingdom I think there were several circumstances which combined to create a state of affairs in power statoin construction that no longer exists.

First the market was limited. The CEGB, The South of Scotland Board, the North of Scotland Hydro Board were not to offended. Secondly, manufacturer's margins were reasonably generous; there was a contribution to development. As a consequence, management afforded the technical professionals a fairly free reign. That was the heyday of the concept of the design team, drawn from all the participants and combining to get the best out of the project. The technical best. Professionals looked on the work as a common interest. Deals on variations were done. On the one hand, reputation was more important than money; on the other, public service was seen as requiring that the suppliers were treated fairly and, so far as was practical, kept in business for the next time.

Admittedly this was not always a perfect system. Delays in power station construction frequently resulted from the design professionals exercising their free reign to improve the work as it went along. "You can have yesterday's improvement today, but implementing today's new idea may take a little longer." Nevertheless, it was a time when employer, contractor and sub-contractor were able to co-operate in the common weal. They created the team – and does not that expression have a familiar ring? Perhaps there is nothing new under the sun after all. That atmosphere was not confined to power station construction, of course. Indeed, in some ways the practice in power generation was a little less flexible than in other fields, because of the monopoly power of the buyers. Nevertheless technical co-operation was the norm.

Now the scene has changed. We have to attempt to re-create those days of technical co-operation by enforcing strict contractual terms, by legislation and by all the panoply of legal and pseudo-legal means at our disposal. Sir Michael Latham and others say that it can be done, that intervention and new forms of contract will make up for the lack of margins, the loss of goodwill and the tide of litigation that has swept over us all. But they cannot change the technical issues and they cannot change the facts of life. All we can hope for is that there will be a move against the tide, but I wonder if I will live to see it.

Endnote

As an endnote to this paper, I would mention one area in which, admittedly, a number of mistakes were made, but within which the level of co-operation was perhaps particularly noticeable. It was that of early nuclear power. It is interesting that the early nuclear constructors all were consortia of companies with related interests, financial and technical. I would suggest one of the advantages of joint venture activities to be that, when the major suppliers all are concerned in the joint venture, there is more scope for co-operation without disturbing the financial pattern. My personal view is that contracts which involve the end user in a joint venture with the major various suppliers ought to provide an optimum way forward for projects which have a high degree of innovation.

Part IV

Damage, Proof and Recovery

16. Containing the Loss: Recent Trends

John Powell QC

Synopsis

This paper deals with loss containment in the context of claims against professionals. It does not attempt to deal with all recent cases but rather to focus on broad trends, including what may be seen in that context as an emerging principle of proportionality.

Introduction

The explosion in the number and size of claims against professionals has focussed attention on the means to contain the exposure. Containment needs to be addressed at various levels including liability, loss and insurance. In the context of loss, containment devices include causation, contributory negligence, contribution and statutory powers to give relief. As a reminder:

- contributory negligence is a defence provided by statute[1] which enables the court, where the plaintiff suffers damage as a result partly of his own "fault"[2] and partly of the fault of the defendant, to reduce the damages recoverable to such extent as the court thinks just and equitable having regard to the plaintiff's share in the responsibility for the damage;

- contribution is not a defence but a right conferred by statute[3] upon a defendant, D1, to recover a proportion of the damages for which he is liable to the plaintiff, from other persons. D2 D3 etc. each of whom is also liable to the plaintiff in respect of the same damage, based on that other person's share in the

---

[1] The Law Reform (Contributory Negligence) Act 1945

[2] Defined in s.4. Pure contractual claims are not covered, but the defence may be raised to a contractual claim where there is concurrent liability in tort: *Forsikringsakieselskapet Vesta v. Butcher* [1986] 2 All ER 488 and on appeal [1989] A.C. 852. The defence may not be raised to a claim for deceit: *Alliance & Leicester B.S. v Edgestop Ltd.* [1993] 1 WLR 1462; or conversion: Torts (Interference with Goods) Act 1977 s. 11(1).

[3] The Civil Liability (Contribution) Act 1978

responsibility for the damage; while each of D1, D2 and D3 is liable to the plaintiff, as between themselves the damages are shared as appropriate e.g. a third each;

- relief is neither a defence nor a right, but a discretionary power given to the court under certain statutes[4] in respect of a defendant who is otherwise liable to the plaintiff, to relieve him from such liability, whether wholly or partly and on such terms as the court thinks fit, on the basis that he has acted honestly and reasonably and that in the circumstances he ought to be excused.

Causation

Causation is a difficult problem and there are more cases on the subject than there is a lifetime to read.[5] The perennial problem is ascertaining whether one or more putative causes link in law the duty breached and the loss claimed. The "but for" test is not necessarily determinant. It is an exclusionary test serving only to filter out non-causal "occasions" for the loss. Putative causes may survive that test but may still not qualify as "effective causes". How does one choose among these?

Causation has recently received attention in two major cases in the House of Lords. I turn now to consider the effect of these cases.

Smith New Court Securities Ltd. v Scrimgeour Vickers (Asset Management) Ltd.[6]

This was concerned with the measure of damages for the tort of deceit or fraudulent misrepresentation, the context being misrepresentations made in the course of negotiations for the sale of a large block of shares. Two points emerge from the speech of Lord Steyn. The first is the impact of the moral factor and the relationship between the nature of the duty breached and the compensatable loss. He addressed "the question of policy whether there is a justification for differentiating

---

[4]   The Companies Act 1985, s. 727 in relation to officers and auditors under that Act and the Trustee Act 1925, s.61 in relation to trustees.

[5]   See further *Hart & Honore* in their classic work on the subject, "Causation in the Law" (2nd. ed. 1985).

[6]   [1996] 4 All ER 769

between the extent of liability for civil wrongs depending on where in the sliding scale from strict liability to intentional wrongdoing the particular civil wrong fits in". He answered the question affirmatively concluding that "the exclusion of heads of loss in the law of negligence, which reflects considerations of legal policy, does not necessarily avail the intentional wrongdoer" for reasons of both of morality and deterrence.[7]

The second point made by Lord Steyn was there was no "single satisfactory theory of causation" capable of solving "the infinite variety of practical problems" confronted by the courts. Judges sometimes applied a pragmatic test of asking whether the condition in question was a substantial factor in producing a result and others asserted "common sense" as the guiding criterion. There was no material difference.[8]

Banque Bruxelles Lambert SA v Eagle Star Ins. Co. Ltd.

But despite the fact that "our case law yields few secure footholds",[9] judges keep striving; those in Australia perhaps harder than in this country, at least, that is, before the other major recent case, *"BBL"*.[10] The House of Lords there considered a number of consolidated appeals concerning the loss recoverable against valuers by lenders who had lent money in reliance on negligent valuations of the properties providing the mortgage security. The lenders sought to recover the shortfall between the amounts of their loans and recoveries effected against defaulting borrowers. The valuers contended that the lenders were not entitled to recover the element of the shortfall which they said was caused not by their negligent valuations but by a subsequent "fall in the market". The argument failed before the Court of Appeal but succeeded before the House of Lords to the extent that the loss recoverable was held to be limited to a maximum representing the

---

[7] *Ibid.* at 790.
[8] *Ibid.* at 794-5
[9] *Ibid.* at 794
[10] *Banque Bruxelles Lambert SA v Eaale Star Ins. Co. Ltd.* reported at [1996] 3 W.L.R. 87 *sub. nom. South Australia Asset Management Corp. v York Montague Ltd.* Lords Goff, Jauncey, Slynn and Nicholls all agreed with Lord Hoffman who delivered the only reasoned speech.

difference between the valuation actually given and an accurate valuation (i.e. the mean within a range of competent valuations). *BBL* has considerable ramifications for professional negligence cases generally, including claims against financial advisers and accountants. So the reasoning merits closer analysis.

Lord Hoffman started from a moral premise: "Normally the law limits liability to those consequences which are attributable to that which made the act wrongful." Applied to a case of negligence for providing inaccurate information, he characterised that as "liability for the consequences of the information being inaccurate." Some, including myself, would cavil at that and rather characterise it as "liability for the consequences of failure to exercise care". Thus the bargain made with a professional man is normally the exercise of reasonable skill and care and not a warranty as to the accuracy of the information or advice given. Lord Hoffman's answer to this is that it would be paradoxical and not fair and reasonable that the liability of a person who warranted the accuracy of the information should be less than that of a person who gave no such warranty but failed to take reasonable care. The riposte to this is that it is a false paradox and merely a consequence of the particular bargain struck, namely for the exercise of care.

Lord Hoffman then goes on to define a difference in terms of causative potency between information and advice:

> "*The principle thus stated distinguishes between a duty to* **provide information** *for the purpose of enabling someone else to decide upon a course of action and a duty to* **advise** *someone as to why course of action he should take.*
>
> *[a] If the duty is to advise whether or not a course of action should be taken, the adviser must take reasonable care to consider all the potential consequences of that course of action. If he is negligent, he will therefore be responsible for all the foreseeable loss which is the consequence of that action having been taken.*
>
> *[b] If his duty is only to supply information, he must take reasonable care to ensure that the information is correct and, if he is negligent, will be responsible for all the foreseeable consequences of the information being wrong.*"

Applied to the facts, what the valuers provided was characterised as information and not advice and hence the recoverable loss was subject to the limit of that recoverable if they had warranted its accuracy.

I have considerable reservations as to the reasoning as opposed to the particular result.[11] The first relates to the warranty cap. In the case of negligent information it sets an artificial limit for loss by reference to that recoverable based on a different contractual bargain. It seems particularly anomalous where the basis of the duty is exclusively tort and not contract, but to deny the application of the limit to a claim based on a duty of care in tort would create a greater anomaly, as it would place the recipient of free information in a better position than one who paid for it pursuant to a contract.[12]

The second reservation relates to the information/advice dichotomy. To relate recoverability in professional negligence cases to whether the professional gave information or advice:

- creates major problems of characterisation and uncertainty;
- belies not only what many profess to provide (e.g. legal advice), or their self-description (e.g. investment advisers) but also the normal understanding and expectation of the public at large;
- underrates the causative potency of what may be properly characterised in a particular case as only information;
- encourages the invertebrate professional if not the Pontius Pilate: I can tell you this and that, but to go ahead is entirely a matter for you, Mr Client, and your other professional advisers.

---

[11] A similar conclusion could have been arrived at by alternative conventional rationalisations based on: foreseeability: *Overseas Tankships (U.K.) Ltd. v Morts Dock & Engineering Co. Ltd. (The Wagon Mound)* [1961] AC 388 PC: *Hadley v Baxendale* (1854) 9 Ex 341: and the restorative principle and characterising what P would have done given competence by D: *Livingstone v Rawyards Coal Co.* (1880) 5 App. Cas. 25,39: *Dodd Properties (Kent) Ltd. v Canterbury City Council* [1980] 1 WLR 433 (CA): *County Personnel v Pulver* [1987] 1 WLR 916 (CA). In *BBL* the latter route was not open to the House of Lords given how the cases were advanced in lower courts

[12] See further Stapleton, J., (1997) 113 LQR 1.

Consider the application of the dichotomy in a financial context. Take the pension mix-selling review. Should compensation for mix-selling be limited on the basis that what was provided may have been information and not advice? Probably not in most cases. The commission incentive to effect an actual sale of a private pension would doubtless persuade a court that advice and not mere information was given.

What about the negligent architect? Is the architect who negligently fails to discover a construction defect and who negligently issues a final certificate having the effect of precluding recourse against the builder to be taken as having given negligent information? Or to the extent that he failed originally to discover the defect and to recommend corrective action, is he to be taken as having failed to give proper advice as opposed to information?

My third and major reservation is that the very specificity of the information/advice dichotomy diverts attention into an over-mechanistic and potentially misleading test in the context of causation and away from the primary importance of evaluating purpose. By that I mean the importance of evaluating the reason why the particular defendant was engaged and the potency of his role in relation to the transaction in question and to each element of loss claimed. The point is summated in the question: was the particular loss "within the reasonable scope of the dangers against which it was the [defendant]'s duty to provide protection"?[13]

I suspect the information/advice dichotomy will in practice prove not a barrier but a circumventable obstacle. Adherents of the American

---

[13] *The British Racing Drivers Club Ltd. v Hextall Erskine & Co* [1996] 3 All ER 667 per Carnworth J. Similarly in an Australian case, *Barnes v Hay* [1988] 12 NSWLR 337, 355, where the solicitors' negligence consisted of failing to complete a commercial lease agreement before the acquisition of a freehold by a Landlord who proceeded to harass the lessee to the point that his business collapsed, Mahoney JA in holding that the tenant was entitled to recover his consequent losses from the solicitor said: "The reason why the law imposes liability for that loss in such a case is, not because there is, in the abstract, a group of conditions sufficient to produce the loss, but because defendants are to be held responsible for that which it was their duty to seek to avoid."

school of jurisprudence will doubtless have no difficulty in making a choice to reflect their view of justice in a particular situation.

A more general perspective of *BBL* is that it represents a judicial attempt to carve out of causation what is sought to be achieved by statutory relief provisions. By the latter the court may limit a defendant's liability in damages for breach of duty to such degree as the court thinks fair and just having regard not only to causative potency but also moral culpability.[14] It is highly questionable, however, whether causation lends itself to such fine tuning. In any event, *BBL* has and will continue to encourage exploration of the frontiers of liability and loss recoverability.[15]

Causation and reliance

Reliance is a manifestation of causation. Specific reliance is a prerequisite to a claim based on negligent misrepresentation or the provision of negligent information or advice. However, it is not essential to claims based on negligent action or inaction or omission.[16] In such cases foresight of loss or damage may suffice.[17] An alternative

---

[14] Although still limited in scope and application: Companies Act 1985 s. 727; Trustee Act 1925 s. 61.

[15] Note *Machin v Adams* (1997) CILL 1273 (CA) (Architect held not liable primarily since no reliance. But also held that no duty of care owed by architect to purchaser of property in respect of information contained in letter sent to vendor even assuming that it was foreseeable that it would be shown to purchaser, in the absence of knowledge of the purpose for which the purchaser required by purchaser. *Hartle v Laceys* (1997) CILL 1255 (interrelationship between BBL principle and damages for loss of a chance).

[16] [1995] 2 AC 207 at 272 D-G, per Lord BrowneWilkinson: "it does not follow that in all cases based on negligent action or inaction by the defendant it is necessary in order to demonstrate a special relationship that the plaintiff has in fact relied on the defendant or the defendant has foreseen such reliance. If in such a case careless conduct can be foreseen as likely to cause and does in fact cause damage to the plaintiff that should be sufficient to found liability." See also *Edwards Karawacki Smith & Co Pty Ltd. v Jacka Nominees Pty Ltd.* (1995) 13 ACLC 9 (Supreme Court of Western Australia) at 23-29 (refusal to strike out claim by defrauded investors in finance broking company against its auditors) (cf. *Anthony v Wright* [1995] 1 BCLC 236.).

[17] *Ibid*

analysis in professional negligence cases is that the plaintiff relied on the defendant to exercise due care and skill, i.e general reliance.[18] But even absence of general reliance is not always fatal to the success of a claim.[19]

Interplay of causation, contributory negligence, contribution and statutory relief

This is illustrated by a recent auditors' negligence case in Australia, *AWA Ltd. v Daniels t/a Deloitte Haskins & Sells*.[20] The auditors of a company were held negligent in failing to discover severe internal control deficiencies and concealment of vast losses arising from foreign exchange hedging transactions by an employee. The auditors alleged contributory negligence on the part of the company and sought relief from liability under the Australian equivalent to section 727 of the Companies Act 1985 and made contribution claims. Rogers J. at first instance reduced the damages by 20 per cent. on account of contributory negligence on the part of its senior management. As to the contribution claim against the chief executive, the judge held that the auditors had a right to elect either to have his negligence taken into account as part of the company's contributory negligence or to claim contribution from him. The auditors elected the latter and the company's loss was apportioned 90:10 between the auditors and the chief executive.

Given the reduction of the claim for contributory negligence, statutory relief was not granted to reduce further the auditors' liability in damages to the company. However, the judge concluded that the relevant statute providing for relief was an appropriate provision for allocation of fault.

---

[18] *Henderson v Merrett Syndicates* [1995] 2 AC 145 at 180F-G, *per* Lord Goff.

[19] For example *White v Jones* [1995] 2 AC 207 at 262C-D, 268A-B *per* Lord Goff: he rationalised liability on the basis of deemed assumption of responsibility reflecting foresight of loss: see esp. 268C-E.

[20] (1992) 7 ACSR 759. Supreme Court of New South Wales, Commercial Division.

On appeal[21] the New South Wales Court of Appeal varied the decision of Rogers C.J. in various respects. It held that the auditors were not entitled to elect as to treatment of the chief executive's negligence. Apportionment for contributory negligence had to be taken into account before consideration of contribution between defendants. The Court reduced the damages by a third on account of AWA's contributory negligence, the relevant negligence being that of the whole board of directors (including the chief executive) and senior management. The auditors having secured partial relief by way of a finding of contributory negligence, they were not additionally entitled to contribution from the chief executive as they would otherwise "unjustly receive double compensation".[22]

A more recent New Zealand case, *Dairy Containers Ltd. v. NZI Bank Ltd.*[23] also illustrates the interplay of causation, contributory negligence, contribution and statutory relief in an auditors' context. It is especially instructive given Thomas J's emphasis of the management role of directors and his analysis of criteria to be taken into account in assessing the appropriate discount for contributory negligence in a claim against auditors. On the facts, a 40 per cent. discount was made.

Contributory negligence

The operation of what may be seen as a principle of proportionality in the context of contributory negligence is best illustrated in this country in recent years in the context of valuers. The reckless enthusiasm among lenders to take advantage of the property boom in the late 1980s bore a bitter harvest of default. Valuers were in the front line of recovery actions against professionals as naive and sometimes unscrupulous sought to treat a negligent valuation as tantamount to an indemnity against the financial consequences of default, irrespective of the prudence of the original lending. But the increasing success of the defence of contributory negligence based on the lender's own failure to exercise appropriate prudence in the original lending, is demonstrative of the courts' desire to achieve a fairer allocation of loss more

---

[21] *Sub nom. Daniels v Anderson* (1995) 16 ACSR 607 Supreme Court of New South Wales, Court of Appeal. Clarke, Sheller and Powell JJA.

[22] *Ibid.* at 735

[23] [1995] 2 NZLR 30

proportionately related to the original share of blame. Plaintiff lenders have had their damages reduced significantly for contributory negligence. Where the recklessness of the Plaintiff has been such as to suggest a higher deduction than that, claims have frequently been abandoned.

The successful experience of valuers in invoking contributory negligence has lessons for other professional especially accountants and the building professions. As the law currently stands contributory negligence is only available to a defence to a claim in contract where D's liability in contract is the same as his liability in the tort of negligence independently of the existence of the contract.[24] In most professional negligence cases this criterion is satisfied because the duty is one of care both in contract and in tort. It only poses a problem where the professional has undertaken a stricter duty.[25] The Law Commission has in 1993 reported on the subject of contributory negligence as a defence in contract a paper so entitled.[26] It recommended that the availability the defence to claims in contract should be extended.

Contribution

Contribution claims between wrongdoers have been commonplace for years, and increasingly so since the Civil Evidence (Contribution) Act 1978 extended the basis of contribution beyond joint tortfeasors to contract breakers and others. The appropriate allocation depends very much on the facts of the particular case and there are many illustrations in a building context and to a lesser extent as between solicitors and surveyors.

Statutory relief

As to statutory relief, the *AWA* case in Australia is one of the exceptional instances of its application, albeit as an alternative basis for reducing damages to contributory negligence. Section 727 of the

---

[24] *Forsikringsakieselskapet Vesta v. Butcher* [1986] 2 All ER 488 at 508

[25] As, for example, the defendant architect in *Barclays Bank v Fairclough Building Ltd.* [1995] 1 All ER 21 (C.A.).

[26] Law Commission No. 219, published 6 December 1993.

Companies Act 1985 enables relief to be given to an officer (e.g. a director) or an auditor appointed as such by the company. Thus it gives the court a discretion in any proceedings against such a person for negligence, default, breach of duty or breach of trust, to relieve him wholly or partly from his liability if certain criteria are satisfied. These are that, in the opinion of the court, he has acted honestly and reasonably and that, in the circumstances of the case, including those of his appointment, he ought reasonably to be excused. It would seem that such relief is only available in respect of a claim against him by the company.[27] Even then it remains to be tested in this country whether and to what extent a person who has been found to be negligent and thus to have failed to exercise *reasonable* care and skill may be relieved whether wholly or in part of liability on the basis that he has acted honestly *and reasonably.*[28]

An emerging principle of proportionality?

At this point may I make an observation? As I have sought to illustrate, frequently detectable in attempts to contain the loss by the operation of the defence contributory negligence and contribution claims, is a striving to give effect to a principle or concept of proportionality. That is a principle that the extent of a defendant's liability in damages for breach of duty should bear a reasonable relationship to the extent of his error or cuplability. I would contend that English law as it currently stands is deficient in lacking the means, at least in certain circumstances, to give full effect to this principle.

Apportionment criteria

The deficiency is brought out by focussing on the apportionment criteria applicable as between plaintiff and defendant in the context of contributory negligence and as between co-defendants and other

---

[27] See *Customs and Excise Commissioners v Hedon Alpha Ltd* [1981] 2 All ER 697 (C.A.)

[28] See doubts as to the application of relief in such circumstances expressed in *Diamond Manufacturing Co. Ltd. v Hamilton* [1969] NZLR 609 at 631, 640 and 645 (NZ C.A.) and *Pacific Acceptance Corporation Ltd. v Forsvth* (1970) 92 N.S.W. (W.N.) 29 at 119, 124-125.

wrongdoers in the context of contribution. The criterion is essentially the same, namely what the court thinks is just and equitable having regard to the extent of the responsibility for the damage of the plaintiff in relation to contributory negligence and the other defendant(s) or wrongdoer(s) in relation to contribution. Responsibility embraces two factors:

- relative culpability; and
- causative potency.[29]

But note that once a defendant is shown to be culpable and the loss too is shown to have been caused by that fault, the defendant, subject to sharing of the loss with the plaintiff or other defendant, is responsible for the whole loss however large and however apparently disproportionate the amount of the loss to the degree of error – unless relief provisions can be successfully invoked. To illustrate the point I need only mention without commenting further as the merits the recent judgment for £65 million against the defendants in *ADT v BDO Binder Hamlyn*.[30]

Giving effect to a principle of proportionality

How can effect be given to such a principle of proportionality? There are a number of alternatives.

Contract

I anticipate there will be an increasing tendency for professionals to seek to limit or define their liability by appropriate contractual limitation clauses. Already standard forms of engagement for architects and engineers incorporate clauses which seek to limit their liability to a plaintiff in circumstances where they are liable along with others so as to limit their liability to what is their degree of fault relative to those others. In other words the clauses seek contractually to turn the statutory contribution right *qua* other defendants into a partial defence *qua* the plaintiff. These clauses remain to be judicially tested. More

---

[29] See for example *Stapley v. Gypsum Mines Ltd.* [1953] AC 663 at 682, *per* Lord Reid.

[30] May J. 6 December 1995.

conventional limitation clauses limit liability to a particular amount or a particular ascertainable amount, perhaps related to the amount of available insurance cover.

Unfair Contract Terms Act 1977

Quite apart from problems of incorporation in the contract and construction, contractual limitation clauses are subject to statutory restrictions. Applicable across the board is the Unfair Contract Terms Act 1977. Liability for death or personal injury cannot be excluded or limited and few would wish to alter that. As regards other loss or damages, liability for negligence cannot be excluded or limited unless the relevant clause or notice is reasonable. In my view there has been too much pessimism as to the threat the criterion of reasonableness poses for clauses which seek to limit liability for economic loss in commercial as distinct from consumer contexts. Nevertheless, there is a strong case for minor amendment of the 1977 Act to give more confidence in the efficacy of limitation of liability clauses in commercial contexts, including by providing for the amount as well as the availability of insurance cover to be taken into account in assessina reasonableness.

DTI/Law Commission: Feasibility Investigation of Joint and Several Liability

This brings me to the paper published by the DTI, the Feasibility Investigation of Joint and Several Liability by the Law Commissioner, Professor Andrew Burrows and the Common Law Team of the Law Commission. The report considers and rejects the introduction of "full proportionate liability" i.e. a new statutory regime whereby the defendants would be liable to plaintiffs only for the amount of damages equal to their proportionate share (i.e. relative to other defendants or wrongdoers) of the fault in the plaintiff's loss. The main grounds for rejection advanced are that (1) it is unfair for a legally blameless plaintiff to have to bear the risk of a defendant's insolvency and (2) it is misleading to say that defendants can currently be called upon "to provide 100 per cent. of the damages even though they are only 1 per cent. at fault" since the principle of joint and several liability is that relative to the plaintiff each defendant is 100 per cent. responsible for the whole of the loss.

For various reasons the paper also comes down against various forms of modified proportionate liability. One form would be reallocation of the share of an insolvent wrongdoer between other wrongdoers and the plaintiff where the latter is contributorily negligent – a solution favoured by Professor Glanville Williams. The report provides a useful summary of the law in other common law jurisdictions. Variants of proportionate liability have been introduced in the U.S.A., Ireland and Australia.

As many will be aware, the paper attracted strong responses from professional bodies related to building and accountancy. The new government's response is awaited. Perhaps building professionals would benefit most from a proportionate liability regime, owing to the structure of contracts for building projects in this country. Thus a building project brings together what may be viewed as temporary coalition of professionals and others with a diversity of skills and financial strength. Many may incur liability if something goes wrong although the fault of one may be relatively slight. There may be little or no scope for a defence of contributory negligence. Instances are legion of insured professional defendants being left carrying 100 per cent. of the loss without being able to obtain contribution from an insolvent corporate contractor who was most at fault.

Accountants may find themselves in a similar situation. However, in the context of auditors it should be borne in mind, as the *AWA* case illustrates, that the negligence of potential contributants (e.g. directors and senior management) may also and more usefully be attributed to the company and hence invoked by way of a defence of contributory negligence. The utility of successful invocation of that defence is that it reduces the amount of the defendant auditor's liability. Hence almost invariably it will be more useful to invoke the negligence of directors and senior management as a defence rather than a basis for seeking contribution, since they may not be good for the money. Accountants would be wise to take up the hint of support in the DTI report for modification of section 310.

The regulatory analogy

Auditors may wish to invoke the regulatory or quasi-regulatory nature of certain functions which they perform (especially if statutorily required as in the case of the company audit) in favour of a measure of statutory protection. This may take the form of a statutory capping of liability in performing statutory functions or of a modification of section 727 of the Companies Act 1985 to provide more explicitly for a discretion to a court to limit liability, perhaps by reference to a criterion of proportionality as outlined above. While auditors may not be deserving of immunity to the extent accorded to certain financial services regulators under section 187 of the Financial Services Act 1991 (and other regulators under other statutes), that section provides fruitful analogy for arguing that their (albeit lesser) regulatory role be recognised and rewarded with a degree of protection.

The regulatory analogy may not be quite so close or apposite in the case of architects and engineers. But the supervisory element of their work, where execution and control are the responsibility of others (usually protected by limited liability), is a deserving candidate for legislating to enable a measure of damages limitation on the basis of capping or discretionary relief.

17. Liquidated Damages: A New Role for an Old Remedy

Jonathan Hosie

Synopsis

This paper examines the existing and future role of liquidated damages in the construction sector. Conclusions are drawn as to how the remedy is in practice used to fulfil a variety of different aims. Proposals are formulated as to how greater use can be made of this remedy to provide certainty in the event of default.

Introduction

Liquidated damages are used extensively in construction contracts as a tailor-made and pre-determined remedy to compensate one party for the cost of delay in late performance of the contract caused by the other. In *Temloc v. Errill Properties,* [1] Croom-Johnson LJ said:

> *"There is every reason why parties to building contracts should agree to liquidated damages for non-completion. Proof of such loss is often difficult to achieve and agreement in advance is a saver of disputes."* [2]

The learned judge could have gone on to extrapolate the further benefit of the liquidated damage provision, namely that it brings certainty to the construction process. It enables the tenderer to price a known risk and to produce a reliable price for the works rather than to have to price for an unquantifiable contingency. Conversely the employer is better able to compare and evaluate tenders which have (at least to this extent) priced the contingency of delay in a uniform way. Furthermore, by agreeing a finite measure of compensation for delay, a contractor is able to calculate the cost of forfeiting liquidated damages to the employer as against the cost to himself of putting greater resources into the project to accelerate progress and alleviate delay.

---

[1]   (1987) 39 BLR 30
[2]   *Ibid*, p.38.

Whatever the rationale for the use of liquidated damage provisions, such have been used in construction contracts for many years and continue to be used to compensate for the cost of delay.

The existing state of play

One of the earliest reported cases concerning a building contract with a liquidated damages provision is that of *Holme v. Guppy*.[3] In that case there was a contract to construct a building within a specified period and a provision for payment of liquidated damages for failure to complete within that period. However, the owner of the property failed to give possession of the site when due thereby preventing the contractor from completing on time. When the employer nevertheless sought to impose liquidated damages for delay, the Court held that the contractor was not liable to pay damages for late completion as he had been prevented from completing on time by the acts of the owner.

The House of Lords, some 144 years later in *Percy Bilton Ltd v. GLC*,[4] applied the same principle where the employer had delayed in nomination of a new sub-contractor. Lord Fraser of Tullybelton stated the general rule that the main contractor is bound to complete the work by the date for completion stated in the contract. If he fails to do so, he will be liable for liquidated damages to the employer. This however is subject to the exception that the employer is not entitled to liquidated damages if by his acts or omission he has prevented the contractor from completing his work by the completion date.

Any discussion of the origins of liquidated damages should start with first principles. These are to be found in the House of Lords' judgment in the case of *Dunlop Pneumatic Tyre Co Limited v. New Garage & Motor Company Limited*.[5] In that case, the House of Lords set out a series of guidelines against which to check whether a sum stated in a contract as compensation payable for a party's breach was unenforceable as a penalty or valid and enforceable as a contractually agreed measure of loss. The guidelines run as follows:

---

[3] (1838) 3 M&W 387

[4] (1982) 20 BLR 1

[5] [1915] AC 79

- whether a sum is a penalty or liquidated damages is a question of construction to be decided upon the terms and circumstances of each particular contract judged at the time of making of contract not at the time of breach;

- to assist in this task of construction, the following tests may be used:

  (a) if the sum is extravagant and unconscionable in amount in comparison to the greatest loss that could conceivably be proved to flow from the breach, the sum will be held to be a penalty;

  (b) if the breach consists only in paying a sum of money and the sum is greater than the sum which ought to have been paid, it will be held to be a penalty;

  (c) where a single sum is made payable by way of compensation on the occurrence of one or more of several events some of which may occasion serious damage and others but trifling damage, there is a presumption that it is a penalty; and

  (d) the fact that the consequences of the breach are such as to make precise pre-estimation almost an impossibility does not mean that the sum is a penalty. On the contrary this is just the sort of situation when it is probable that pre-estimated damage represents the true bargain between the parties.

Of particular note for the purpose of this paper, is the fact that in delivering judgment and stating the law, their Lordships in the *Dunlop* case said they were doing so by reference to precedent and existing decisions of the Court.

Indeed, ten years previously there had been another important case in shaping the remedy of liquidated damages, *Clydebank Engineering & Shipbuildings Co Limited v. Don Jose Ramos Yzquierdo Y Castaneda*.[6] That case concerned a contract for the provision of four torpedo boats which contained a liquidated damages clause of £500 per week for a delay in delivery of those boats. There was a serious delay in supplying

---

[6]   [1905] AC 6

the torpedo boats and the total liquidated damages for the period of culpable delay amounted to some £67,500. The shipbuilders sought to escape liability for this sum arguing that there could be no measure of damages in the case of late delivery of a warship that had no commercial value. The shipbuilders estimated the actual loss to the Spanish Government at only £3,126.

The House of Lords held that the sum of £500 per week was to be regarded as a valid liquidated damage figure and not an unenforceable penalty, reasoning that it was just in this sort of situation (where the precise pre-estimation of actual loss was impossible) that the use of a finite figure for damages for delay represented a sensible and workable solution.

Unfortunately, there is nothing in the *Clydebank* judgment to show how the parties arrived at the liquidated damage figure although it was noted that the figure had been put forward in the contract negotiations by the shipbuilders themselves. Interestingly, injury to a State, as a matter of law, was considered to be expressible in terms of money albeit extremely difficult to quantify in practice. The House of Lords gave examples of how difficult the assessment of damages could be, requiring the cross-examination of every person connected with the Spanish navy and military administration to assess delay damages. Lord Robertson said:

> "*It would be preposterous to expect that conflicting evidence of naval or military experts should be taken as to the probable effect on the suppression of the rebellion in Cuba or on the war with America of the defender's* [Clydebank's] *delay in completing and delivery those torpedo boat destroyers.*"[7]

The judge also referred to "*the magnitude and complexity of the interests involved*".

The corollary of this approach is that the party suffering the delay does not have to prove actual loss. It is sufficient that the parties have agreed a liquidated damage figure in their contract and that this figure represents a reliable pre-estimate of their loss.

---

[7]   *Ibid*, p.20.

How accurate is the pre-estimate required to be?

In arriving at a reliable pre-estimate of loss, parties to a contract would be expected to ask themselves what possible losses could flow, both as a natural consequence of delay and as a probable result of such delay. These are, of course, the so-called first and second rules in the assessment of damages under *Hadley v. Baxendale*.[8] In addition, if there are special circumstances known to both parties that could increase the ambit of the recoverable damages, then the damages may indeed be increased. In practice, however, it is almost invariably the party seeking to include the liquidated damages in the contract that puts forward the rate. It is not often the case that this rate is accompanied by any explanation as to how it has been arrived at.

The rules of *Hadley v. Baxendale* have been judicially recognised as being of relevance in the calculation of liquidated damages in a recent first instance decision of the New South Wales court in Australia, *Multiplex Constructions Pty Ltd v. Abargus Pty Ltd.*[9] The judge in that case had this to say on the subject:

> *"It is important, in my view, to recognise the stages in a development project and the place which the construction contract occupies in that project. That is because agreement between the proprietor and the builder in the building contract regarding liquidated damages payable for tardy performance need not encompass all damages which in truth the proprietor may, although not necessarily will, suffer from late performance. An agreement for damages limited to a segment of possible total damage may itself indicate an acceptance by the parties that other aspects of loss might occur but were treated by the parties, implicitly or explicitly, as not being losses which would arise in "the ordinary course of things" as contemplated by the first rule in* Hadley v. Baxendale *(1854) and may, by design or default, not have been brought to sufficient attention of the builder by the proprietor so as to satisfy the second rule in* Hadley v. Baxendale*."*[10]

---

[8]   (1854) 9 Ex. 341
[9]   (1992) 33 NSWLR 504
[10]   *Ibid*, p.519.

In the *Multiplex* case, the contract contained an elaborate formula for the calculation of a liquidated sum rather than specifying a pre-determined figure. The contract provided for interest to be paid *"at a rate per annum equal to the maximum rate of interest then charged by Trading Banks on overdraft accounts over $100,000 calculated on daily balances of the total of"* a series of holding costs for the uncompleted development, which were identified in the contract. The court held that specifying such a rate was not out of all proportion to the damage likely to be suffered as a result of the delay. Nor did the fact that the formula might not encompass all costs of the owner, derogate from its integrity as a valid liquidated damages clause.

The contractor's attack on the liquidated damage clause in the *Multiplex* case is, however, illustrative of the pre-occupation with the idea that liquidated damages have to be *"a genuine covenanted pre-estimate of damage"*. These words come from the *Dunlop* case, but are often quoted out of context. The Court in *Dunlop* was not laying an exhaustive statement as to what constitutes liquidated damage, it was simply concerned to distinguish a penalty expressed as payable for a breach of contract from liquidated damage, namely whether a sum payable for a breach of contract was a penalty or not. As Lord Dundedin said in *Dunlop*:

> *"The essence of a penalty is a payment of money stipulated as in terrorem of the offending party; the essence of liquidated damages is a genuine covenanted pre-estimate of damage."*[11]

The recent case of *J.F.Finnegan v. Community Housing Association*[12] is another example of an unsuccessful attack on a liquidated rate on the grounds that it was not an accurate sum. In that case, however, the contractor claimed the inaccuracy was in the nature of an over-estimate, thus rendering the clause penal in effect and unenforceable as a result. In that case, it was found on the evidence that the liquidated damages rate of £2,500 per week which had been inserted in the contract had been computed on the basis of various estimates of delay-related expense which had then been rounded up by a total of some £65 more per week than the original estimate. The contractor argued that this rounding up

---

[11] [1915] AC 79, 86
[12] (1993) 65 BLR 103

was wholly inconsistent with the idea of reliably pre-estimating the loss. However, Judge Carr sitting as an Official Referee declined to hold that the rounding up process so distorted the figure as to produce an unreliable pre-estimate of cost and dismissed this aspect of the contractor's attack.

As a percentage, the rounding up in *Finnegan* represented an excess of some 2.6 per cent. of the liquidated rate. Is 2.6 per cent. a permissible margin of error or does it depend on the magnitude of the figures involved? There is as yet no further case law on this area but what we can say, on the basis of *Finnegan*, is that absolute certainty and precision in the calculation of the liquidated rate is not a pre-requisite for the calculation of the valid liquidated damages figure. It is suggested that it will be a question of degree in such circumstances as to whether the rounding up of sums in excess of their actual estimates constitutes the sum as a penalty or not.

Liquidated damages as an exhaustive remedy

Many of the cases on liquidated damages were concerned with defining the scope of character of the remedy. *Clydebank* said it was appropriate to use liquidated damages where the assessment of damages under usual *Hadley v. Baxendale* principles would be very complex and difficult. In that sense, liquidated damages are used as an agreed contractual measure of loss. In *Dunlop*, the court was concerned with the question of whether a particular agreed damages rate in a contract was void as a penalty or an enforceable damages clause. Guidelines were given to help the parties determine the difference between these two.

More recently, the exhaustive nature of the remedy has been emphasised. The case of *Temloc v. Errill Properties*[13] caused a great deal of concern to those in the construction industry involved in the drafting of contracts when the decision was published in 1987. What may have appeared as a matter of harmless contract drafting intended to exclude the use of liquidated damages and allow for general damages turned out to cap the damages for delay at zero.

In that case, the Court of Appeal had to consider whether clause 24 of the JCT 80 form of contract dealt comprehensively with the employer's right

---

[13]   (1987) 39 BLR 30

to damages for late completion. The appendix to the contract has to be completed by inserting the words *"£[nil]"* opposite the item referred to as *"liquidated and ascertained damages at the rate"*. The Court concluded that this meant the parties had agreed the employer was entitled to *"£[nil] damages"* for delay caused by the contractor. Lord Justice Nourse stated:

> *"I think it clear, both as a matter of construction and as one of common sense that if (i) clause 24 is incorporated in the contract and (ii) the parties complete the relevant part of the appendix, either by stating a rate at which the sum is to be calculated or as here, by stating that the sum is to be nil, then that constitutes an **exhaustive agreement as to the damages** which are or are not to be payable by the contractor in the event of his failure to complete the works on time."*[14] (emphasis added)

The importance of this decision is that clause 24 was found to represent an exhaustive damages regime governing the parties' rights to damages for delay even to the exclusion of general or unliquidated damages for failure to complete within a reasonable time. The employer therefore was entitled to *"nil"* liquidated damages for the contractor's culpable delay.

Temloc v. Errill is to be contrasted with the decision of the Supreme Court of New South Wales in the case of *Baese Pty Limited v. A R Bracken Building Pty Limited*.[15] The contract appendix in that case had also been completed using the word *"nil"* when referring to damages for non-completion. However, unlike the JCT 1980 form, the contract terms in *Baese Pty* made it clear that the question as to whether or not to apply liquidated damages was simply an option for the employer; its operation depended on a provision whereby the *"architect **may** give a notice"* of non-completion (emphasis added). Thus, if the architect gave no such notice, the employer in effect was electing not to recover liquidated damages but without relinquishing its right to claim general damages for delay. The liquidated damage provision in that case was not therefore an exhaustive remedy for damages for delay and the employer was able to seek general damages against the contractor in culpable delay.

---

[14] *Ibid*, p. 31.
[15] (1991) 52 BLR 130

It is thus a matter of construction of the contract terms in the circumstances of each case as to whether the liquidated damages provision in a contract will be construed as an exhaustive remedy or not.

Liquidated damages as a limit on liability

Temloc v. Errill illustrates the use of liquidated damages remedy as an exhaustive remedy. It can also be seen to illustrate the remedy as a cap or limit on liability for the cost of delayed completion. Adoption of the remedy in this form is often founded on commercial considerations; the liquidated figure represents a purposeful under-liquidation of the amount of loss a party is prepared to forfeit for delay.

This is not a new approach to liquidated damages. Consider the facts in *Cellulose Acetate Silk Co. Ltd v. Widnes Foundry (1929) Ltd.*[16] In that case there was a contract for delivery and erection of an acetone recovery plant. The contract provided that the contractors should pay by way of a penalty £20 for every week that completion was delayed beyond a stipulated date. The contractors were some 30 weeks late and the actual damages suffered by the plant owner by reason of non-operation of the plant amounted to some £5,850, far in excess of the £600 penalty payable under the terms of the contract. Notwithstanding this, the Court accepted the commercial practice and sense whereby parties to a contract agreed that the actual cost of delay in supply of a piece of equipment for operation of a revenue-producing project could be enormous and therefore agreed to the purposeful under-liquidation of the loss. Lord Atkin said this about the liquidated damages of £20 per week:

> "*Except that it is called a penalty, which on the cases is far from conclusive, it appears to be an amount of compensation measured by the period of delay. I agree that it is not a pre-estimate of actual damage. I think it must have been obvious to both parties that the actual damage would be much more than £20 per week; but it was intended to go towards the damage, and it was all that the [contractors] were prepared to pay.*"[17]

---

[16] [1933] AC 20

[17] *Ibid*, p.25.

The continuing use and approval of liquidated damages

Liquidated damage provisions received a large measure of support by the Privy Council in the case of *Philips Hong Kong Limited v. Attorney General of Hong Kong.*[18] The case concerned a contract which identified certain key dates for certain sections of the work with liquidated damages at a daily rate if the key dates were not met. It also provided that if any section of the work had been completed and taken over, the liquidated damage figure would be reduced *"in proportion which the value of the section so [completed] bears to the whole of the works"*. The contract also provided for liquidated damages at a minimum daily rate for failure to complete the whole works. The clause was a complicated one.

At first instance, the Court found that the provision of a minimum liquidated damage figure offended against the idea of reliably pre-estimating the loss due to non-completion of the works. The Court also found that the formula for reducing liquidated damages in proportion to the value of the sections of work completed could not possibly amount to a genuine pre-determination of any financial loss likely to arise. The damages would be a function of arithmetic rather than a representation of loss. It was therefore concluded that the provisions amounted to a penalty and were accordingly void and unenforceable.

As to minimum liquidated damage figures, such provisions are commonly found in international construction contracts under the FIDIC conditions. The rationale for this minimum figure is the fact that the employer is likely to incur continuing supervisory costs so long as the works, albeit only a small proportion perhaps in value, remain incomplete. Indeed, such costs may be wholly disproportionate to the value of the work which has not been completed. The First instance decision in *Philips Hong Kong* had been criticised for this reason but the problem could have been avoided by a statement of the reason for the minimum liquidated damages. It was also criticised as being based on a narrow approach to *Dunlop* in holding, *inter alia*, that a minimum figure by itself constituted a penalty. It has been argued that such an approach ignores the need to assess whether, in all the circumstances, the clause is exorbitant, extravagant or unconscionable and is at variance with the *Dunlop* and *Clydebank* decisions.

---

[18] (1993) 61 BLR 41

The Government of Hong Kong was successful before the Hong Kong Court of Appeal, although the Court did not have to decide the matter of whether the damages were a penalty or not because it decided that the contract did not contain enforceable provisions for sectional completion in the first place and so the questions about the proportional reduction of sectional liquidated damages or the minimum amount of liquidated damages simply did not arise. The reasoning at first instance therefore remained intact.

However, when the matter came before the Privy Council of the House of Lords (in 1993), the earlier penalty finding was set aside with the Court being satisfied that, on the wording of the contract and its application, it was not penal in its effect and, moreover, was workable. Counsel for Philips argued that the formula represented by the liquidated damage provisions could and most probably would result in the Government receiving at least double compensation in some cases, entitling the Government to receive liquidated damages both for the delay which caused the key date to be missed and again when the same delay resulted in the completion date not being met. It was also suggested that such double recovery could occur as a result of the same delay causing two or more key dates to be missed, with the liquidated damages continuing to be paid in respect of the earlier key date after the later date was missed. There were indeed a number of hypothetical situations which, had they occurred, would have caused larger sums to be awarded by way of liquidated damages than the actual loss position. However, the Privy Council decided that this was not a ground for declaring the provisions to be a penalty.

The Privy Council decision in *Philips Hong Kong* is highly illuminating in terms of how the Court may be expected to approach any attack on liquidated damages based on the penalty argument. The underlying basis of the Privy Council's judgment was that parties to contracts should be left free to determine for themselves the consequences of their breach and the Court should not be overly ready to adopt an approach to liquidated damages which could defeat their very intended purpose.

The Court thus rejected Philips' arguments, which were based on a number of *"what if"* scenarios. As Lord Woolf said, delivering the majority judgment:

> *"To conclude otherwise involves making the error of assuming that,*
> *because in some hypothetical situation the loss suffered will be less*
> *than the sum quantified in accordance with the liquidated damage*
> *provision, that provision must be a penalty, at least in the situation*
> *in which the minimum payment restriction operates. It illustrates the*
> *danger which is inherent in argument based on hypothetical*
> *situations where it is said that the loss might be less than the sum*
> *specified as payable as liquidated damages. Arguments of this*
> *nature should not be allowed to divert attention from the correct test*
> *as to what is a penalty provision – namely, is it a genuine pre-*
> *estimate of what the loss is likely to be? – To the different question,*
> *namely are there possible circumstances where a lesser loss would*
> *be suffered?"*[19]

As to the minimum payment provision, Philips argued that it was so
obvious the actual loss would be less than the specified minimum figure,
that to include the minimum figure transformed the liquidated damage
provision into a penalty. On this latter point, the Privy Council simply
did not agree that it was such a type of case: the Court found that the
assumptions of loss upon which the Government of Hong Kong based its
liquidated damage figures were reasonable.

New Uses for Liquidated Damages

There is no reason in principle why liquidated damages provisions
cannot be used for any breach of contract which sounds in damages, not
simply failure to complete on time. Public policy considerations aside,
liquidated damages could be provided for in a contract for breach of a
marriage contract being payable for the failure to marry, so long as the
parties were able to agree upon a reliable pre-estimate of loss at the
outset. Subject to compliance with the guidelines in *Dunlop*, the
provision will be an enforceable contractual measure of the jilted
partner's loss.

Breaches other than delayed completion

Liquidated damages are sometimes used in process engineering contracts
to compensate not just for delayed completion but also for failure of the

---

[19]   (1993) 61 BLR 41, 62.

plant to achieve its contractual performance criteria. The way in which the process engineering industry deals with liquidated damages is of interest for a number of reasons. First, the assessment of a reliable figure to represent a customer's loss is an example of both precision and approximation.

The Model Form of Conditions of Contract for Process Plants published by the Institution of Chemical Engineers ("the IChemE form") provides for liquidated damages as an option for compensating the customer or Purchaser for both delayed construction completion and for failure of the completed plant to achieve performance criteria. The Guide Notes for preparation of the schedules to the IChemE form give some suggested headings of loss for compiling a liquidated rate as agreed compensation for the Purchaser's increased operating costs as a result of the plant's poor performance. An examination of these heads of loss will give a good idea of the degree of sophistication and apparent precision that can go into assessing the liquidated rate:

- Raw material consumption – over a period of 13 years at flow sheet rates;
- Running costs – may actually be lower and savings should be off-set against other additional costs or losses;
- By-products – a shortage could represent a loss or, where these have no commercial value, a saving for the Purchaser in terms of reduced disposal costs;
- Plant capacity – simple apportionment of lost production depends for its accuracy on the assumption that full use would be made of the specified plant capacity;
- Product quality – impurities in the process may affect running costs of the plant;
- Effluent quantity – higher disposal costs can be projected, subject to any absolute limitations imposed by statutory or other authorities;
- Performance criteria – where more than 1 set of criteria are used, they should be grouped and the overall or grouped position assessed; and
- Gross Deficiency – where this exceeds the liquidated rate, the contract terms will need to be clearly amended if the Purchaser wishes to recover any excess from the Contractor.

An appreciation of the above factors illustrates the relative complexity of compiling a reliable pre-estimate of loss in this situation. A certain degree of precision is certainly envisaged by the Guide Notes. However, a countervailing degree of approximation is to be found in practice (and indeed is recorded in the very same Guide Notes) which recognise that it is more usual in practice for such contracts to express liquidated damages as a simple percentage of the contract price (generally between 1 and 5 per cent.).

The second reason why use of liquidated damages in the IChemE form is of interest is that the calculation shows just how many factors have to be considered in order to calculate an accurate figure. Some factors may have a positive effect on the calculation. Others may have a negative effect. Their relative impact may depend on what stage the works have by that stage reached. These considerations do not, however, deter those using the IChemE form from stating a liquidated rate.

Parties to such contracts seem to get around these difficulties in practice by calculating the liquidated rate as a percentage of the contract sum. This does not invalidate the process. Provided that percentage can be checked against and found not to obviously exceed a reasonable assumption of pre-estimated loss, it will be a valid figure.

The use of liquidated damages in complex damage areas

The rationale for the wider use of liquidated damages is perhaps most compelling where the ascertainment of the actual loss would be complex, difficult and time consuming. This much is clear from the *Clydebank* decision. Yet, is this fact commonly recognised by those involved in the drafting of liquidated damage provisions?

The point is perhaps best illustrated by the industry's treatment of delays in the sub-contract tier of contracting. Traditionally, it is rare to see a liquidated damage provision in a sub-contract. The reason normally given for this is that at this tier of contracting, single point assessment becomes impractical and, importantly, precise pre-estimation is no longer possible. For instance; where a sub-contractor is in culpable delay, the main contractor is faced with a variety of losses which arise as a result. Moreover, the ascertainment of those losses does not lend itself to precise pre-estimation. Consider the following heads of loss and their ascertainment:

- the contractor's own extended site preliminary costs caused by a delay will change in intensity and variety as the project proceeds;
- the prolongation of other package contractors may be impossible to accurately pre-estimate because such ascertainment depends on whether the particular sub-contractor in delay is on the critical path of activities or is at the start or at the end of the project;
- the contractor at the top of this tier has the job of trying to predict the affects of delay from a series of interacting site operations which may be affected by the stage that the other sub-contractors have reached in the construction process. These matters cannot be reliably pre-estimated and there are inherent difficulties in expressing such costs as a fixed sum or percentage.

Because of these difficulties, it has traditionally been considered not advisable, nor is it usual in construction projects to provide for liquidated damages in sub-contracts. More usually, sub-contracts provide for an amount to be payable equivalent to the loss or damage suffered by the contractor at the top of the tier as a result of the delay by the secondary tier contractor, such assessment being carried out after the event of the delay has occurred.

If one refers back to the earlier part of this paper, we find that liquidated damages are used to compensate for delay in a number of ways, one of which is where the actual loss would be difficult, complex and costly to prove. Is that not the case with the delays in the sub-contracting tier? If so, why do parties not take a view and use liquidated damages as an agreed measure of loss for delay in each tier of the contractual matrix. All parties would then know precisely their exposure and, more significantly, there would not be any debate over the assessment of prolongation costs. This brings me to my next point.

The liquidation of prolongation and disruption costs

Attempts have been made at fixing the main contractors' own preliminary costs. Liquidated Prolongation Costs ("LPC") appeared some years ago in a consultation draft of the third edition of GC/Works/1. That consultation draft also introduced the idea of liquidating disruption costs by expressing these as a fixed percentage addition to the value of additional work to cover the cost of disruption caused by the Supervising Officer's variation instructions, the so called Additional Variation Percentage ("AVP"). Whilst the construction industry was prepared to accept LPCs, the AVP was considered to be too fraught with difficulty in terms of its accurate prediction and neither found their way into the final form of the third edition of GC/Works/1.

The liquidation of prolongation costs is not, however, dead. Consider the recent case of *Clarksteel Limited v. Birse Construction Limited.*[20] In that case, the sub-contract included an entitlement by the sub-contractors to be paid at extra-overrates for welding of jointed pipework where the gaps between the joints exceeded certain parameters. The sub-contractors claimed that the gaps between the joints were excessive and issued proceedings claiming damages for breach of contract, alternatively a quantum meruit. His Honour Judge Humphrey Lloyd had this to say about the extra-overrates agreement:

> *"Contracts exist, amongst other things, to apportion risks and to provide what is to happen should a defined risk materialise. Such a risk clearly may include a breach of contract. If the parties' intention was that a specific sum or rate should be paid if an event occurred which might otherwise be regarded as a breach of contract, I can see no reason why effect should not be given to that contractual intention.*
>
> *The result is rationalised in legal terms by treating document 7 [the extra-overrates agreement] as the parties' agreement as to what Birse's secondary obligation is to be if it were to have failed in either of its primary obligations to provide or to install pipes which did not give rise to excessive widths. Just like a liquidated damages clause, the effect of document 7 may therefore not merely fix the amount of compensation payable for a breach of contract but effectively limit it (but not to exclude it). This is desirable commercially as both parties will know exactly where they stand, and is of particular value in the construction industry as it serves to reduce the prevalence of claims for breach of contract.*

---

[20] (1996) CILL 1136

Equally, it may be open to Clarksteel to argue that the extra-over rates cover only some of the types of loss flowing from the assumed breach, although since the rates were intended to be used for the valuation of the work they will presumably cover the extra costs and expenses that would be directly incurred."[21]

This judgment is significant because it illustrates how a liquidated rate payable on the occurrence of certain events may be capable of encompassing the various heads of loss that flow from such events. The event in *Clarksteel* was the welding of jointed pipework where the gaps between sections of pipework exceeded certain parameters. The heads of loss resulting from that event were recognised as being capable of including not only the value of the extra work undertaken but also the extra expenses directly incurred in carrying out such work in terms of the contractor's extended preliminary costs. In other words, liquidated damages can be used to fix a contractor's claim to prolongation costs where extra works are instructed.

Distinction between prolongation and disruption costs

The distinction between the different types of loss that flow from delay claims, ie prolongation or time-related costs of the one hand and disruption/out of sequence/unproductive working on the other hand, is an important one. The traditional view of liquidated damages as a remedy is to limit this to prolongation or delay-related costs. For this purpose, the disruption costs are separated out so as to be covered by a general damages regime.

The importance of clearly dissecting prolongation and disruption losses in the context of liquidated damages can be illustrated by considering the case of *M.J. Gleeson plc v. Taylor Woodrow Construction Limited.*[22] As management contractors, Taylor Woodrow entered into a sub-contract with Gleeson for part of the work at the Imperial War Museum, London. Under clause 32 of the sub-contract, liquidated damages were fixed at £400 per day of delay. Clause 11 of the sub-contract further provided that if the sub-contractor failed to complete the sub-contract works on time, he should pay to Taylor Woodrow *"a sum equivalent to any direct loss*

[21] *Ibid*, p. 137.
[22] (1989) 21 Con LR 71

or expense suffered or incurred."

Taylor Woodrow alleged that Gleeson were late in completing their package and gave notice of its intention to deduct £95,360 in respect of *"set-off claims"* of 10 other sub-contractors caused by Gleeson's delay together with liquidated damages of £36,400 for the period of delay. Gleeson conceded the deduction of £36,400 but claimed that Taylor Woodrow was not entitled in addition to deduct the other 10 sub-contractors' claims. The Court agreed with Gleeson; it was found that the liquidated damage provision was the agreed contractual machinery for compensating for Gleeson's failure to complete on time. Those damages were fixed at £400 per day. In seeking to deduct both those liquidated damages and the other sub-contractors' claims, Taylor Woodrow were in effect seeking a double deduction for delay.

Another recent example of the dissection approach to damages is to be found in the Court of Session judgment in the case of *Bovis Construction (Scotland) Limited v. Watlings Construction Limited.*[23] In that case, the sub-contractor's employment was determined by Bovis for failure to proceed diligently with the sub-contract works. Bovis later commenced proceedings claiming damages for breach of contract and in defence the sub-contractors claimed that the recoverable damages were limited to £100,000. In the course of the contract negotiations, Bovis had sought to impose liability for unliquidated damages for delay which the sub-contractor had resisted, rightly recognising that this would have meant *"the extent of the sub-contractor's liability for loss and damage is undefined and unlimited...".* The negotiations were ultimately concluded with the sub-contractor suggesting *"that the contract be amended to allow damages, as proven, to be deducted from ourselves up to a limiting figure of £100,000".* In other words, the contract terms provided for a cap on the sub-contractor's liability similar to a liquidated damages provision for a maximum of £100,000.

On appeal to the Court of Session, it was held that these liquidated damages were contractually applicable only to the sub-contractor's liability for late completion. Significantly, they did not extend to limiting liability for damages for **all** breaches of contract, such as the failure to proceed with the works diligently. The Court found that it would be

---

[23] (1994) 67 BLR 25

stretching the language of the contract unreasonably to say that because damages recoverable for breach of the obligation to proceed diligently are in the character of time-related damages, Bovis should be limited to recovering only £100,000 for such category of damage. This was because the financial consequences of determining a contract for failure to proceed diligently, with the consequent cost of replacing one sub-contractor with another, could far exceed £100,000. The Court reasoned that such an interpretation would for all practical purposes deprive Bovis of their remedy to determine for failure to proceed as adopting such a course would have been too expensive for them.

The lesson of this case is that while liquidated damages may be the exclusive remedy for a party seeking damages for late completion, they do not necessarily cover or limit liability for failure to proceed diligently during the course of the works. Nor will the liquidated damages necessarily cover all the types of loss that flow from an event that causes delayed completion.

For example, if a main contractor is delayed by a sub-contractor, the main contractor may well incur disruption costs both in its own sequencing of the works and that of its other sub-contractors. Provided that such disruption related costs can be identified and linked to the out of sequence work (as distinct from delayed completion) and provided the contract terms provide for recovery of these different heads of loss, then disruption costs can be recovered in addition to liquidated damages. Delay and disruption, whilst inter-linked concepts are not co-extensive.

On the other hand, if the contract is not so worded that the provisions for recovery of delay related costs covers both liability for liquidated damages and liability for the disruption costs of other sub-contractors, then the chosen damages of liquidated damages remedy may be held to constitute an exhaustive cap on the recoverable damages. This is precisely what happened in *Gleeson v. Taylor Woodrow*.

It is suggested that where recovery of a certain sum of damages for delay is required, but an employer does not wish to limit itself solely to the recovery of liquidated damages, the contract documents should identify and dissect the likely delay-related losses into those where quantum can be predicted with reasonable certainty and those which cannot. That will require an identification and listing of the heads of loss which go into making up the liquidated rate and, importantly, those which do not. This would leave the employer able to obtain liquidated damages for the predictable elements of its claim for delay, whilst preserving its option to prove unliquidated or general damages for the other elements.

Conclusion

Perceptions as to the purpose of liquidated damage provisions vary according to the interests of the parties and the size of the project. On a small project where the liquidated rate amounts to an accurate pre-estimate of loss, the parties may properly regard the provision as an incentive to the contractor to complete on time or suffer the consequences. On the other hand, on a large project the parties may purposefully use liquidated damages to cap liability for delay.

The traditional use of liquidated damage or the current state of play then can be summarised as follows; principally, liquidated damages are used in construction contracts to compensate for delay in a number of ways, namely:

- as an accurate pre-estimate of anticipated loss;[24]
- as a pre-determined limit and intended under-liquidation of the actual loss;[25] and
- as a best guess sum representing the parties' bargain, where precise ascertainment may be impossible.[26]

What is perhaps surprising about each of these uses is that they are, to a greater or lesser extent, mutually exclusive. Having said that, certainly the first two approaches could be applied to the same contract and factual matrix producing very different sums, eg. actual loss in one case and a low sum in the other and still, in each case, amount to an enforceable liquidated damages sum.

---

[24] *J.F.Finnegan v. Community Housing Association* (1993) 65 BLR 103
[25] *Temloc v. Errill Properties* (1987) 39 BLR 30; *Cellulose Acetate Silk Co. Ltd v. Widnes Foundry (1929) Ltd.* [1933] AC 20
[26] *Clydebank Engineering & Shipbuildings Co Limited v. Don Jose Ramos Yzquierdo Y Castaneda* [1905] AC 6

On a larger project where there has been a purposeful under-liquidation of the rate for commercial reasons, the parties may regard the liquidated damage provision as a minimum measure of loss for delay but ought not to rely upon that provision to regulate progress. Management techniques and programming considerations take over as the predominant tools under the contract in such circumstances to control and mitigate delay. Damages for delay in such circumstances (be they liquidated or unliquidated) may be commercially oppressive and not in the best interests of the parties.

In many projects, greater use can be made of liquidated damages by providing agreed sums (or at least formulas for the calculation of certain sums), not just in the contracts between employer and main contractor but also in the sub-contracting tier as between main contractor and each of its sub-contractors.

Construction projects are, by their nature, dynamic. Requirements change during the course of the project with extra and varied work introduced. The disputes which this gives rise to are all too well documented. However, there is no reason in theory which prevents the valid liquidation of prolongation costs nor indeed disruption costs. The difficulty of precise pre-estimation is no bar to a valid liquidated damages figure. Indeed, it is just this sort of case that calls out for the use of liquidated damages. If all parties in the contractual chain know the cost of varied and extra works (both in terms of extended preliminary costs and disruption claims), is it naive to suggest these parties will seek to manage their resources within the financial recovery expectation of the agreed damages regime?

Liquidated damages are an old remedy in the construction industry. They save a great deal of time and cost in avoiding the need to prove actual loss. The extension of the remedy in the liquidation of both prolongation and disruption costs in the sub-contracting tier as well as between main contractor and employer could go a long way to changing the dispute culture which continues to prevail in the industry. It may be time to put this old wine in new bottles.

18. Client Demands for Cost Accountability

Colin Gallani

Synopsis

This paper examines construction projects from a contractor's point of view and analyses the factors which lead to cost and time overruns, defects, and the problems associated with controlling them. In conclusion, suggestions are made for reducing the impact of these factors.

Introduction

It is a sad indictment that too many construction projects suffer from cost and time overruns, and from defects. As a result there has been an increasing demand from 'Clients' for cost accountability. This demand has given rise to changes in procurement methods and in the conditions governing them. Many of these changes have centred on the reallocation of risk so that the Client, at least in theory, becomes less vulnerable to cost and time overruns. Hence the movement to Design & Build, Management Contracting, and Construction Management types of contract. At the end of the day, however, the entity that always carries the risk is the one which has control of the factors of production, and which is the only effective project manager: the **contractor**.

Depending upon the type of contract, the contractor can pass responsibility for cost and time overruns upwards to the Client and his consultants and downwards to his sub-contractors and suppliers. Initially, however, the length of the period in which the project is completed and the cost of completing the project are determined by the contractor. Similarly the responsibility for defects can be passed upwards where the defect arises from a design deficiency and downwards where it arises from defective workmanship.

The Contractor as Project Manager

Construction companies, like any other commercial enterprise have an obligation to provide a return on the capital invested by its owners or shareholders. Thus the organisation has to be profitable, and for it to be profitable the objective must be that each project returns a profit. The profitability of a project is wholly dependent upon the management of the resources put into it. Where a construction company differs from most companies is that for each project it needs to set up the means of production (or construction), utilise the means of production to construct the project and then on completion, clear away the means of production.

The resources that are needed to achieve this can be split into a number of categories: first, those that are deemed indirect, such as head office and site overheads; and, secondly, those which correspond directly to the factors of production. When a contractor plans a project and estimates the cost of construction this cost is based on the resources that he considers are required to construct it, both direct and indirect. There is generally an additional resource requirement – finance.

Generally a contractor spends or invests quite large sums of money at the beginning of a project. This investment can be as high as 20 per cent. of the project cost. Income starts to flow when work is produced for which payment is made by the client; the balance point being reached some way into a project, so that when income exceeds expenditure the project becomes self financing. Having planned the project, assembled the resources and commenced work the control of the resources and the time for which they are deployed is essential to ensure that the project is completed within the time planned and within the estimated cost otherwise the project is unlikely to be profitable or as profitable as originally contemplated.

A contractor's basic aim is to expend on the resources the amounts included in the estimate on which the contract price was based, or preferably less. If individual rates paid for labour, plant and materials or if the quantities or periods of time required for these resources are greater than included in his estimate then he is likely to make a loss on the project. Effective control of these resources and the amounts paid for them is therefore a contractor's primary concern. Almost invariably however, factors arise which affect the contractor's control of these resources.

These factors can broadly be divided into three categories:

- factors which are the contractor's sole responsibility;
- factors which are the client's responsibility; and
- factors which are the responsibility of neither contractor nor client.

These categories can further be sub-divided, these subdivisions being the subject of detailed analysis in the following section.

The incidence of one or more of these factors can affect the outcome of the project so the contractor needs to take some action in order to minimise his exposure. The contractor basically has four courses of action open to him:

- re-programme the resources and their costs;
- submit a claim to his insurers;
- submit a claim to the client; or
- claim against a sub-contractor or supplier.

The first of these courses of action would be implemented if the factors encountered were the contractor's own responsibility, but may also be implemented in the event of the occurrence of factors in the other categories, coming under the heading of a general obligation to mitigate. The second only applies to factors for which the contractor carries insurance. It is a sad fact that the third course of action is resorted to irrespective of the strict allocation of responsibility, particularly where the factors occurring on site are a mixture of all categories.

Factors leading to Cost and Time Overruns

At the time of pricing the tender, the contractor will have obtained quotations from suppliers and sub-contractors for materials and specialist trades and produced estimates for the cost per hour of labour and plant to be provided in house or from labour only sub-contractors and plant hirers. Upon obtaining the contract the contractor will firm up these prices and rates trying where possible to use his bargaining power with a signed contract under his belt to negotiate reductions.

The tender will have been based on a programme produced by the contractor's estimating and planning departments. Because of the short tender periods generally prevailing, and of the tentative nature of much of the planning and estimating information, the tender programme would have been provisional. Following the award of the contract the contractor would firm up his programme and this second version would form the programme representing his actual intention for the execution of the work on site.

At the commencement of the project, or shortly thereafter, the contractor will be in a position to establish the sufficiency of his tender and whether he can complete the project within the price quoted. He will establish a budget for the project and a system of cost control to ensure that he keeps within it. Having done all this, if no factors intervened other than those for which the contractor was responsible the project would be completed entirely at the contractor's risk. In the event of a cost and time overrun he would have no recourse to improve the situation except for insurable risks and claiming from his sub-contractors and suppliers.

Factors within contractor's control.

The factors for which the contractor is responsible can be sub-divided into 3 categories:

- normal commercial risk such as under-estimating, weather conditions, ground conditions, labour disputes;
- self inflicted problems such as bad management, bad workmanship; and

- accidental damage to property or persons usually recoverable via insurance.

There can be, and often is a degree of self-infliction of the effects of all categories on cost and time caused by bad management. Where this is the case the incidence of factors which are totally outside the contractor's control exacerbates the problem.

a) Under-Estimate

An under-estimate will invariably mean that the contractor will not be able to execute the project for the rates and prices on which he tendered. Although having been awarded the contract the contractor will be in a good bargaining position to re-negotiate prices of materials, plant and sub-contracts, the rates paid to his own labour will be fixed by some form of wage machinery and not offer much scope for adjustment. The categories where a contractor is likely to concentrate his efforts is in the levels and periods of utilisation of resources. Some improvement may be effected here by re-planning and examination of alternative methods of construction. If, after close examination of all his options the revised estimate of what he considers he can complete the job for is greater than the original estimate then the contractor is going to be in a loss-making situation.

b) Weather and ground conditions which could have been anticipated

Most forms of contract require a contractor to take responsibility for weather and ground conditions which could reasonably have been anticipated. In the event that the contractor encounters bad ground or weather conditions that could have been anticipated from an examination of generally available information or from the documentation provided to tenderers and for which he made an inadequate allowance then he is likely to be put in the situation of a cost and time overrun.

c) Labour disputes

Most forms of contract provide for extensions of time in respect of labour disputes but generally the costs associated with such a dispute are not reimbursable. Thus the contractor has an increase in expenditure for which there is no compensatory income.

d) Sub- Contract Problems

The main contractor of 20-30 years ago is unrecognisable today. Then a main contractor had a core labour force of his own consisting of general foremen, foremen, gangers and key workers and recruited his own labour at the location of the project. The only sub-contractors employed were specialists, or in certain trades where he had no expertise. Nowadays it is not uncommon for the main contractor to be nothing more than a 'holding company' with every trade sublet. Whereas this in itself need not be detrimental, it is often accompanied by a series of factors which inevitably mean that it is detrimental. These factors include:

- the sub-contractor being coerced to accept a price which is not economic, usually by 'Dutch auction'. This leads to generally lower standards in both materials and workmanship and often deliberately sub-standard. It often leads to bankruptcies of sub-contractors and the loss to the industry of skilled specialists. Delays inevitably result when a new sub-contractor has to be engaged or the work taken over by direct employees. The new prices for this work will invariably be greater than those in the original sub-contract.

- lack of supervision of the sub-contractor by the main contractor; this invariably leads to poor workmanship and poor management of the project. The project is then driven by the sub-contractors, rather than being driven by the main contractor

- the contractor is presented with claims and/or requests for re-negotiation of rates

- the contractor levies contra-charges against sub-contractors.

e) Non or Late Payment of Sub-Contractors or Suppliers.

There has been much talk of late of the injustice of 'pay when paid clauses'. The late or non payment of sub-contractors and/or the use of imaginative contra-charges have plagued the industry for years. Many sub contractors would be only too pleased if they were paid when the main contractor was paid.

f) Non Standard Sub-Contract Forms.

Over the years the industry has introduced standard forms of sub-contract which were intended to be used between main contractor and sub-contractor and on which both parties could rely for a fair deal. It has always been the case that either the supplier or specialist sub-contractor has insisted on special wording incorporated in his standard quotation or the main contractor has introduced non standard forms or amendments to the standard forms. Whereas the amendment of standard forms is often a necessity to cater for some special provision, some of the non-standard forms are horrendous and impose almost impossible conditions on sub-contractors. It is all very well saying that a sub-contractor should not sign or accept such a document, but, particularly in today's economic climate, he often has no option.

g) Claims

A tradition has grown up in the industry of the presentation of claims for additional moneys and time, which are either based on spurious grounds and/or are grossly inflated. To some extent this has been fuelled by the economic climate where margins are so low that the only way of making a profit is to ensure an income from claims. The prevalent claims culture tends to encourage, if not lead to, a refusal to negotiate. A claim which is discussed at a meeting between client's consultant and contractor and rejected as having no grounds or lack of substantiation, and which the contractor knows has little real chance of success, crops up with remarkable regularity at future meetings.

h) Workmanship

Many projects contain workmanship of a less than adequate standard such that well after the project's completion the client is obliged to undertake extensive remedial work and attempt to recover the cost from the contractor. Invariably this results in litigation involving sub-contractors and designers against whom counter allegations are made.

To my mind there are three basic causes of defects:

- contractor and/or sub-contractor working to a price that is totally unrealistic;
- lack of supervision by the contractor; and
- lack of supervision by the consultant.

The second category is often associated with extensive sub-contracting and also the quoting of unrealistic prices.

i) Bad Management

Bad management of a project encompasses; lack of adequate planning and programming, ineffective quality control, poor supervision and record keeping, poorly drafted sub-contracts and purchase orders, and lack of contractual notices. The presence of one or more of these elements of bad management may result in overruns of cost and time and in the incidence of defects, or in the inability properly to pursue contractual entitlements for time and money.

j) Damage to the Works, Persons or Property

These are generally insured risks and the contractor is able to recover the damage from his insurers except for the usual excess. It is important however that a contractor considers recovery on insurance as important a source of income as the client. Too often this is not the case and giving notice to insurers is inadequately dealt with.

Factors within client's control

It is obvious that a contractor must have systems in place for controlling the resources which, if not controlled, will lead to overruns of time and cost. These systems must cater for the situation where the project runs smoothly and is unaffected by any of the factors referred to previously as being his responsibility. This is also the case where the project is affected by factors which are the responsibility of the client, or resulting from circumstances which could not have been foreseen by either party. However, in order for the system to work the contractor must be in a position to plan for the incidence of such factors. Therefore, it is of paramount importance that information, instructions, decisions, extensions of time awards and payment is transmitted to him as soon as is possible so that the full consequences can be assessed, additional materials and resources allocated and the effect on the project minimised.

a) Unforeseen Conditions

Many projects suffer from being affected by ground, seabed, marine and weather conditions which could not have been anticipated. Whether the conditions could have been anticipated depends upon the adequacy of the information contained in the documents issued to tenderers, and upon general information in the public domain and therefore accessible to any tenderer. Too often there are arguments as to whether a contractor could have anticipated the conditions encountered.

The contractor of course has to overcome these conditions in order to complete the project. Whether he will be paid any extra or be awarded extra time to complete, will depend upon whether the client's consultants accept that the conditions could not have been anticipated. Many of these arguments could be avoided if more and better information was provided to contractors at the time of tender.

b) Variations

A variation in the work defined in the specification and on drawings for a project will invariably require an adjustment of the resources and duration of the individual activity or activities affected by the variation and possibly of the project as a whole. The consequence of a variation is usually not only an increase in the direct cost of executing the work but also the disruption of the directly affected activity and other associated activities and possibly delay to the project. It follows that to ensure a minimum effect on cost and time the primary objective should be to minimise the number of variations. They should be instructed only when absolutely necessary.

The timing of a variation and its proper instruction is also important if its effects are to be minimised. There are still too many changes required by the Client at too late a stage. Changes instructed before the construction contract is let but at a late stage in the preparation of the design and the tender documents invariably result in the change not having been adequately defined, such that there is a need for further amendment after the construction contract has commenced.

Variations are too often issued to correct shortcomings in the consultant's design. In these circumstances there is an obvious reluctance by the consultant to accept responsibility and to issue the appropriate instructions for their rectification. Such design shortcomings are caused either by the designer not having spent the necessary time on a design to ensure its completeness prior to the project being put out to tender, or the use of inexperienced staff on the design in an attempt to keep within budget.

c) Ambiguities/Discrepancies in Contract Documents

Ambiguities and discrepancies arise because of lack of co-ordination of the contract documents by the client's consultants. This is usually caused by insufficient time having been spent on the preparation and checking of contract documents or the use of inexperienced staff in their preparation. There is often a reluctance by the consultant to admit to such discrepancies or ambiguities because to admit to their existence is to admit to a failing. Nevertheless, most forms of contract make provision for the correction of ambiguities/ discrepancies in the contract documents and the issuing of appropriate instructions. The forms also make provision for compensation of the contractor in both time and money, should the correction have a direct effect on the work.

An argument is often presented as to the time at which discrepancies and ambiguities should have been discovered by the contractor. Contractors generally do not have teams of people looking through contract documents for discrepancies at an early stage. Discrepancies tend to be found when the pre-construction activities for an element of construction are commenced. By definition, depending upon the seriousness of the discrepancy and the need for instruction, this is too late to avoid some disruption.

d) Late Information, Instructions, Drawings

Late information is usually associated with an under developed design or with ambiguities/discrepancies in the contract documents. When information is requested, there is invariably an argument as to whether it should have been, either requested earlier, supplied in accordance with the original or current programme, or supplied in keeping with current progress, which may of course be behind or ahead of programme.

In recent years the advent of the facsimile machine has meant that information is often supplied virtually as work is progressing on site. A programmed activity does not start with construction or erection, it starts with the planning of the work, is followed by procurement of the resources and materials, and finishes with construction or erection. Information supplied during construction or at any time after commencement of planning in most instances causes disruption.

e) Nominated Sub-Contractors

A contractor experiences a number of problems associated with the process of nominating sub-contractors. First, a relationship is established between client and sub-contractor often well before the appointment of the main contractor. This results in difficulties in the chain of command. It is frequently the case that the client communicates directly with the sub-contractor and vice-versa often without the knowledge of the main contractor. Secondly, The conditions of contract that the sub-contractor wishes to use or even insists on using, are totally incompatible with the main contract. Alternatively the sub-contractor insists on conditions that are not acceptable to the main contractor. And, thirdly, the sub-contract is usually for some specialised piece of plant or equipment which has been designed by the sub-contractor and the conditions of the main contract do not include design.

f) Defective Design

Many instances of defective design are corrected by the client's consultants by the issue of revised drawings or specifications and covered by variations. Often however design defects do not come to light until there are allegations of defective workmanship by the contractor following handover of the building or facility. On researching these workmanship defects, it is discovered that the damage was caused not by defective workmanship but by defective design or by a combination of the two.

Factors without the control of both contractor and client

Although these factors are without the control of both contractor and client the means of dealing with them are not; *i.e.* the client or his consultants still have a responsibility to issue the appropriate instructions for dealing with the factors and the contractor has a responsibility to control the resources required to deal with the factors that have arisen in the most effective way.

a) Unforeseen Conditions

The incidence of ground, seabed, marine and weather conditions which could not have been foreseen by either party are relatively rare. Most claims for unforeseen conditions arise from lack of comprehensive investigation of the site before the award of the contract and could have been avoided by the spending of an adequate amount of time and money on such investigation.

b) Changes in Legislation

Changes in legislation can affect the safety regime on site, the disposal of waste, the prices of labour, plant and materials, import duties etc. Most contracts make provision whereby the contractor is able to obtain reimbursement of his additional costs or an extension of time for the effects of such changes.

The Effects

The effect of the factors examined above include:

- Contractor pays higher rates and prices for labour plant and materials than was included in his tender.
- Contractor is obliged to introduce additional resources of labour and plant than was included in his tender.
- Contractor requires to extend the period for resources beyond that included in his tender.
- The productivity of the contractor's labour and plant is substantially reduced from that on which his tender was based.
- Contractor is obliged to re-plan and re-programme his activities and/or introduce alternative methods of construction.
- Contractor is forced to increase his overdraft facilities to finance construction for which income is either not forthcoming or does not match the rate of spend.
- Progress on activities, sections of the works and/or the whole of the works is delayed.
- Contractor works excessive hours of overtime with accompanying loss of productivity.
- Activities which should have been completed in favourable seasons and in good weather conditions are forced into unfavourable seasons and into periods of inclement weather with a resulting shortening of working hours.
- Morale of both labour and staff affected.
- Relationship between contractor and client and/or his consultants deteriorates.

- Too much of the management time of involved parties is taken up with argument on contractual issues, claims and money.
- Head Office personnel and facilities engaged on project related matters for a period in excess of that included in tender.
- Site and head office resources which it was anticipated would be available for other projects remain tied up.

These in turn lead to an increase in a project's cost and/or duration, and/or to a completed project subject to defects. Whether this consequence arises in the first instance from factors which are the contractor's responsibility is not relevant for a number of reasons. First, if a contractor is in a loss making position on a project there will be pressure to attempt to recover as much of this loss as possible. Thus claims will be presented on the flimsiest of grounds, or claims which have some validity will be inflated so as to include those losses which should have been borne by the contractor. Secondly, whether a project is delivered late as a result of factors which are the responsibility of the contractor or the client it is still late and this is not to the client's advantage. Thirdly, the incidence of factors which are not the contractor's responsibility give rise to effects which are the same as those arising from factors which are. It is therefore difficult to distinguish between the effects of the two categories of factors.

The combination of all or some of these factors gives rise to a project which is delivered to the client later than he had anticipated and for a sum in excess of the amount he had budgeted for. It is also likely that the facility which has been constructed will include defects which will come to light in later years. As if this is not bad enough, the client will probably find himself spending more money in litigation or arbitration either to defend himself against claims, or to prosecute claims arising from these factors.

Recommended Solutions

For a solution to be efficacious it has to remove a factor or minimise its effects. The amendment of conditions of contract and methods of measurement have not and will not cure the problem. Changes in the type of contract merely recognise that there are problems and move the goalposts so that the risk to the client of cost and time overruns and defects are minimised or passed to others. Similarly, the introduction of new and improved means of dealing with disputes merely recognises that problems exist which are generating more disputes in the industry but does not deal with the problems.

The problems which lead to cost and time overruns and defects are caused by the action or inaction of one or all of the participants in the construction process, *i.e.* the client, designer, contract administrator (architect, engineer or project manager) contractor, sub-contractor and supplier.

Suggestions

Some suggestions as to the means of solving the problems or at least reducing the effects of the factors previously referred to are set out below.

1. The client should increase the tender period so that contractors have adequate time to research the conditions likely to be encountered on the site.

2. The contractor should ensure that all sub-contractors are adequately supervised. He should not rely on the client's consultant to identify defective workmanship but on his own supervision.

3. The contractor should not sub-let all trades. Consideration should be given to maintaining at least certain elements of trades such that he provides a buffer between sub-contractors. Alternatively the client should insist on approval of all sub-contractors including the sub-contract arrangements.

4. Consideration should be given to the incorporation of a provision whereby all approved sub-contractors can be paid directly if main contractor fails to pay within a certain period.

5. The contractor should ensure that the project is adequately planned and programmed. The programme should include all pre-construction or lead-in activities of procurement, temporary works design etc., and should not contain more activities than can be properly monitored.

6. The contractor should produce proper written notices of events in order to obtain entitlement to additional cost and time.

7. The client and his consultants should ensure that comprehensive information about the site of the project is obtained and issued to the contractor. This should include not just geotechnical and marine investigations, but all information that could be of assistance to a contractor.

8. The client and his consultants should ensure that the design, as expressed by drawings and specification, is complete and fully developed.

9. The client and his consultants should ensure that contract documents are properly prepared, co-ordinated and integrated without discrepancies and ambiguities. It is recommended that debriefing sessions are held with the administrators of previous projects. This would draw attention not only to actual discrepancies in previous sets of documents but perceived discrepancies. ie matters which created problems between contractor and contract administrator which although not finally admitted as discrepancies leading to cost and time adjustments could nevertheless be improved.

10. The clients' consultants should ensure that variations are kept to an absolute minimum. Client should be encouraged not to change his requirements once contract has been let.

11. The clients' consultants should ensure that information, instructions, directions and drawings are issued promptly and well

in advance of the contractor's needs. The contractor should ensure that his programme includes lead-in periods for procurement, temporary works design and other pre-construction activities so that the client's consultants are fully aware of the need for and timing of information.

12. The client should pay promptly all sums certified by his consultants.

13. The client's consultants should acknowledge the principle of an entitlement to additional payment promptly and certify the appropriate sums due once in possession of sufficient information to substantiate such sums. He should not necessarily wait for all substantiating information to be provided by the contractor but make his own assessment.

14. The client and his consultants should avoid the nomination of sub-contractors. If a specific or specialised piece of equipment has such a long delivery period that it needs to be ordered before commencement of the main contract the client should place a separate contract for its design, manufacture and supply. The installation or erection will then be the subject of a normal sub-contract.

15. The contract administrator (Architect/Engineer) should not be an employee of the client. On the face of it this would mean that less biased decisions are made, or that they would be made more speedily. There is however a disadvantage in appointing as contract administrator the client's consultant designer. It is submitted that the better solution is to appoint as contract administrator a person or entity that was not involved in the design process and did not have a hand in the preparation of the contract documents. This is the only way of ensuring that the contractor obtains an unbiased opinion or decision.

16. Consideration should perhaps also be given to changing the tendering procedure. The consequences of accepting the lowest bid were set out by John Ruskin many years ago and his words have been trundled out so often in discussions on this topic that they have become a cliché. He stated:

> " *It is unwise to pay too much, but its worse to pay too little. When you pay too much, you lose a little money-that's all. When you pay too little, you sometimes lose everything, because the thing you bought was incapable of doing the thing it was bought to do.*
>
> *The common law of business balance prohibits paying a little and getting a lot-it can't be done. If you deal with the lowest bidder, it is as well to add something for the risk you run, and if you do that you will have enough to pay for something better.*"

17. Consideration should also be given to the deployment of more contracts of the cost-plus type, particularly for projects with elements of high risk. These types of contract have the advantage that the means of overcoming all contractor's risks are reimbursed at cost. The target cost type has a particular advantage in that it encourages the contractor to implement proper control of resources and penalises him for cost and time overruns.

   For cost-plus contracts to be effective the purchaser must be involved in the procurement process and 'recoverable cost' has adequately to be defined. In a pure cost plus contract the problem is competition. This is usually based on the fee which is charged on the cost. In target cost contracts the competition is on the target itself which is generally derived by the pricing by tenderers of a relatively simple bill of quantities.

18. The conditions of contract, specification and drawings constituting the contract should be amended so as to include the appropriate amendments included, or alluded to, in the invitation to tender, instruction to tenderers, tender amendment letters, tender submissions, pre-contract meetings, checklists and all such documents so that the contract executed is complete in all respects.

Conclusions

The suggested solutions resolve into two discrete types; to ensure that existing procedures are better administered, and/or to introduce new or improved procedures. If the client is demanding cost accountability and not unreasonably projects which are completed on time and within budget then he must first put his own house in order. It is not coincidence that the majority of the factors leading to cost and time overruns for which the client or his consultants are responsible are recognised by the existing forms of contract. These forms provide measures for dealing with these factors including the means of recompensing the contractor for their effects. In most instances, these measures and means are perfectly adequate. It is their non-, or ineffective, implementation that causes problems.

The factors, however, need to be kept in control. If they are kept in control and properly administered there is no need to deviate from the existing forms and types of contract. There was a time when they served the industry well and there were very few projects that ran substantially over time and over budget. In respect of those that did, disputes were settled relatively easily and painlessly without the need for arbitration and litigation.

There has been a fundamental change in attitudes of consultants which manifests itself as a lack of acceptance of responsibility and a lack of decisiveness. Architects and Engineers seem most reluctant to accept responsibility for errors and shortcomings in their designs and to issue the appropriate instructions for their rectification. To some extent this has been brought about by the introduction of fee competition so that in many instances the designer cannot afford to spend the time necessary on a design to ensure its completeness prior to the project being put out to tender or he is obliged to use inexperienced staff on the design in an attempt to keep within budget. There is a similar reluctance to recognise variations, to award extensions of time and recognise contractors claims.

There has been a change in attitude of contractors which can be best described as the introduction of the claims culture. To some extent this has been a reaction to the change in attitudes of consultants but also has arisen from the poor economic state of the construction industry where jobs are often obtained at cost and the only chance of making any profit is to adopt a very hard attitude from day one and claim for everything in sight. The introduction of new or revised forms of contract will not change these attitudes. What is needed is re-education. In the current discussions post-Latham, much has been said about the adversarial nature of construction contracts. Surely it is the parties, and their attitude towards the administration of construction contracts, that have become adversarial.

19. Loss of Profit and Head Office Overheads in Construction Disputes

Christopher Lemar

Synopsis

This paper examines the characteristics of overheads in construction, discusses the type of evidence needed in support of such a claim, and comments on the benefits of applying formulae to quantify the claim.

Introduction

Within the Construction Industry, the successful resolution of appropriate claims can play a significant part in the well being of a contractor. Formulating such claims in a proper way can often be a key contributor to achieving this goal. One aspect of claims formulation which is commonly misunderstood is the claim for loss of contribution to head office overheads and profit. This paper seeks to provide guidance on the issues to be addressed in evaluating such claims and comments on the relevance and usefulness of formulae to establish such heads of loss.

In this context it is helpful to keep in mind the legal principles which underpin the award of damages. In contract, damages comprise the sum of money to put the claimant into the position he would have achieved had the contract not been breached. In tort, damages are of a more compensatory nature, that is to say they seek to put the claimant back in the position he would have been in had the tort complained of not been committed. Finally, as far as breach of contract is concerned, the losses claimed should have arisen from the breach and should have been foreseeable.

The Nature of Head Office Costs

Typically, claims for loss of overheads and profit are combined as one head of loss. While this is not necessarily inappropriate, it is important to consider the characteristics of head office overheads and thus to recognise when they can be distinguished as a separate head of claim from loss of profits. Head office costs, sometimes referred to as home-office costs, are typically associated with the overall management of the business. They will usually include property costs, rent, rates, heat and light together with other central services and utilities. They also include the cost of head office staff, the directors and other senior management and support staff, their salaries and other benefits including cars and pension payments; the cost of information systems, finance and accounting departments, perhaps the in-house legal team and secretariat; and, often, include the cost of a central QS/design team as well as related selling and marketing costs.

Accountants often refer to these types of costs as "fixed costs" (as opposed to "variable costs") in the sense that they do not tend to go up or down in response to an increase or decrease in sales revenue. The significance of the "fixed" nature of such expenses, in the context of a claim for loss and expense through delay or variations, relates to the question of "causation". How can a claimant legitimately argue that such "fixed costs" are caused by the matter complained of, when the costs would have been incurred in the normal course of events?

But are these costs really fixed? A helpful exercise to test this hypothesis is to examine a company's published accounts and compare the trend in its overhead costs with the trend in its turnover over a number of years. It will often be apparent that overhead costs and turnover do in fact tend to move broadly in line with each other if one looks at the medium to long term relationship. By 'medium term' in this context I mean two to three years and more. The reason for this is fairly simple. As turnover goes up and the business gets busier management start to take on a higher overhead burden. Partly this is through necessity. More managers are needed to run the growing business. More office space is acquired to accommodate them, together with all the underlying office support costs. Growth will also create an environment where there is a greater willingness to spend money, for example on more sophisticated computer systems, training, corporate hospitality and so on. Conversely in an extended period of reduced sales activity companies will take steps to reduce the overhead burden. Management and support teams will be down-sized. Opportunities to sell or sub-let surplus property will be taken.

It is apparent therefore that even so called "fixed costs" vary with sales in the medium to long term. It is important, therefore, when considering the appropriate way to formulate a claim for head office overheads that the time period covered by the claim is taken into account.

In the short term, a delay or an extension to a job may well not cause extra overheads to be increased or alternatively may not prevent the contractor from saving overheads that might otherwise have been curtailed. But in a claim which covers the medium or longer term, it may well be possible to show that, but for the delay, the contractor could have reduced its overhead cost and therefore, as a result of the delay in the contract, it has suffered unnecessary costs. Furthermore it seems to me that such losses are a natural consequence of medium to long term delay and are reasonably foreseeable.

Does this analysis mean that for relatively short delays there is no place for a claim for head office overheads? The answer to this is, "not necessarily", but it does, in my view, depend on identifying specific increases in overhead expenses which can be directly linked to the problem contract. Examples of the type of additional costs which might be claimable include extra travel costs, telephone charges, insurance costs, professional consultancy, overtime payments to head office staff.

Such costs sound very straight forward but it is surprising how rarely contractors' accounting records are kept in a way which facilitates the identification of such costs by reference to the underlying problem contract. Of course, there is a trade off to be made between (a) the cost of setting up and maintaining records with sufficient particularity and (b) the amounts actually claimable. Nevertheless contractors wishing to smooth their path to recovering such costs in claims would be well advised to ensure that their accounting systems and record keeping are capable of identifying such extra costs.

Recovery of Overheads and Profit

So far in this paper I have been considering overheads as additional costs, ie as additional costs of working. I now turn to examine the concept of claims for "recovery of or contribution to overheads and profit".

It is here that what appear to be two heads of loss, namely lost overheads and loss of profits in fact become one. In essence, the logic behind a "contribution claim" is that, as a result of delay or disruption to a given contract, head office resources become inevitably involved in dealing with the problems that arise in managing the contract in such circumstances. This will divert management resources from other duties, including the efficient and profitable running of other contracts, and perhaps, more importantly, looking for and winning new work.

Both of these diversions can lead to a reduction in the claimant's loss of profit, through inefficiencies on other contracts or through failure to obtain contributions towards the overheads and profit of the business from new work.

It is worth noting here that much the same result can arise in a delay claim where the company's direct resources, namely its labour and plant are idle. These resources are not generating any income, so not only do they fail to cover their own cost but also they fail to generate income to contribute to overheads and provide profit to the business.

The concept of lost contribution to overheads and profit is fairly straight forward to argue. But it is often a different matter producing sufficient robust evidence in a particular case to prove loss, even on the balance of probabilities. Again much will depend on the extent and quality of the claimant's records; and here I do not just mean its accounting records. It can be equally important to be able to furnish contemporaneous records demonstrating the impact of the contract disruption on other parts of the business. Such documents can range from diary notes and records of telephone calls through to detailed accounts of consequence to other contracts. They could include schedules of tender opportunities not taken up or perhaps an analysis showing a reduction in tender success rate. Factual witnesses may do their best to recall such issues at a later date, but when there is no contemporaneous documentation, such evidence may not be sufficiently persuasive.

Calculation of the loss

Where there is sufficient evidence to justify a claim for lost contribution to overheads and profit how should it be calculated? This question has taxed the preparers of claims and judges alike over the years. By its very nature as a hypothetical loss there is no single right figure for any given claim. The extent to which certainty must be established to obtain damages is dealt with in case law. The following statements demonstrate the court's present attitude:

- The fact that damages cannot be assessed with certainty does not relieve the wrongdoer of paying damages.

- Where the precise evidence is obtainable the court naturally expects to have it; where it is not, the court must do the best it can.

- As much certainty and particularity must be insisted upon, both in pleading and proof of damages, as is reasonable having regard to the circumstances and to the nature of the acts themselves by which the damage is done.

- Damages can be received for future or projected loss – if reasonably anticipated – as a result of the defendant's wrong, whether such future damage is certain or contingent.

Formulae

To overcome the problem of lack of detailed records in support of loss of overhead and profit claims in the construction industry, claimants have turned to the use of formulae as a surrogate. Attached to this paper, by way of amplification, is a short commentary on the pro's and con's of certain of the formulae used in construction claims.

To appreciate the relevance of formulae it is worth considering their history. In broad terms these formulae have been developed and applied successfully in periods of high economic activity. There is a good rationale for this. It is in such conditions that the court will feel more comfortable to accept a "broad brush" approach to proving lost opportunity. In an active economy it is reasonable to argue that distractions on a particular contract will inevitably cause a loss of opportunity to take on other profitable work, (which in a time of high activity will be readily obtainable).

In such circumstances there is less need to prove specific causation and the use of a suitable formula to establish a reasonable measure of loss of contribution to overheads and profits from lost work is often accepted by courts and by arbitrators. Conversely, in times of recession the court will, not surprisingly, tend to want explicit evidence of lost opportunities. However, where such opportunities can be shown by records to have existed, I believe that formulae, suitably chosen for the given case, can fairly be applied to compute the value of lost contribution to overheads and profit.

There are some who say formulae should never be used to compute damages in this way. I disagree. For the court to expect every pound of overhead and lost profit claimed to be proved by reference to specific costs or contracts is not only excessive in detail but, I believe, would represent a lack of understanding of the way the contracting business operates. To achieve the necessary detail would require very sophisticated accounting systems and record keeping and impose an unreasonably costly burden on the construction industry. The court should, and typically does, recognise that problem contracts do divert and distract head office management. It would be irrational to assume that such management would not be actively doing other things to benefit their business had they not been so distracted. The most sensible way to reflect what would hypothetically have happened is to look at "normal" levels of activity. The claimant should try to establish by reference to past accounts and management information what might be regarded as the normal level of contribution to head office costs and profit from the company's contractual work. Formulae clearly play a useful role in such an exercise provided the result passes the test of "reasonableness". A claimant who applies formulae "blindly" does so at his peril.

Conclusion

In conclusion, the essential ingredients to a well argued claim for lost overheads and profits are good contemporaneous records, together with a proper appreciation of the nature and causation of the overheads and profit being claimed.

Annex
Building Contract Disputes: Overhead Formulae

In the body of this paper I have referred to occasions when formulae might be used to evaluate overheads to be included in a building contract claim. In this section we introduce four such formulae which are used from time to time in construction disputes. They are representative examples of formulae used to compute what proportion of overhead costs to include in a contract claim. I comment also on some of the pros and cons of the use of these formulae in practice.

"The Hudson Formula"[1]

The formula takes the percentage allowance made by the contractor for head office overheads and profit in his original tender ('HO'), divides it by the original contract period and multiplies the result by the period of the contract extension:

$$\frac{\text{HO Profit percentage}}{100} \times \frac{\text{Contract sum}}{\text{Contract period (weeks)}} \times \text{Period of delay}$$

The formula is a very broad brush approach to dealing with claims for overheads. It is designed to deal only with overruns in contract time. It compensates for both overhead expenses and profits. It may not be appropriate to claim for loss of profit unless there is a clear indication that the contractor would have been able to earn profits on other contracts but for the overrun. Also it uses as its base, overhead and profit percentages taken from the original tender. These may not properly reflect the contractor's true overhead cost and profitability.

---

[1] Source: Hudson's Building and Engineering Contracts (11th edition, 1994) Sweet and Maxwell.

"Emden's Formula"[2]

Emden's formula applies the percentage that the contractor's total overheads and profit bear to total turnover ('h') to the proportion of the original contract sum ('c') represented by the period of delay ('pd') — the original contract period ('cp'):

$$\frac{h}{100} \times \frac{c}{cp} \times pd$$

The advantage of this formula is that it uses a head office overhead percentage based on the contractor's total business rather than on the specific contract in dispute. Again it does not necessarily reflect the real effect on overhead costs arising from the delay, but it may provide a reasonable approximation particularly if some simplistic approach is looked for to assist in negotiating an out of court settlement.

Direct cost allocation

The direct cost allocation method expresses the contractor's total overhead costs over a period as a rate per of direct costs. This 'average' rate of overheads per unit of direct cost is then applied to the total additional direct costs associated with the contract claim.

Although simple, this method implies that overheads vary proportionately with direct costs. This is not necessarily the case. Some contracts will consume very high levels of labour or valuable materials which should not have a corresponding effect on overheads and can distort the implicit average relationship between overheads and direct cost.

Specific base allocation

The specific base allocation method relates, as far as possible, individual categories of overheads to specific categories of direct cost. For example, site preliminary costs may be related to direct labour hours. This method can overcome the problems associated with the broad-brush total cost allocation methods. However it is dependent for its success on the existence of reliable detailed cost analysis.

---

[2] Source: Emden's Construction Law, Butterworths

Recent developments in accounting practice relating to overheads may also be relevant. As a result of cheaper computing power, it has been possible to introduce relatively complex systems of accounting for overheads costs which relate more precisely the costs incurred to the activities which generate these costs. Such systems include 'activity-based costing' system. If a contractor employs such a system in his management accounts it may be that this will provide an alternative method of dealing with overheads preferable to any of the above bases.

Conclusion

It is important that the expert accountant is aware of the application of formulae in construction claims to compute the amount of overheads to be recovered. However, we would urge caution in the blind application of such formulae. Their individual suitability will depend on the circumstance of each case.

Part V

Disputes and their Resolution

20. Why are there so many Arbitrations in Construction?

Phillip Capper

Synopsis

This paper examines how arbitration has become recognised as the dispute settlement mechanism in construction. It goes on to examine the characteristics of construction disputes and how the industry can make use of other methods of dispute resolution to streamline the settlement process.

Introduction

The construction industry uses arbitration as its principal, final mode of dispute resolution for a number of reasons. These go beyond the usual attractions of arbitration, such as privacy, speed, flexibility, and choice and location of tribunal. There are three main reasons why arbitration has become the norm in the British construction industry:

- the prevalence of arbitration clauses in standard forms of contract;
- the technical content of disputes, leading to the use of arbitrators skilled in technical disciplines; and
- the need in many disputes to have a tribunal empowered to open up, review and revise decisions, or certificates, arising from the professional judgment of the contract administrator during the project

In this paper I deal with these issues in turn.

Arbitration clauses in standard forms

A distinctive feature of the construction industry in Britain, as compared with many other industries, is the widespread – almost universal – reliance on a small set of published standard forms of contract conditions. The two principal families of such forms both have their origins in the interest groups of the consultant professionals who have traditionally acted as construction contract administrators: architects and civil engineers.

There are other widely used published standard forms in particular sectors. For example, government contracts and those let by some major utilities have traditionally used the GC/Works/1. There is a model form of general conditions of contract recommended by the Institution of Mechanical Engineers, Institution of Electrical Engineers and Association of Consulting Engineers for use in connection with electrical, electronic or mechanical plant contracts: the form is called MF/1. Similarly, the Institution of Chemical Engineers publishes model forms of conditions of contract for Process Plant: known as the Red Book and Green Book. All of these provide for arbitration as the final form of dispute resolution.

A new integrated set of standard forms suitable potentially for all works sectors is also published by the Institution of Civil Engineers. These are the NEC[1] forms comprising various components of the New Engineering Contract system. The NEC Contract achieved the encouragement and support from Sir Michael Latham's Final Report[2] of the Government/Industry Review of the Procurement and Contractual Arrangements in the UK construction industry *"Constructing the Team"*. The NEC is unusual amongst standard forms of construction contract in the UK in not making arbitration the mandatory final mode of dispute resolution. Rather, though it does make provision for arbitration, this is optional and the choice of "tribunal" (court, arbitration, or whatever) has to be specified by the parties in the contract data.

---

[1] The Engineering and Construction Contract: a New Engineering Contract Document 2nd Edition, November 1995: Thomas Telford Services Ltd, Thomas Telford House, 1 Heron Quay, London E14 4JD

[2] Latham, M (1994) *Construction the Team*. HMSO, London

All these forms provide for arbitration as the method of ultimate dispute resolution. The dominance of their use has produced a *de facto* universality of arbitration as the normal method, no doubt on many occasions without much critical thinking as to the choice of that method. However, the nature of the multi-party involvement in construction procurement can militate against the appropriateness of the choice for certain kinds of dispute, unless a great deal of care has been taken in making prior provision for consolidation of arbitral proceedings.

Technical disputes demanding technical arbitrators

The construction industry is not unique in generating disputes that arise from matters of considerable scientific or technical difficulty. However, two factors explored below combine to increase the technical content of construction disputes, and to increase the use of technically qualified arbitrators in their resolution. A further common factor lies in the degree of discretion vested by the traditional standard forms of contract in the consultant contract administrators: the architects and engineers.

The first main factor is that the JCT forms, and the ICE forms even more so, tend to postpone matters of uncertainty under the contract, rather than seeking to determine them by prior contractual provision. They are therefore left to the later discretion and judgmental evaluation of the architect or engineer. Uncertainty may permeate matters so fundamental as the scope of the work to be undertaken, the schedule by which it should have been completed, or the amounts of money that should be paid for it. Though legal and contractual issues may arise, disputes typically turn on these matters of technical evaluation. Those evaluations are likely already to have been the subject of a disputed determination by the architect or engineer, acting as contract administrator.

The second main factor flows inexorably from the first. These *ex post facto* technical evaluations, required by the contract style, involve not only the contract administrators and parties, but also – in Britain at least – an army of specialists and advisors skilled in various associated disciplines. These advisors promote, prepare, argue, defend and appeal from claims disputing technical evaluations. Such is the frequency and experience of these disputes that the participants themselves aspire to become more specialist in their resolution, and to make their careers in the pursuit of construction arbitration.

The circle is therefore completed: the contract style exacerbates the occurrence of technical disputes; the disputes require specialist technical support; the supporters aspire to become career dispute resolvers; and, construction arbitration can become an industry in itself. The principal recursive element in all of this is that the JCT forms, and the ICE forms even more so, are influenced in their drafting by professional interest groups strongly committed to the resolution of technical uncertainties arising on projects by the technical specialist themselves. This commitment affects both first stage resolution and ultimate dispute resolution by arbitration.

Even in those projects where the contract is not executed using the basis of one of these published standard forms, it is likely that the bespoke contract entered into will have derived from or be coloured by the style and practices of the published standards. Indeed so prevalent is the use in the industry of these standard forms that the tertiary education and in-service training of industry professionals proceeds largely on the assumption that these forms (and JCT or ICE especially) are not just contracts but descriptions of good (if not universal) practice. This again reinforces the tendency towards arbitrations being conducted on certain set assumptions flowing from practice in technical disciplines.

The challenge of new procedures post-1996

The challenge for the construction industry, particularly after the Arbitration Act 1996, is to keep these factors in proper balance and perspective. Undoubtedly construction disputes will frequently turn on technical issues and, of course, specialists will be required to facilitate their resolution. Indeed this is reflected even in English High Court practice, where construction disputes are dealt with by the specialist Official Referees. However, there remains considerable scope for improvement in the drafting of construction contracts for the prevention and avoidance of disputes; and where they do arise, for their better management and resolution. There is also scope for more rapid and effective arbitration of construction disputes by better attention to their technical elements and appropriate modes for their evaluation.

Empowering a tribunal to revise project decisions, certificates, etc.

Arbitration has become the essential mode of dispute resolution for certain kinds of construction dispute since the decision in the Court of Appeal in *Northern Regional Health Authority v. Crouch.* [3] Until that decision it had been widely assumed that Official Referees were not fettered in their determination of construction disputes by the fact that an engineer or architect had issued a certificate or otherwise formally determined the parties' rights and obligations pursuant to powers vested in the engineer or architect under the contract. Indeed, Official Referees had come to judgments which had contradicted the earlier such decision of an architect or engineer.

The effect of the Crouch decision

The decision in *Crouch* changed that, though its effects are in danger of being exaggerated. [4] The Court of Appeal drew a fundamental distinction between the powers of arbitrators and the powers of the court. Arbitrators were given by the standard forms of construction contract the express power to "open up, review and revise" certificates, decisions, etc., of the engineer or architect. In the view of the Court of Appeal, no such power was within the court's jurisdiction, nor could it – at that time – be conferred on the court by agreement of the parties.

More recently, Parliament has permitted parties to agree to confer such a power on the court. [5] However, most standard forms of construction contract continue to require reference to arbitration, and this explicit

---

[3] [1984] QB 644

[4] *Great Ormond Street Hospital NHS Trust v Secretary of State for Health & others* [1997] unrep; *University of Reading v Miller Construction Ltd* (1994) 75 BLR 91; *John Barker Construction Ltd v London Portman Hotel Ltd* (1996) 50 ConLR 43.

[5] Section 43A Supreme Court Act 1981: though all parties to the arbitration agreement must agree so to empower the court.

empowering of arbitrators, rather than of the courts.[6] Given the inherent unlikelihood of parties in dispute then to agree to confer such a power on the court, it follows that every construction dispute will under the current law have to be submitted to arbitration if it requires for its resolution the revision of an earlier certificate, decision etc. of an architect or an engineer exercising professional judgment.

Distinctive features of construction contracts

Whatever contractual documents are used, there are a number of characteristics which are common to, and largely distinctive of, almost all construction projects. It is generally in these characteristics that the seeds of eventual disputes lie, and which explain not only the higher occurrence of disputes in the industry, but also the traditional particular mechanisms for their resolution.

Construction procurement differentiated from other commercial supplies

The delivery of a product in construction is a process, not an event. The process requires many participating entities. Even where the main contractor takes on design responsibility, the client employer is likely still to have a consultant team. Also, key elements of supply, such as plant and machinery, may have to be sourced from a specified sub-contractor. Typically, in practice, the participants in a construction project will include at least the client employer organisation, advised by architects, engineers from various disciplines (civil, structural, mechanical, electrical, etc.) and costs consultants (or quantity surveyors); a main contractor perhaps with sub-consultants; and a host of sub-contractors and suppliers – at one extreme, some specialist and more substantial than the main contractor itself and, at the other, individuals employed for their labour only.

---

[6] For an example of an agreement to confer such powers on a court, unusually occurring in a published standard form of contract, see the I ChemE Yellow Book, clause 46.6 (Institution of Chemical Engineers, Model form of Conditions of Contract for Process Plant, Subcontracts, 2nd Ed, 1997.

The two most significant other approaches to construction procurement are management contracting and construction management. In both of these variants the construction contractor's expertise is harnessed more like a consultant team to manage the construction activities of other contractors carrying out particular works packages. In management contracting the management contractor still stands in contractual line between the client employer on the one hand and all the works package contractors on the other, but the management contract form relieves the contractor from many of the commercial and performance obligations that it would have in respect of its domestic sub-contractors on a traditional project. Construction management goes further, as there the construction manager is engaged like consultants by a side contract to advise: the works package contractors are then engaged directly in privity of contract with the client employer.

Whatever contract may be used, the actual works on almost all construction projects exhibit recurrent distinctive characteristics:

- the prototypical nature of the works;
- split responsibility for specification and/or design;
- high degree of inter-activity between purchaser and supplier;
- expectation of, and provision for, substantial levels of change to the specified scope of work;
- complexity of sequencing of activities, and dependencies on other activities/supplies;
- site specificity;
- interaction with neighbouring fixed infrastructure;
- exposure to, and dependence on, weather conditions;
- longevity of the products, and lateness of revelation of defects; and
- the diversity and sheer volume of evidentiary material.

Apart from some volume house-building, and certain structures such as agricultural buildings, the great majority of construction projects produce structures which are, if not unique, still a prototype. Construction generally does not enjoy the benefit of other industries that can design out the problems in a prototype phase, and only then move on to serial production of finished items. The prototypical characteristics of construction accentuates the significance of responsibility for design.

Responsibility for both specification of principal supplies and design of the structure itself has traditionally been the province in British construction of the consultant engineer or architect engaged by the client employer. The employer's team designed the works, specifying what was to be built and how: the general contractor then built it according to those instructions, contributing his skill in labour and workmanship. If a structure were simple, or the commercial circumstances ideal, one could imagine the design being complete to detail before the contract was let, and the price and programme fixed. Typical reality is very different. The other characteristics set out above would often require change to the design in its implementation. More realistically, budget considerations and a myriad reasons for the design not actually being complete on letting the contract, leads in most cases to change and evolution in the scope of the work during its execution. This is the case even in traditional employer-designed works. The trend more recently has been to move away from this traditional approach to design. Increasingly, construction works are let on the basis of "design and build". The project may even be a turnkey project, where the principal contractor is providing a package-deal supply of all the principal services within his own scope of works: design, construction, commissioning and testing etc. A major difficulty in the transition from traditionally designed works to a new environment of design and build, or turnkey contracting, is that industry practices lag behind the obligations as stated in new forms of contract. Even in a turnkey project, the employer client must specify in some way what it is that he intends to buy. Frequently, the employer client will have advisors or consultants at least checking the contractor's design, and more likely intervening in that process with potentially disastrous results in terms of responsibility for out-turn results.

The high degrees of inter-activity in the design and construction process, between employer client, his appointed consultants and agents, and the contracting team distinguishes construction from many other industries. Construction does not lend itself to a clear and fixed specification by a purchaser, only then to be executed by a contracting organisation without further communication until completion and handover. Even so-called "turnkey" projects do not enjoy such simplicity. Communication during the course of the project is essential both for the developing definition of the eventual work and for the management of its execution, relative to time and budget. The difficulty however that arises from such inter-activity is a fluidity in definitions. The scope of obligations changes. But the causes and evidence of such changes may lie in a host of communications as often oral and informal, as formal and contractual.

Change in the delivered scope, or in the manner or sequence in which it is carried out, must to some degree be inevitable. This is the result of designing and constructing a complex prototype on a particular site, where its function includes communication with external environment. Changes in fact arise for many reasons other than technical problems in fulfilling the contemplated design. Worse, the freedom to make changes after the contract has been let has become a hallmark of traditional construction practice on British forms of contract. The architect or engineer is given the power. The power to order change is exercised. Its impact on the time for completion of the works, and their out-turn cost can be greatly disproportionate to the extent of any particular change. The cumulative effect of such instructed changes can undermine the whole economy of a project. A weakness of the traditional JCT and ICE forms (beginning to be corrected under the influence of more modern forms such as e.g. NEC) is that these contracts provide for changes to be implemented before their impacts in time and/or cost have been resolved. *Ex post facto* claims, arguments, justifications, and eventual disputes over what is an appropriate adjustment to the contract programme and contract price are hardly surprising results. These form, perhaps more than anything else, the stuff of arbitrated construction disputes.

Traditional weakness of contract forms as to programme obligations

Programming of the complex sequences of activities, and their dependencies, is of course one of the principal skills of the successful contractor, or construction manager. All but the most simple of projects will proceed from some such programme. That is obvious. Yet it is a further weakness of the traditional JCT and ICE forms of construction contract that the contractual provisions on programming of activities involve little obligation. Unlike GC/Works/1 and NEC, the traditional forms make little contractual provision to integrate the programming of activities into the structural obligations. It is not an unfair generality to say that the contractors' time-based obligation under the traditional forms comprises only an obligation to complete the totality of the works by a particular date. This weakness compounds with the previous one in regard to the instructing of changes. Delay in eventual completion affects great many projects. There is little, if anything, by way of obligation to identify the causes of such delays at the time they occur. Eventual claims to justify additional time and money to be awarded to the contractor again become the norm.

Site specificity

The characteristic of site specificity goes beyond the uniqueness and prototypical nature of most construction works. The nature of the site can be tested often only to a limited degree economically. The carrying out of the works themselves may well reveal unexpected features, or difficulties to be overcome. These have their consequences in the development of the design, the interactions leading to change and programme consequences summarised above.

Interaction with neighbouring fixed infrastructure

Unlike many manufactured items, whose physical existence and utility (such as a book) may exist for all practical purposes in isolation from others and its environment, almost all of the products of the construction process cannot sensibly exist or be used without communication, in the wider sense, and interaction with the neighbouring external environment. Furthermore, that neighbouring environment is likely also to be owned by others. So, the process of design and carrying out of construction works is constrained and affected by many third party influences, particularly through the laws relating to planning, nuisance, environmental impact and neighbouring proprietary interests. There are the practicalities of securing supply by third party utilities of essential services. And, unlike a mass-produced road vehicle which will have gained its regulatory approvals for design, construction and use long before its first predecessor left the factory, the construction industry equivalent gets its fire safety certification, building regulation approvals, and other regulatory signing-off appropriate to its sector, only as the works progress or are completed. In all of these steps there is the potential for questioning of design, or of its execution, and all the resulting impact on time and cost referred to above.

Weather conditions

The unpredictability of English weather is incontrovertible. That it affects many construction processes is not surprising. Traditional forms of construction contract leave this risk as one to be resolved in the eventual discretion of the contract administrator. But views will differ as to the fairness and appropriateness of the exercise of that discretion. Other solutions could be adopted. The NEC forms seek to base the evaluation of compensation for such events on more objective data. Contracts could conceivably be drafted which require the prior pricing of such contingent risks. That has not been the traditional practice of the British construction industry but nor has the postponement of resolution of uncertainties been limited only to weather. Therein lies one of the clues to the frequency of construction disputes, eventually demanding arbitration.

Longevity of the products, and lateness of revelation of defects

The products of the construction process present special problems for a system of law (and limitation) based around more immediate consumption of traded goods. The passage of time also accentuates the difficulty of retrospective forensic identification of the sources of causes of defects, especially where design responsibility has been split from that for workmanship.

The diversity and sheer volume of evidentiary material

Masses of record materials are produced even on relatively small construction projects, many of them as crucial as they are informal: such as eg the pencilled scribblings of a gang member on daywork sheets, or the mud-stained cards recording a piling set. Project records may be as diverse as site investigation reports, feasibility studies, specifications, drawings, tender submissions, estimating and pricing details, diaries, minutes of meetings, formal instructions, test data, payment applications and certificates, weather records, job sheets, inspection reports, programming data and reports, and so on. To all of that is added great chains of correspondence between the participants, management reports in each of the entities, and the usual periphery of any business activity: from management accounting to press publicity.

It is haphazardly in these various forms of contemporary record that are to be found the clues as to the causes of disputed matters.

Payment arrangements under construction contracts

A rational system for the determination of the price for construction works might involve three principal elements: (i) the tendered price for which the contractor is willing to do the work; (ii) some method of assessing the suitability of that price, by way of a breakdown; and, (iii) a method or schedule for pricing any additional works or changes to be made to the scope within the tendered price. Thereafter the timing of payment of the price would be a matter for negotiation upon a number of factors, with each side looking for a form of security as working in progress is delivered into capital value. Any such system is likely to involve payment in stages, against identified milestones including perhaps some retention of a final stage for the assessment of outstanding works or defects.

In many industries it is the suppliers that have the special expertise in the design and construction of their products, and their capitalisation is strong enough to secure in large measure the financing of their production until their products are delivered to their customers. For mass produced, or serial production items, the design costs and regulatory approvals at least, if not some or all of manufacturing costs, will be financed by the supplier as part of its work in capital.

The history of the British construction industry has produced a very different pattern. We have seen above that traditionally the expertise in design has been exercised by consultants engaged as agents of the employer client. The works are designed by the employer's team. Indeed, in former times, but in most cases no longer, such skills were beyond contracting organisations. So the traditional contractor built what he was told to build. Market entry qualifications for those offering contracting were therefore low, and commensurately sound capitalisation of the contractor could hardly be expected. Though the major contracting entities of today have moved far from those origins, the structural arrangements of the British construction industry have remained largely unchanged, save perhaps for more recent initiatives in the provision of privately financed infrastructure works. These traditional payment systems again have the characteristic of postponing the resolution of uncertainties until late stages, or even after completion, of the project. Meanwhile, the financing of the contractors' work is achieved by interim payments assessed by judgmental evaluation. Every such judgment is capable of argument, contradiction, claim and eventual dispute.

Payment arrangements that may foster disputes

There are also structural elements in the payment arrangements for British construction which exacerbate the uncertainty of the sums eventually due. Fixed prices (or "lump sums") even for the initially contracted for scope of work are not the normal pricing method in many projects. On small projects, works of uncertain extent are let to contractors working on day rates; and arguments will arise as to the efficiency of the works carried out and the accuracy of the hours recorded to justify the rates claimed. Major projects for civil engineering works have traditionally been treated as so uncertain in their scope, by definition, that the traditional ICE forms are drafted on the basis that they will not be tendered for a fixed price. Rather, the payment system is based on "remeasurement".

The remeasurement system

In summary, the engineer, on behalf of the employer client, designs the works so far as is possible from information known as to the site. From those designs another specialist construction industry professional, the quantity surveyor, prepares a statement of the contemplated activities and materials. These are expressed in a Bill of Quantities. The relevant quantity is expressed, as a unit or item, and the estimated number or volume is shown. It is this document, the Bill of Quantities, which the tendering contractor quotes against by stating his prices – thereby binding himself on acceptance to a rate or price per unit for each of the components which go to comprise the overall works. Already this summary over simplifies the technical expertise which has gathered around these practices: for, such Bills will normally be prepared in accordance with a standard method of measurement which itself becomes an arcane field of expertise in its own right. The contract is called a "remeasurement" contract because the actual quantities of work and material supplied are remeasured as the project progresses. The price payable to the contractor is therefore the product of that actual remeasurement multiplied by the unit rates tendered in the priced Bills of Quantities. In other words, the tender price total has little real significance to the pricing of the actual work: the project proceeds with initial uncertainty and the sums eventually to be due to the contractor flow only from intervening professional activity and judgment. The latter, in hard cases, will be challenged.

If the Bills of Quantities were used only as such, they would of course satisfy our criterion (ii) above of an adequate tender price breakdown for the assessment of the suitability of a tender. Unfortunately, the ICE form of contract goes further in using the same Bills as a schedule of prices for changes in the scope of the works. It may be thought that the functions of our two payment mechanisms (ii) and (iii) above are incompatible. The arcane skills of estimators and quantity surveyors can become pitched in a mysterious game at tender time in pricing Bills of Quantities so as better to guess the outturn actual quantities. From this rates may be loaded to improve margins reality on the project may be very different, and commercial imperatives will arise to find justifications to recover substantial additional costs incurred by the contractor and initially refuse to be paid by the contract administrator on behalf of the employer client. The remeasurement system promotes a judgmental and interim approach to all payments during the progress of the works. The more they are interim, the more they may be argued over.

These specialised uses of Bills of Quantities, the resulting specialist expertise of quantity surveying, and the interim assessment of payments have permeated widely the British construction industry and its derivatives. They extend beyond remeasurement contracts into the normal practice also of building contracts, such as the JCT forms, even though the latter are let as lump sum contracts at tender time. So, even building contracts whose initial scope is agreed for a fixed price are paid for on account, during the progress of the works, by a system of interim measurement. Similarly the changes in the scope of those works are valued by reference to the rates stated in the Bills of Quantities.

Characteristics of the disputes that arise in construction

The archetypal disputes in the British construction industry arise of course from contractor's claim to be paid more for the increased time and cost of additional works; and, the claims of building owners in respect of defects. The latter especially may involve many parties as responsibility is sought to be attributed between designers, suppliers and contractors; but even the former apparently more simple money claims are likely to be multi-party disputes as sub-contractor's interests and responsibilities have to be taken into account.

The low capitalisation of contracting organisations in the British industry has made cash flow critical to the life of the organisations and the projects they undertake. This has received the recognition of the courts. The construction industry is exceptional in being allowed by English law to recover financing charges by way of damages for the late or non-payment of a money sum.[7]

Conversely, until the exploration of private funding for infrastructure works, social services and utilities, many significant projects were public works. Public accountability and scrutiny by audit commissions allow less room for the resolution of disputes by commercial trade off. In the public sector, determination of a dispute by a competent tribunal through a transparent process may be more important to the public body than the extent of the financial responsibility thereby found against it.

Dispute resolution procedures in construction

Partly because of the public sector influence, the architect and engineer in traditional procurement under JCT and ICE respectively have come to be recognised by English law as having a dual role. They are not just the agent of the client employer. The contract forms give them independent powers of evaluation and decision. These latter powers must, as a matter of law, be exercised fairly. Indeed, it is precisely the evaluative and determinative characteristics of the powers which by

---

[7]   *President of India v Lips Maritime Corp* [1988] AC 395; *Holbeach Plant Hire Ltd v Anglian Water Authority* [1988] CILL 448, (1988) 14 Con LR 101.

their contract the client employer and contractor have agreed to vest in the architect/engineer that have led to the perceived difficulties from the decision in *Crouch*.

Conclusiveness preventing disputes arising

We have seen above that the perceived effect of the *Crouch* decision is greatly to increase the significance in arbitration of the decisions, or certificates, of the engineer, architect or project manager. The powers of these contract administrators may go further. Their decision, or certificate, may in some circumstances be contractually conclusive: see for example *Crown Estate Commissioners v Mowlem*.[8] Attempts have even been made to achieve degrees of conclusiveness where an independent consultant professional is not being used as contract administrator: see for example *Balfour Beatty v Docklands Light Railway*;[9] *Tarmac Construction Ltd v Esso Petroleum Ltd*;[10] and, *Beaufort House Developments v Zimmcor (International) Inc.*[11]

First-tier dispute resolution

The ICE contracts, and their FIDIC derivatives, go further. The Engineer has a dispute resolving power beyond these initial evaluative and determinative powers. There is formal provision for a reference to the Engineer of any dispute arising under or in connection with the contract for his decision. This procedure is a mandatory precondition for any subsequent reference of the matter to arbitration. In these traditional and still very widespread arrangements lies the basic structure of multi-stage dispute resolution that now characterises construction projects world-wide. The credibility of the independent aspect of this dual role is today challenged. NEC and FIDIC contracts have substituted a third party independent adjudicator for the formal decision stage which under ICE remains with the Engineer.

Adjudication as a first tier mandatory form of dispute resolution in construction contracts was made a statutory right by the Housing

---

[8] (1994) 70 BLR 1

[9] (1996) 78 BLR 42

[10] (1996) 51 ConLR 187

[11] (1990) 50 BLR 91

Grants, Construction and Regeneration Act 1996. The legislation flowed from some of the recommendations of Sir Michael Latham's Final Report of the government/industry review of procurement and contractual arrangements in the UK construction industry *"Constructing the Team"*.

Growth in multi-stage procedures

The growth in modern times of interest in other ADR techniques, such as mediation or conciliation, also influences the published revisions to standard forms of construction contract. The ICE forms provide for conciliation before arbitration. The contracts for the Airport Core Programme for the major new airport in Hong Kong provide for multi-stage dispute resolution,[12] including steps for mediation and for adjudication. In Britain, bespoke contracts for public infrastructure works provide for complex multi-stage procedures, with stepped opportunities for review by an engineer of decisions, followed by conciliation, and if necessary eventual arbitration by an appointed Official Referee, or even by a court empowered by the contract to open up, review and revise project certificates etc.

Adjudication and expert determination

The movement towards adjudication as the mandatory first tier of dispute resolution by a third party neutral (instead of a formal decision by a traditional engineer) has been influenced by such a system for the Channel Tunnel.[13] The contract for the design and construction of the Fixed Link between England and France was derived from the FIDIC form. However, it provides for disputes first to be settled by a Panel of Experts. The contract for the second Dartford Crossing similarly provided for adjudication by a body appointed for the duration of the project. These models, reinforced by statutory right under the Housing Grants Construction and Regeneration Act 1996 have focused particular attention on the use of another know ADR technique: expert determination. Just as architects and engineer's decisions have

---

[12] Lewis, D., "Dispute Resolution on the New Hong Kong International Airport" (1993) *International Construction Law Review*

[13] *Channel Tunnel Group Ltd and another v Balfour Beatty Construction Ltd and others* [1993] AC 334

generated a substantial jurisprudence culminating with *Crouch*, so also the decisions from expert determinations have provoked some jurisprudence as to the extent of their reviewability.[14]

Potential conflicts of jurisdiction in multi-stage procedures

Construction contracts normally provide for multi-stage dispute resolution procedures to be activated in an orderly sequential fashion, at least in regard to any one particular dispute. As with all dispute resolution, informal agreements will intervene to attempt parallel negotiations, and other ADR techniques. The statutory imposition of adjudication, particularly on well established traditional published standard forms of contract, may lead to some degree of parallel jurisdiction, e.g. as between adjudicators and arbitrators. Even with orderly prior provision, conflicts between the stages may still arise.

Conflicts of powers or jurisdiction between the elements of a multi-stage procedure are likely to be reduced if the recommendation of Sir Michael Latham's Report is accepted, that final resolution of a dispute e.g. by arbitration, is postponed until after completion or termination of the works. Such postponement of arbitration was required in the contracts for the Hong Kong airport and for some major infrastructure works in Britain. A degree of postponement is also provided for in the JCT form of contract, by allowing only some questions to be referred to arbitration before completion or termination of the works. There is a delicate balance to be judged in deciding whether such postponement is desirable in contract planning. It is said that references to arbitration during the progress of the works (as the Channel Tunnel contract allowed) might unduly interfere with the satisfactory progress of the works and distract the participants from that. It might also diminish the force and value of interim stages such as adjudication. However, the postponement of the reference of dispute to arbitration until after the works has a number of disadvantages, including a festering of those problems, defensive conduct of the remainder of the works, and all the evidentiary difficulties that arise from the passage of time.

---

[14] See for example *Jones v. Sherwood Computer Services* [1992] 1 WLR 277; *Nikko Hotels (UK) Ltd v MEPC plc* [1991] 28 EG 86; and, *Mercury Communications v Director General of Telecommunications* [1996] 1 WLR 48.

Arrangements for arbitration in the construction industry

There is a curious tension and dilemma that arises from the dominant use of standard forms of contract in the British construction industry, and their provision for arbitration. On the one hand, it would much benefit the industry and those that advise them to have the guidance on decisions on the meaning and effect of provisions in the contracts, and practices arising therefrom. On the other hand, the very nature of arbitration, and its privacy save where matters are reviewed in the courts, prevents institutional dissemination of decisions.

This tension is mitigated somewhat by the substantial informal network of contacts of those servicing arbitration in the construction industry. There is a Society of Construction Arbitrators. Also, the Society of Construction Law brings together a great many individuals specialising in arbitration and the construction field, and its meetings and published papers assist in that regard. Similarly, the many meetings and publications of the Chartered Institute of Arbitrators, and its branches, contribute to understanding and learning in the field. It is also to the Presidents of the various professional institutions, Royal Institute of British Architects (RIBA), the Institution of Civil Engineers (ICE) and the Royal Institution of Chartered Surveyors (RICS), that applications are typically made for appointments of arbitrators in default of agreement by the parties. Membership, communications, and networks that arise from these professional institutions again contribute to understanding and learning in the field.

Out of this diversity has arisen, particularly after the passing of the Arbitration Act 1996, a common sense of purpose in regard to arbitration rules. We have seen above that there are many features which particularly distinguish construction contracts in Britain, the nature of disputes likely to arise, and the procedures that are therefore appropriate to deal with them. There have been published in 1997 for the first time the Construction Industry Model Arbitration Rules (CIMAR).[15] These are for use with arbitration agreements under the

---

[15] *Construction Industry Model Arbitration Rules* for use with arbitration agreements under the Arbitration Act 1996: Society of Construction Arbitrators, 1997

Arbitration Act 1996. They were prepared following an initiative of the Society of Construction Arbitrators. In their published form, they have been produced with the approval of a very wide range of institutional bodies and interest groups across the breadth of the British construction industry. It is likely that they will be adopted by those drafting construction contracts, and in due course may well replace the published standard separate arbitration rules which each of the JCT and ICE presently issue for use with their respective contract forms.

Opportunities and challenges in multi-stage procedures

We have seen from the above that multi-stage procedures for dispute resolution are already normal in the ICE, NEC and FIDIC forms. The introduction by the Housing Grants, Construction and Regeneration Act 1996 of a statutory right to Adjudication is likely to impose a multi-stage procedure also in the JCT forms. The refinement of those processes produce opportunities and challenges. They are likely also to cause reconsideration of the true limits of the *Crouch*[16] decision, and the true nature of a "dispute".[17]

Appropriate procedures for different kinds of dispute

The opportunities are to recognise the appropriateness of different forms of dispute resolution to different kinds of dispute. The challenge is, in summary, to avoid the initial stages becoming expensive sideshows or cynical fishing expeditions before an eventual, old-fashioned style of litigation conducted before arbitrators in the private sector.

The distinctive features of construction contracts and their circumstances, discussed above, demonstrate that special consideration has to be given to the achievement of fair resolution of construction

---

[16] *Great Ormond Street Hospital NHS Trust v Secretary of State for Health & others* [1997] unrep; *University of Reading v Miller Construction Ltd* (1994) 75 BLR 91; *John Barker Construction Ltd v London Portman Hotel Ltd* (1996) 50 ConLR 43

[17] *Hayter v Nelson* [1990] 2 Lloyds Rep 265: cf *Cruden Construction Ltd v Commissioner for New Towns* (1994) 46 Con LR 25; *Balfour Beatty v Docklands Light Railway Ltd* (1996) 78 BLR 42

disputes without unnecessary delay or expense. The almost inevitable involvement in disputes of contested professional judgment on technical matters, set in a context of a mass of record material, calls for expert evidence.

The Official Referees have been in the vanguard, even before Lord Woolf's report, in encouraging expeditious procedures, and the Court of Appeal has also been pointing the way in construction cases.[18] It would be odd if any construction arbitrator did not go at least as far in seeking to streamline and simplify the procedures towards final resolution of a dispute. Arbitrators must now approach their task afresh, and not to be unduly influenced by English court procedures which themselves have anachronistic shadows of procedures more appropriate to civil jury trial. Most published procedures for arbitration, for use with the standard forms of contract, already encourage parties away from formal pleadings to more appropriate statements of case, and of defence, etc. Similarly, they already encourage parties to consider approaches to the disclosure of documents which is commensurate with the nature of the dispute, rather than encouraging the parties to embark on full scale discovery.

The provisions of the Arbitration Act 1996 in regard to costs and interim orders offer real potential for construction disputes to become managed in arbitration appropriately for the issues and sums at stake. The industry's experience of other methods of dispute resolution, such as adjudication and expert determination will assist in this process. Many an arbitration in the construction industry might benefit greatly from the identification of preliminary technical issues, for reference to an expert determination in support of the overall arbitral procedure.

---

[18] *British Airways Pension Trustees Ltd v Sir Robert McAlpine & Sons Ltd* (1994) 72 BLR 26; and see *GMTC Tools & Equipment Ltd v Yuasa Warwick Machinery Ltd* (1994) 73 BLR 102.

21. The Contractor, the Sub-Contractor, the Legal System and the Lawyers: Construction Survey Results

Penny Brooker & Anthony Lavers

Synopsis

This paper reports upon a major research project carried out at Oxford Brookes University into attitudes within the contracting and sub-contracting sectors to dispute resolution and focuses on the legal system and the role of legal advisors. Analysis and comment are advanced on attitudes to a range of issues and some conclusions are offered on the likely effect of these attitudes on the future development of dispute resolution mechanisms.

Introduction

Sir Michael Latham in his reports[1] has placed emphasis on the pivotal role of the client in the construction process, yet reminded the supply side of the industry of the continuing need to focus on achieving and maintaining the satisfaction of the parties financing the process. This eminently sensible approach is translatable, at least by analogy, to construction law. The client of the professional advisor and the consumer of services in the dispute resolution process deserve similar attention to the issue of their levels of satisfaction.

The four-year Oxford Brookes' project began with an extensive review of the UK and US literature on dispute resolution. The field work phase ended in 1996 and analysis of the results was completed during

---

[1] Latham, M. *Trust and Money* Interim Report of the Joint Government/Industry Review of Procurement and Contractual Arrangements in the UK Construction Industries, HMSO, London, 1993; Latham, M. *Constructing the Team* Final Report of the Joint Government/Industry Review of Procurement and Contractual Arrangements in the UK Construction Industries, HMSO, London, 1994.

the first half of 1997.[2] The field work began with an Indicator Exercise designed to identify the principal area of conflict within the construction industry. Interviews were conducted with representatives of the main professional bodies and trade associations within the industry, for example, the RICS, RIBA, CIOB, Chartered Institute of Arbitrators, the Federation of Association of Specialists and Sub-contractors (FASS) and the British Property Federation.

The Indicator Exercise clearly identified the contractor/sub-contractor 'axis' as the principal area of dispute within construction. Accordingly, the second element of the field-work, the questionnaire survey, concentrated on contractors and sub-contractors (taking due account of the fact that some organisations appear in both roles in different projects). A total of 500 contractors and sub-contractors were selected, representing large, medium and small turnover categories. The average response rate of 42.5 per cent[3] gave a final number of respondents of 229. This makes the project one of the largest conducted in this area in terms of sample size[4] with one of the highest response rates.[5]

Follow-up interviews were then conducted with a sample of respondents to explore further the attitudes and general level of satisfaction of contractors and sub-contractors towards litigation (and arbitration) and their perceptions about the role of legal advisors in dispute resolution. Then, to provide an additional perspective, interviews were conducted with legal advisors. The sample comprised seven construction solicitors from major London and provincial firms, five practitioners at the Construction Bar and two claims consultants.

---

[2] This is reported more fully elsewhere, see, for example, Brooker, P. and Lavers, A. 'Perceptions of ADR as constraints upon its use in the UK Construction Industry'. *Construction Management and Economics* (1997) 15, Issue 6.

[3] 46.3% main contractors and 38.7% sub-contractors.

[4] Newman, P. *Construction Litigation Tactics* CLT Professional Publishing, Birmingham, 1996, cites a survey of 400 firms by Herbert Smith.

[5] Fenn, P. & Gould, N., *Dispute Resolution in the UK Construction Industry* International Multidisciplinary Conference on Dispute Avoidance in the Construction Industry, 1994.

The National and International Context

In conducting the research, and in preparing this paper, the authors were conscious of the fact that the responses received could not be viewed in isolation, either within the UK or beyond it. It is almost superfluous to note that Sir Michael Latham found dissatisfaction with the 'culture of conflict', its *"toll on morale and team spirit"* and the effect of ready recourse to legal advice and legal action. Lord Woolf was more scathing about civil litigation itself:[6] *"it is too expensive in that the costs often exceed the value of the claim; too slow in bringing cases to a conclusion and too unequal: there is a lack of equality between the powerful, the wealthy and the under-resourced litigant. It is too uncertain: the difficulties of forecasting what litigation will cost and how long it will last induces the fear of the unknown; and it is incomprehensible to many litigants"*. Such findings must be regarded as generally authoritative, but were not focused upon the views of the construction sector.

There is sufficient evidence from other jurisdictions to imply disquiet, to put it no more strongly, with the legal process. Gaede described the US situation as involving courts which are *"overcrowded, the cases are more and more complex, and the costs both in monetary and organisational terms have become excessive"*.[7] There is evidence that the volume of reported cases at least in Singapore and Malaysia is growing,[8] but that this is not congenial to Asian cultural mores: *"our Chinese mentality ... abhors any attendance in a court of law"*.[9] Nor is arbitration universally perceived as an eligible solution to these criticisms. Latham found *"general dissatisfaction with arbitration as a*

---

[6] Lord Woolf *Access to Justice* The Interim Report to the Lord Chancellor on the Civil Justice System in England and Wales, Lord Chancellor's Department, 1995; Lord Woolf *Access to Justice* The Final Report to the Lord Chancellor on the Civil Justice System in England and Wales, Lord Chancellor's Department, 1996.

[7] Gaede, A., 'ADR: the USA experience and some suggestions for international arbitration: the observations of an American lawyer' [1991] ICLR 5

[8] Robinson, N., Lavers, A., Tan, G. & Chan, R., *Construction Law in Singapore and Malaysia* (2nd edn.), Butterworths (Asia), 1996.

[9] Koh K.C., *Arbitration for the Construction Industry: The Singapore Scene* Proceedings of the Joint Conference of the Singapore Institute of Arbitrators and Chartered Institute of Arbitrators, Singapore, 1981.

method of dispute resolution" while in the US, a study for the Forum for Construction of the American Bar Association found that "*in many cases arbitration does not provide efficient, economical and expert justice.*"[10]

It is almost universal knowledge that the UK's legislature tried to address some of these criticisms in the Arbitration Act 1996 and, to a limited extent, in the adjudication provisions of the Housing Grants, Construction and Regeneration Act 1996. Parallel, although not identical attempts have been made in many other comparable jurisdictions; further evidence, if it were needed, that dissatisfaction with the litigation process generally is an international phenomenon. In the US, the wholesale re-examination of its procedures by the prestigious 'Triple-A', the American Arbitration Association, has led to the appointment of a Drafting Committee of the National Conference of Commissioners on Uniform State Laws to consider reform to the Uniform Arbitration Act, which is the model for most American states.[11]

In Australia, the comprehensive reforms of construction law generally in the states of Victoria and New South Wales have also had to respond to criticisms of the traditional dispute resolution process. Legislation was introduced to create a specialist tribunal in the Domestic Building Contracts and Tribunal Act 1995 to deal cheaply and expeditiously with smaller-scale disputes involving contractors.[12] Even in Singapore, where arbitration was given the fillip of the setting up of the Singapore International Arbitration Centre in 1991, by 1995 a mediation system had been set up, confusingly called the Renovation Conciliation and Arbitration Procedure (RECAP) to provide a simpler, cheaper and more expeditious means for resolution of disputes involving renovation contractors.

---

[10] Stipanowich, T., 'Rethinking American Arbitration' *Indiana Law Journal* 63:425 (1988).

[11] Stipanowich, T., 'At the Cutting Edge: Conflict Avoidance and Resolution in the US Construction Industry' *Construction Management and Economics* (1997) 15, Issue 6.

[12] Jenkins, P. & Lovegrove, K., *A Users Guide to the Domestic Building Contracts and Tribunal Act 1995*, Melbourne, 1996.

The overall picture, then, both nationally and internationally, contained at least indications of dissatisfaction with the role of litigation and to some extent arbitration as means for dealing with the construction industry's disputes. The purpose of the research reported in the remaining sections of this paper was to examine in greater detail the attitudes of contractors and sub-contractors to the legal process and to consider the important balancing element, namely the response of construction lawyers to the criticisms inherent in these attitudes.

Attitudes of Contractors and Sub-Contractors

We now turn to examine some of the trends disclosed by the survey responses and which were further investigated through the agency of the interview part of this research. In this part, we are particularly concerned with the issues which serve to negative the effect of private dispute resolution.

Adversarial Procedures

Earlier research[13] had indicated that the major criticisms about the formal systems of dispute resolution (litigation and arbitration) in the construction industry centre around the issues of cost and time (both in management time and the delay in settling disputes). However, almost as frequently cited were the adversarial, threatening, complex nature of litigation and arbitration. Both formal procedures have, as is well known, traditionally used an almost entirely adversarial approach[14] which tests the disputants' arguments through formalised procedures of examination, cross examination and challenge by the opposing side. This is regarded as confrontational for many people, who are not experienced in the procedures, and as threatening. Further, there exists in the construction industry a perception that the formal procedures are used tactically to create delay and force an unfavourable settlement on

---

[13] Brooker, P. & Lavers, A., 'Perception of the Role of ADR in the Settlement of Construction Disputes: Lessons for the UK from the US Experience' in *Construction Conflict: Management and Resolution*, CIB Publication 171, International Council for Building Research, 1994, pp. 49-69.

[14] The 1996 Arbitration Act has sought to minimise the use of this approach, although the effectiveness of arbitrators in adopting more flexible procedures under the duty given to them under clause 33 (1)(b) remains to be seen.

the financially weaker party. This problem has received considerable coverage in the construction literature. It was also the subject of investigation in the Latham Review and condemned as a practice in the Woolf Report on Civil Litigation. There has been extensive criticism of the role of lawyers in both the formal systems of dispute resolution. Lord Woolf, in his Interim Report on Civil Justice severely criticised the legal professions for causing much of the delay and costs in litigation because of their adoption of what Lord Woolf has termed an *"excessive(ly) combative environment"*, which is used to wear the opponent down. Many of the problems of arbitration in the construction industry are perceived to be due to the involvement of lawyers, who are accused of hi-jacking the process and *"slavishly"*[15] following litigation with confusing procedures, which results in dependence on legal professional and excessive legal costs. The Departmental Advisory Committee (DAC), which was set up to steer through the 1996 Arbitration Act, observed the bullying tactics of arbitration lawyers, who try to force the non-legal advisors to take particular courses of action by, *"seeking to blind him with legal science."*

One objective of the postal survey and follow-up interviews with respondents was to test the attitudes and general level of satisfaction of main contractors and sub/specialist contractors in relation to arbitration and litigation and their perception about the role of legal advisors to the construction industry in the dispute resolution process.

The postal survey reveals extensive disillusionment with the adversarial models, with over 80 per cent. of respondents agreeing that the construction industry needs to move away from them. Many of the interviewees perceived that the dispute is taken out of the hands of the parties, who have to relinquish control of the complex procedures to the professional legal advisors. Interviewees described their *"bitter experiences"* of arbitration and litigation and many of those surveyed, who had gone through either formal system, were disinclined to repeat the experience. The confrontational nature of arbitration and litigation was summed up by one respondent in the follow-up interview to the postal survey:

---

[15] Departmental Advisory Committee on Arbitration Law *Report on the Arbitration Bill*, DTI, London, 1996.

> *"Well, it's like war...you know you are going to get hurt....It's like when you go to a boxing match, you know you are going to get hurt."*

This censure of the adversarial system is leading to a perception that there are other, less antagonistic, procedures that can be used to resolve disputes. After litigation which ended up in the Court of Appeal, an interviewee said:

> *"...it was crazy that we had got ourselves into that situation to keep a lot of barristers, lawyers and judges in business over a civil matter which really two heads should have been able to resolve."*

Cost

A concern which has been better documented in both the literature and the indicator interviews is the cost involved in running a dispute through arbitration or litigation. The postal survey exposed overwhelming dissatisfaction with the costs of both procedures. Over 90 per cent. of the respondents believed that litigation costs too much and nearly 80 per cent. agreed that arbitration costs too much. This attitude was confirmed extensively both in comments made in the postal survey and in the follow-up interviews, by both main contractors and sub/specialists. A picture emerges of escalating costs, which are frequently perceived to outstrip the value of the dispute.

A significant part of the cost of using the formal procedures is caused by the rules governing discovery, which result in huge quantities of paperwork. This paperwork is costly, in both management and monetary terms, and interviewees and respondents identified the lawyers as responsible for generating the supposed need for it. As an interviewee, who was the head of an in-house legal department of one of the largest main contracting companies in the UK explained: *"The trouble is, of course, that most of it is irrelevant, but the lawyers say, 'Well you have got to see everything, there may be something there.' Of course, this is where the cost of litigation goes storming up."* The adversarial approach used by litigation and arbitration, with its insistence on technical procedures and complex rules, adds to a sense of helplessness on the part of the beleaguered contractor. As one medium-sized contractor complained:

> *"I just feel the crux of the point just gets submerged in an absolute mass of trivia. It all takes time and there is more paper. Of course, every bit of paper has got to be read and the costs just go up. The man-hours spent by the legal people reading and re-submitting and considering and responding and pleading. It is just horrendous and crazy."*

Those surveyed attached considerable blame to the legal profession, who are perceived to be the beneficiaries of the adversarial approach. Comments made in the survey, together with the follow-up interviews, illustrate the concern respondents have with the legal costs involved in both litigation and arbitration:

> *"Too much money is being siphoned off from the industry in legal fees which are wholly disproportionate to the amount in dispute."*

> *"...if you are going to issue a writ, you are stuck with a lawyer and not only do you have the solicitor but you have the barrister and the barrister's assistant, so you are in for the whole tribe.... all at a very expensive rate per hour."*

Time

The level of dissatisfaction about the costs of the formal systems is matched by the concern revealed about delay in reaching settlement when disputes have arisen. Indeed, in the Herbert Smith survey, the concern about delay was even higher than that about cost. Over 89 per cent. of the respondents agree that construction industry disputes need a quick decision, which clearly signifies the level of importance awarded to the issue of resolving disputes expeditiously. The respondents and interviewees not only perceive that the formal systems are manipulated to create a deliberate delay, the procedures themselves are seen to be drawn out, time consuming and slow to come to fruition and again the view was expressed by those interviewed that such an approach is to the benefit of the lawyers themselves. A legally trained interviewee representing a large main contracting firm observed:

" I think nowadays the legal profession has become much more of a business and I am afraid that one does get the impression, on occasions, that a lot of people are running arbitration, and litigation for that matter, more for their own interests than perhaps their clients' interest. It is an impression that I know a number of people have. "

Respondents and interviewees maintained that there is an *"urgent need for a cheaper method for resolving disputes."* Over 78 per cent. of respondents believed that less money is spent on lawyers when using ADR and 73 per cent. stated that they would resolve a construction dispute without seeking advice from a legal advisor. The predominant reason given for this emphatic response is the costs involving legal professionals. As one contractor asserted:

"The main problem with most dispute resolution processes is the involvement of the legal profession. Costs escalate sometimes out of all proportion to the dispute, non-issues become major stumbling blocks....We need a bold new resolution procedure which will not be hi-jacked by the legal profession. "

Manipulation

Added to the adversarial, expensive and delay-ridden perceptions held about the formal systems, a more serious allegation has been made in both the construction literature[16] and the indicator interviews. It is claimed that both arbitration and litigation are manipulated as levers for negotiation by the legal advisors and their clients. Due to the expense and time involved in both procedures, the threat of either can be tactically exploited. These attitudes are confirmed by the respondents to the survey and the interviewees. Sub/specialists testified to the manipulation of the formal systems *"by unscrupulous main contractors"*, who have the financial power to draw out the legal procedures which can result in the sub-contractor going out of business. Main contractors had nothing to lose by *"insisting"* on litigation or arbitration, knowing that it would take too long and cost

---

[16] Departmental Advisory Committee on Arbitration Law *Report on the Arbitration Bill*, DTI, London, 1996.

too much for the sub-contractor to fight his claim.

The counter argument proposed by main contractors is that sub/specialists use the formal systems to put pressure on them to reach settlements in disputes which are often only of a nuisance type. The sub/specialists were frequently portrayed in this tactical game as unsophisticated players. In any disagreement, even over *"stupid things"*, their first reaction is to send out for a writ. Main contractors accuse them of using a 'hammer to crack a nut' in order to get the main contractor to take action about their claims:

> *"The next thing you have is some claims man coming in. Nobody wants to solve anything, they just want to blackmail you. Cost pressures. Okay, you can deal with that but it is a waste of resources."*

Overall levels of satisfaction

The perceptions held by contractors of excessive costs, delay and the manipulation of the arbitration and litigation have resulted in high levels of dissatisfaction with both. Over 60 per cent. of the respondents disagreed with the proposition that litigation is a satisfactory procedure. The follow-up interviews and the survey comments support the findings that there is general agreement amongst contractors that litigation is an unsatisfactory procedure and there is evidence to suggest that it can be used only by those who have the money to back up their arguments. A main contractor who was interviewed perceived litigation as a 'game of poker', which the party with the greater resources and nerves is likely to win:

> *"...it may be pure tactics at the moment.. I mean a lot of Court actions are...It's a poker game isn't it? It's who is prepared to or who has the guts. When you actually have the nerve and are prepared to go to court, you do frighten people but you have to have big bucks behind you."*

The survey findings for arbitration, however, are more ambiguous. Nearly one third of respondents disagreed that arbitration is a satisfactory procedure to resolve construction disputes and conversely, nearly another third agreed. There is a high level of neutrality expressed (one third) about satisfaction with arbitration as a procedure for resolving disputes. Despite substantial levels of dissatisfaction with its costs, confrontational and time consuming procedures, there is an indicative level of support for it, in comparison with litigation. This may be an instrumental factor in the potential development of ADR and the neutral attitudes towards arbitration could be swayed in its favour, if the major flaws are eradicated or at least reduced by the 1996 Arbitration Act.

The survey and interviews concerning the perceptions of arbitration and litigation reveal a picture of substantial dissatisfaction towards the formal systems and the attendant costs upon the involvement of the legal profession. This is reflected in the numbers willing to use ADR. Over 70 per cent. of the respondents affirmed that they would consider using it to resolve construction disputes. In those areas where the formal systems are seen to be failing the industry: its costs, delay and adversarial approach, the perception in the contracting sector of construction is that ADR must be a better option. Statements made on the survey questionnaire and interviews by both main contractors and sub/specialist contractors alike attest to this perception:

> *"Any system is better than the existing systems of litigation and arbitration. These systems have been taken over by the lawyers!!! They control the process and the costs. The participants pay with time, money and time!!!"* (Exclamation marks given by the respondent.)

The response of the legal advisors

One objective of the legal advisor interviews was to take the principal themes, which were identified from the survey data and follow-up interviews, and compare and contrast legal professionals' perceptions and experiences of these issues. The survey and interviews disclosed that there is considerable dissatisfaction with arbitration and litigation and with the role of the legal advisors in the dispute process, who are perceived by many contractors to profit from the adversarial approach.

Many of the legal interviewees recognise that the attributes of arbitration and litigation are unpalatable to the construction industry and they confirm that the criticisms of the costs and time involved are in many cases justified. Further, they accept that the costs could be taken up by issues which frequently are not relevant. Although it was admitted that this could sometimes be the fault of a poorly prepared advocate, blame is apportioned, in some instances, to the clients, who may have given misleading information or instructions. A barrister explained the problems created by the adversarial approach:

> *"Well, there can be a great deal of time taken up with points which may not at the end of the day have a great deal to do with the case. Whether this is the fault of the advocate, because he has not prepared his case properly, or whether it is because he is doing it on instructions or has been misled in some ways by his clients; it is always difficult to say, but that is certainly one process, or part of the process, which I can see fairly commonly."*

Notwithstanding an acceptance of some of the perceived problems that the adversarial system has, many of the legal advisors defend the approach, as its primary function is to reveal the truth about the arguments which the parties put forward. There is a recognition that this approach may not be appropriate for all disputes, particularly where commercial settlements are required, but there was a general acknowledgement, from nearly all the interviewees, that both litigation and arbitration have their place when there is a need for a final, binding solution which has been tested for the truth: *"If you are trying to get the final resolution...without the adversarial approach, you are not going to get at that truth. You are not going to destroy the junk that has been piled up."*

Where large amounts are in dispute, the legal advisors are of the opinion that the advantage of arbitration and litigation is that the adversarial approach enables the strengths and weaknesses of a case to be ascertained, with the added bonus of vindicating the disputant 'in the right':

"If you are talking about the sort of big amount.....it is really best to leave the parties to act as adversaries....if the adversarial approach is adopted, it can have the effect of a bloodletting.....The disputants feel that they have stood up for themselves and had it out."

A notable perception voiced by all the legal interviewees but one is that it is their experience that the client are, themselves, adversarial. By the time the legal advisor is consulted, the parties are polarised into their positions and, as far as most of the clients are concerned, the legal advisor cannot be adversarial enough. For many of the legal interviewees, the claim that contractors in the construction industry want to move away from the adversarial approach is merely *"lip service"* to a theoretical idea which is prevalent in the media. For some legal advisors, being adversarial is the role that they are trained for. A leading QC at the Construction Bar stated that his function is to satisfy his client by giving the opposition a gruelling examination in court:

"Somebody walks in when he is owed money, steam coming out of his ears. Suddenly, you can't get too adversarial. I think the interesting thing is it is not the lawyers who are adversarial, it is the parties who are adversarial. This may be another reason why they like the aggressive lawyer, because it is a catharsis for them. They can vent their venom at the other side. I mean, I have to confess that one plays to the gallery in cross-examination, because you know that you are giving enormous satisfaction to your client. One of the reasons your client is retaining you is because he wants you to give Joe Bloggs, who sat opposite him at a negotiating table two years before and raised two fingers at him, he want you to give him a hard time and you are being paid to do that....It is perfectly ethical as long as it is in my client's best interests and I am not acting in any way contrary to the Code of Conduct laid down. I am happy to do it. It is part of my job. So to say:. 'Let's be less adversarial' so far as lovely phrases can go but is completely untrue in practice."

This view, that it is the client that is adversarial, was shared by barristers, solicitors and claims consultants who were interviewed. One claims consultant described his perception of what the client wanted from him:

> *"I think most parties that come to us want us to put forward their best possible case. Punch the other chap on the nose."*

The allegations of the manipulation of the formal systems by the legal professional for their clients, (either acting for the main contractor or the sub/specialist) were not denied by the legal advisors. Part of this process is the utilisation of arbitration and litigation by using the threat of either to indicate the seriousness of, and commitment to, the dispute. Due to the expense and time involved in both procedures, the threat of either can be tactically exploited. The tactics of this process were described by a construction solicitor in the indicator interviews:

> *"One factor that frequently arises amongst contractors is tactically issuing or facing a writ. So they recognise the tactics, which don't carry a sense of commitment to long running dispute. If they issue a writ, they are beginning a process where there will be high costs to get out. It is part of the contractors' culture. ADR has no alternative to this."*

These tactical manoeuvres which are played by both protagonists to the dispute were recognised by main contractors and sub/specialists in the survey. There is support for the view that some disputes require the force of the formal systems, as they *"require stronger action than ADR."* One sub/specialist contractor commented:

> *Some disputes are so intractable and long established that the due processes of the law are the only procedures that can effect a result enforceable on both parties."*

Contractors in the survey perceived the formal systems to be more appropriate in some situations, because they force the parties to assess their disputes and be realistic:

> *"I think there is a place for litigation and arbitration which makes all parties concentrate their minds on the reality of their case."*

Often, it is perceived by the main contractor that there is no intention on the part of the sub/specialist of *"going the distance"*, but the formal systems are used as a *"signal"* to the main contractor that they want the issue resolved. A sub-contractor interviewed admitted to using this ploy:

> *"We have used the threat of arbitration to at least get a meeting with the contractors and get some money out of them."*

The legal advisors who represent sub/specialist contractors imparted a strongly held attitude that it often takes the weight of either arbitration or litigation to force the main contractors to take their clients' claims seriously and that ADR is unlikely to be a suitable choice of dispute resolution procedure when their clients have not been paid. In this situation only a *"writ"* would suffice. A solicitor whose clients are principally sub/specialist contractors explained that he recommends litigation or arbitration when the main contractor is refusing to take his client's claim seriously:

> *"More often than not, a case comes into us because someone has not been paid and he has not been taken seriously....Somebody is just being plain bloody-minded and often deceitfully bloody-minded as well. Someone is deliberately orchestrating things and making life difficult. Very often, in my view, to talk about bringing in the heavy guns of litigation and arbitration basically because it concentrates their minds and that is often my perception of the best way forward to make people take my clients' claims seriously."*

Central to most of the legal interviewees' judgment about recommending dispute resolution processes is that by the time the dispute reaches them, it is too late to advise conciliatory methods. The parties have already become entrenched in their positions and are demanding an adversarial approach. A solicitor who represents main contractors predominantly denied that the adversarial stance is one adopted by the lawyer; it is one that they are presented with by the client, who arrives in the office having become personally involved in the dispute:

> *"There is an assumption that lawyers are responsible for that (adversarial approach) but, actually, I am not sure that is the case, because it comes back again to the fact that a lot of our*

clients get involved very personally and feel very aggrieved and a lot of site negotiations appear to be based on that, rather than a co-operative approach. They come to us expecting an adversarial approach...Not only is it what they expect and demand from us, but they have already set it up themselves, so that it has become an adversarial position."

The legal advisors interviewed are aware of the problems which are inherent in the adversarial approach, which result in the perceptions held by contractors of the excessive costs, delay and confrontational nature of the formal systems of dispute resolution. Nevertheless, there are situations when this approach is deemed to be appropriate. Many of the legal interviewees will continue to recommend the formal systems when the *"heavy guns"* of litigation and arbitration are required because their client's claim is not being taken seriously and when the adversarial approach is one which their clients demand of them.

Conclusions

The authors do not claim to be the first commentators to suggest that the traditional formal systems of dispute resolution contain deficiencies nor even that there is dissatisfaction with them within the construction industry. Reference was made to recognition in a number of other jurisdictions, such as the US, Australia and Singapore, that the construction industry needs additional mechanisms as a result of perceived inadequacies in litigation and arbitration. The findings of Latham and of Woolf would be sufficient to cast doubt on the likelihood of complete satisfaction in the UK industry with the available routes for conflict resolution.

The research has sought to achieve something which is at once less and more than the sector-wide studies referred to. It focuses entirely on two groups of producers, namely contractors and sub-contractors and obtains from a large sample detailed articulations of their attitudes and perceptions. While it produces little which is inconsistent with previous work, the findings may make disturbing reading for those concerned with the efficient administration of justice and perhaps for the suppliers of legal services.

Specifically, the combination of very high percentages of agreement by respondents on the undesirability of adversarial procedures, cost and delay with the damning descriptions of experiences of litigation by the interviewees leave little room for further speculation as to the views of these important groups of clients/consumers of legal services. An area of criticism which has not been the subject of so much attention previously as time and cost is that of manipulation. Sub-contractors in particular see litigation as a game played often under very unequal conditions, from which considerable financial advantage can be extracted by the skilful player, a perception which seems to bear little relation to concepts of justice or effective dispute resolution.

The overall level of satisfaction with litigation in the survey would not surprise Lord Woolf; some two-thirds of respondents would not accept the word 'satisfactory' to describe it. The response to arbitration was less predictable and interestingly split approximately into thirds, representing satisfaction, dissatisfaction and an unusually high level of neutrality. It will be desirable to revisit this area once the reforms effected by the Arbitration Act 1996 have had time to be appraised.

The authors wish this paper to present a balanced picture and the research into the responses of the legal advisors, who are engaged in operating the litigation and arbitration processes, are intended to provide an important additional view to those of the contractor/sub-contractor clients. Perhaps the most notable feature of this element of the research is the extent to which the legal advisors supported some of the main criticisms by the contractors and sub-contractors. This was certainly true of delay and cost, where the legal advisor interviewees broadly accepted that both arbitration and litigation had bad reputations with construction industry clients in these respects and that in many cases their criticisms were justified.

Different perspectives emerged, however, in two other vital respects. The legal advisors were generally resistant to an image of an adversarial legal culture and conflictual procedures souring relationships and dragging the parties down the route to confrontation. The strong feeling was that the parties themselves generate the adversarial heat, which is then largely channelled by the dispute resolution systems. The allegations of manipulation were not denied by the legal advisors; on the contrary, they were confirmed. However, whereas the suggestion by the contractor and sub-contractor respondents were that this was a 'lawyer's game', the legal advisors saw it as a necessary weapon in the hands of their (often contractor and sub-contractor) clients for defeating the nefarious purposes of an opponent. Lawyers continue to recommend litigation and arbitration as powerful antidotes to delay or evasion on the other side.

What the findings have to say about the future of dispute resolution can be summarised as follows.

- Lawyers seem as committed to the benefits of litigation and arbitration in appropriate cases as they were, while recognising the justice of criticisms of excessive cost and delay in those processes. This suggests a willingness, at least, to try to make 'reformed' arbitration work and perhaps to enter into the spirit of post-Woolf reforms of the litigation process.

- Contractors and sub-contracts as a client group are very unhappy with the range of perceived features of litigation and, to some extent, of arbitration. They express a strong desire for alternatives, which will not embody these attitudes. Some of them see an irony and little cause for optimism in the concentration of lawyers in the ADR processes. Ronald Davies of FASS has given the opinion that "*it is essential that the activities relating to adjudication should be designed in such a way as to keep the activities of lawyers to an absolute minimum...if one looks at the present ADR scene it is disturbing to see a predominance of lawyers yet again and what is more likely to ensure the failure of a scheme than?*"[17]

The most pessimistic interpretation of the conclusions of this paper is that contractors and sub-contractors are dissatisfied with the dispute resolution services supplied to them by the systems and the legal professionals who operate them. The most optimistic interpretation is that there is a public relations shortfall to be made up if the legal

---

[17] Davies R., 'Construction Conflict – The Specialist Contractors View' in *Construction Conflict Management and Resolution*, Fenn, P. & Gameson, R. (eds), E. and F.N. Spon, London, 1992.

profession is to continue to operate as successfully as it has done previously.

The authors conclude with the view that the legal profession's involvement in ADR in construction and the construction industry's continued consumption of its services in litigation and arbitration will be jeopardised if the negative perceptions of the client groups studied are not addressed.

22. Costs of Construction Disputes: Recent Developments

Mike O'Reilly

Synopsis

This paper considers Lord Woolf's proposals in outline and discusses briefly the benefits in terms of costs which will flow from their implementation. The paper focuses principally on the Arbitration Act 1996 which contains a number of features which affects costs in arbitrations.

Introduction

The costs of construction disputes adversely affect the industry in a number of ways. They represent a drain on resources causing reduced efficiency; they prevent access to justice and allow both the wealthy and the reckless to exploit the risks of litigation. Costs and disputes also create an atmosphere which sours relationships in the industry.

A significant feature of allocating costs in practice is the disparity between their monetary importance and the time spent dealing with them. Frequently, the parties spend many weeks arguing the substantive issues before a judge or arbitrator, while the costs hearing will last just a couple of hours, even though the costs may involve greater sums than the substantive claims. I am not of course suggesting that the time and cost spent on dealing with costs be increased; rather I hope that the amount of costs incurred on substantive issues might be reduced, so that the time spent dealing with costs will come into proportion.

A number of developments over recent years and months provide new opportunities for providing a more sensible approach to the costs of disputes in the construction industry. These include the adjudication provisions of the Housing Grants, Construction and Regeneration Act 1996 which will lead to many potential disputes being settled at an earlier stage. The recommendations of the Woolf Report also provide grounds for optimism that there will be more control of costs through case management. The Arbitration Act 1996 also contains welcome new powers in respect of costs.

Lord Woolf's proposals

In the opening paragraphs of Chapter 7 on Costs, of his comprehensive review of the civil justice system in England[1] Lord Woolf says:

"I began the chapter in the interim report by saying: "The problem of costs is the most serious problem besetting our litigation system." The year which has elapsed since the interim report has not caused me to alter that assessment.... The adverse consequences which flow from the problems in relation to costs contaminate the whole civil justice system... Costs are central to the changes I wish to bring about.

Annex III to the report gives statistics on costs obtained by the Supreme Court Taxing Office. The figures for Official Referees' business shows that there was a mean claim recovery of £112,000 and a mean costs recovery by the winning party of £36,000. Assuming that the losing party's costs were the same as those of the successful party, and that the recovered costs were only 80% of the total costs incurred, this means that for every £100 paid out under judgments, approximately £80 are paid out in costs. This is, of course, slightly misleading because most cases settle and so the costs bill will be much lower. Nevertheless, the statistics about the cases which go to judgment show that the prospective costs bill for the loser must play a very significant part in many decisions to settle cases.

In order to control costs, we need to use management principles, including "case management" and procedural decisions informed by "cost-benefit" considerations. Lord Woolf has made a number

---

[1] *Access to Justice, Final Report to the Lord Chancellor on the Civil Justice System in England and Wales,* HMSO, London, 1996.

of proposals, for example that small cases be placed on a "fast track", with case management conferences and pre-trial reviews. Larger or more complex cases will be on a "multi-track" and will be closely managed by the judges."

The Woolf Report is significant not because of its individual suggestions or recommendations, but because it envisages a new culture in litigation. It envisages judges taking decisions about discovery etc. based on cost-benefit in addition to the traditional criteria. It imagines clients being fully informed about projected costs and risks; it imagines clients being empowered (in practice as well as theory) to take informed decisions about the litigation. It requires lawyers to be accountable to their clients in a more formal way than hitherto.

This culture change will require judges and lawyers to become familiar with a number of management techniques, which are currently used as a matter of course by construction professionals (some of which are used in construction dispute evaluation and hence are already familiar to the Official Referees). The specific example of scheduling techniques was cited by Lord Woolf;[2] computer programs designed specifically for litigation management are now becoming available. An example is *Dispute Manager* which enables the user to schedule the tasks which make up a case; it enables him to input cost projections and estimated probabilities of success on each head of claim in order to estimate the range of possible outcomes. It also enables the analysis of uncertainty using well-established project simulation techniques. Programs such as this will enable clients to be much better informed about the risks associated with running a piece of litigation or arbitration and will, I believe, assist in bringing about the culture change advocated by Lord Woolf.

These innovations will not, of course, prevent construction disputes from arising; however, it is hoped that the sea-change proposed by Lord Woolf, supported by the analytical tools now coming onto the

---

[2]   *Ibid* at 290.

market, will reduce the cost of disputes. In particular, it is to be hoped that an additional awareness by both parties as to the risks of litigation will encourage reasonable settlements.

The costs provisions of the Arbitration Act 1996

Arbitration, particularly in the construction industry, often closely mirrors litigation. Under the 1950 Act, the position as to costs was largely the same as for litigation. The new Act makes some innovative proposals which will, hopefully, reduce the costs in arbitrations.

The provisions as to costs are set out principally in Sections 59 to 65, though provisions affecting costs are also found in a number of other sections. These include:

- Section 24(4): order of the court as to fees and expenses upon removal of the arbitrator;
- Section 25: fees of an arbitrator who resigns;
- Section 28: joint and several liability of parties to arbitrators for fees and expenses; and reduction by the court of the arbitrator's fees;
- Section 37(2): fees of assessors, experts etc. appointed by the tribunal;
- Section 38(3): security for costs;
- Section 39(2)(b): example of a provisional award dealing with costs;
- Section 56: power to withhold award in the case of non-payment;
- Section 70(5),(6): costs associated with challenging the award;
- Section 75: charge to secure payment of solicitor's costs.

Agreements of the parties as to costs

The Act contains a number of distinct types of provisions as to agreements as to costs:

- provisions which specifically allow agreement between the parties as to costs;[3]
- provisions which provide powers to the arbitrator, subject to a different agreement between the parties;[4]
- provisions which render invalid certain agreements between the parties.[5]

General background and the definition of recoverable costs

The basic rule is given in s. 63(1) "The parties are free to agree what costs of the arbitration are recoverable". The term "Costs" is give a wide meaning in s. 59, including the arbitrator's and parties' fees and costs of or incidental to the proceedings.

As an aid to interpretation we must also consider Section 1, which sets out general principles. This provides, inter alia:

1.   The provisions of this Part are founded on the following principles, and shall be construed accordingly:...

(b)   the parties should be free to agree how their disputes are resolved, subject only to such safeguards as are necessary in the public interest;

---

3   For example, section 63(1).
4   For example, section 38(3).
5   For example, section 60.

This is further elaborated upon in Section 4

> 4. *(1) The mandatory provisions of this Part are listed in Schedule 1 and have effect notwithstanding any agreement to the contrary.*
>
> *(2) The other provisions of this Part (the "non-mandatory provisions") allow the parties to make their own arrangements by agreement but provide rules which apply in the absence of such agreement.*

The sections listed in Schedule 1 include Sections 28, 56, 60 and 75.

It is my view that (subject to the restriction in Section 60, which will be discussed below) the parties are now free to make any agreement as to recoverable costs which to them seems convenient in their arbitration agreement. They may, therefore, agree:

- that there is to be a specified costs ceiling; or
- that the maximum costs are to be related to the sums claimed or recovered.

The potential scope of the agreement allowed for in s. 63(1) is further illuminated by the remaining subsections of s. 63, which apply "If or to the extent there is no such agreement..." – s. 63(2). There are items as to the "basis" on which costs are awarded and "the items of recoverable costs and the amount referable to each". This is widely drawn and would, it seems, entitle the parties to agree, for example, that the costs recoverable will be limited to a specified proportion of the sum recovered or the respondent's successful offer, whichever is the higher. Such agreements must, however, not offend against Section 60, which is discussed below.

The event

Section 61(2) provides: "Unless the parties otherwise agree, the tribunal shall award costs on the general principle that costs should follow the event...". The expression "the event" has the ring of a term of art. But the cases show that it means no more than "success", which is often difficult to define. Sections 1, 4 and 61(2) suggests that parties are free also to depart from the traditional concept of "the event" and write in their arbitration clause a narrowly drawn definition, for example, based on offers made by each party.[6]

There are two basic concerns over the traditional definition of the event.

- The imprecise meaning of "the event" creates an additional layer of uncertainty which is not conducive to informed decision-making. For example, when a claimant recovers (say) 5% of the amount claimed, some arbitrators might treat him as successful, while others might not. Clearer definitions of what is meant by "winning" and "losing" help us to size up the risks involved and to take appropriate decisions.

- The current process does not drive a sensible settlement. Consider an alternative: if both parties were required to put in an offer at the close of pleadings (which offers are available for acceptance) and (if the matter were to proceed to an award) the closest to the award was adjudged "successful", both parties would be forced to sit down at an early stage, before the majority of costs were incurred and seriously consider the real value of their case and the attendant risks of proceeding. This would, I suggest, make settlements more likely and the settlements would be reached earlier.

These arrangements – and more sophisticated arrangements, such as sliding scales of costs – could readily be incorporated into standard form contracts as an option. No one would be forced to use them, by the more enlightened and commercially sensible, may wish to do so.

---

[6] See (1995) 61 JCIArb 1, p. 27 for a discussion as to the terms of such costs agreements.

The meaning of Section 60

Section 60 in the new Act is based on Section 18(3) of the 1950 Act. It provides:

> 60.　An agreement which has the effect that a party is to pay the whole or part of the costs of the arbitration in any event is only valid if made after the dispute in question has arisen.

This section relates to what might be termed "prior agreements" and the discussion below refers exclusively to such agreements.

During consideration of the Arbitration Bill, concerns were expressed that Section 18(3) of the 1950 Act may render invalid agreements as to recoverable costs ceilings. While the present section differs somewhat from Section 18(3), the problem remains unresolved. The argument is that a costs ceiling means that any costs incurred by the successful party over and above that level rank as "part of the costs" and would be have to be borne by him "in any event".

It is submitted that this argument goes too far and that Section 60 does not generally make agreements as to costs ceilings invalid. It is submitted that Section 60 merely provides that any attempt to get a party to pay his own (or the other party's) costs, irrespective of the outcome is invalid. Therefore a costs ceiling which is so low that it clearly has this intention is invalid. It is submitted, however, that a costs ceiling which is reasonably proportionate to the sums in dispute and which allows reasonable costs to be allocated on the basis of success is valid. Such a proposal is, after all, exactly what Lord Woolf proposes for fast track cases for reasons of fairness and the promotion of good policy.

In any event it is submitted that the term "costs of the arbitration" in Section 60 is to be read as "recoverable costs of the arbitration" and this is referable to any agreement made: and Section 63(1) provides that parties are entitled to make such an agreement.

If we cannot take the liberty of reading the expression "recoverable costs of the arbitration" into Section 60, we may be left with an inconsistency between Section 60 and Section 63(1). However, Section 1(b) states the general principles of construction that "the parties should be free to agree how their disputes are resolved, subject only to such safeguards as are necessary in the public interest." This principle suggests that agreements which do not obviously offend against the spirit of Section 60 are valid and enforceable; the test is whether the level of costs recoverable are proportionate and whether the agreement allows the recoverable costs to be allocated on the basis of success.

By way of example, it is submitted that an agreement which provides:

> *the successful party will recover his costs from the other party; but the recoverable costs will be limited to 30% of the amount recovered by the claimant or the sum offered in settlement by the respondent (whichever is the higher)*

is valid. Agreements limiting each party to the costs of (say) a single lawyer at hearings appear to be valid in accordance with Section 63.

Arbitrator's power to limit the costs of the proceedings

Section 65 of the new Act is an important provision in the control of costs. It provides:

> 65   *(1)*   *Unless otherwise agreed by the parties, the tribunal may direct that the recoverable costs of the arbitration, or any part of the arbitral proceedings, shall be limited to a specified amount.*
> *(2)*   *Any direction may be made or varied at any stage, but this must be done sufficiently in advance of the incurring of costs to which it relates, or the taking of any steps in the proceedings which may be affected by it, for the limit to be taken into account.*

Section 65 allows the arbitrator to take a firm line as to the costs in the proceedings, provided that a party is not caught unawares. It is to be hoped that the power given by the section will be widely used. Just as the judges are enjoined to manage cases in the courts, so should arbitrators manage cases in arbitration. I suggest the following guidelines for the exercise of the power in Section 65:

- While the power in Section 65 may properly be brought to the parties' attention by the arbitrator, it is thought that the arbitrator should be slow to exercise it unless requested to do so by one of the parties.

- The arbitrator must make a direction under Section 65 only after proper consideration. It is appropriate for him to invite submissions as to whether the exercise of the power is appropriate, and, if so, the appropriate limit on costs. If the proposed limit is considerably less than one would historically expect for the costs bill in such an arbitration, the arbitrator may properly call a short hearing so that oral representations may be made.

- It is submitted that the prime consideration is whether, in all the circumstances, it is in the interests of justice (which includes not imposing undue financial burdens or risks on the parties) and the parties that the limit be imposed. In order to determine this, the following matters may properly be taken into account:

    (i)   the sums in dispute;
    (ii) the importance of the case to each of the parties;
    (iii) the cost-benefits of extensive enquiries or discovery
    (iv) the cost-benefits of expert and other professional advice/evidence;
    (v)   the complexity of the issues and the risk of injustice being done if the costs actually spent are limited to the proposed limit.

- A number of difficulties may arise with the above criteria. For example, while the limit would normally bear some relation to the "sums in dispute", it is not always easy to determine the real amount in dispute before evidence is heard. Claims are frequently exaggerated and it may be unfair to the respondent to have a high costs limit imposed merely because the claimant chooses to make an exaggerated claim. The arbitrator must not, of course, prejudice himself by taking an early view as to the proper value of the claim. However, it may be possible for him to state in his order that the costs limit is based, in part, on the amount claimed and if it is shown that the claims were exaggerated he reserves the right to take that into account when the question of costs comes to be decided.

- The exercise of the power in Section 65 should be treated independently of other powers available to the arbitrator. An example which may arise is where an application is made under Section 38(3) for security for costs against a claimant. The claimant may submit in his response that any security ordered should be limited to a "specified amount" determined in accordance with Section 65. The arbitrator now has two distinct applications which should not be coupled. The arbitrator should probably first consider whether a costs limit is appropriate and, if so, he should make his direction. He should then go on consider whether the conditions for ordering security have been met; the maximum sum which the claimant must provide is the amount of costs which are likely to be due if the respondent wins; in the event that a costs ceiling has been directed, that sum has now been determined. If the arbitrator orders security for costs, he may make his order on terms that he will entertain an application in the event that the costs limit is varied in accordance with Section 65(2).

Appeals on costs

There was some confusion following the 1979 Act as to the appropriate method for challenging an award as to costs. It was eventually resolved that, in the absence of misconduct, the challenge was essentially to be characterised as an appeal on the grounds of an error of law and could be made only under Section 1 of the 1979 Act.[7] Accordingly the guidelines laid down in *The Nema* [8] and *The Antaios* [9] apply and significantly restrict the right to have the matter raised before the court. Furthermore, an exclusion agreement would make it impossible to raise the matter.[10]

Under the 1996 Act, this remains the case. A challenge on the grounds of "serious irregularity" as defined in Section 68 may be made in appropriate circumstances, but ordinarily the challenge will be that the arbitrator has misapplied the law and so the challenge will be under Section 69. The restrictions on appeals remains pretty much as before and the effect of an exclusion agreement will, likewise, be as before.

Security for costs

Under the Arbitration Act 1950 Act, an arbitrator has no power to order security for costs unless the parties had clothed him with such power. An application was made to the court under Section 12(6) of the 1950 Act. Most published rules of procedure provide the arbitrator with power to order security for costs.

The 1996 Act entitles (and indeed encourages) the parties to agree rules of procedure. But in the event that they do not provide the arbitrator with power to order security, Section 38 will do so. It provides, *inter alia*:

---

[7]   *Blexen v. G. Percy Trentham* (1990) 54 BLR 37

[8]   *Pioneer Shipping Limited v. BTP Tioxide Limited 'The Nema'* [1982] AC 724

[9]   [1985] AC 191

[10]   *King v. Thomas McKenna Ltd* [1991] 2 QB 480

38 - (1) The parties are free to agree on the powers exercisable by the arbitral tribunal for the purposes of and in relation to the proceedings.
(2) Unless otherwise agreed by the parties the tribunal has the following powers.
(3) The tribunal may order a claimant to provide security for the costs of the arbitration.

This power shall not be exercised on the ground that the claimant is

(a)   an individual ordinarily resident outside the United Kingdom, or
(b)   a corporation ... outside the United Kingdom.

Furthermore, the court will not be able to order security for costs. Section 44 sets out those powers which the court may exercise in support of arbitral proceedings. Orders for security for costs are not mentioned. This is consistent with Section 44(5) which sets out a general principle that the court will not exercise powers which are available to the arbitrator.

The principles which an arbitrator should consider when an application for security for costs is made are broadly those set out in *Sir Lindsay Parkinson* v. *Triplan* [11] as explained by later cases.[12] Note, however, that under the 1996 Act, the residence of the claimant is a factor which is not to be taken into account – Section 38(3) proviso.

Arbitrators' fees

Under the 1950 Act, there was some uncertainty about a number of aspects of the fees due to arbitrators. There was, for example, some doubt about whether parties were jointly and severally liable for the

---

[11]   [1973] 1 QB 609
[12]   See generally, O'Reilly, M.P., *Costs in Arbitration Proceedings*, 2nd Edition, LLP Ltd, London, 1997.

arbitrator's fees; by Section 28(1) (which is a mandatory provision) parties are now jointly and severally liable for his fees. There were also doubts about the position where the arbitrator was removed or resigned; these situations are now dealt with by Sections 24(4) and 25 respectively. Furthermore, the position where an arbitrator awarded himself fees which a party considered excessive was troublesome as it appeared only challengeable by Section 19 of the 1950 Act (which applied only to cases where a lien was claimed) or by appeal on a point of law under Section 1 of the 1979 Act (which created major hurdles for the applicant); now Section 28(2) allows a party to apply for a reconsideration and adjustment of the arbitrator's fees. Further useful clarifications include the provision in Section 37(2) that the fees of arbitrator-appointed experts, legal advisers and assessors are expenses of the arbitrator to be paid by the parties.

Conclusion

The cost of resolving construction disputes are frequently excessive and out of proportion with the sums at issue. It is hoped that the introduction of the adjudication provisions of the Housing Grants, Construction and Regeneration Act 1996, the culture change proposed by Lord Woolf, the use of management techniques and the upgraded powers in the new Arbitration Act 1996 will each play their part in reducing costs and making costs more proportionate to the substantive issues to which they relate.

23. ADR of Commercial Disputes and the English Courts†

Michael Black QC

Synopsis

This paper examines the attitude of the English Courts to the use of Alternative Dispute Resolution (ADR) in relation to commercial disputes.[1]

Introduction

Binding arbitration is not regarded in England as an "alternative" to adjudication in Court. While there are differences of opinion among academics and judges as to the extent to which it is both desirable and permissible for the Courts to intervene in domestic and international arbitration, the relationship is, at least, now governed by a single statute.[2] It is suggested that since the English Courts will rarely (if ever, following the 1996 Act) refuse to stay litigation to enable a reference to arbitration, it is correct *not* to consider litigation and arbitration as true alternatives, but rather as complementary to each other.

English law does not yet by statute recognise any alternatives to litigation or arbitration.[3] The Courts however will, on an *ad hoc* and case by case basis, enforce the bargain between the parties to a contract

---

† This paper was first published in *The Bulletin of the Swiss Arbitration Association*, March 1997 and is reprinted here with kind permission.

[1] Excluded from the scope of this paper are family, consumer and labour disputes. The position stated is that at 1 February 1997.

[2] The Arbitration Act 1996, in force 31 January 1997.

[3] The Housing Grants, Construction and Regeneration Act 1996, which came into force in May 1998, will introduce the concept of "Adjudication" into contracts for works of construction carried out in England, Wales or Scotland. The procedure allows an impartial Adjudicator appointed within seven days of a dispute arising to ascertain the relevant facts and the law and to make a quick enforceable decision. The Adjudicator's decision may be revised by an Arbitrator appointed in respect the same dispute or by the Courts if there is no arbitration agreement.

under which they have chosen a form of dispute resolution other than, or prior to, arbitration or litigation.[4] Consequently there is no single source of information to which resort might be had to determine the volume of matters passing through the Courts which have or will be referred to some form of ADR, or the attitudes of the Judges. The decisions cited above have turned upon the construction of particular contracts rather than any judicial policy. In an already considerable volume of literature in England about ADR (which seems to increase daily) there is no authoritative study of the relationship between the Courts and references to ADR.

There *have* been statements of practice concerning ADR, but they have not led to any reported decisions of any Court. Leaving aside various "pilot schemes" and the initiatives of individual Judges, the following directions have been issued.

- On 10 December 1993, Mr Justice Cresswell, the Judge in Charge of the Commercial List, issued a Practice Statement[5] stating that the Judges of the Commercial Court expressed their wish to encourage parties to consider the use of ADR as a possible additional means of resolving particular issues or disputes. The Judges would not act as mediators or be involved in any ADR process but would, in appropriate cases invite parties to consider whether their case, or certain issues in their case, could be resolved by means of ADR. The Clerk to the Commercial Court would keep a list of individuals and bodies that offer mediation, conciliation and other ADR services. The Pre-trial Check List annexed to the Guide to Commercial Court Practice was amended to include additional questions to ensure that legal advisors in all cases considered with their clients and the other parties concerned the possibility of attempting to resolve the particular dispute

---

4   See by way of example – *Drake & Scull Engineering v. McLaughlin & Harvey plc* (1992) 60 BLR 102; *Channel Tunnel Group Ltd v. Balfour Beatty Construction Limited* [1993] AC 334; *Mercury Communications Ltd v. Director General of Telecommunications* [1996] 1 WLR 48; *The Glacier Bay* [1996] 1 Lloyd's Rep 370; *British Shipbuilders v. VSEL Consortium plc* [1997] 1 Lloyd's Rep 106; *Conoco (UK) Limited et al v. Phillips Petroleum Company United Kingdom Limited et al* (1996) CILL 1204.

5   [1994] 1 WLR 14.

or particular issues by mediation, conciliation or otherwise. It was stated that legal advisors should ensure that parties are fully informed as to the most cost-effective means of resolving the particular dispute.

- On 24 January 1995 the Lord Chief Justice and the Vice-Chancellor issued a new Practice Direction *(Civil Litigation: Case Management)*. It brought the practice in all civil disputes in line with the practice of the Commercial Court. In particular it obliged the parties to lodge with the Listing Officer no later than two months before the date of trial a completed Pre-trial Check List in the form annexed to the Practice Direction. The Check List made reference to the Commercial Court Practice Direction referred to above and contained the following questions:

> 10. *Have you or Counsel discussed with your client the possibility of attempting to resolve this dispute (or particular issue) by Alternative Dispute Resolution?*
> 11. *Might some of ADR procedure assist to resolve or narrow the issues in this case?*
> 12. *Have you or your clients explored with the other parties the possibility of resolving this dispute (or particular issues) by ADR?*

- In April 1995 the Chancery Guide[6] reminded parties that there exist alternative methods of dispute resolution which do not involve the Court but which may provide a more suitable or cheaper or quicker method of resolving disputes in a particular case. Reference was made to the list of the individuals and bodies that offer ADR services held by the Clerk to the Commercial Court.

- On 7 June 1996, Mr Justice Waller, the Judge in charge of the Commercial List issued a Practice Statement[7] saying that the Judges of the Commercial Court considered that it was now desirable that further steps be taken to encourage the wider

---

[6] Paragraph 14.3.
[7] *Practice Statement (ADR) (No.2)* [1996] 1 WLR 1024.

use of ADR as a means of settling disputes pending before the Court. The Practice Statement empowered the Judge to adjourn proceedings in order to enable parties to utilise ADR and, after discussion with the parties' representatives, offer early neutral evaluation either by himself or another Judge. It also made provision for the giving of directions necessary for the resolution of the dispute by means of ADR.

- In the *Commercial Court End of Year Statement* made 4 October 1996, Mr Justice Waller said that following the recent Practice Statement on ADR it should now be the norm before matters reach Court for legal advisors to have discussed with their clients and for their clients to have considered whether ADR might not be more cost effective than litigation.

The Commercial Court is the most "international" of the English courts. It deals principally with actions in the fields of shipping, insurance, banking, international carriage of goods, international trade, commodity trading and the operation of international markets and exchanges. Further, all applications to appeal arbitral awards or to remove arbitrators are made in the first instance to the Commercial Court, which may then release the application to other specialist Judges. The Commercial Court has shown itself ready to adopt procedures from other jurisdictions and from international commercial arbitration to save time and cost. By the nature of the work, the users of the Court are likely to be among the most "sophisticated" litigants. Thus, if one wished to examine the Court most likely to have embraced ADR not only in word, but also in deed, the Commercial Court would be the natural choice.

Methodology

The Practice Statement of June 1996 could represent a significant change in the way in which English Judges approach their task – if its provisions were followed. It is, however, too soon to tell. The Practice Statement of December 1993 was far more limited in its scope, but was in operation for two and a half years before the second Practice Statement was issued. This should be a sufficient time within which to assess its effect.

How then may one assess that effect? The Practice Statement was directed to Judges "inviting parties to consider" the use of ADR, rather than making any order. Since Court files usually record only orders made, it is unlikely that any examination would reveal when invitations had been made. The files would reveal the identity of the Judges and the parties in each case. Several judges and deputies will have sat in the Commercial Court between December 1993 and 1996, many of whom have moved to other jurisdictions or have retired. It is suggested that without the benefit of records Judges are unlikely to have any independent recollection of discussions about ADR in individual cases. Attempting to contact parties' representatives in each case would, for much the same reasons, be unlikely to produce useful data – if ADR were merely raised at a directions hearing, depending upon the accuracy of any notes, it would be necessary to identify the particular individual who attended the hearing. The individual may no longer be with the relevant firm or may have been independent Counsel. In addition to the foregoing problems, any discussions concerning settlement of actions[8] would be confidential and would require the consent of both (or all, if more than two) parties for any information to be revealed.

The approach adopted in the preparation of this article has been to contact all the individuals and bodies offering ADR services on the list held by the Clerk to the Commercial Court and to ask what enquiries they have received under the 1993 Practice Statement. This will not disclose where Judges have suggested ADR but the parties have chosen not to pursue the suggestion. It will not disclose where the parties have decided for or against ADR before the case came to Court, or otherwise

---

[8] Whether pending or not.

independently of judicial intervention. It will not disclose that applications to members of the list have been made following a recommendation by the Court, where the applicants do not reveal that they have been recommended. It should however give some indication in general terms of the volume of references, if not a precise number.

The Commercial Court List

The Practice Statement emphasises that it would be inappropriate for the Commercial Court to recommend any individual or organisation. This is, of course, proper but the list is uncontroversial and includes the major English institutions providing ADR services. The list is in three parts: retired Commercial Court Judges; bodies offering ADR services and bodies offering arbitration and other services in connection with particular commodities and businesses.

Of the first group, sadly Lord Roskill died during the research for this article and one of the retired Judges (The Rt. Hon. Sir Roger Parker) offers arbitration only. The other members of the group are The Rt. Hon. The Lord Ackner, The Rt. Hon. The Lord Donaldson of Lymington, The Rt. Hon. Sir Michael Kerr and Sir Peter Webster.

The second group comprises the following

- Academy of Experts
- Advisory Conciliation and Arbitration Service (ACAS)[9]
- Centre for Dispute Resolution (CEDR)
- Chartered Institute of Arbitrators
- City Disputes Panel
- IDR Europe Limited
- London Bar Arbitration Scheme
- London Court of International Arbitration (LCIA)
- London Maritime Arbitrators Association
- Securities and Futures Authority.

The third group comprises several trade associations. All the members of the first and second groups replied to the enquiries, but not all the members of the third group. Those replies received suggested that the trade associations were primarily involved in the provision of binding arbitration rather than ADR. This article therefore confines itself to a consideration of the replies of the first and second groups only.

---

[9] ACAS provides advisory, conciliation and arbitration services in the field of industrial relations and industrial disputes. The Department of Employment first established a voluntary conciliation and arbitration service in Britain in 1896. In 1919 a standing Industrial Court was formed to offer voluntary arbitration. In 1960 the functions became known as the Industrial Relations Service but remained part of the Department of Employment. It was re-named the Conciliation and Arbitration Service in 1972, when the duty to conciliate in complaints of unfair dismissal under the jurisdiction of Industrial Tribunals was added. On 2 September 1974, ACAS first came into being. Re-named as the Advisory Conciliation and Arbitration Service, ACAS was established as a statutory body on 1 January 1976. The functions of ACAS fall outside the scope of this paper, but the most recent statistics of its activities are interesting

- actual and potential individual claims in the Industrial Tribunal – 91,568
- collective conciliation – 1,321
- cases referred to single Arbitrator – 129
- cases referred to Board of Arbitration – 1
- cases referred to single Mediator – 5.

The Responses

None of the retired Judges reported having received a reference as a result of the 1993 Practice Statement, although one reported having received references from the ICC, LCIA and City Disputes Panel. Another expressed doubts whether there was scope for a scheme of court-annexed ADR in the Commercial Court as the litigants in that Court were very sophisticated and may be expected to have considered and rejected the possibility of ADR before pursuing their remedies by litigation.

Of the bodies in the second group, only the City Disputes Panel reported having received any references under the 1993 Practice Statement. They have received two.

While CEDR were not aware of any references under the 1993 Practice Statement, they observed that parties may not inform them that they have approached CEDR at the suggestion of the Commercial Court. CEDR reported an increase of referrals in the last twelve months that could have been contributed to by the 1993 Practice Statement and that they have had two inquiries since the June 1996 Practice Statement arising from comments of a Judge of the Commercial Court.

The Academy of Experts experienced an upsurge of interest for several months following the publication of the 1993 Practice Statement, but that interest did not lead to an increase in appointments. Their general experience was that the act of appointing a "neutral" itself often acted as a catalyst for settlement.

Conclusions

For the reasons stated above it is impossible to obtain a definitive picture, but certain conclusions may be drawn in terms of general impression. The volume of Court-related ADR activity in connection with the Commercial Court would appear to be substantially less than has been reported in other English-speaking jurisdictions.[10] It is clear from the June 1996 Practice Statement and the remarks in the October 1996 that the Judges of the Commercial Court consider that greater use should be made of ADR. It may therefore be deduced that the use of ADR following the 1993 Practice Statement was less than originally anticipated.

While giving all due weight to the observation that Commercial Court users may be assumed to have considered ADR before instituting proceedings, if any litigants as a group are likely to be more receptive to judicial suggestions for the efficient and economical resolution of their disputes, it is suggested that it would be the members of the international business community who use the Commercial Court. It is therefore unlikely that there is greater ADR activity associated with any other English Court where there will be less formalised and well-publicised procedures.[11]

There is evidence that the June 1996 Practice Statement may lead to an increase in activity. A further incentive to parties to consider alternatives to litigation is a very recent substantial increase in Court fees, although English Court fees remain lower than those in other jurisdictions and lower than the costs of arbitration.

In summary, the English Courts do appear to exhibit an enthusiasm for ADR, no doubt at least in part for similar reasons to other jurisdictions, namely to reduce the pressure of work upon them. That enthusiasm does not appear to be wholly shared by litigants, although pressure from the Courts and other changes may alter their views. There are no current proposals for mandatory ADR in commercial disputes and it is suggested that until such time as there is, consumer resistance may remain a limiting factor on the growth of the use of ADR in England.

---

[10] Much of which is anecdotal, but see *Alternative dispute resolution in Australia* by David A Netwon published in *A Handbook of Dispute Resolution* (1991); *Alternative dispute resolution & the Ontario court experiment*, a paper delivered by The Hon Mr Justice James Farley at the IBA Conference Lagos, Nigeria, 28 February 1995; *1994 Construction Industry Survey on Dispute Avoidance & Resolution* (1995), Stipanowich & O'Neil (University of Kentucky).

[11] Only in the field of labour relations are there any established procedures. Various pilot schemes have been launched for limited periods, for example at the Patents County Court.

Select Bibliography

Bailey, S.K. & Tudway, R.H. *Electricity Law and Practice*, Sweet & Maxwell, London, 1992

de Smith, Woolf & Jowell, *Judicial Review of Administrative Action* Fifth Edition, Sweet & Maxwell, London 1995

Hart, H.L.A & Honoré, A. *Causation in the Law*, Second edition, Oxford Uniiversity Press, 1985.

Latham, Sir Michael *Constructing the Team*—Final Report of the Joint Government/Industry Review of Procurement of Contractual Arrangements in the UK Construction Industry, HMSO, London, 1994.

May, A. *Keating on Building Contracts*, 5th edition, Sweet & Maxwell, London, 1991.

McGregor on Damages: 15th Edition, Sweet and Maxwell, London, 1988.

Montague, A. *Build-Own Transfer: A Re-Evaluation*, Linklaters and Paines, London, 1989.

Mustill, M.J. & Boyd, S. *Commercial Arbitration 2nd Edition*, Butterworths, London 1989.

O'Reilly, M.P. *Costs in Arbitration Proceedings 2nd Edition*, LLP Ltd, London, 1997.

Odams, A.M.(Ed.) *Comparative Studies in Construction Law: The Sweet Lectures*, Construction Law Press, London, 1995.

Trepte P-A. *Public Procurement in the EC*, CCH, London, 1993

Uff, J. & Capper. P (eds) *Construction Contract Policy – Improved Procedures and Practice*, Centre of Construction Law, King's College London, 1991.

Uff, J. & Odams, A.M. (Eds)   *Risk, Management and Procurement in Construction,* Centre of Construction Law & Management, King's College London, 1995.

Vinter, G.   *Project Finance A Legal Guide*, Sweet and Maxwell, London, 1995

Wood, P. and Vinter, G. *Project Finance*, Allen & Overy Publication, London, 1992

Woolf, Lord   *Access to Justice, Final Report to the Lord Chancellor on the Civil Justice System in England and Wales,* HMSO, London, 1996.

Index